Trade and Gunboats

STEVEN C. TOPIK

Trade and Gunboats

THE UNITED STATES AND BRAZIL
IN THE AGE OF EMPIRE

STANFORD UNIVERSITY PRESS
STANFORD, CALIFORNIA

Stanford University Press
Stanford, California
© 1996 by the Board of Trustees of the
Leland Stanford Junior University
Printed in the United States of America

CIP data are at the end of the book

To my parents

Kurt Topik and Gertrude Krizsanich Topik

Who instilled in me a love of history and justice

Acknowledgments

This study has been a long time coming. I would like to thank Richard Graham and Lewis Gould for suggesting the topic and helping me in the early stages. I have also had the benefit of comments on some chapters from José Murilo de Carvalho, Lewis Gould, Kenneth Hagan, R. Hal Williams, Spencer Olin, David Rankin, Keith Nelson, Mira Wilkins, and an exacting and perceptive anonymous reader for Stanford Press. Jeffery Dorwart kindly shared his expertise on naval intelligence with me, and Todd Diacon shared an important unpublished source. Maria de Lourdes Mônaco Janotti helped me understand Brazil's monarchists. Bill Billingsley, Guillermo Pastrano, and Eric Zimmerman provided valuable research assistance. Julia Cristina Topik and Natalia Marcy Topik aided in constructing the bibliography and in proofreading. My mother, Trudy Topik, was also a great help in proofing. Most important, Martha Marcy Topik generously applied her mastery of the English language to this manuscript, lending it whatever grace it might have. Unless otherwise specified, I have done the translations.

I have also been fortunate to receive grants that allowed me to research far-flung archives. A summer fellowship from the National Endowment for the Humanities in 1987 and a full-year fellowship from them in 1990–91 allowed me to visit the National Archives and the Library of Congress in Washington, D.C., as well as the British Public Record Office and the N. M. Rothschild Archive in London. In 1989–90 I received a University of California President's Fellowship in the Humanities that permitted me to research at the Arquivo Histórico de Itamaraty in Rio de Janeiro to supplement the research I had done in Brazil as a member of the faculty of the

Universidade Federal Fluminense between 1978 and 1981. An invitation from the Ecole des Hautes Etudes en Sciences Sociales in Paris to serve as Directeur d'Etudes in the spring of 1990 afforded me the opportunity to use the Ministry of Foreign Affairs' Quai d'Orsay archive. I researched Mexico's Ministry of Foreign Relations archive under an invitation from the Colegio de Mexico and with funds from the University of California Irvine's School of Humanities' Committee on Research and Travel in 1988. I would also like to thank the staffs of Rio de Janeiro's Biblioteca Nacional, Arquivo Nacional, Arquivo Histórico de Itamaraty, Centro de Pesquisas e Documentação, Fundação Casa Rui Barbosa, and Instituto Histórico e Geográfico Brasileiro; the Archivo Histórico of the Ministério de Relaciones Exteriores in Mexico City; the archive of the Ministère d'Affaires Etrangères and the Bibliotèque Nationale in Paris; the Public Records Office in Kew Gardens and the N. Rothschild archive in London; the University of Texas's Nettie Lee Benson Library; UCLA's University Research Library, especially Larry Lauerhass; and particularly Pam La Zarr and the rest of the extremely helpful and friendly interlibrary loan staff at the University of California Irvine.

Parts of Chapter 3 were previously published in "Brazil's Bourgeois Revolution" in *The Americas* 48, no. 2 (October 1991): 245–72, and an overview of the project in the proceedings of the Congresso Internacional América 92, Raízes e Trajetórias, held in Rio de Janeiro, August 23–26, 1992.

This book is dedicated to Kurt Topik and Gertrude Irene Krizsanich Topik, my parents. They have been models of honor, integrity, and energy. I have been very lucky.

Contents

Ten pages of photographs follow page 92

Tables and Maps

Tables

Maps

Trade and Gunboats

Introduction

T rade rivalries have become one of the most contentious and prominent international issues since the Cold War ended in the early 1990's. The United States faces increasingly self-contained European and Asian trading blocks. Latin America, feeling somewhat left out of the new order, is turning to inter-American commercial alliances. These actions are guided by the new discourse that exalts "free markets" and limited government. Too often commentarists announce that this configuration constitutes a new world, unlike the past. They are not looking back far enough.

Let us return to the end of the nineteenth century, at the beginning of the second industrial revolution when many similar issues, clothed in different language, preoccupied politicians and businessmen. The United States first projected itself onto the international stage, hoping to stake out a sphere of influence in Latin America just as the largest of Latin American countries, Brazil, ending a 67-year-long monarchical regime, struggled to redefine its relationship to the world economy. Debates raged between liberals and corporatists, between free traders and protectionists. When the trajectories of these two unequal giants collided, their interaction revealed much about the international economic and political affairs of their day that bears on today's "new world order."

On a cold, wet January 30, 1891, Salvador de Mendonça, Brazil's minister plenipotentiary to the United States, and James G. Blaine, the U.S. secretary of state, braved the inclement weather to sign a commercial trade agreement. The pact is now largely forgotten, but at the time it was hailed enthusiastically by the U.S. press. The *Washington Post* saw it as a master stroke by Blaine. The wily strategist conceived of the agreement as the first step toward extending U.S. prestige and economic control over Latin America and eventually Asia to contest Europe's hold on their vast empires. Blaine also saw the accord as a means of winning greater popularity at home for the Republican Party by appealing to free trade sentiment. The Brazilian press, however, was far less pleased with the pact. Many newspapers called for its abrogation because it offended congressional prerogatives and undermined the industrialization drive that Brazil was undergoing. Legislation conceived and drafted in Washington looked very different in Rio de Janeiro.

The agreement's welcome in Washington was easy to understand. It was indeed of considerable moment, although the actual document seemed fairly innocuous. In exchange for permitting Brazilian sugar, coffee, and hides duty-free entry, the United States won duty exemptions or a 25 percent customs reduction on a long list of manufactured and agricultural goods.

But the document's symbolic importance was great. It was the first commercial pact signed between Brazil and the United States. This was no small matter. Latin America's largest country was the world's fourth largest exporter to the United States and its major non-European trade partner. In fact, U.S. trade with Brazil was four times larger than its business in the much-coveted China market and almost the equal of all U.S. commerce with Asia and Africa combined.[1]

The Blaine-Mendonça Accord also signaled the beginning of what E. Bradford Burns has termed the "unwritten alliance" between the western hemisphere's two most populous countries that lasted into the 1970's.[2] The two countries developed a special relationship in which "Brazil and the United States were natural allies in facing the Spanish-speaking states [of Latin America]."[3] The agreement also cemented a friendship between the Brazilian military and the United States, since the army ruled Brazil during the years in which it was in force (1892–94).

Although Brazilian trade and friendship were important to the United States, the Blaine-Mendonça Accord enjoyed a warm reception in the U.S. press more because it constituted the first step in a broader strategy. The pact was one of the first concrete results to issue from the initial Pan American Conference, which took place in Washington, D.C., in 1889. Blaine and other influential U.S. politicians sought to carve out an American[4] sphere of influence to contest the rapidly expanding European colonial empires. Unfortunately, from Blaine's point of view, the Latin American representatives refused to cast off their economic ties to Europe and submit to a U.S.-dominated free trade zone. They were willing, however, to recommend bilateral trade agreements such as the Blaine-Mendonça Accord between individual participants. Thus the agreement was a test for Pan-Americanism. U.S. policy makers hoped that it would lead to greater inter-American economic integration. This vision was not to be. It proved ironic that the

Blaine-Mendonça pact grew out of a desire to create a Pan American market. For Brazilians, the agreement was motivated by the desire to gain special privileges over their American neighbors in the United States market rather than representing a first step in integrating the economies of the Americas.

Symbolically too, Pan-Americanism was part of a larger question. By the 1890's, a growing number of Americans reconceptualized the U.S. mission and role in the world. No longer content to be a new world experiment as a "city on a hill," nor satisfied that the country's manifest destiny was to span and develop the continent from the Atlantic to the Pacific, they began to look outward. Ever more Americans were seduced by foreign markets, territories, naval bases, and potential religious converts.

The extent of this expansionist sentiment and its origins have been much debated. There is no dispute that in the "Gay Nineties" the United States gained over 100,000 square miles of overseas territories as it made colonies or protectorates of Cuba, Guam, Hawaii, the Philippines, Puerto Rico, and Wake Island while preparing itself to become "policeman of the Caribbean." There is disagreement, however, over whether the territorial acquisitions were a historical accident or an inevitable component of capitalist development and an integral result of the structure of American society and thought. The conflation of "expansionism" and "annexation" has prevented historians from studying closely the market-oriented initiatives that had no territorial aspirations.[5]

Proponents of the view that it was accidental hold that foreign relations did not interest politicians, businessmen, or the U.S. public. The home market and domestic politics consumed their attention. In contrast to imperialist Europe, foreign affairs were of limited, marginal, and sporadic importance in the republican United States.[6] Only after the overseas territories fell into the considerable American lap did citizens of the new empire wrestle with defining the new international role of the United States.

Other historians such as William Appleman Williams, Walter LaFeber, and Thomas J. McCormick argue, to the contrary, that the nineteenth century witnessed a fundamental transformation of the U.S. economy and society that made expansionism abroad necessary.[7] Part of their argument follows Charles Beard's notion of the evolving national interest; it also rests on American exceptionalism. The U.S. frontier, which did so much to forge the nation's character, was popularly perceived to have closed in the 1890's. This generated fear that the democratic "safety valve" was off; popular unrest, already evident in the rise of the Knights of Labor and the Grange and Populist movements, might explode without the frontier alternative. The American missionary zeal that preached the country's destiny was to fill the continent now believed that the country's white men should take on the burden of uplifting the uncivilized peoples of other countries so that the United States could "spread the American dream."[8]

Another part of the expansionist argument of Williams, LaFeber, and McCormick argues that U.S. foreign policy was subjected to the same economic forces that guided European imperialism. They maintain, as did J. A. Hobson and Rosa Luxemburg in their studies of European imperialism, that the new expansionism was a manifestation of the need of the developed capitalist countries to find new markets. New markets became necessary because as capitalism reached its monopoly stage, it concentrated wealth in the hands of the capitalists and deprived workers of sufficient purchasing power. As the crushing depression of the 1870's demonstrated, markets became glutted and prices plummeted. In addition to the problems of sated commodity markets, there was an oversupply of capital, which drove down interest rates. Advanced industrialization required greater and more dependable raw materials, and declining prices demanded cheaper inputs. Luxemburg, Hobson, and Lenin believed that advanced capitalism thus drove the European powers toward colonialism.[9] In the United States many observers became worried that European colonization and international trade dominance were closing out Yankee traders' potential markets in Africa, Asia, and Latin America.

More germane to the American experience are the studies of Ronald Robinson and John Gallegher who, in studying the British empire in Africa, maintain that the assertion of political pressure to gain economic advantage did not necessarily require formal colonies. Indeed, the "imperialism of free trade" that won access to markets without direct political control was preferable in many ways to the entanglements of direct rule.[10] Many late-nineteenth-century U.S. policy makers shared this opinion.

The Blaine-Mendonça Accord was a result of a U.S. effort to establish the mechanisms of free trade imperialism. The commercial agreement was the first agreement, and generally held to be the most important one, signed under the conditions of the McKinley Tariff of 1891, the country's first reciprocal tariff act. The McKinley bill was not a marginal piece of legislation; the tariff had been the central issue of the 1888 presidential election. Emily Rosenberg asserts that the form it took, the quid pro quo of offering privileges in the U.S. market in return for privileges in the Brazilian market, represented a new economic role for the U.S. state. Previously, U.S. tariff policy had concentrated on protecting the home market for domestic producers. Now the "promotional state" attempted to open foreign markets to U.S. products.[11]

Many historians who dispute the causes of the new direction of U.S. policy agree that the state began to take a new activist role. LaFeber maintains that "the 1890s may correctly be called a major watershed in American history."[12] Robert Beisner sees the decade as the beginning of the "new diplomacy" with a foreign policy rather than piecemeal responses.[13] Specifically, President Benjamin Harrison and his secretary of state, Blaine, are often viewed as the originators of the new diplomacy. LaFeber notes that they "formulated the strategy the builders of the new empire followed during the remainder of the 1890s."[14] Samuel Flagg Bemis concludes that the "new Manifest Destiny found expression during the Administration of Benjamin Harrison," while John Grenville and George Young assert that "Harrison was the first President since the Civil War who fully recognized the need to co-ordinate the strategic, diplomatic and economic factors of policy."[15] David Pletcher suggests that the reciprocity treaties were the precursors of Dollar Diplomacy.[16] Surprisingly, given the interest in U.S. economic expansion, no case studies of the McKinley Tariff have been done. In fact, there are no historic studies of Latin American trade negotiations or of Latin American commerce with the United States in the nineteenth century.[17] This study breaks new ground.

An equally serious lacuna in the debate over U.S. expansionism has been the tendency to frame it entirely in terms of U.S. concerns and interests. Other nations are largely treated as billiard balls, only of interest when they collide with the United States. Some, such as the European Great Powers, appear as cue balls that initiate the momentum; others, such as the Latin American nations, simply rebound when struck. The sparse Latin American literature on those countries' history of international relations also tends to view the United States as a hemispheric cue ball that is distinctly white.[18] It is the aggressor and the Latin Americans are the victims, victims either of U.S. force or of domestic comprador elites.[19] In fact, much more complex and enlightened perceptions often were involved. Latin American leaders were often concerned with national sovereignty and the national interest and were fairly successful in protecting them.

This work departs from most studies of U.S. foreign relations because it takes Brazilian actions and motivations seriously; indeed, it places them at center stage. As a historian of Brazil, I have researched Brazilian archives—not only the foreign ministry, but also archives on domestic politics and economics. I have also researched archives in the United States, Mexico, England, and France. I have delved into the Brazilian side of this story because this study is not conceived of as diplomatic history or international relations, focusing mainly at the point where the two countries meet. Rather, it is an analysis of international political economy, one that examines primarily domestic issues in each country and their effects on the interrelationship of the two countries. I attempt to employ what Stephen Gill has termed Gramscian "non-structural historicism" that understands historical change as the result of collective human activity.[20]

Just as war is an extension of politics, so too are international relations. International regimes shape the discourse and the rules of the game, but priorities are set by domestic concerns.[21] Robert Putnam has aptly described international relations as a "two-level game":

> At the national level, domestic groups pursue their interests by pressuring the government to adopt favorable policies, and politicians seek power by constructing coalitions among those groups. At the international level, national governments seek to maximize their own ability to satisfy domestic

pressures, while minimizing the adverse consequences of foreign developments. Neither of the two games can be ignored by central decision-makers,
so long as their countries remain interdependent, yet sovereign.[22]

Their concerns are imbedded in traditions, class interests, and ideological
discourses. The realist and neorealist positions in international relations
rarely look inside the "black box" of domestic politics. If they do peek in,
they see a monolithic rational state defending the ill-defined "national interests" that have, in fact, little to do with historical reality. International
relations are not determined simply by rational choices.[23] Indeed, irratio-
nality, or at least a rationality diffused through the prism of cacophonous
domestic interests and perceptions, is more the rule. This was certainly true
in the United States and Brazil of the 1890's when the states were parsimonious, and the foreign offices were small and underfunded. Thus I do not
treat Brazil as merely an arena to test U.S. penetration and resolve; Brazilians are important and central actors in their own right.

Taking Brazilian politicians seriously also runs counter to a strong
trend in Brazilian history that discounts the abilities and allegiances of its
leaders during the era of exports. The position was perhaps most starkly
stated by André Gunder Frank, who denounced the "corrupt state of a non-
country."[24] Others denounce the "comprador" elite and its subservience to
European and American interests.[25] The liberalism these leaders obeyed
was simply an ill-advised formula to sell out the country for the sake of
enriching a few strongmen and planters.

This position has come increasingly under attack in recent years as the
complexity and contradictions of export regimes are exposed. A growing
number of historians have come to see liberalism as adaptable and reasonable. They recognize that many of the participants in the export regimes strove for, and occasionally achieved, national development.[26] Liberals were not knee-jerk, laissez-faire free traders who spoke with a British
accent and hoarded their money in Paris. Very serious debates and earnest
challenges to the export model were posed. Their resolutions were not obvious nor predestined. The debates that raged in Brazil in the 1890's over
alliance with the United States demonstrate the wide diversity of interests
and perspectives that was present in many parts of Latin America.

Brazil's willingness to sign the Blaine-Mendonça Accord was not whole-
hearted nor was it clear-cut. Brazil had not signed a trade pact with any
other nation for 65 years. The last one it had signed with Great Britain
in 1826 was generally viewed as onerous and detrimental to the national
interest.

But the United States was different. In many ways it was a logical choice
for Brazil. After all, like Brazil, the United States was an excolony with a
continental-size expanse that had exploited a large slave sector. To add
appeal, the United States was no threat to Brazil. The trade balance between
the two countries was in Brazil's favor, and there was almost no U.S. invest-

ment nor immigrants in Brazil, nor were there any diplomatic arguments between the two countries.

Moreover, the overthrow of the Brazilian monarchy and the founding of a republic in 1889 excited interest in the U.S. political system as well as in its economy. Of particular interest was American federalism.[27] Decentralization was one of the primary goals of Brazilian republicans who opposed the monarchy's concentration of power. Brazilians were also attracted to the U.S. economic model. They found congenial the "corporate liberal" system that assigned the state the role of promoting the expansion of private enterprise.[28] Long complaining of the stifling effects of the imperial patrimonial state, Brazilian entrepreneurs sought greater freedom of action. At the same time, the state maintained a small budget, a smaller staff, and little real regulation of the economy.

Ironically, and unfortunately for Blaine and Mendonça, the same reasons that led Brazilians to imitate the American model also militated against acceptance of the trade agreement. That is, the means by which the pact was negotiated and ratified and the privileges it awarded to U.S. exporters contradicted the very features of the American system that Brazilians admired. Rather than respecting the urge for decentralization, the treaty was decreed in an autocratic manner and imposed on the Brazilian states. Rather than respecting Brazil's nascent industries' call for tariff protection, the treaty reduced the customs barrier.

The tension between Brazilian developmental goals and friendship with the United States crystallized during the rule of Marshal Floriano Peixoto (1891–94). Floriano has been generally regarded as one of Brazil's most developmentalist and nationalistic presidents. Numerous historians have asserted that only with his regime did an industrial bourgeoisie come to power, an alliance that supposedly forged a developmental policy that sharply contrasted with the laissez-faire, free trade programs of the planter-dominated Empire. One would have expected this to jeopardize relations with the United States, particularly since coffee planters have been seen as the main architects and supporters of the rapprochement with the United States. At the same time, the marshal was hostile to most European powers, particularly the British and the Portuguese, whom he suspected of supporting a restoration of the monarchy. Somewhat surprisingly, he and his most radical followers, known as the Jacobins, regarded the republican United States, the Monroe Doctrine, and Pan-Americanism much more approvingly. They viewed the United States as the anti-imperialist alternative. Floriano had to weave a convoluted path around his contradictory aims and supporters to maintain friendship with the United States.

By 1893 the trade accord lost diplomatic importance, and the next year Democrats in Washington rescinded it. In its place, the friendship between the United States and Brazil was put on a naval footing as Floriano's regime was imperiled by a naval revolt in Rio de Janeiro's harbor and a civil war in the country's south. He needed military help. It is here that the issues of commercial expansion and the construction of the U.S. "New Navy" merged. Economic and strategic concerns revealed their interrelationship. The Brazilian naval revolt was the first time that the New Navy was successfully used to defend American merchant vessels and supplant the other great powers—particularly the British.[29] The intervention has been largely ignored by historians of the U.S. Navy and U.S. foreign policy, though William Appleman Williams cites it as one of the nine key events that helped "crystalize the agrarian and metropolitan consensus on market expansion."[30] Even though Democratic President Cleveland won election in 1892 by attacking the McKinley Tariff and Republican "jingoist," adventurist foreign policy, Anglophobia and some proexpansionist sentiment in the Democratic Party forced him to intervene in action—if not in word—in Brazil. The forceful action of Admiral Benham in Rio Bay, not Cleveland's annulment of Harrison's seizure of Hawaii, would be the prototype of future U.S. foreign policy. Where the McKinley Tariff's reciprocity trade treaties presaged Dollar Diplomacy, the actions in Guanabara Bay foreshadowed Gunboat Diplomacy in the age of steam and steel.

The naval drama in Rio had a second, less known, act that involved one of the principal protagonists of this story: Charles R. Flint. His participation casts light on central controversies in U.S. history. The debates over U.S. foreign relations have turned on such issues as the relative importance of economic, political, and strategic considerations as well as the relative weight of social structures or the instrumentality of specific individuals in dictating foreign policy. Generally, historians who stress economic motivations for foreign policy use class analysis and point to the structural needs of an expanding economy. Historians of politics, on the other hand, are much more partial to the machinations of individuals to explain outcomes. Military historians concern themselves with technological exigencies but also emphasize the pivotal thought and actions of key individuals or class of officers. When taken to the international arena these same trends are noticeable. To stress economic causes is to discuss structures; to emphasize political causalities is to speak of individual politicians. Military affairs turn on military hardware and strategists. Businessmen are not well represented. Indeed, the general view is that they did not concern themselves with foreign affairs until after the end of the depression of the 1890's.[31] Even those who argue the significance of the expansionist thrust of the McKinley Tariff's reciprocity provision maintain that politicians were in advance of the business community. In fact, however, Charles Flint, a major exporter, importer, shipper, trust promoter, and arms dealer, demonstrated that there was a small group of New York– and Boston-based merchants who were very much interested in foreign affairs and very effective in lobbying for an expansionist state policy. These men orchestrated a campaign in the Pan American Conference and in the U.S. Congress to push the country outward.

This is not to posit a conspiracy theory, but rather to widen Martin Sklar's concept of corporate liberalism to include foreign policy. In the Gilded Age private "blue-ribbon" committees and advisory boards took on quasi-governmental functions since Americans were loath to fund and empower an expanded federal bureaucracy. These businessmen naturally saw the national interest as their own private interest writ large.

Flint, a U.S. representative to the Pan American Conference, key figure in the reciprocity campaign, an architect of the Blaine-Mendonça Accord, and a diplomatic representative of several Latin American governments, merged business, government, diplomacy, and naval warfare. In 1893, when Floriano was under attack, the Yankee trader assembled a mercenary fleet in New York replete with Annapolis-trained officers, U.S. seamen, and the latest American martial technology. He sought influence and concessions in Brazil, and a profit from selling arms. Never before studied, this fleet played a decisive role in crushing the insurrection and cementing U.S.-Brazilian friendship. Flint's tangle of martial, industrial, and diplomatic activities presaged the emerging military-industrial complex.[32] It also marked an important watershed in the transition away from the nineteenth-century filibusterers and economic adventurers who could, as V. G. Kiernan observes, "get their way as a rule by bribing local bosses as they were accustomed to do at home."[33] Flint and friends foreshadowed the twentieth-century "entrepreneurs" who used the U.S. state to get their way abroad.

This study attempts to take a middle ground between the instrumental view of the state and its foreign projections and the state-centric one. The state was not simply the central committee to defend the common interests of the bourgeoisie because the owners of capital were greatly divided among themselves in terms of interests, perceptions of those interests, and notions of the proper role of the state. Moreover, state administrators, somewhat insulated from the civil society by the welter of contradictory interests, also had their own interests and their own views of the national interest. Bureaucratic politics were important in the fragmented and divisive U.S. state. Yet the participation of New York and Boston merchants behind the scenes makes me stop short of Stephen Krasner's "intellectual vision that sees the state autonomously formulating goals that it then attempts to implement against resistance from international and domestic actors."[34] Both the state and civil society were important in formulating U.S. foreign policy in Brazil.

In the short run, the naval aid was more important than the trade agreement in the rapprochement between the unequal giants. Even though the commercial results of the Blaine-Mendonça Accord did not live up to their high expectations, however, the pact charted the way for future U.S. expansion, particularly once the 1893–96 depression demonstrated the risks in depending too greatly solely on the U.S. home market. Another lesson would also have to be learned before the United States could mount its export campaign: simple access to markets without government subsidies and assistance in building a commercial infrastructure was doomed to failure.

For Brazil, the trade treaty was an important element in a new alliance that allowed the fledgling Republic to reduce British diplomatic influence, consolidate the new regime, and chart a more independent course internationally. Both American and Brazilian diplomats sought to strengthen their nation's position. Brazilians demonstrated that an alliance could be forged that did not carry with it dependence or subservience; the nascent imperialistic urge within the United States was blocked in Brazil by pragmatic Brazilian nationalism.

This study, then, explores a number of dimensions and implications of the Blaine-Mendonça Accord and the following military alliance. Chapter 1 discusses the growing tide of expansionism in the United States and its relationship to the tariff issue and the struggle between Republicans and Democrats. Pan-Americanism and the political jockeying to construct the McKinley Tariff are central concerns of Chapter 2. The third chapter shifts the focus to Brazil where the exceptional conditions of 1888–91 are examined. In this three-year period slavery was abolished, the monarchy overthrown, a republic established, and military rule imposed. This political ferment occurred against the backdrop of a vigorous economy and a transformed class structure. The cleavages in Brazil's political economy and the perceptions of the United States were revealed in the arguments for and against the commercial agreement, which are the subject of Chapter 4. Chapter 5 next examines the rise to power of Marshal Floriano Peixoto and his perceptions of the treaty and U.S. friendship.

Then the story returns to the United States in Chapter 6 to explore the electoral failures of the Republicans, the position staked out by the Democrats and Grover Cleveland, and the repeal of reciprocity. Chapter 7 examines the naval revolt in Rio Bay and the actions there of the U.S. Navy. The creation of the mercenary "Flint's Fleet" and its travails and triumphs follows in Chapter 8. Chapter 9 evaluates the economic consequences of the Blaine-Mendonça Accord. It considers how interested, energetic, and successful American traders were in the Brazil market, and how much promoting the U.S. promotional state actually did and which Brazilian interests were injured. Chapter 10 carries the story forward because this drama—with its free trade debates, governmental attempts at commercial promotion, voter fear of strong government, bruising international rivalries, secretive arms dealing, and grasping entrepreneurs—continues today.

CHAPTER I

The United States in the Gilded Age

The Gilded Age conjures up images of robber barons lighting cigars with hundred dollar bills, farmers plowing the Great American Desert into a wheat basket, miners striking pay dirt, and factories belching black, prosperous smoke across a countryside closely knit together by rail and canal. It was a time of excess and contrast: abundant crops followed by drought, industrial boom leading to glut, silver bonanzas cheapened by dwindling prices, wealthy captains of industry in palatial mansions employing impoverished immigrants and freedmen who dwelt in slums.

Perhaps most important, it was a time of transition, as the years between 1876 and 1900 witnessed the triumph of the city over the countryside and industry over agriculture. It saw the bipolar North versus South rivalry become more complicated with the addition of the Midwest, the Southwest, and incipiently the Pacific West. The Jeffersonian yeoman farmer yielded to the corporate financier as the prototypical North American. As the continent filled with Euro-Americans, ever more people, hoping that the United States would join the ranks of the great powers, began to cast an eye over the horizon toward other lands. The Gilded Age, thus, fostered the transition from continentalism to globalism. An important step in expanding the United States into a world power was the McKinley Tariff and the commercial treaty with Brazil that issued from it.

U.S. Expansionism

The United States had long been an expansionist nation. From the arrival of the colonists at Jamestown, British subjects slowly crept along the coast and into the interior of the vast North American continent. But after almost 200 years of British rule, the colonies had fewer than three million inhabitants, mostly huddled by the Atlantic with few interior outposts. Then, in the first six decades of the nineteenth century, the young United States acquired and seized territory at one of the fastest rates in history. Purchases from Spain, France, and Russia and seizures from Mexico extended Washington's de jure, if not de facto, authority from the Atlantic to the Pacific. Foreign affairs concerned mostly the protection of the shores from the European powers and the conduct of bloody wars against the indigenous inhabitants of those lands that had been so easily ceded by distant European powers. The United States swelled with the greatest transoceanic immigration in history that brought some 25 million Europeans. At the same time, the Euro-American population enjoyed one of the highest natural growth rates in the world. The population doubled every 23 years. Waves of people moved onto the lands of the Native Americans, pushing the Europeanized border ever westward.

With the country's borders secure from the great powers of England, France, Germany, Russia, and Austria-Hungary, the 35 years after the Civil War were a time of consolidation and economic integration. Between 1865 and 1900 as much land was put under the plow as had been farmed in the previous two and a half centuries.[1] Three times as much land was in cotton in 1890 as had been during the height of the antebellum period. Cultivation of corn, wheat, and tobacco more than doubled.[2] Manufacturing over the same period expanded more than fourfold, causing agriculture's share of the Gross Domestic Product (GDP) to fall from one-third in 1869 to under one-fourth in 1890.[3] The domestic market became the largest in the world as manufacturers and commercial farmers were linked up by the largest rail network, which quadrupled between 1870 and 1890.[4]

This allowed the country's demographic center of gravity to move westward. The original thirteen states, which held 93 percent of the Europeanized population in 1800, contained only 50 percent 60 years later, and 41 percent in 1890. The Midwest almost equaled the eastern seaboard's inhabitants in that last year.[5]

The westward expansion, in the national psyche, was more than a demographic movement: it was a national mission. The citizens of the United States viewed their onslaught not as a war of conquest but as a divinely appointed mission to people the "empty" continent and tame the frontier. Anticipating Herbert Spencer, many Americans viewed continental conquest as evidence of righteousness and virility, of their appointment as God's chosen people. As President James K. Polk proclaimed, occupation of neighboring lands was the manifest destiny of the United States. This continentalism was generally viewed as nation building, not empire building. (Unlike Russia, which was advancing at the same time on the peoples of Central Asia and integrating them as units of the empire, the United States marginalized, banished, or exterminated its less complex and numerous indigenous peoples.) Because the conquest of the West was done mostly by settlers rather than through army campaigns, the prevailing image of the frontier was the hardy, self-sufficient pioneer homestead rather than the battlefield and military garrison.[6] The march to the Pacific did not create an imperial bureaucracy with legions of soldiers and tax collectors as nation building did in Europe; rather, it yielded decentralized, localized rule, referred to by Ann Markusen as the "territorialized state."[7] Americans were suspicious of the far-removed national government. The peculiar frontier style of U.S. nation building meant that the conquest of neighboring peoples was seen as an organic internal civil process, not a foreign affair of state. Hence, despite a heritage of conquest and expansion, Americans regarded overseas colonies and an imperial state warily.

Consequently, before the 1880's the United States viewed itself as isolationist in foreign relations even though it was in fact intimately involved in international trade, investment, and immigration. Interactions with foreigners were usually viewed as part of an endogenous process of state and nation building. The actions undertaken mostly related to protecting and expanding U.S. continental designs. The seizure of California after the defeat of Mexico in 1848, however, redefined continental interests. The discovery of gold in 1848 transformed the sleepy, sparsely populated Pacific coast into a magnet, drawing many other peoples to it. Within a year of John Marshall's gold strike, California's nonindigenous population swelled from 14,000 to 100,000. It almost quadrupled in the next decade. Chinese laborers, Chilean wheat, and Salvadorean corn arrived to meet the booming demand.

The new-found wealth tilted the United States a bit toward the west. Now national interests included defending the West Coast; moreover, with the United States now a Pacific power, Asian countries were as much neighbors as were the Europeans. Admiral Perry's forced opening of Japan in 1854, following quickly on the heels of the English opening of the China market through the Opium Wars, demonstrated the new U.S. concern and self-image. Perhaps most important, the U.S. transcontinental expanse demanded means of connecting the two coasts. Before the railroad joined together the east and west at Promontory Point, Utah, in 1869, U.S. and British companies vied for canal and railroad routes across Mexico, Nicaragua, and Panama. Thus Central America became a strategic concern of the United States. Similarly, the Caribbean islands gained strategic importance as the potential sites of naval bases to defend the contemplated canal. However, Caribbean and Central American policy were generally conceived as extensions of domestic policy rather than as qualitatively different foreign affairs.

Slowly, the urge for expansion abroad grew out of the consolidation of the U.S. occupation of the continent and economic problems at home. The period between 1873 and 1896 has been termed the first "Great Depression." Even though real per capita Gross National Product (GNP) grew by some 50 percent during the period, the era was punctuated by the greatest depression the country had ever known between 1873 and 1877, contraction between 1887 and 1891, followed by a more severe downturn between 1893 and 1895.[8] The principal problem was the dramatic decline in industrial and agricultural prices after the Civil War. Between 1873 and 1895 the wholesale price of all goods fell by 45 percent, affecting textiles, metal products, cotton, and wheat alike.[9] At the time, many victims of the contractions blamed the inadequate money supply, leading to the call for the free minting of silver coins. Milton Friedman and Anna Schwartz's research lends some credence to the monetarist view that an insufficient money supply retarded growth.[10] Yet a more structural and more global explanation has greater force.

Economic Joys and Woes

Throughout the industrialized world these years were marked by price declines, particularly in agriculture. The 1873 depression was the first "world depression," impressing contemporary observers with the extent to which world commodity and capital markets had become intertwined. For the entire 1873–96 period, prices fell 32 percent in Great Britain, 40 percent in Germany, and 43 percent in France, all comparable to 45 percent in the United States.[11] The United States faced problems similar to those of the other industrialized nations.

The economy's illness was simply overproduction. Technological revolutions had greatly increased productivity, but increasing amounts of capital went into machinery. Workers—by and large unorganized and politically weak in the oligarchic regimes of the industrialized countries—and farmers received an ever smaller share of revenue. Department of Agriculture statistics showed that average wages fell in every section of the United States roughly 20 percent between 1866 and 1892 while the country's wealth steadily grew.[12] Meanwhile, the number of millionaires climbed exponentially.[13] Unsurprisingly, demand for industrial products could not accompany increased supply. Competition for the sated markets drove prices down farther. Agriculture also suffered gluts as new areas were drawn into the world economy by the Suez Canal, the steamship, and European investments in rural production. U.S. cotton and wheat, in particular, faced stiff challenges from Argentina, Australia, Canada, Egypt, India, and Russia.

That the United States should be greatly affected by world market trends seems unlikely at first glance. The U.S. economy of the nineteenth century is generally viewed as fairly autonomous. Exports contributed only about 7 percent of the GNP. But when one considers exports as a percentage of moveable products, they become more significant, as they constituted about one-eighth of the total produced. For a number of important manufactures such as petroleum and kerosene, sales abroad were the difference between net profit or loss.[14]

In 1887 more than one-third of the wheat crop and two-thirds of cotton harvested were shipped overseas.[15] For farms as a whole, exports accounted for as much as one-fifth of income; they constituted the difference between solvency and bankruptcy. Moreover, when the world market had been healthy, foreign markets had customarily strengthened prices in the domestic market by absorbing sufficient surplus in years of overproduction to prevent domestic prices from falling.

The United States had already become intimately involved in the international economy. By 1880 it vied with Germany and France for second place in world trade, each with about 10 percent of the total. The United States was also the world's largest borrower.[16] Clearly it could not afford to ignore the rest of the world and look just to internal development. The future of the United States became inextricably linked to a world of empires.

The Age of Empire

After the depression of 1873, the major European powers turned to defensive methods to secure parts of the world market. Although international commerce continued to balloon, doubling between 1870 and 1890, free trade was abandoned for protective tariffs in France, Germany, Austria-Hungary, Italy, Belgium, and Russia. Lord Salisbury complained that England was suffering relative decline because of the number of protective tariffs "growing up on all sides of us constantly in the nature of protective duties limiting and, to the utmost of their ability, stifling our trade."[17] A corollary to protectionism was an increase in colonial systems as the "Age of Capital" became the "Age of Empire," or in Lance Davis's and Robert Huttenback's term, the period of "high imperialism."[18] The Age of Empire "was essentially an age of state rivalry" as Great Britain lost its overwhelming superiority.[19] New opportunities for its European competitors—and for the United States—arose.[20]

The European powers rushed to divide up the world. Between 1876 and 1915 about one-quarter of the globe's land surface was distributed or redistributed as colonies among great powers. A French free-trading economist noted the reason and the consequences of the spread of empire in 1889:

> It is in the colonies, in the still unexploited markets, that one seeks to extend Europe's commerce. Africa is attacked on all sides; it is being partitioned. The rivalries between nations is equally lively on the seas. In light of the digging of the American isthmian [canal] all maritime peoples want to

have rest and coaling stations there. In Indochina the English and the French are searching a route to penetrate the heart of China. Russia, which is more an Asian than a European power, regularly annexes . . . barbarian countries to the civilized world.[21]

In addition to commercial and colonial expansion, the Age of Empire was characterized by a frenzy of European investments abroad. Joseph Schumpeter noted that "foreign and particularly colonial enterprises and lending was the dominant feature of the period."[22] The excess of capital at home had made investments in far-off, riskier, yet potentially lucrative lands more appealing. Not only the City of London, but stock markets in Paris, Berlin, Frankfurt, Amsterdam, Vienna, and Lisbon actively traded in foreign stocks and bonds. The urge to invest brought European capitalists into increasing competition with each other. The century's high-water mark for European foreign investments came in 1889.[23]

The European partition of the world worried North Americans. Yes, the United States was a new nation and still by far a net debtor (foreign investment in the United States was five times greater than American investments abroad in 1890). But it had enjoyed a steeply rising trajectory of economic development in the nineteenth century that convinced many in the New World and the Old that before long the United States would become a major international player.[24] After all, in 1890 the nascent power already had a larger population than any major European country (almost equaling France and Britain combined), and its GNP trailed only Britain's.[25] But now the protective barriers built around the main European economies, such as Great Britain's growing preference for products from its own colonies, threatened the U.S. commercial future. Some influential Americans also began to worry that the United States was being left out of the new world order. They feared that by the time the country faced the economic necessity of foreign markets and sufficient naval capacity to exploit them, the world would already be divided up by its European competitors.

International affairs became increasingly immediate and pressing. By the late nineteenth century the globe had become largely known. Scientists and naturalists mapped remote areas, most dramatically represented by Stanley's and Livingston's plunge into the heart of Africa. The incredible advances in transportation technology that allowed one to go around the world in fewer than 80 days, and communications that linked continents in a matter of minutes, shrank the world. Now the results of the English Derby could be known in Calcutta within five minutes of the race's end. The steamship upended people's sense of space. As one reporter observed already in 1839, "We have seen the power of the steam suddenly dry up the great Atlantic Ocean to less than half its breadth. . . . The Mediterranean . . . has before our eyes shrunk into a lake . . . and the great lakes of the world are rapidly drying into ponds."[26] Newspapers relied on international wire services to keep their readers abreast of late-breaking events across the globe. Thomas Cook's first grand tour, conducted in 1856, ignited a flourishing tourist trade that helped make the exotic more accessible. The world began to seem in a very tangible way finite and the race for its riches and souls a zero-sum game.[27]

Concern over the extending global reach of U.S. rivals was not limited to the economic sphere. As Eric Hobsbawm has keenly remarked, "Economic development is not a sort of ventriloquist with the rest of history as its dummy."[28] The international triumph of Great Britain or Germany would have had psychic costs to the United States as well as economic ones. Since the founding of the Massachusetts Bay colony, many Americans believed that they were creating a "city on a hill," a new, moral model that would serve as a beacon for corrupt old Europe. Although there was much disagreement over the nature of the U.S. model, a strong proselytizing strain remained in the nineteenth century. It preached Protestantism and the uniqueness of American culture. As the frontier was pushed back, the purveyors of redemption and the American dream such as Josiah Strong began to look abroad. Senator Albert J. Beveridge voiced the beliefs of many when he proclaimed ingenuously: "He [God] has marked the American people as His chosen nation to finally lead in the regeneration of the world. This is the divine mission of America, and it holds for us all the profit, all the glory, all the happiness possible to man. We are the trustees of the world's progress, guardians of its righteous peace."[29] Thus the struggle for international influence was, in the minds of many, a struggle for salvation as well as profit. It was also a battle against the corrupt, Anglican British. This was an important consideration because anti-British sentiment for many was the nineteenth-century equivalent of twentieth-century anti-Soviet feelings.[30] The partition of the world in the last decades of the nineteenth century, then, threatened the U.S. mission and, hence, its claim to uniqueness.

The perception of the closing of international opportunities was probably more significant in explaining growing expansionist sympathies than the sense that the American frontier was closing. Gilded Age expansionism rarely was territorial. Colonies were generally taken reluctantly and did not serve as surrogates for the frontier escape. Few Americans ever migrated to them, and, except for Cuba, there was relatively little investment there. Nor could one argue that territorial expansion would protect U.S. democracy. Indeed, more often the argument, made on racist grounds, was that colonials were incapable of democracy and their incorporation threatened the national system. Moreover, the cost of a large navy to defend colonies would overly strengthen the central government.[31] Trade, not territory, drove U.S. expansionism. As Thomas Jefferson Coolidge, an influential millionaire who represented the United States at the first Pan American Conference, put it, "We will buy from you and we will sell to you, but we will not federate with you and we will not govern you."[32]

U.S. Economic Growth

The expansion of U.S. influence and economic activity promised to address the woes of Gilded Age America. First, of course, were the problems of industrial and agricultural overproduction. The 1870's depression and downturns in the 1880's caused captains of industry to worry about structurally determined and recurrent business cycles. For the first time they feared that crises might not be occasional and accidental but rather inherent in the modern economy.[33] Structural responses had to take the place of ad hoc remedies.

In the United States, industrialists sought solutions in the private sphere. A higher protective tariff and trusts, mergers, and syndicates were fashioned to protect manufacturers from foreign and domestic competition. Indeed, the United States had the best-formed trusts and syndicates in the world.[34] As Paul Holbo has pointed out, the robber barons concentrated on combinations at home, which they could bring about by themselves, more than on expansion abroad, which required state assistance. Indeed, the spokesmen of the haute bourgeoisie such as Andrew Carnegie and John D. Rockefeller opposed and feared state involvement because they believed that it was more likely to work against the interests of big business than in its favor.[35] Yet private solutions were also risky; industrial combinations were inherently unstable. The higher prices that they created invited new competitors.[36] Moreover, they were politically unpopular because they symbolized the concentration of wealth and power and were counter to the ideological justification for profit from interest: that it was payment for risk. Small-scale producers who did not have the capacity to form combinations or establish their own foreign policy needed public help.[37] Hence commercial expansion struck many industrialists as an ever-more-attractive solution. Abram S. Hewitt, a New York industrialist and member of the House Ways and Means Committee responsible for crafting the tariff, observed in 1890: "I think that the calculation that has been made of this country's ability to produce in six months what we consume in a year is not exaggerated. We need a market for the products of the other six months and the great market that our Spanish American brothers offer us is at our doorstep."[38]

Overseas markets for manufactures were also important because of rising labor militancy during the Great Depression of the 1870's. The Knights of Labor, who counted over 500,000 members in 1886, the American Federation of Labor, which reached 630,000 in 1890, and a surging anarchist movement threatened not only to cut into profits but to assume political power. Labor increasingly demonstrated its force in the polling booth as well as in the factories. The European example of growing working-class political parties, particularly the German Social Democratic Party founded in 1875, alerted capitalists to the perceived menace. In the pivotal state of

New York, where a few thousand votes could determine the presidential victor, the Labor Party vote grew from 2,800 in 1886 to 70,000 in 1887. In Cincinnati a labor ticket did well, and in Chicago socialists garnered many votes.[39]

Anarchist actions in the United States, the most publicized being the Haymarket affair of 1886, underlined the seriousness of the challenge.[40] The U.S. Commissioner of Labor found that between 1881 and 1886 the United States suffered 3,902 strikes in 22,304 establishments involving 1,323,203 employees and another 2,214 lockouts with 160,823 workers. The *Economist* of London concluded from these statistics: "This discloses an extraordinary amount of discontent and dissatisfaction among the operative classes of America which is altogether inconsistent with the generally accepted opinion that they are so very much better off in that country than in Europe." The journal concluded its October 1888 article: "Industrial disturbances in the United States have shown a tendency lately to multiply and increase in an extraordinary manner."[41] Strikes reflected the serious maldistribution of American wealth. It has been estimated that by 1890, 80 percent of the population lived on the margin of subsistence, while 20 percent controlled almost all wealth.[42] A healthy, growing economy could blunt class warfare. Increasingly more observers believed that foreign markets could reinvigorate the ailing economy of the United States.

Politically potent farmers, frustrated by low prices, also began to look overseas for buyers. Their votes, especially in the new Midwest and western states where they predominated, became especially important in the Gilded Age because of the equilibrium in national elections. Democrats and Republicans routinely exchanged the presidency and control of Congress. The elections of the 1876–96 period were the closest in U.S. history with the winner of the popular vote twice losing in the electoral college. With a solid Democratic South and a largely Republican North, the Midwest usually held the swing votes.[43] Southern and midwestern farmers were not only politically important, they were angry over the sharp drop in farm commodity prices and the drought that began in 1887 in the plains states. Many farmers decided to raise less corn and more hell. They organized the Grange and the Farmer's Alliance, the latter claiming two million well-organized members in 22 states by 1890.[44] In 1891 they formed the People's Party, which would win over a million votes the next year. Their principal concerns were railroad rates, bank loans, and the free minting of silver, but William Appleman Williams has shown that increased foreign markets for their goods was a vital part of midwestern and southern farmers' agenda.[45]

Although structural problems in agriculture and industry as well as the political stalemate between the parties and growing politicization of marginalized groups would seem to demand an expansionist economic policy, ideology in 1888 had not yet accompanied the economic transformations. Certainly most people agreed that the United States should expand its prestige and its exports internationally, but there were sharp differences over the means and the acceptable costs of such an expansion. Strong and somewhat contradictory beliefs in states' rights and tariff protection, and fear of government bigness and corruption, hamstrung expansionist efforts. Congress refused to cede its authority and control of patronage to the executive, thus creating a cacophony of local demands and little harmony of national interest. Big business feared government would regulate and hinder rather than aid capital, while workers and farmers feared that government action would enrich politicians' wealthy friends. It took the struggle over the tariff in the late 1880's and early 1890's to redefine the terms of the debate over the state's proper role in guiding economic expansion.[46] The reciprocity plank served as a catalyst for crystallizing debate and indeed creating vocal organized support for public export promotion.

Debate on the Tariff

The debate over U.S. foreign expansion centered not on territorial acquisition or foreign investment, but on trade, more specifically, on the tariff. The tariff had always been an important issue. It was certainly one of the major points of contention between the North and South in the antebellum period, but it usually assumed a subordinate position to more riveting concerns such as the debate over slavery. Only in 1880 did it become a major political issue when the Republican Party discovered that with the end of Reconstruction, waving the "bloody shirt" no longer guaranteed them the northern vote. James G. Blaine, who became the principal exponent of Pan-Americanism and reciprocity, argued that the tariff provided a useful rallying point to tie together the party's heterogeneous following. For the next fourteen years, as Tom Terrill has noted, "Tariff positions became the litmus paper test for political affiliation."[47]

Through stressing a protective tariff, Republicans could distinguish themselves from the Democrats, emphasize what they believed were their most compelling virtues, and at the same time diminish or ignore internal differences. Blaine, and successful Republican candidates for the presidency James Garfield and Benjamin Harrison, argued that the tariff brought the United States prosperity. Industry and agriculture had both flourished behind the protection of high duties. The tariff aided all classes, not just the bosses. The American worker's wages had increased because his employer did not need to compete with cheap labor from Europe, and this, in turn, created a large domestic market for farmers and other manufacturers. Moreover, the high tariff showed the Republicans to be the party of union, protecting all American producers, not just regional interests (though they claimed that the West in particular would benefit). Additionally, protection illustrated Republicans' active assistance for the development of the private sector.[48]

Through the tariff, Republicans appealed to nationalism to overcome the ethnic rifts that threatened the party. As one of their leading spokesmen, William McKinley, proclaimed: "Stand by the protective policy, stand by American industries, stand by that policy which believes in American work for American workmen, that believes in American wages for American laborers, that believes in American homes for American citizens."[49]

The nationalist face of protection also provided a useful weapon against the British. The *New York Times* recognized that "the hatred of England constitutes a considerable percentage of the political capital of protectionists, and they are bound to make it go as far as they can."[50] The Anglophobia that ran strong in parts of Gilded Age United States was the harvest not only of the two wars the United States had fought with its former masters, but the control English capitalists exercised over large parts of the U.S. economy. Englishmen owned almost 80 percent of all foreign investment in the United States and were also important in finance and trade. Many of the great financiers such as the Rothschilds and the House of Morgan were accused of constructing an international conspiracy and a shadow government centered in the City of London.[51] Farmers blamed the British for the demonetarization of silver and the closing of European markets to U.S. goods such as beef. Agriculturalists pushed for measures against English ownership of railroads, land, cattle, and meat- and wheat-processing plants. The Irish, who usually voted Democratic, expressed particularly vehement opinions of the British. Blaine, an Irishman but a Republican, was a leading Anglophobe; he wooed the Irish vote by arguing that the tariff wall protected U.S. producers from the British and was thus a blow to their commercial pretensions.[52]

The presidential election of 1888 transformed the tariff from an important point of contention to the main issue in the campaign. The Democrat Grover Cleveland, in office since 1884, searched for an issue to bring together his fractured party, which was suffering "a notable relaxation of discipline."[53] As a "goldbug" who firmly believed in the gold standard, he was particularly concerned with blunting or distracting the rising call for the free coinage of silver from the western members of his party. In his 1887 presidential address to Congress, he took the unprecedented step of devoting the entire message to just one issue: the tariff. The risky idea of placing the tariff so prominently was Cleveland's, not the party's.[54] He hoped to transform the American political terrain, his goal to rally a divided Democratic Party to appropriate tariff reform—formerly a Republican issue—as a central plank in their platform.[55] Cleveland galvanized the public. According to the *New York Times*, "There has not been for a quarter of a century any such forcible and practical arousing of public attention as followed that message."[56] Cleveland was not responding to public opinion so much as attempting to form it.[57] The battle lines were drawn.[58] It is important to underline that the controversy over the tariff, which reshaped the terms of the debate over U.S. commercial expansion and heightened awareness of foreign markets, developed out of *domestic* political concerns, not international rivalries. The tariff issue galvanized public opinion because it appealed *both* to traditional concerns and to the country's new social and political realities.

Cleveland naturally contested the Republican version of the benefits of protection while, at the same time, refusing the "free trade" label Republicans attempted to attach to him.[59] The tariff for Cleveland and the Democrats, as for the Republicans, was more than an economic issue. It touched on a constellation of beliefs that formed the core of their ideology. Democrats tended to be classical liberals. Champions of states' rights and the private sector, they feared a strong, centralized state. They saw the protective tariff as evidence of state activism and centralization. The revenues it brought, which provided most of the federal government's income, encouraged further federal "interference" in society. Duties were taxes that were appropriating the hard-earned income of the taxpaying victim, and taxes were excessive. Revenues had been building up in recent years to the extent that the Treasury held a $105 million surplus with forecasts that it would continue to grow at the rate of $92 million a year.[60] This greatly concerned Democrats (a concern hard to fathom in our deficit-ridden times).

In fact, influential Democrats in Congress argued that the central issue *was* the treasury surplus, not tariff reform.[61] Cleveland maintained that these funds were keeping money out of circulation, which was contributing to the depression of prices. He wanted to remove the funds from the private banks in which they had been deposited to avoid the charge of favoritism and overly close relations between the government and the business community (which was a popular Democratic charge against the Republicans). Cleveland did not want to reduce excise taxes on liquor and alcohol for fear of offending the growing prohibitionist movement.[62] He ruled out buying back Treasury bonds early because that would encourage speculation. Opposing state economic intervention, he refused to expend the funds in more public works projects.[63] Instead, he advocated lowering public customs revenues to reduce the government's income. The surplus would be spent in normal expenditures.

Cleveland employed populist rhetoric in defending his stand on the tariff. He aimed particularly at issues on which the Republicans were especially vulnerable: political corruption and trusts. Since the days of Grant, the Republicans had been branded the party of the pork barrel and patronage. Cleveland protested that greater customs duties only provided them more money to misappropriate for political purposes. High customs duties also encouraged the state to favor influential companies much more than the average citizen. Most seriously, tariff protection aided trusts that feared international competition and indeed required protection to be able to survive. In short, duties too often took from the many deserving taxpayers and gave to the few undeserving rich. Cleveland was posing the Jeffersonian republican model of the state and society to attack the newly emerging Republican corporate liberalism that promoted coordination over competition and organization over individualism.[64] He was extending to international trade his platform of honesty in government, public economy, limitation of corporate privilege, and reduction of federal powers. Cleveland promoted tariff reform because of its strategic political usefulness and the manner in which it welded together the Democrats' discourse. Government promotion of trade expansion was a secondary issue.[65]

Even though the effect of tariff reform on foreign commerce was a subordinate concern for Cleveland, the logic of his argument required that trade play a more central role in his defense of reform. Thus trade expansion became propelled, almost accidentally, into a prominent role in national discourse. Inchoate public interest in international commerce began to take form in the crucible of domestic politics during the election of 1888.[66] Cleveland argued that protection had not brought prosperity, but depression. The problem was a glut of industrial and agricultural goods. The solution was exports. Foreign markets would take the surplus, but only if the tariff were lowered. This followed from the Democrats' barter view of international trade. They believed that foreign countries could not import from the United States if they could not export there. Cheaper imports provided the added advantage of lower prices for U.S. consumers. Democrats included the benefits for industrial exports in their arguments for freer trade: manufacturers could import cheaper raw materials, which in turn would make them more competitive abroad. U.S. producers for the most part would not be hurt by the lower tariff because they had come of age and could compete. Those that could not win in the free marketplace generally did not deserve to, for they were surviving essentially through a subsidy from the consumer. The export argument was now turned to Anglophobic uses by maintaining that through free trade American producers could wrestle away British foreign markets.[67]

The Election of 1888

Republicans regarded the election as a referendum on tariff reform when their candidate, Benjamin Harrison of Indiana, defeated Cleveland. The Democrat had backed away from the tariff question and refused to campaign during the summer of 1888, while Harrison issued speeches almost daily in favor of protectionism to the almost 200,000 people who trooped to his Indiana home.[68] The result was a victory that "was the most decisive in nearly twenty years."[69] The Republicans not only regained the White House, but also won a majority in both houses of Congress. They set out to shore up the protective wall.

But as the GOP would discover two years later—and some far-sighted Republicans such as Blaine already recognized—the election had not really been won because of the protectionist plank. The margin of victory for the presidency was razor thin. Democrats complained that it was due as much to fraud as to popularity. Only two states, New York and Indiana, changed their presidential votes from 1884 when the Democrats had won. In those two states Harrison only won 1 percent more votes than had the Republican loser, Blaine, in 1884.[70]

Although analysts at the time certainly attributed Harrison's victory to his stand on the tariff, historians more recently have cast that view into doubt.[71] Richard Jensen's study of the election in the crucial state of Indiana led him to conclude that Harrison's arguments made little difference. "Rather it [the Republican victory] reflected, for the last time, the stabilizing influence of party loyalty and army-style campaigns."[72] Paul Kleppner examined mining and lumbering counties in the Midwest and found no relationship between economic interests and party vote; party loyalty was dictated much more by ethnicity and religion.[73] Clarence Miller also found in the Northwest that the issues were "too befogged to permit of any rigid interpretation"; the tariff's main contribution was the "solidification of tariff attitudes within party lines."[74] In California, according to R. Hal Williams, although Cleveland's tariff reform message was well received and improved Cleveland's vote, it could not overcome the influx of Republican voters into the south of the state.[75]

This is what historians tell us. But in politics, perceptions count more than realities—in the short run. (Two years later the Republicans would discover just how unpopular their high protective tariff actually was.) In 1888, however, Republicans perceived that the tariff was their savior. They therefore set out to revise it.

Reciprocity

It has been argued that the reciprocity provision of the 1890 McKinley Tariff demonstrated Republican awareness of the need for state promotion of exports, but in fact the party was concerned almost exclusively with protecting the domestic market. As H. Wayne Morgan has noted, in the election of 1888 "the real symbolism in a tariff campaign [was that] the Republican party had moved from the war's residue of moral questions to economic issues, centering on protection."[76] Only one influential Republican realized that his party was vulnerable to the new Democratic position on tariffs, especially in the Midwest where exports were likely to appeal more than protected internal markets. But that man made a great difference; he was perhaps the most popular and politically able politician of his generation, James G. Blaine (1830–93).

The aging, stately Blaine had long enjoyed a position of preeminence in his party. He had been a leader in the House for fourteen years including six years as Speaker, secretary of state under Garfield, and party standard bearer in 1884 when 600 votes in New York would have propelled him to victory over his opponent Grover Cleveland.[77] Blaine was a master politician and a magnetic speaker. He had been the leading candidate for the Republican presidential nomination again in 1888 before he withdrew from the race, ostensibly because of ill health. A large sector of the GOP adored him.

Harrison himself had supported Blaine for twenty years, which led him to appoint Blaine secretary of state. Blaine had the additional advantage of a reputation as the quintessential Republican and fervent protectionist. He was a man to be trusted on the tariff,[78] one who would employ his vast influence to carve out an expansionist economic policy.

During the election of 1888 Blaine played a key role in defending protectionism. When he returned to the port of New York from a European vacation in August 1888 he was greeted by fireworks and crowds chanting "Blaine, Blaine, James G. Blaine/No, No, No free trade."[79] He immediately took to stumping around the country for the protective tariff while Harrison entertained crowds at home. When the two finally met in Indianapolis, 25,000 marchers and a crowd of 100,000 turned out in what some claimed was the largest parade ever to take place outside of New York.[80] With this outpouring of affection for Blaine, one could easily have been confused whether it was Harrison or Blaine who was the presidential candidate.

While Blaine was the champion of protection, he was also a man who recognized the importance of foreign trade: he had long had his eye on widening commerce with Latin America. In Congress he had been a staunch supporter of subsidies to expand the U.S. merchant marine; in his first term as secretary of state he had attempted to convene the first Pan American Conference; and as presidential candidate he had made increased exports an important plank in his platform.[81] Defeats on all these initiatives no doubt impressed upon Blaine that he was ahead of his party in his support for international economic expansion. But he believed that he once again had to push for export promotion because he feared that the logrolling of his overconfident party colleagues, flush with their apparent mandate in the 1888 election, was leading to a high, unreformed tariff that would invite Democratic attacks. He therefore led the effort to retain the essence of protectionism while making gestures to trade expansion.

His vehicle was reciprocity. Reciprocity was a policy of country-by-country negotiations for specific trade concessions reciprocal to those offered by the United States. Blaine contended that it was necessary for the country to protect nascent industries and farmers while still seeking new markets abroad for more competitive producers. The Democrats were wrong, he lectured, to believe that simply lowering trade barriers would provide foreign markets: "In the trade relations of the world it does not follow that mere ability to produce as cheaply as another nation insures a division of an established market, or indeed, any participation in it at all."[82] In other words, active state promotion, not laissez-faire, was necessary to provide markets.

Blaine had to walk a fine line. He could not disavow the Republicans' decades-long contention that the domestic market was huge and that its protection guaranteed prosperity, particularly since he had been instrumental in crafting the argument. Yet he could also not let the Democrats steal the commercial expansion issue. He hoped that reciprocity would allow him to argue that the Republicans were actually extending the protective wall to South America rather than—as most Democrats and even Republicans first argued—undermining the wall by admitting the importance of international trade.

Reciprocal trade agreements were not new; they had been successfully used earlier with Hawaii and Canada. But the broader efforts under President Chester Arthur (1881–85) to apply reciprocity to Latin America failed to gain congressional approval. Even with the lobbying of Arthur, his secretary of state, Frederick Frelinghusen, and a note of urgency from the Treasury and important industrialists, Republican congressmen had refused to ratify the 1881 treaty with Mexico and five other circum-Caribbean countries. The refusal to strike an agreement with Mexico was particularly surprising given that several American railroad magnates were busy building lines, principally financed by the Mexican government, to connect the United States with the heart of its neighbor. Nonetheless, Republican leaders such as William McKinley and Thomas Reed rejected the treaty, fearing that it was an attack on the protective system. Mexico's negotiator at the time, Matias Romero, concluded that the reason that the treaty was rejected was "because industrial production in the United States still has not reached the level that makes it necessary to take measures to open foreign markets and therefore, efforts made could not succeed because they were premature."[83]

Romero was wrong about the political importance of industrialists for changing tariff policy, however. The Republicans were more concerned about the western farmers in their expansionist policy. This is certainly contrary to the leading European analyses of the growth of imperialism, be it of the free trade or colonial variety. Luxemburg, Hobson, Bukharin, Lenin, and Robinson and Gallegher all stressed that the new stage of monopoly capitalism demanded expansion because of its large and overly productive factories. This is understandable, because in no European country was agriculture as fully capitalist and technologically sophisticated as in the United States. The advent of advanced agricultural machinery such as the McCormick reaper, the spread of rural credit, and the expansion of a railroad network so dense that, by 1890, 90 percent of the farmhouses in Illinois were within five miles of a railroad station created an agro-industry qualitatively different from the peasant or sharecropper production of Europe or South America.[84]

These American farmers, together with smaller producers of semiprocessed goods, wanted public help to coordinate their splintered interests and find markets overseas. Large-scale, technologically sophisticated industries rarely sought state assistance since they had the financial and organizational ability to forge their own solutions. American economic policy was not prescribed by some abstract, teleological logic of capital accumulation that recognized that farmers and basic materials producers were destined to furnish an ever smaller share of United States exports while sophisticated manufactures expanded. Rather, Blaine was responding to politics, pure and simple.[85] Farmers and raw material producers represented many votes in swing states; proportionately they were much more likely to vote than factory workers.[86] Reciprocity promised to find consumers abroad for agriculturalists.[87]

Blaine also realized that Republicans had to blunt the attacks on the GOP's alleged support of trusts and high taxes. Moreover, they had to find a way to diminish the Treasury surplus. Blaine hit on the idea of offering to remove the duties from raw sugar in return for reciprocal trade concessions from sugar exporters. Sugar was responsible for fully one-fourth of all customs revenues, so the Treasury surplus would decline and consumers would notice the difference at their breakfast tables. Moreover, the attack on sugar protection had the additional virtue of popularity. The recently organized U.S. Sugar Refining Company trust was one of the most pervasive and reviled in the country.[88] Thus the action could be viewed as antitrust legislation as well, though in fact it was not.

The McKinley Tariff

The McKinley Tariff that the Republicans ultimately passed in 1890 was a transitional document that embraced contradictory tendencies. Eric Hobsbawm sees it as the end result of a nineteenth-century process focused on the domestic market. He notes that after beginning in Germany and Italy in the late 1870's, "protective tariffs became a permanent part of the international economic scene culminating in the early 1890's in the penal tariffs associated with the names of Méline in France (1892) and McKinley in the U.S.A. (1890)."[89] Emily Rosenberg, on the other hand, views it as the first "barter tariff" signifying the intent of the state to use this weapon to find new trade. David Pletcher, in the same vein, considers the tariff a dry run for the dollar diplomacy of the early twentieth century.[90] To reconcile these somewhat contradictory impulses behind the McKinley bill required a masterful tightrope walk.

Blaine faced the problem that neither Congress nor Harrison shared his enthusiasm for expansion. The tariff that issued from the labyrinthine negotiations was rather disappointing. Blaine initially hoped to make all imports free from countries awarding sufficient trade concessions to U.S. products, thereby creating a Pan American customs union. Defeated, he then sought an extensive free list of agricultural and industrial products to use to gain reciprocal reductions. These goods would retain high duties unless other countries awarded the United States reciprocal trade concessions in which case they became duty free for that country. Even this list was rejected. Instead, the original bill that issued from the Ways and Means Committee in April included only sugar, coffee, tea, molasses, and hides. Since coffee and tea, which were not produced in the United States, had been free since 1872, this was not much of a concession. More disappointing to

Blaine, these goods were made free to everyone, so there was no carrot to dangle to open foreign markets.[91]

Congress was able to add sugar to the free list because Louisiana producers, once responsible for supplying 60 percent of U.S. consumption, had fallen to producing under 10 percent. Most sugar was imported, duty exempt or not. Moreover, Louisiana growers were granted a bounty to compensate for the lower price of imported sugar. The sugar trust, which reputedly invested hundreds of thousands of dollars in the 1888 campaign and helped draft the legislation, was content with the bill because only raw or semirefined sugar was made free.[92] Therefore, they would purchase their raw material free of duties but still not face competition from foreign sugar refiners. Other goods found their rates raised almost across the board, with many agricultural goods receiving tariff protection for the first time. Although McKinley had promised reform to remove the tariff's inequities and inconsistencies, he settled for the unsatisfying remedy of a blanket increase.

A coherent tariff was difficult to forge because the territorialized nature of the U.S. state and regional economic specialization led congressmen to represent primarily their local interests, not to be concerned with a coherent national program. This is not a surprising result. Recent econometric studies of tariffs have found that they are inherently conservative; historical precedent outweighs the power of lobbies or displacement costs in setting duties.[93] David Lake has suggested that because of the decentralized nature of government (and one could add the weak executive of the nineteenth century) the U.S. Congress found it more difficult to resist protectionist pressures from local interests than did the governments of France or Germany.[94]

More seriously for Blaine, even though the Republicans had promised commercial expansion in the 1888 election, the original form of the McKinley Tariff did not include reciprocity at all. Blaine was so infuriated at the draft of the new tariff that he protested to the Senate Finance Committee that it did not contain "a section or line of the bill that opens a market for another bushel of wheat or barrel of pork" and smashed his fist into his silk hat.[95] McKinley, in later years a leading advocate of U.S. expansion and Blaine's competitor for Republican leadership, was irritated by Blaine's attack. He responded that "This is a domestic bill; it is not a foreign bill."[96] Later he added, "The markets of the world in our present condition are a snare and a delusion. We will reach them whenever we can undersell competing nations and no sooner."[97]

The standoff between McKinley and Blaine was more than a clash of prospective presidential candidates. It demonstrated that even though the Republicans had been increasingly centralized and had expanded the power of the federal state in the nineteenth century, they had not overcome the territorialized nature of the state. Congress adamantly defended its perquisites against executive intrusion; it also tended to be localist and nationalist, while the executive favored a more internationalist stance. Republican congressional corporate liberals had come to subscribe to two-thirds of the trinity of Charles Conant, economist and Republican consultant: concentration and integration. They were still reluctant to join the executive on the third: expansion.[98]

The state and its relationship to civil society were only slowly being reconstructed. LaFeber notes that "In 1889 James G. Blaine had led and the businessmen had willingly followed. But after 1893 the businessmen played at least an equal role in focusing attention southward"; here he emphasizes only one dimension of the restructuring of the state.[99] The other key transformation was the executive's seizure of the upper hand in foreign policy.

Ironically, the president who took the first steps to enhance executive power on trade issues did not initially favor reciprocity. The *New York Times* noted in April 1890 that Harrison preferred the McKinley draft without reciprocity. In June the paper reported that Republicans were angry with the secretary of state for publicly proclaiming Harrison's support for reciprocity when the president was opposed. They began denouncing Blaine as a bull in a China shop.[100] Even when Harrison presented Blaine's proposal for reciprocity to Congress in June, the *Times* noticed that "he did so with a contemptuous sneer and practically proclaimed that it would reduce American labor to the foreign level."[101] Blaine complained to Mexico's minister to the United States, Matias Romero, in July that his own efforts to convince the president and Congress had failed. He feared that reciprocity was dead and that the Democrats would win the next election. Romero, who had spent parts of three decades in the United States trying to encourage trade and investment with Mexico, agreed with Blaine's assessment. He thought no reciprocal treaty was possible in the United States given "the current state of public opinion."[102] This astute observer thought the nation was not yet sufficiently expansionist. He also believed that some Republicans opposed reciprocity because they viewed it as Blaine's attempt to win popular support and prepare a run for the presidency in 1892. Newspapers noted in July that Harrison was ignoring Blaine, apparently in hopes of forcing the secretary of state to resign.[103]

By August, however, papers were reporting that Blaine had convinced Harrison of the need for reciprocity. The president in turn brought McKinley around.[104] What had happened? Two things. The first is fairly well known. Blaine went public with his campaign. His most dramatic move was an open letter to Senator Frye of Maine in which he wrote:

> The charge against the protective policy which has injured it the most is that its benefits go wholly to the manufacturer and the capitalist and not at all to the farmer. You and I will know that this is not true, but still it is the most plausible and therefore the most hurtful argument made by the free trader. Here [reciprocity] is an opportunity where the farmer may be bene-

fitted—primarily, undeniably richly benefitted. Here is an opportunity for a Republican Congress to open the markets of forty million people to the products of American farms. Shall we seize the opportunity or shall we throw it away![105]

Blaine then administered the rhetorical coup de grace when he argued that reciprocity was not a Democratic free trade bill in disguise, but a fundamentally Republican protectionist act: "Every free trader in the Senate voted against the reciprocity provision. . . . They know and feel that with a system of reciprocity established and growing, their policy of free trade receives a most serious blow. . . . The enactment of reciprocity is the safeguard of protection. The defeat of reciprocity is the opportunity of free trade."[106]

Blaine's leadership and eloquence have usually been given the credit for swaying Congress, but a second, less known, strategy was employed that was equally as important in the victory of reciprocity. Despite LaFeber's assertion that Blaine was in front with businessmen tagging along behind, this strategy was directed by some major businessmen. They undertook both public and clandestine publicity campaigns.

The most conspicuous public platform for expounding the merits of trade expansion was the Pan American Conference that took place in Washington, D.C., from October 1888 to May 1890. A six-week-long, six-thousand-mile junket through the Midwest and the East with a luxurious banquet at every stop guaranteed the attention of local and national press. Local businessmen extolled the virtues of Pan American trade in speeches and in print while leading the delegates through tours of their factories. Blaine used the conference to drum home the importance of trade.[107] The conference's resolution on reciprocity was read to Congress by President Harrison. William E. Curtis, head of the commercial bureau established by the Pan American Conference and "indirectly connected" with the State Department, also turned his pen to the cause of reciprocity, issuing hundreds of bulletins to the press around the country.[108]

The covert campaign was also an outgrowth of the Pan American Conference. Charles R. Flint, one of the "most successful merchants" in New York City and perhaps the largest rubber dealer in the United States, had been appointed a representative to the Pan American Conference because of strong pressure by New York merchants.[109] A member of the conference's commercial committee, Blaine had charged him with drafting a reciprocity proposal when Blaine's hoped-for customs union met with strong opposition. Some people close to the events, such as the Uruguayan minister to the conference, believed that Flint was the author of the idea of reciprocity; the *New York Times* wrote later in Flint's obituary that he was known as the force behind reciprocity.[110] At the time, however, the short, 39-year-old New York merchant acted behind the scenes to keep his role largely secret. He spoke quietly and carried a big typewriter. The clandestine campaigns to influence public opinion seem to have misled the otherwise astute British observor James Bryce to conclude that while specialists were responsible for opinion making in Great Britain, in the United States opinion "grows up in the nation at large."[111] In fact, special interests worked very hard at winning their way.

Certainly Flint, a Democrat but a protectionist, was a strong advocate of reciprocity. As early as October 1889 he had made the principal speech at a large reception for the Pan American delegations in Chicago where he argued that the "dealings between the peoples of the Americas should be direct—without foreign intervention. We should declare our commercial independence. . . . Now that American capital is in a position to look abroad for investment, now that our 'infant industries' have grown up and have become 'overproducers' we must prepare for a new future."[112] To prepare for that future, Flint, together with millionaire business magnate Thomas Jefferson Coolidge, unofficially negotiated a reciprocal trade treaty with Brazil's delegate Salvador de Mendonça during the Pan American Congress (and an unsuccessful one with Argentina), but their agreement was endangered by Congress's initial refusal to offer reciprocity provisions.[113]

To create support for reciprocity, Flint set out on an aggressive speaking and letter-writing campaign aimed at the country's chambers of commerce and boards of trade. As a leading member of the New York Board of Trade and the Spanish American Commercial Union, he enjoyed considerable influence.[114] He wrote to the board's members asking them to petition their congressmen and to secure from their own organizations resolutions in favor of reciprocity because "this simple business question has, unfortunately, become involved with politics and personal interests."[115] (The quote is ironic in light of Flint's personal interests in the treaty that we will explore later.) He convinced his uncle to present a pro-reciprocity resolution to the San Francisco Chamber of Commerce that was unanimously endorsed, and then proceeded to write some 2,000 letters to businessmen and associations across the country along the same lines, though he did not always use his own name.[116] Flint coordinated his actions closely with Blaine to whom he explained, "If the businessmen can only be stirred up on this question a sentiment will be shown most favorable to your ideas, and the way to have these views expressed is through meetings of Boards of Trade."[117] Flint also had articles favorable to reciprocity placed in the *New York Times* and other newspapers.[118] No doubt other private individuals and politicians were also lobbying for reciprocity, but only Flint's substantial correspondence appears in Blaine's archive, and his are the only discussions of a publicity campaign in the records of the U.S. delegation to the Pan American Conference.

The campaign was a success. The *Baltimore American* reported in September that "the endorsements are pouring in." The *Minneapolis Times* attributed Blaine's success to "the irresistible pressure of public opinion" as well as Blaine's "statesmanship," and the *Philadelphia Press* noted that "every Republican state convention since July has approved [reciprocity]. . . . The leading daily papers that represent them are of a like mind."[119] Indeed, resolutions in favor of reciprocity arrived from commercial associations spanning the country: from New York to Indianapolis, Pittsburgh, Cincinnati, Minneapolis, Los Angeles, and San Francisco.[120] The Plumed Knight, as Blaine was known to his admirers, had once again asserted his mastery over the Republican party, leading the *Baltimore News* to remark, "You must be sure your old lion is really down for good before you begin to dance on him."[121] While it is true, as LaFeber suggests, that Blaine led and businessmen followed on reciprocity, it is also true that businessmen, as much as Blaine, convinced Congress and the president to agree to an export expansion plank in the tariff.

The reciprocity measure stated:

> That with a view to securing reciprocal trade with countries producing the following articles, and for this purpose, on and after the first day of January, eighteen hundred and ninety two, whenever, and so often as the President shall be satisfied that the government of any country producing and exporting sugars, molasses, coffee, tea and hides, raw and uncured, or any such articles imposes duties or any other exactions upon the agriculture or other products of the United States which, in view of the free introduction of such sugar, molasses, coffee, tea and hides into the United States, he may deem to be reciprocally unequal and unreasonable, he shall have the power and it shall be his duty to suspend, by proclamation to that effect, the provisions of this act relating to the free introduction of such sugar, molasses, coffee, tea and hides the production of such countries for such time as he shall deem just.[122]

This was certainly far short of Blaine's objective of a Pan American free trade zone, but it reflected Harrison's position. Harrison wrote Blaine: "We should confine our reciprocity negotiations with such limits as not to attack the protective system—in other words, to the admission to our markets of non-competing products, as much as possible."[123] Little new was added to the free list of the previous tariff, and very important items for obtaining trade concessions, such as wool, were left off. Two free trade critics of reciprocity complained that the possibilities reciprocity offered for freer trade were "nullified" by the unwillingness to make "it apply to articles of some degree of importance."[124]

For all its shortcomings, the McKinley reciprocity provision was an important victory for Harrison and Blaine. First, it constituted Republican acknowledgement of the importance of promoting exports. It also established that expanding exports was a duty for the state, not just the private sector, and it recognized for the first time the supremacy of the executive in formulating foreign policy. The wording specifically established that retaliation would be forthcoming "whenever and so often as the President shall be satisfied." Congress had granted the executive a coercive weapon and the right to determine for himself when to employ it. Moreover, it was the president who interpreted whether trade concessions made by negotiating countries constituted reciprocal measures. Thus Harrison could enter into trade agreements without congressional approval and could thereby avoid repeating the embarrassment of Chester Arthur when Congress had rejected his reciprocal treaties.[125]

The Democrats naturally denounced the McKinley Tariff. Cleveland portrayed it as "an unjust tariff which banishes from many humble homes the comforts of life, in order that in the palaces of wealth, luxury may more abound."[126] The free sugar provision was seen as a sop that would in fact strengthen the sugar trust by providing it with free raw materials while refined sugar still faced a 0.4 cents per pound duty.[127] Since the U.S. Sugar Refining Company would come to control 95 percent of the market at the end of the McKinley Tariff in 1895, the Democrats appear to have been correct.[128] They were particularly perturbed about the president's power to enter into reciprocal treaties without congressional approval. A weak executive had long been a cherished Democratic institution. They challenged the tariff in the courts, but the Supreme Court disappointed them when it found the reciprocity clause constitutional.[129] The president was not entering into trade treaties, but rather "arrangements" or "agreements" because he promised no special treatment to nations offering reciprocal tariff advantages; his power was restricted to punishing with higher duties nations that refused to provide reciprocal favors.[130]

The reciprocity provision came under attack along with the high McKinley Tariff itself. Republicans, who gave first priority to protection of domestic production, feared reciprocity would be a wedge against protective tariffs. Democrats, who favored the expansion of foreign trade, believed reciprocity was a palliative meant more to defend protectionism than to stimulate international trade. The particular form that the McKinley Tariff's reciprocity took struck them as inappropriate. Democratic critic William L. Wilson observed, "It is not reciprocity at all. It is retaliation, and, worst of all, retaliation on our own people."[131]

On the other hand, an impressive number of important organizations hailed the tariff's reciprocity provision: the National Board of Trade, the National Livestock Exchange, the National Association of Wool Manufacturers, the Southwestern Winter Wheat Millers' Association, the American Paper Makers Association, Baldwin Locomotive Works, the B. F. Goodrich Company, National Cash Register Company, and the National Association of Manufacturers. It is interesting how many manufacturers were on the list since Blaine's main intent in forging the provision was to encourage agricultural exports, which, after all, constituted some 80 percent of all U.S. exports. Now that the reciprocity provision had finally been pushed through Congress, it had to be applied to foreign markets to gain entry for American products. The logical place to look for commercial expansion was to the south.

CHAPTER 2

Target: Latin America

The tariff's free list, which almost exclusively contained tropical agricultural goods such as coffee, sugar, and cocoa, reflected the fact that Latin America was targeted for trade expansion. Reciprocity, after all, had partially grown out of the first Pan American congress. Historical, geopolitical, and economic reasons all argued for closer U.S.–Latin American relations.

The United States had historically had close, if not always amicable, relations with Latin America. In the colonial period and early republic, the triangular trade had brought American traders to the Caribbean and Brazil in considerable numbers. Later U.S. settlers and soldiers battled Mexicans for control of Texas and then for much of the western half of what is now the United States. The discovery of gold in the newly conquered California territory brought the Caribbean and Central and South America into the commercial orbit of the United States. American fortune hunters and merchants filled the clippers that rounded Cape Horn or the trains that traversed Panama and Nicaragua. Some of them, such as William Walker who briefly was president of Nicaragua, were so ungracious as to attempt to conquer parts of Central America.

After the Civil War, U.S. diplomats largely replaced American armies, filibusterers, and traders as agents of foreign policy. Their most important victory was in Mexico in 1866–67, where American threats to the French and ammunition supplies to Benito Juarez led to the defeat of Emperor Maximilian and the resumption of Mexican rule.

Despite a long history of relations with Latin America and the advantage of proximity, the United States in 1889 was far from exercising a sphere of influence in the continent. In virtually every country, Europeans were the principal trade partners and the main investors. Nonetheless, Latin America was still attractive to the United States for geopolitical reasons: it was the underdeveloped area least under European control. Whereas none of Oceania was independent and only 3 percent of Africa's territory was sovereign, 32 percent of North America (because of Canada) and 43 percent of Asia were independent, fully 92 percent of Central and South America was ruled by independent states.[1] It was the part of the world where it would be easiest to be a "free rider on free trade" by taking advantage of an international system dominated by British free traders.[2] Moreover, Latin America had a centuries-long tradition of incorporation into the Atlantic economy. Consequently, its leaders shared the prevailing notions of private property, individual liberty, and the sanctity of contracts.[3] Commodity and stock markets as well as courts replaced the need for gunboats to extract surplus. Thus in Latin America it was possible to wage an economic struggle with the European Great Powers without entering into military combat or constructing the expensive apparatus of empire; it was possible, but increasingly difficult.

Latin America loomed important in the 1880's because Europeans, particularly the British, were rapidly expanding their presence on the continent. Direct colonialism was slight after the French effort to place the Austrian prince Maximilian on Mexico's throne was defeated. Britain added formally only the rather inconsequential colony of British Honduras and informally the Mosquito Coast of Nicaragua. But trade and investment swelled. Britain tripled its exports to the continent's richest nation, Argentina, in the brief period between 1880 and 1885, while buying an ever larger share of Argentine wheat, corn, wool, and meat, all of which began replacing U.S. exports of these goods to Great Britain.[4] British capital investments in Latin America also grew sharply, and an increasing share were in direct ownership of private resources rather than loans to states. Englishmen in the 1880's and early 1890's came to control the railroads of Argentina, the nitrates of Chile, and mines and railways in Mexico.[5] The French began investing heavily in the 1880's in Latin America; their most spectacular undertaking, which most troubled American politicians, was the ailing Panama Canal company.[6] Even the Germans, Dutch, Belgians, and Portuguese began to invest in Latin American companies in the 1880's. Increasing European control in the one area of the world free from European colonialism worried U.S. policy makers.[7]

Blaine and other politicians were also concerned about the more direct economic importance of Latin America to the United States. The U.S. trade deficit in the 1880's was directly attributable to its failure in Latin America. In 1889, despite a net surplus of $129 million with the rest of the world, the United States suffered a negative net trade balance because of its deficit of $142 million with Latin America.[8] It purchased a vast amount of raw materials such as coffee and sugar from Latin America but exported relatively little to the south. Particularly worrisome was that the total share of U.S. exports to Latin America had fallen from 14 percent in 1868 to only 9 percent in 1888.[9] Something had to be done to increase exports to its southern neighbors. Since the U.S. market was of much greater importance to the countries of Latin America than to any other part of the non-European world, threats to close the American market if reciprocal favors were not forthcoming appeared best suited to Latin America.

Latin America was attractive, then, because it was intimately integrated into the world market and it offered possibilities for reciprocal trade treaties. Latin American per capita exports were greater than those of southeastern Europe in the late nineteenth century, almost three times Asian totals, and over four times those of Africa.[10] More to the point for U.S. policy makers, imports were similarly greater in Latin America. As Blaine pronounced, "While the great powers of Europe are steadily enlarging their colonial domination in Asia and Africa it is the especial province of this country to improve and expand its trade with the nations of America."[11]

President Harrison made clear his interest in Latin America when he appointed Blaine secretary of state. Inviting Blaine into his cabinet, Harrison noted that he was "especially interested in the improvement in our relations with Central and South America."[12]

Blaine and Latin America

Blaine was a leading advocate of a more aggressive Latin American policy. Indeed, his daughter believed that closer relations between the United States and Latin America was the one thing he "really cared about."[13] As secretary of state briefly for President Garfield in 1881 he had demonstrated unusual diplomatic energy and Anglophobia. He sought to secure the western hemisphere as a U.S. sphere of influence, both diplomatically and commercially. To accomplish this he anticipated the Roosevelt Corollary by seeking to become the policeman of the hemisphere. In his opinion, if the United States did not resume its efforts to secure peace in South America some European powers would be forced to perform that friendly office.[14] In the case of the 1881 Mexican-Guatemalan dispute over Chiapas, Blaine as secretary of state took an even more aggressive stand: the United States would exert its influence and, he intimated, perhaps even use force "for the preservation of the national life and integrity of any one of them [Latin American nations] against aggression, whether this may come from abroad or from another American republic."[15] When the Colombian government asked various European powers to guarantee the sovereignty of the Isthmus of Panama, Blaine pointed out that the U.S. treaty with Colombia of 1846 stipulated that its sovereignty was already protected and warned Colombia that no other nation's help was needed or desired. In Nicaragua, Blaine negotiated a treaty to build an isthmian canal, hoping to repudiate the Clayton-

Bulwer treaty with Britain that had promised the English a share in any such undertaking. Blaine also interceded in the War of the Pacific, which he believed was "an English war on Peru with Chile as the instrument."[16] He attempted to pressure Chile into recognizing a concession held by a U.S. citizen to nitrate beds that Chile had recently conquered.

The capstone to Blaine's efforts to establish U.S. diplomatic supremacy in Latin America during his tenure as Garfield's secretary of state had been his abortive attempt to organize a Pan American conference. There were precedents, to be sure, but none had included significant U.S. participation.

Latin Americans had called three previous meetings of the American republics to forge hemispheric unity. In 1826, shortly after independence from Spain, Simon Bolívar had called the Congress of Panama to establish cordial relations between the Americas and establish joint defense against European reconquest. The United States, which had lent some moral and material aid to the independence movements and had expressed its support for the sovereignty of the new nations three years earlier in the Monroe Doctrine, had sent observers (who arrived after the conference had ended). Congress would not agree to mutual defense treaties, however.[17] In 1856 Peru had initiated the Continental Treaty to prevent inter-American hostilities, which nine Latin American nations signed. The United States was not invited to participate.[18] Colombia invited its Latin American neighbors for a conference on arbitration, but the war raging at the time in the Pacific between Chile and Peru (1879–83) demonstrated that the Latin American efforts to arbitrate hostilities were not graced with success.

Blaine's first attempt at a Pan American conference was no more successful than the previous Latin American efforts. He called it for the "purpose of considering . . . the methods of preventing war between the nations of America."[19] Blaine also wanted to "cultivate such friendly, commercial relations with all American countries as would lead to a large increase in the export trade of the United States. . . . To obtain the second object, the first must be obtained. . . . Peace is essential to commerce."[20] Although several Latin American nations had already accepted the invitation to the conference and some others were favorably inclined, the meeting was aborted when Blaine resigned following the assassination of President Garfield. His successor, Frederick Frelinghusen, canceled the conference. Blaine argued that the reason for cancellation was Congress's refusal to fund the $10,000 necessary to conduct the meeting, while his wife believed that Frelinghusen "attacked from behind" for personal reasons. Latin American lack of enthusiasm for the congress, particularly because of the failure of U.S. diplomacy in the Chilean-Peruvian war, also contributed to the withdrawal of invitations.[21]

None of the other Latin American initiatives of Blaine's first term produced results. His failure reflected the tenuous and inconstant nature of U.S. Latin American policy in the nineteenth century. The stalemate between the parties, the weakness of the executive, and the territorialized nature of the state led to a bewildering assortment of false starts, U-turns, and unfulfilled promises. As Allen Peskin quipped, "If, as has been suggested, a country without a foreign policy is a happy country, the United States must have reached the peak of its felicity between the Civil War and the turn of the century."[22] Only with the Harrison administration did that giddiness begin to abate as a seriousness of purpose and a consistent and forceful Latin American policy started to take shape.

The First Pan American Conference

When Blaine returned as secretary of state to Harrison in 1889, conditions were ripe for a Pan American conference. In 1885 Chester Arthur had sent a three-man commission to ascertain commercial and diplomatic possibilities in South America; they returned with a glowing report.[23] Opportunities for commercial expansion were enhanced by the construction of several underwater telegraph cables in the 1880's that connected the United States to the west coast of Spanish-speaking Latin America down to Valparaiso, Chile, and to the Caribbean and Rio de Janeiro on the east coast. Northern Mexico was brought more tightly into the American economic sphere through railroads that linked Texas to the northern states. In 1886 the Monterrey Chamber of Commerce complained that because of the new railroad local citizens now preferred to satisfy "all the necessities of life with American articles and products."[24]

International diplomatic events also increased the appeal of Pan-Americanism. Numerous international conferences took place in the last two decades of the century that largely excluded the United States. Just before the Washington Pan American Conference, the South American countries convened in Montevideo to focus on international civil and commercial law, copyrights, trademarks, patents, and penal and procedural law. They agreed that only Latin countries be invited. Consequently, while France, Italy, and Spain became signatories to the copyright agreement, the United States was left out.[25]

Europeans were even more active than the Latin Americans in meeting and agreeing to common laws and standards. There were meetings in 1883 and 1887 in Paris on trademarks, 1886 in Bern on copyrights, and 1884 in Paris on time zones. Economic meetings such as the 1878 and 1881 monetary conferences in Paris and Brussels and the 1880's treaties against sugar bounties became common. Perhaps most threatening to the United States was the Berlin Conference of 1884–85 in which it was invited to observe as the European colonial powers partitioned Africa. Certainly the boldest and most grandiose European statement was the 1889 Parisian exposition that brought representatives and products from the entire world under the shadow of the newly erected Eiffel Tower.[26]

Europe provided not only a challenge but a model. The United States responded by attempting to Americanize international conferences and expositions, organizing not only the 1889 Pan American meeting in Washington, but also an international maritime conference the same year and an international monetary conference in 1891. By far the most imposing and expensive of these gatherings was the Chicago Columbian Exposition, intended to celebrate the four-hundredth anniversary of Columbus's "discovery" of the New World. The multi-million-dollar exposition drew more than twenty million visitors at a time when the population of the United States was only 75 million.

Intellectually, Pan-Americanism derived in good part from the nationalist trends of nineteenth-century thinkers such as Herder and Fichte who stressed Pan Germanism, the creators of the Pan Germanic League, as well as the Pan Slavic movements and Mazzini and Garibaldi's Italian consolidation movements. Of course, the cultural difference between the Latin Americans and the Anglo Americans vitiated the applicability of cultural nationalism.[27] But a stress on the distinctive features of Americanism—newness, vast frontiers, racial melding, republicanism, and opposition to European colonialism—resonated in parts of Latin America, particularly, as we shall see, in Brazil.

These precedents converged to produce the first Pan American Conference in 1889.[28] For once there was bipartisan agreement in Washington. In 1888 Congress authorized $100,000, and Cleveland issued the invitations and set the agenda. The actual conference would commence after Harrison took office. The guest list sent a message to the European powers: no European colonies—not Cuba, Martinique, or Canada—were invited. Hawaii was included in this creative redefinition of the Americas when Blaine somewhat belatedly invited the king of Hawaii to send a delegate. The *New York Times* saw the tardy invitation as an "inferential notification to whom it may concern that the Sandwich Islands are a part of America and are accordingly not to be gobbled up by European powers."[29] Clearly the conference was an effort to mark out a sphere of influence for the United States.

Representatives of all independent Latin American nations except the Dominican Republic met in Washington on October 2, 1889.[30] The composition of the delegates and the agenda displayed a difference in expectations between the United States and the Latin American nations. Representatives from the southern hemisphere were political and cultural figures. The United States sent businessmen. Indeed, some Latin Americans felt that the U.S. representatives not only were "not the best fitted for the mission" but "that their selection was an act of disrespect to the Latin American nations."[31]

The U.S. Delegation

James G. Blaine had a weakness for plutocrats. While Speaker of the House he had taken a large loan from the Union Pacific; he had defended the railway so forcefully against repaying government subsidies that some critics labeled him "Jay Gould's errand boy." He represented the maritime companies of Collis P. Huntington and John Roach—for a fee—in the same manner. Roach, the organizer of the first United States and Brazil Mail Steamship Company and a leading investor, along with Huntington, in the second company of that name, continued his support for Blaine, contributing $100,000 to his abortive campaign in 1887.[32] Blaine loved to rub elbows with the rich, befriending men such as Jay Cooke and Stephen Elkins—who served as his investment advisor—while making extended visits to Andrew Carnegie's castle in Scotland. Indeed, Blaine's reputation as defender of the trusts probably cost him the presidency in 1884 when the "Mulligan letters" cast doubt on his honesty.[33]

But avarice did not guide the secretary of state's advocacy of big business as much as ideology did. He was what Jeffrey Lustig would call a "corporate liberal."[34] The state, not the unfettered market, had the obligation to promote economic development by funding and regulating the private sector. Productivity and efficiency, not competition and equality, were his principal values. He wished to be the pastor presiding over the marriage of capital and the state.[35]

His public advocacy of private interests had caused him trouble in the past. In his first term as secretary of state he had suffered a scandal and six-month-long congressional investigation on charges that U.S. consular officials were personally involved in business transactions in Peru.[36] So he decided now for the Pan American Conference to choose men who did not hold office. Instead, he nominated men of business. The use of wealthy businessmen on blue-ribbon official committees was a new feature of American politics that he was helping usher in in the last decades of the nineteenth century.[37]

The composition of the U.S. delegation reveals much about Blaine's hopes for the conference. Of the ten men chosen to represent the United States, only three had been politicians and just one was a diplomat. The career diplomat was Henry Trescot, a close friend of Blaine's. Trescot had attempted to settle the Peruvian-Chilean war during Blaine's first tenure at the State Department and had negotiated a reciprocal trade treaty with Mexico under Frelinghusen.[38]

Most of the members were representatives of Big Business, well connected to the merchant community. Several students of the Gilded Age have argued that the great magnates were absent from the political debate, except for Andrew Carnegie (who was a member of the Pan American delegation).[39] Ernest May, studying the "foreign policy establishment" of the 1890's, found that it "was not identifiable with what a C. Wright Mills of the day would have labeled its 'power elite.'"[40] Rather than the "titans," May maintains it was secondary businessmen who took a hand at forming public opinion. May goes on to contend that even this second rung often concentrated on foreign policy rather than domestic and kept their minds more on their railroad shares or manufacturing plants than on politics.[41] In fact, however, delegate Thomas Jefferson Coolidge was closer to the mark when he observed that the delegation consisted of "the leading businessmen of the country."[42] Moreover, the businessmen on the Pan American commission saw politics as intimately tied to their economic ventures and regarded domestic and foreign issues as connected as well. Unfortunately, the extent of their influence on public opinion is difficult to gauge because so much of their maneuvering was intentionally behind the scenes.

Cornelius N. Bliss was certainly among the most important businessmen in the country. Head of the "great" wholesale dry goods firm of Bliss, Fabyan and Co. and vice president of the Fourth National Bank, he was, according to the *New York Herald*, "first a merchant prince, and second a banker and—shall we say it—third a politician. . . . [He was] a munificent contributor to republican campaign funds."[43] He also had been a major textile manufacturer for more than twenty years.[44]

Clement Studebaker was a millionaire carriage maker from Indiana whose stagecoaches and farmers' wagons were sold all over the world. His company was soon to branch into automobile manufacturing.[45]

T. Jefferson Coolidge, grandson of Thomas Jefferson, was a leading member of Boston's economic elite. He also was, according to May, "a prototype member of what today we call the foreign policy establishment."[46] Starting as a partner in the mercantile house of Gardner and Coolidge, he became manager of his father-in-law's factory, Amoskeag Mills, the largest cotton-spinning establishment in the United States and the supplier for Levi Strauss jeans. (His father-in-law, William Appleton, was a director of one of the country's largest and most prestigious publishing houses, D. Appleton, which published, among other things, the *North American Review*.) Coolidge later became a director of Merchant's Bank, the Chicago, Burlington, and Quincy railroad, and for a short time he was the president of the Atchison, Topeka, and Santa Fe railroad. He also founded the Old Colony trust company and had interests in several other Boston financial organizations that involved him in the financing of railroads, telegraph and telephone projects, and one of the precursors of the General Electric Company. He later helped organize the United Fruit Company over which his son in later years presided as chairman of the board.[47] Coolidge explained in his memoirs what had driven his early life: "Everybody was at work trying to make money, and money was becoming the only real avenue to power and success both socially and in regard to your fellow-men. I was ambitious and decided to devote myself to the acquisition of wealth."[48] That wealth, however, necessarily involved him in politics as well.

Henry G. Davis, ex-senator from West Virginia, was an owner of coal mines and president of the West Virginia Central Railroad, as well as a banker. He seems to have been appointed because of the recommendation of Baltimore merchants where he now lived. His relationship to his son-in-law,

Stephen B. Elkins, who ran Blaine's 1884 presidential campaign and was a partner in the Bering Straits sealing company Harrison was fighting hard to protect, did not hurt Davis's candidacy for the conference.[49]

John Hanson, owner of the Bibb Manufacturing textile company and the Macon (Georgia) *Advocat* was the only representative of the South. His newspaper was one of the South's most vocal defenders of protectionism.[50]

Andrew Carnegie was an experienced railroad executive in Pennsylvania before he became the wealthiest steel manufacturer in the country, if not in the world. He was also a widely read author and one of the country's most respected political commentators.[51]

The group was notable for the absence of representatives of the Midwest, the Southwest, and farming interests. This was a strange oversight in light of the importance placed on farmers and the western part of the country in Blaine's arguments in favor of reciprocity. Only Morris Estée, a lawyer and politician but also one of the leading fruit growers on the Pacific coast, had roots in the soil at a time when the majority of Americans still lived in the countryside. Even Estée was considered by the *New York Times* a "representative of railroad companies."[52] John Henderson had made a fortune in Missouri real estate, but then lost it and turned to law, which he had been practicing in Washington for two decades.[53]

Personal politics were certainly clear in the absence of representatives from Louisiana and Alabama, two southern states anxious to increase their commercial ties with Latin America, but dominated by the Democrats and hence uninteresting to Republicans. Brazil's consul general, Salvador de Mendonça, noted in 1887 the struggle for commercial supremacy between New Orleans, the natural entrepôt for Brazilian coffee because most consumers were accessible along the Mississippi, and New York. New York had captured the trade because of superior capital, railroad networks, and government concessions,[54] but the delegates to the Pan American Conference, especially the representatives of New York and Boston (Bliss, Flint, and Coolidge), worked hard to protect the advantages of their ports.

The most active member of the delegation, and the man most germane to our story, was the New Yorker Charles R. Flint. Flint was a fascinating and complex man who has received little historical attention. His versatility is demonstrated by the fact that the very few historians who have mentioned him point to different aspects of his career, like blind men describing an elephant. Alfred D. Chandler terms him a "leading promoter of industrial mergers" and a "financier and speculator."[55] V. G. Kiernan describes him as the "world roving embodiment of it [private enterprise] and of the arms trade in particular."[56] Alfred Thimm, on the other hand, refers to Flint simply as "a representative of the newly developing managerial class."[57] Although still less than 40 years old in 1889, Flint brought over two decades of experience in Latin American markets to the conference. The son of one of Maine's largest sailing ship builders, he had begun in shipping and trade, soon becoming a 25 percent partner (later 35 percent) in the W. R.

Grace shipping company. He then became a commission agent, which made him the "largest buyer in this country of miscellaneous manufactured products for export."[58] He also became an arms dealer helping the Peruvian government procure five naval war vessels in 1869 and providing them with munitions later for their war with Chile. He served as financial agent to the Peruvian government as well as consul for Chile, Costa Rica, and Nicaragua.

In addition to his quasi-diplomatic relations with Latin America, Flint became, in the words of a Chicago newspaper, "the Father of Trusts."[59] He perhaps conceived of the advantages of consolidation and cooperation as U.S. agent of the Nitrate Company in Peru, which sought to create an international nitrate trust years before Rockefeller established the first American trust. This was the company that Blaine had tried to defend after Peru lost its nitrate fields to Chile.

Flint applied his experience to the United States. In 1879 he became president of the U.S. Electric Lighting Company, which—after he left the directorship—joined with competitors to become Westinghouse. At the time of the Pan American Conference Flint was busy cornering the New York rubber market and bringing together rubber manufacturers in what would become in three years U.S. Rubber.[60] In subsequent years Flint served as organizer or expert in the formation of 24 consolidations.[61]

Flint personified the overlap between foreign and domestic business, the interrelationship between transportation, commerce, and manufacturing, and the alliance between business and government. As an advocate and director of trusts he favored protection but as an owner of one of the country's principal trading and shipping companies he also wanted to expand trade. He believed both that "it is very desirable that we should do everything possible to extend our markets abroad" but the home market could also be protected. The principal way to make U.S. industry internationally competitive, he believed, was through greater efficiency brought by combinations.[62] In his mind there was no contradiction between greater concentration at home and greater competition internationally. Indeed, the first was necessary for the second to become possible. This is a view that Carnegie and most of the other delegates shared, but it was not the view of small businessmen and farmers who hoped to solve their domestic problems through exports.

Blaine's appointment of Flint to the delegation should have come as no surprise, nor could the leadership role he later assumed together with Coolidge and Bliss have startled any informed observer. Flint and Blaine's relationship reflected the overlap of business, diplomacy, and politics. Blaine no doubt already knew the Flints from their shipbuilding operation in his home state of Maine, but the connection became stronger when Flint, as Nicaragua's consul in New York, participated in the 1881 negotiations between Blaine and Nicaragua for a U.S. canal across the isthmus. As mentioned earlier, Flint was also a principal in the controversy between Peru

and Chile. These were two of Blaine's most important foreign policy initiatives. In addition, Flint was a director of the United States and Brazil Mail
Steamship Company, which was directed by two of Blaine's most generous
contributors, John Roach and Collis P. Huntington.[63]

The Pan American delegation as a whole mirrored Flint's multiple roles.
Many of them had close ties to commerce, finance, industry, and transpor-
tation. Bliss was president of the New York Chamber of Commerce, and,
with Flint, a director of the Spanish American Commercial Association.
Coolidge was closely tied to Boston merchants through the Boston Fruit
Company and Davis to Baltimore merchants.

Some were politically important. Davis had been a senator from West
Virginia, and John Henderson had been senator for Missouri as well as chair
of the Republican national convention in 1884. Coolidge would serve as
U.S. minister to France in 1892. Bliss, a boyhood friend of Harrison's vice
president Levi P. Morton, was chairman of the New York Republican state
committee and of the American Protective Tariff League, one of the country's leading advocates of protectionism. He later graduated to Republican
national campaign treasurer from 1892 to 1904. He would serve as McKinley's secretary of the interior in 1897 and 1898 and reportedly turned down
that president's offer of the vice presidency in 1900. (Had he accepted he
might today be more famous than Theodore Roosevelt.) Estée chaired the
Republican national convention in 1884.[64] They were, by and large, men
like Flint who supported protection but saw advantages in reciprocity.[65]
These men also reflected the more general American experience in that
none of them besides Flint had experience in Latin America, though several
such as Bliss and Coolidge had interests in Latin American commerce or
railroads. They were men hoping for a changing relationship with Latin
America, and they hoped to personally profit from it. But their personal
fortunes, with the possible exception of Flint, did not at this point depend
upon Latin American trade and investment.

Pan American Negotiations

The American objective in convoking and funding the Pan American
Conference was clearly to bring Latin America into the U.S. sphere of influence. After a brief session in Washington that saw the election of Blaine as
president of the conference, the delegates (except the Argentines who refused to participate) were taken on a six-week, six-thousand-mile junket
from New York and Boston as far west as Omaha, Minneapolis, and St.
Louis. Revealingly, Southern cities were not included in the original tour,
and an effort to bring the delegates south after the conference fell through.[66]
The *Charleston News and Courier* was not surprised that the entourage ignored the South since the impending conference was "just for our protected
manufacturers that have outgrown the home market and have no other."

With few factories, the South was really not included in the "scheme."[67] Solidly Democratic, the South also held little political promise for the Republican administration. The critical Midwest, on the other hand, received great attention.

The common interpretation of this tour of factories and banquet halls is that it was meant to impress the Latin Americans with American prosperity and might. The visitors were supposed to develop a taste for the fine American goods they were shown in what amounted to a traveling trade fair and become greedy for the vast American market. Blaine's not very hidden agenda for this grand tour, however, was to divert the attention of the U.S. Congress, which was debating the McKinley Tariff as the Pan American delegates dined, to the markets of the southern republics. He hoped to whet Congress's appetite for reciprocity.

The American press responded to this effort in contradictory ways. Some papers, such as the *Chicago Inter-Ocean*, the *Omaha World-Herald*, the *San Francisco Examiner*, and the *New York Tribune* expected important results improving commerce, transportation, and international arbitration.[68] Some, such as the *St. Paul Press* and the *San Francisco Chronicle*, were hopeful but unsure.[69] The *New York Herald*, on the other hand, denounced the conference as "folly." *Bradstreet's*, a leading commercial journal, warned that "immediate practical results from the conference are not very hopefully anticipated in commercial circles." *Harper's* captured the paradox of the situation: "No event involving the possibilities of large result ever aroused in advance less general attention" and noted that "The assembly has been regarded with much more interest even curious anticipation in Europe than in this country."[70]

Americans thought little and knew less about the countries to the south, particularly those farther south than Cuba and Mexico. Ignorance reached into the highest levels, as it usually does. One member of Harrison's cabinet gave a speech shortly before the beginning of the conference in which he referred to Buenos Aires as capital of Brazil, and a Supreme Court justice asked what language was spoken in Chile. There simply was little public knowledge of Latin America. Even William E. Curtis, one of the trade commissioners who had traveled to South America in 1884 and who would become the leading propagandist for Pan-Americanism, admitted before the conference, "It is not expected that any immediate or direct results will follow the meeting. . . . The results of the conference will be largely sentimental."[71] Blaine and the U.S. delegation would attempt to create interest, not respond to it.

Not all Latin American delegates were pleased by the experience of being a traveling publicity campaign. Some harbored the fears of the Cuban newspaperman, future hero of Cuban independence, and journalist assigned to the conference, José Martí, who depicted the conference in alarming terms:

Never in America, from its independence to the present, has there been
a matter requiring more good judgement or more vigilance, or demanding
a clearer and more thorough examination, than the invitation which the
powerful United States (glutted with unsalable merchandise and determined to extend its dominions in America) is sending to the less powerful
American nations (bound by free and useful commerce to the European
nations) for the purposes of arranging an alliance against Europe and cutting
off transactions with the rest of the world.[72]

While perhaps a bit strident, Martí was not far off the mark. Certainly
other writers—and delegates, especially those from Argentina and Chile—
shared his opinion.[73] Blaine's list of seven objectives for the conferences
demonstrated the U.S. preoccupation with trade. He sought (1) the prosperity of the American nations (through greater trade, of course), (2) an
American customs union that would lower duties to American countries
but raise them to European competitors, (3) greater communications between the ports of the Americas (to encourage commerce and provide subsidies to steamship lines), (4) a uniform customs system (to facilitate trade),
(5) uniform weights and protection of patents and trademarks and literary
property (to protect royalties), (6) common money based on silver (to sub-
stitute New York for London as the hemisphere's financial center), and (7)
obligatory arbitration (to prevent involvement of European powers).[74]

Despite the seemingly clear and coherent purpose of the American delegation, its performance at the conference betrayed the amateurish and privatized nature of diplomacy in the early years of corporate liberalism.[75]
Only Trescot and Flint had had first-hand experience with Latin America.
Only one of the ten U.S. delegates could speak Spanish reasonably well,
and only one member had diplomatic experience representing the United
States. Unfortunately they were not the same person and neither of the two
was in charge of the delegation. Indeed, it soon became clear—to the dismay
of the Latin American representatives—that no one was really in charge.

Although Blaine had written to leading industrialists and to the boards
of trade and chambers of commerce of the country for their views on the
conference's agenda, he failed to even attempt to hammer out a unified position in the large U.S. delegation.[76] Certainly the men had a unified vision in
the sense that eight of them were Republicans (three had served on national
or state Republican committees) and all believed that the business of government was business; but they differed markedly on the particulars.[77]

The professional diplomats among the Latin Americans found this particularly frustrating. Mexican and Argentine members worked hard to deci-
pher the U.S. position on important issues, but to no avail. The Mexican
delegate, Matias Romero, complained: "We have noted very clearly not only
the lack of agreement among the United States delegates but also the disorganization and almost anarchy among them. Frequently what one proposes
is opposed by others [of the same delegation]."[78]

The U.S. delegates tended to give their own personal opinions rather than representing any larger constituency. Somewhat surprisingly, even in handpicking men favorable to commercial expansion Blaine had created the same cacophony in his delegation that was frustrating so many of his initiatives in Congress. Clearly there was a great difference of opinion over means as well as ends.

Not surprisingly, the eventual resolutions of the Pan American Conference were disappointing to Blaine. The *New York Evening Post* announced that "all of Blaine's proposals have been defeated."[79] This was an overly pessimistic appraisal. Still, the results of the meetings demonstrated the relatively weak position his country still exercised in the hemisphere. The agreements that were reached on international private law, extradition codes, patents, and trademarks were based on agreements Latin Americans had reached in Montevideo the year before without U.S. advice. The sanitation codes were accepted from an 1887 international convention in Rio and projects from the 1889 congress in Lima.[80]

On the three most important issues—a common monetary standard for the continent, obligatory arbitration of international disputes, and, most important, an inter-American customs union—the U.S. position was undermined by the Argentines as well as by the divisiveness within the North American ranks. Blaine sought to create a coin common to all the Americas based on the silver dollar that would allow New York to replace London as the hemisphere's financial center. The Argentine delegate, and most of the Americans, preferred gold. Consequently, the conference agreed to the advisability of an international conference the following year to discuss a common coin but did not comment on whether it should be silver or gold.[81]

The delegates likewise agreed to the principle of arbitration, but insisted it be voluntary at the discretion of participating nations. At the suggestion of the Argentine delegation, they defeated a measure to create a permanent tribunal in Washington. Mexico, wary of past experiences with its northern neighbor, also inserted a clause foreswearing the right of conquest in the Americas, which outraged Blaine. The secretary of state fought it energetically, but eventually also conceded this to the majority.[82]

The customs union, to be based on the model of List's German Zollverein, was rejected as "utopian." Again the Argentinians led the way. The Latin American members were unwilling to isolate their principal trade partners in Europe with a customs wall for the benefit of trading with their neighbors whose economies were more competitive than complementary. Argentina's Saenz Pena argued that the United States was clearly not yet able to provide goods as cheaply as Latin America's European competitors or to purchase enough to compensate for lost markets. Besides, if the United States was truly interested in increasing trade, why was it at that very moment busy increasing the tariff wall that caused Argentina to import twice as much from the United States as it exported there?

The Argentine case was exceptional since the country's main products—wool and meat—were competitive rather than complementary to U.S. products and were therefore kept out of the United States by the tariff.[83] Flint attempted to demonstrate the fallacy of the Argentinian position but could not overcome the reality that the various Latin American countries had sharply differing relations with the world economy, both in products and in trading partners. Moreover, the governments of Latin America depended heavily on customs duties to finance themselves.[84] Thus one customs union with minimal duties for all was doomed to failure. A compromise position was offered, however: American nations were encouraged to engage in bilateral trade treaties. The compromise held out this possibility:

> If . . . the results [of reciprocity] should be as satisfactory as is to be expected, the number of articles on the free list might be enlarged in each case from time to time until . . . the development of the national elements of wealth should have enabled each nation to obtain or increase its revenue from domestic sources, unrestricted reciprocity or a free trade among all or some of the American nations should at last be attained.[85]

The American delegation enjoyed more success in drumming up conference support for steamship subsidies, a Pan American railroad, and an inter-American bank because these would be financed largely by the United States and would not infringe on Latin American sovereignty. Steamship subsidies had been important to Blaine for more than twenty years. He had fought fiercely thirteen years earlier to continue subsidies, but Congress had refused. Now he took up the fight again, and the company he had previously defended, the U.S. and Brazil Mail Steamship Company, was pleased.[86]

Under free market forces, the American merchant marine had gone into eclipse. In 1856, 75 percent of all U.S. trade was carried in American ships, but by 1888 the percentage had fallen to a mere 13.5 percent. Indeed, the total U.S. sail and steam fleet registered for international trade at the time of the Pan American meeting was 6 percent *less* than it had been in 1810.[87]

Blaine hoped to use the Pan American Conference to pressure Congress to return to steamer subsidies. It was probably not coincidental that an international maritime conference convened in New York at exactly the same time.[88] The *New York Times* predicted that the Pan American Conference would create "a great hunt for steamship subsidies"; apparently both Blaine and President Harrison were indebted to steamship owners who made large campaign contributions.[89] The conference agreed to recommend to their governments steamship subsidies for lines plying the Caribbean, Gulf, and South Atlantic trades. In the South Atlantic, 60 percent of the subsidy would be paid by the United States, and all ships would be built there.[90]

All of the conference's participants also agreed that their governments should finance the surveying of a Pan American railroad. U.S. companies had already built lines thousands of miles into Mexico and were planning one to the Guatemalan border, as well as railways in Costa Rica and Peru. Blaine hoped for Congress to pay as much as $20 million for the Pan American line—to be built by private concessionaires—if the Latin American governments guaranteed the bonds and ceded land and mines. The U.S. representative, Henry Davis, saw the railroad as a method of opening Latin American markets. He hoped and expected, he said, "to live to see this road built from here to the southern-most part of South America and the balance of trade turn in our favor."[91] The American proposal, however, was more ambitious than the Latin Americans cared for, but they were willing to commit a minimal amount for surveying.[92]

The delegates supported the idea of an inter-American bank as well, that is, a private bank that could operate in Latin America. At the time, there was no U.S. bank in Latin America. American merchants had to discount all of their notes on London, which was costing almost $1 million a year. A bank authorized by the U.S. government would facilitate inter-American trade.[93]

Opinions differed on the net success of the Pan American Conference. W. R. Grace, who probably had more business experience in Latin America than any other man in the United States at the time, was pessimistic. He believed that because the agenda for the conference sent out by Cleveland had stressed diplomatic issues, because the Latin American countries had sent diplomats rather than businessmen, and because the American delegates knew so little of Latin America, little of use to business was achieved. Of course his view was probably colored by the fact that his commercial rivals Charles Flint (who had fallen out with Grace) and Cornelius Bliss were appointed to the delegation while Grace—a former Democratic mayor of New York—was pointedly excluded.[94]

But the secretary of state shared Grace's misgivings. Blaine lamented in private to Matías Romero in July that if Congress did not pass reciprocity, the conference was a failure. The delegate from Mexico concluded, on the other hand, that while the results might appear "disappointing" in reality, the conference's "success has been greater than there was any reason to expect" because it improved international relations.[95] The response of the press ranged from the *Philadelphia Press*, which trumpeted the "great importance of the meeting," to the *Boston Post*, which dismissed the conference's deliberations as "visionary schemes."[96] In either case, the conference seems to have influenced Congress to take some remarkable initiatives that would begin the transformation of the state's relationship to export promotion.[97]

Shortly after the end of the conference, Congress passed the Sherman Silver Purchase Act, which strengthened bimetallism in the United States.[98] Congress also authorized funds to survey the Pan American railroad and passed a steamship subsidy bill the next year.[99] Most important, it passed a reciprocity provision to the McKinley Tariff, which led to a series of bilateral treaties between the United States and Latin American countries.

The conference also indirectly stimulated interest in an isthmian canal, a colony in Hawaii, and the China market.[100] The Frenchman Ferdinand-Marie de Lesseps's attempt to build a Panama Canal and his failure in 1889 offered both a threat and an opportunity for the United States to build a canal. Congress authorized a private Nicaraguan canal company in 1889, which began construction. The Republican 1892 platform would call for a federal guarantee of the project and U.S. government control.[101]

Congress agreed to institutionalize this southward thrust by funding the International Union of American Republics (the predecessor to the Organization of American States) and the Commercial Bureau of American Republics. The first was to serve as a forum for international issues, and the second was a trade bureau intended to encourage U.S. exports. Most of these projects were mostly symbolic because Congress provided meager funds. Characteristically, the single greatest expenditure was made by a private individual: Andrew Carnegie contributed most of the $1.1 million required to build the Pan American headquarters.[102]

It should not be surprising that a delegate personally funded the international organization given the individualistic nature of the diplomacy the U.S. delegation had conducted at the conference. In fact, it appears that the American representatives came to the conference as much to advance their own personal interests as to represent their country. Flint and Bliss acted more as lobbyists than diplomats. They assailed the conference members with petitions and invitations from U.S. businessmen and orchestrated the delegates' commercial tour.[103] An embarrassed journalist complained of the extent to which Studebaker touted his own products.[104]

The American delegates stood to benefit personally from some of the conference's provisions. Davis hoped to participate in the Pan American railroad. Both he and Carnegie became members of Pan American railroad committees and lobbied hard for federal funding. Carnegie offered to raise $200 million personally for the line if Congress refused to participate. Their advocacy could be seen as visionary patriotism, but the man responsible for first conceiving of the Pan American railroad denounced them as "cunning and conniving and . . . crafty and clandestine conspirators."[105]

The clearest example of corporate liberalism, the private appropriation of public powers, was the Inter-American Bank. The U.S. delegates, most of whom were financiers or capitalists, were the intended concessionaires.[106] The man who would have most benefited from the bank was Flint who, as a member of the banking committee, urged its approval. He personally applied for the twenty-year charter and lobbied Congress for years. The bank was conceived as a commercial bank to encourage trade. The committee particularly discussed the advantage of a Pan American bank for financing the rubber trade, which was booming since Dunlop's invention of the pneumatic tire the year before. Flint owned a small rubber-manufacturing company. More important, he was perhaps the largest rubber dealer in the United States. He was already contemplating the merger he would bring about two years later of the nine largest rubber manufacturers in the United States. Then he became treasurer of the resulting United States Rubber Company, and his New York Commercial Company became its sole importing agent.[107] Commercial credit in Brazil was important to him.[108]

One of the companies most likely to benefit from the steamship subsidy was Collis P. Huntington's U.S. and Brazil Mail Steamship Company. Its predecessor had been the only U.S.–Latin American line to be granted a congressional subsidy, and the 1891 shipping bill made it one of two lines to receive a subsidy. One of its principals was Flint, who also personally owned a large fleet of vessels. The stipulation that subsidized ships had to be made in the United States would have helped Carnegie's steel.[109] On a related issue, Carnegie and Bliss became large stockholders in the Nicaragua canal company. Flint, who had served as Nicaragua's consul, was also involved in the canal and owned 20 percent of the stock in the Nicaraguan railroad.[110]

The contradictory political and economic impulses behind Blaine's Latin American initiative and the personalistic manner in which it was conducted were revealed in the maneuvers to increase U.S. business with Latin America. These forces were evident in their most crystallized form in the largest Latin American country, the country with which the United States did the most trade, the country in which Flint had the greatest commercial interest, and the first country to sign a reciprocal trade treaty: Brazil.

CHAPTER 3

Brazil: From Monarchy to Republic

Ayellow and green stars and stripes replaced the monarchy's flag soon after the royal guard surrendered to Marshal Deodoro da Fonseca's rebellious troops in Rio de Janeiro's Campo de Sant'Anna on November 15, 1889. The new republican banner was a conscious imitation of the U.S. flag. Although the new-born Republic soon adopted a different pattern for its flag, it did not cease imitating the northern republic. The country's name was changed to the United States of Brazil, and the new constitution promulgated in February 1891 was openly drafted on the U.S. model.[1] Brazilian historians have laid great diplomatic importance on the change of regime; but as this chapter demonstrates, joining the ranks of republics merely formalized on the institutional level Brazil's reorientation toward the United States that had been already under way during the monarchy. First, the possibilities offered by economic development and diversification under the prospering Empire and then diplomatic and internal political threats suddenly faced by the wobbly republican regime convinced Brazilian statesmen of the wisdom of closer relations with the United States. However, when they agreed to a reciprocity arrangement with the United States, they were not acting as representatives of republican coffee-exporting planters as has been generally assumed;[2] rather, support for the accord came, ironically, from champions of industrialization and "modernization"—some of whom were quite suspicious of foreigners— as well as exmonarchist sugar barons. They hoped that the United States would help them weaken the British grip on Brazil. The United States now appeared as more than a friend or an exemplary model; it presented an anti-imperialist alternative.

Retrospective

Although the United States had experienced little interchange with colonial Brazil before King Dom João VI threw open the Portuguese colony's ports to international trade in 1808, some Brazilians had already noted the similarities between the two. Like Brazil, the United States was a former European colony, a huge continental settler colony that relied on European immigrants and African slaves rather than its own marginalized indigenous population. Both countries' character was shaped in good part by their frontiers, and both expanded their borders continuously at the expense of native peoples and competing European colonial powers, which led to a considerable degree of de facto local control.[3]

Early political relations between Brazil and the United States were as amicable as they were infrequent once the United States became the first power to recognize Brazilian independence. Shortly thereafter the declaration of the Monroe Doctrine excited Brazilian hopes that the United States would enter into a mutual defense treaty to protect Brazil from Portuguese recolonization; but the U.S. Congress refused to commit itself to such a large and impossible undertaking (particularly because the Portuguese were close allies of the British). Nonetheless, American clipper ships were able to aid the Brazilian slavocracy by including Brazil in their triangular trade with the West Indies and Africa. By the 1840's, the United States was second only to Great Britain as Brazil's largest commercial partner.[4] As the English withdrew from the slave trade and attempted to end it because of proscriptions at home, American ships replaced them. When ships flying the Star-Spangled Banner, which were exempt from British search, delivered slaves to Brazil, this was seen not only as an economic godsend, but as a twist of the British lion's tail. It was part of a greater pattern of U.S.-British rivalry that was playing itself out in South America in the early nineteenth century and would return to play a central role in the diplomacy of the 1890's.[5] Although the United States signed a treaty with Great Britain in 1842 promising to end the trade in human beings, ships flying the U.S. flag continued to deliver 20 percent of all slaves in 1848 and fully half in 1850. In that year, however, the British clamped down hard on the traffic, and U.S. ships withdrew.[6]

The 1840's and 1850's marked the low point of U.S.-Brazilian friendship in the nineteenth century because of fear of North American expansionism.[7] Brazilian politicians were aware of the doctrine of Manifest Destiny, the Texas and Mexican-American wars, and the numerous Yankee filibuster assaults on Central America. Brazilians viewed these with more than passing interest because the motivation behind the attacks was the southward expansion of American slavery. Brazil, a slave country well suited to major U.S. crops such as cotton, rice, tobacco, and sugar, was especially coveted by some American slave holders.

Of particular concern was the Amazon area, which, although potentially wealthy, was underpopulated and unprotected. To defend it, Brazil closed the area to international commerce and travel. Some feared that the U.S. Navy, which opened Japan to trade in 1854, would attempt a similar operation in the Amazon. These fears were not entirely unfounded. In 1849, a U.S. Navy lieutenant, Mathew Fontaine Maury, called for the opening of the Amazon and its colonization by Americans. This received a warm reception in southern conventions in New Orleans and Memphis. The House of Representatives considered the question and published his report. In response to Maury's initiative, various proposals to settle U.S. slaves in the Amazon were formulated in the 1850's. The navy also became interested in the issue and sent two lieutenants to explore the Amazon. These explorations and pronouncements prompted Brazil to sign a treaty with Bolivia and Peru that forbade U.S. ships from trade or navigation in the Amazon basin. Brazilian fears were not assuaged by two groups of American filibusterers that attempted to seize part of the Amazon in 1855.

The tensions between the two countries finally relaxed with the outbreak of the Civil War and then the abolition of slavery in the United States. The destruction of the war diverted U.S. attentions to internal reconstruction. Afterward, 3,000 exconfederates settled in the states of Pará, Espirito Santo, and São Paulo, but they no longer appeared the advance guard of a conquering civilization. Rather, they now represented the defeated stragglers of an exhausted way of life. None of their colonies enjoyed much success. The colonists of Americanus, São Paulo, for example, who had dreams of resurrecting slave plantations, instead scratched out livings selling watermelons.[8] Brazilians became sufficiently convinced that the U.S. threat had disappeared that they opened the Amazon to free international navigation and commerce in 1867.

Relations between the two countries once again became cordial. The United States became the single largest market for Brazilian coffee after it was made duty free in 1861. (Great Britain, in contrast, had placed prohibitive duties on coffee imports to protect their tea-producing colonies.) Brazilian exports to the United States, standing at only U.S.$8 million in 1850, nearly tripled by 1870, making them second only to Cuba among Latin American exporters to the United States. In the 1870's, Brazil's exports to the United States doubled again.[9] Communications became closer as well. A steamship line between New York and Rio was subsidized by the two governments beginning in 1865, and two telegraph cables were laid in the 1880's.[10]

The friendship between the western hemisphere's two most populous countries was cemented when Emperor Dom Pedro II traveled to Philadelphia in 1876 for the centennial exposition that he inaugurated with President Grant. There, he was greatly impressed by Yankee culture and ingenuity, meeting such notables as Henry Wadsworth Longfellow, John Greenleaf Whittier, and the young Thomas Edison and Alexander Graham Bell. In turn, he charmed his American hosts with his enthusiasm. A dabbler in Arabic and biology, Dom Pedro struck many as a philosopher-king rather than a despot. His declaration that he wished to see in Brazil not cannons, but modern industrial and agricultural machinery, strengthened his image.[11] Indeed, upon returning to Brazil he had the country's first telephones installed in his palaces.

In a number of areas Americans were becoming recognized in Brazil for their technological sophistication. Brazil's first street railway system in Rio's Jardim Botânico was built by a U.S. company in 1869, and the most sought-after railroad locomotive was the American Baldwin (with Charles Flint as the selling agent in Brazil).[12] Americans also made inroads in the cultural sphere during the Empire's last decades. American ballroom dancing was replacing the French styles, and James Fenimore Cooper was overtaking Sir Walter Scott in literature. The pianist Louis Moreau Gottschalk also made a great impression.[13]

This rapprochement manifested itself in the diplomatic field in 1887 when President Grover Cleveland proposed a customs union between the two countries. Surprisingly, despite the great trade between the two countries, no commercial pacts had been previously attempted. Indeed, when Secretary of State Frelinghusen had negotiated six reciprocal treaties with Latin American countries and colonies in the early 1880's, Brazil was not included,[14] and when Congress sent a trade delegation to Latin America in 1884, it visited every major west coast nation but ignored Brazil. Even though the delegation's ship passed through Rio, Cleveland, anxious to cut the minimal expenses of a stay in Rio, had ordered them to return immediately.[15] By 1887, however, Cleveland's interest in Brazil apparently had grown. He suggested that both countries reduce duties, pool the revenues earned, and divide them evenly. Cleveland was particularly interested in protecting major U.S. exports to Brazil: kerosene (98 percent supplied by the United States but facing a growing Russian challenge), wheat (in which the Argentines were beginning to make inroads), and lard. Dom Pedro approved of the plan, but his minister of finance opposed it. Parliament had long been reluctant to enter into treaties because of the onerous stipulations of the last treaty Brazil had signed in 1826.[16] When that treaty lapsed in 1844, no other commercial treaties were signed until the end of the Empire despite overtures by European powers.[17]

Dom Pedro persisted in searching out a trade agreement. In the Empire's last year the emperor sent his delegation to Washington for the Pan American Congress with two charges: to represent Brazil at the conference and to negotiate a trade treaty with the United States.[18] At first, it seems odd that the monarch would recommend a trade agreement with the northern republic when he refused to negotiate with European monarchs, some of whom were relatives. But, then, much about Dom Pedro was enigmatic. He certainly often acted as an autocrat. The liberal deputy Tavares Bastos complained of an "extremely powerful state," and the entrepreneur the Visconde de Mauá objected to "undue government interference."[19] On the

other hand, many of Dom Pedro's supporters accused him of being too lib-
eral and tolerant, because he sometimes professed republican sympathies.[20]
He appointed a leading republican as tutor to his children and other republi-
cans to high office. Indeed, two of the three men he appointed to represent
Brazil at the Pan American Congress, Lafayette Pereira and Salvador de
Mendonça, had been members of the first Republican Party directory and
had written for its newspaper.[21] Thus political differences did not prevent
Dom Pedro from seeking closer relationships with the United States.

Boom of the 1880's

What most induced Dom Pedro to seek a commercial agreement with
the United States was a general program of economic diversification that
began in the early 1880's. It was fostered initially by the imminent abolition
of slavery and a downturn in international commodity markets, and it ac-
celerated at the decade's close as world financial markets became more
abundant. Diversification meant turning away from the overwhelming superiority exercised by the British. In the mid-1880's the British commanded
about half of all trade with Brazil and probably 80 percent of all foreign
investment. All foreign loans had been placed with N. Rothschild in London for three decades, and most of the internal debt was held by Englishmen. M. L. Mulhall, the world's most respected statistician at the time,
estimated British capital invested in Brazil at £93 (U.S.$452) million.[22] The
most important banks, railroads, and commercial houses were British.[23]
This began to change in 1888.

The boom that later became known as the "Encilhamento" began under
the Empire. It was built on the foundation of an economy that was rapidly
developing in the 1880's. Agriculture regained its earlier preeminence in the
latter part of the decade as prices for coffee spiraled upward and rubber
exports surged. Such favorable market conditions combined with the release of capital from the slave trade in the aftermath of emancipation to
encourage planters to diversify their investments. They turned to railroads,
industries, and other urban pursuits. The countryside echoed with the clang
of iron track being laid as railroads were constructed at the most furious
pace of the nineteenth century; indeed, building in the 1880's was the second greatest in absolute terms in Brazil's entire history. Only eight countries in the entire world laid more track in the decade than Brazil. By the
end of the decade, Brazil had the largest rail network in Latin America
and trailed only India in the entire underdeveloped world.[24] Factories also
sprang up throughout the Empire in the 1880's at an unprecedented rate,
and its cities were beginning to receive the benefits of gas, electrical, sanitation, telegraph, and tram companies.[25] Brazil was entering the modern
world.

Brazil's international standing was particularly high in the Empire's last
two years. With the price of coffee at the highest point in a decade and

rubber the highest ever, exports reached record levels. This in turn created impressive trade surpluses.[26] What was stunning about these achievements is that they were accomplished in the years that slavery was abolished. Brazil's ability to come through emancipation so smoothly and peacefully, without the social upheavals or the economic disruptions experienced by Haiti, Cuba, or the United States, reinforced European confidence in Brazil and its monarchy. One manifestation of European optimism was that the greatest wave of immigrants that Brazil had yet seen entered between 1887 and 1889.[27] Another consequence was that European capital flowed to Brazil in unprecedented amounts.

The world economy was awash in capital in the late 1880's, and Latin America was a principal destination for investments. Recovery from the 1870's depression had made available much capital that was seeking overseas markets for the first time. By one estimate, 1889 was the nineteenth century's high-water mark for foreign investment.[28] British investment to Latin America grew fivefold in the 1880's, and now that investment was risk capital as well as loans and commercial credit.[29] At the same time French, German, Dutch, Austrian, and Portuguese capitalists became more aggressive and more interested in Latin American ventures. Even American investors began—in a small way—to participate in the Brazilian market.[30]

Brazil became one of the Latin American countries most attractive to European investors, partly as part of a ripple effect of the maddened rush to invest in the Southern Cone between 1886 and 1890. The *Money Market Review* concocted this financial recipe in 1889: "What can an investor desirous of getting 4 to 5 percent interest . . . do better than spread it over a selection of Argentine state and railway guarantees, throwing in a mixture of Brazil and Chili?"[31] After all, Brazil's economy was doing splendidly, the major political problem, emancipation, seemed to have been easily resolved, and the country had a long history of punctually servicing its debt. Indeed, its credit rating not only surpassed most of its Latin American neighbors, Brazil's bonds sometimes enjoyed a lower discount rate than the bonds of many European nations.[32] Consequently, in the underdeveloped world Brazil trailed only Argentina in foreign investment received in these bountiful years.

Most of the funds continued in the traditional form of government loans. In 1889 Brazil was able to secure its largest loan up to that point, a £20 million (U.S.$97 million) consolidation loan, as well as float a 100,000 conto (about U.S.$53 million) internal bond issue, partly in Europe. The provinces and municipalities began for the first time to borrow abroad as São Paulo, Bahia, and Santos took up over U.S.$8 million in loans.[33]

The influx of gold was so great that Brazil's currency, the milreis, rose above par for one of the few times in history, and the pound sterling became legal tender in Brazil. The London paper the *Daily Mail* reported on November 18, 1889, that "Already large sums of gold have been sent from London leaving this money market in a bare condition at a critical moment. Indeed, had not gold from Russia, from France and from New York been obtained by the agency of the large financial houses, the Brazilian drain of gold might have proved one of the most embarrassing on record."[34] For one of the few times in the nineteenth century, Brazil had a positive balance of payments.

The eagerness of European investors coupled with Brazil's apparently bright future prospects led native capitalists, for the first time, to stray from government loans and plunge into bonds and risk ventures on a large scale. Some of the investments went into European-run companies, but a surprisingly large share went toward financing companies organized and run by Brazilians. At the end of 1888, well before the Encilhamento began, there were already 95 companies on the Rio stock market totally owned and administered by native capitalists.[35] At least a dozen of them borrowed from Europe the equivalent of U.S.$34 million in 1888 and 1889.[36]

These loans reflected a broader effort by Brazilians to use European capital to develop the economy *and* wrest it away from European—particularly British—control, much as Americans had begun to do in the second half of the nineteenth century.[37] Brazilian optimism and generous capital markets inspired monumental projects. The Sorocabana railroad, for example, sought financing abroad to build a line connecting São Paulo's interior to the port of Santos, thereby breaking the British San Paulo railroad's monopoly of that route. On an even grander scale, a railroad was floated that would have connected Recife, the capital of Pernambuco, with Valparaiso, Chile, opening up the continent's interior to Brazilian trade.[38]

Part of the effort to forge a more autonomous development manifested itself in the diversification of borrowing. Since independence Brazil had been a virtual financial and commercial colony of Great Britain. However, in October 1889 the *Financial News* reported, "Intelligence in Brazil explains that the issue in Portugal of a loan to build a new Bourse in Rio de Janeiro is part of a policy of endeavoring to render Brazil independent of English capitalists by the establishment of relations with the Portuguese, French, and German money markets."[39] In fact, the province of Bahia borrowed the equivalent of U.S.$4 million in France, the Oeste de Minas railroad floated bonds worth 22 million marks in Berlin, the internal debt bond issue opened up an office in New York, and Portuguese bankers sank large sums into Brazilian companies. The Paris stock market began giving official quotes to Brazilian national government bonds in late 1888 as well. Continental lenders were more attractive to Brazilian capitalists than the British because they were more willing to invest in Brazilian-administered companies, while British investors tended to restrict their participation to loans to state entities or shares in British-run companies.[40]

Public policy took advantage of the surpluses in international capital markets to diversify dependence. For example, French companies now received Brazilian state concessions to build the port of Rio Grande do Sul and to expand existing railroad companies into a national network that would connect Uruguay with São Paulo. A more central thrust of state policy, however, was to privilege Brazilian entrepreneurs. Sometimes European companies were nationalized and then rented to Brazilians. At other times new concessions were issued to Brazilians who secured financing at home or abroad. The result of this policy was a dramatic decline in British participation. For example, whereas in 1886 Englishmen owned four of five sugar mill concessions in Brazil with guaranteed interest payments, by 1889 Brazilians owned 90 percent of them.[41]

In the Empire's last year, and particularly after the Visconde de Ouro Preto was named president of the Council of Ministers in June 1889, state policy sought to exploit the advantageous international setting by making Brazil more self-reliant. While he hoped to calm planters after the emancipation of the slaves, Ouro Preto was particularly concerned with strengthening the newly emerging financier class, of which he was part.

Financiers would play a previously unparalleled role in the politics and diplomacy of the 1889–94 period. Since the 1870's the portfolios of merchants and planters had converged. Prosperity, growing monetarization of the economy, and the railroad had led more and more planters into commercial, financial, and urban investments.[42] At the same time that the traditional landed aristocracy was gradually becoming more bourgeois, the bourgeoisie was rapidly becoming aristocratic. But only at the end of the Empire did the aristocratic bourgeoisie join economic and political power and redefine their mission. These financiers were to be the principal planners and participants in the Encilhamento. They were also the principal intermediaries for continental European investors. Their rise promoted a change in Brazilian foreign policy. Unlike the planter elite, which had been content to rely on British commercial credit, Brazilian financiers sought greater autonomy and space to maneuver by contacting French, German, Portuguese, and even some American investors.

Between the abolition of slavery on May 13, 1888, and the end of the Empire, the Rio stock market saw as much trading as it had in the previous 60 years. The *Jornal do Commércio* captured the feverish energy on the Bolsa: "The subscription of stocks was done not only with excitement, but with madness, with delirium, with swooning and drunkenness."[43] Great waves of foreign capital rolled into Brazil to participate in the new banks, just as they did in Argentina. The first German bank in Brazil was founded in 1888, Portuguese financiers such as the Conde de Alta Mearim played leading roles in numerous Brazilian banks, and the leading Parisian investment bank, the Banque de Paris et Pays Bas, was the guiding force behind the Banco Nacional. In fact, many Argentine investors moved north to Rio when the Buenos Aires frenzy subsided. The luxurious carriages they brought with them were soon imitated by Rio's new rich. These ornate coaches rolling through the elegant Largo de São Francisco signified the ascendancy of financial capital over commercial and agricultural capital. Financiers' new eminence was reconfirmed when one stock market nouveau riche rented Princess Isabel's summer palace in Petropolis, and the banker Francisco de Paula Mayrink purchased the Catete palace (which would later be the residence of Brazil's presidents) from one of Brazil's wealthiest coffee barons.[44]

The Empire's last years, then, witnessed unprecedented development and diversification. Brazil's flourishing economy and enviable international standing allowed state policy makers more space to maneuver than they had ever before enjoyed. Imperial statesmen sought to seize the moment by loosening the British grip on the economy. European continental markets increasingly provided Brazilian entrepreneurs with capital, while the United States supplied the market for Brazilian exports. Dom Pedro's quest for a trade treaty with the United States was part of a grander strategy to increase national sovereignty and autonomy. It came at a time of strength. Brazil's emperor was by no means forced into trade negotiations.

Proclamation of the Republic

The establishment of the Republic on November 15, 1889, eventually tightened the bonds of friendship between Brazil and the United States forged by Dom Pedro. The diplomat Manuel Oliveira Lima remembered later, "When the Republic was proclaimed the United States enjoyed the most enviable popularity."[45] Brazilian republicans looked to the United States because it was the only developed country besides France that was a republic. The French had to pass through the violent social upheaval of the French Revolution to abolish their monarchy. Conservative Brazilians, in charge of a state with little popular legitimacy or popularity and ruling a society with enormous inequities, were frightened of the French experience. American bourgeois republicanism was much more appealing. So was American economic development. The United States had attracted more foreign investment than any other country in the world and had capitalized on those resources together with a flourishing export sector to develop a sophisticated industrial base. Brazil, even more than the United States, had been a creation of the world economy; European rulers and capitalists combined African labor and Asian and African crops (sugar and coffee) to create one of the world's premier export economies. Now Brazil, like the United States, was attempting to expand the domestic market and forge industry. But the overthrow of the monarchy endangered the boom.

The Empire's collapse was dimly viewed in the most "civilized" nations and not particularly well received at home. The advent of progressive republicanism was not applauded as apologist historians of the regime subsequently argued. Rather, the Republic faced grave external and internal vulnerability. This, much more than the similarity of political institutions or sudden enlightenment, made U.S. friendship more important than ever for the nascent Brazilian Republic, and the Republic dealt with the United States from a weaker position than had the monarchy.

Foreign investors reacted with hostility to the monarchy's demise. European capitalists, monarchists and republicans alike, had viewed the imperial state as a guarantor of their investments. They found centralization of authority, social peace, and a sound currency reassuring. The overthrow of the monarchy provoked alarm and a precipitous drop in the value of Brazilian bonds and currency. To European investors, the military dictatorship that replaced the Empire appeared not as the "bourgeoisie on stage" in Nelson Werneck Sodré's term, but as a Spanish American caudillo regime. The *Times* of London reported three days after the coup:

> A revolution of the usual Spanish-American type—that is, a hybrid between Radical politics and military insubordination—has broken out with at least momentarily complete success in Rio de Janeiro. . . . The most probable result is the breaking up of what has hitherto been the Brazilian monarchy into a number of separate States, united by a federal bond or merely by treaties of alliance.[46]

The Rothschilds cut off the Brazilian Treasury's foreign credit, and the Banque de Paris et Pays Bas refused to advance foreign exchange. Other foreign investors also began to shy away from Brazil.[47]

European states mirrored the shock and distrust of their investors. None was willing to recognize the Republic's provisional government. They were particularly frightened by the implications for Europe of the overthrow of a monarchy headed by a member of a European royal family. As an observer in the *North American Review* noted, "When the Brazilian revolution was announced, a momentary tremor passed through European capitals, lest Portugal should follow her former dependency's example."[48] There was fear that successful republicanism in Portugal would ignite Spain, which would in turn arouse republicans in Italy and from there spread northward. When Portuguese republicans, inspired by the Brazilian experience, conspired with soldiers to stage a failed republican revolt in Porto, on January 31, 1890 (and again a year later), this did nothing to win friends for Brazil's republicans in the royal courts of Europe.[49] Brazilian republicans, in turn, feared that Europeans would attempt a monarchist restoration.

The United States minister to Brazil, Robert Adams, Jr., on the other hand, initially was heartened by the monarchy's overthrow. He believed that the establishment of a republican form of government would bring the two countries closer together and distance Brazil from the European monarchies. He urged immediate recognition of Brazil so that the United States could be the first power to do so. The head of the U.S. delegation to the Pan American Conference sparked a controversy when he also quickly proposed—without first consulting Blaine—recognition of the Republic.[50] However, U.S. recognition, so treasured by Brazil's embattled republicans, would be used as a bargaining chip to win Brazilian consent to the Blaine-Mendonça agreement.

President Harrison initially withheld recognition because he professed concern about the new regime's lack of democracy.[51] Marshal Deodoro da Fonseca's first actions alienated Harrison (who was also a general, but maintained civilian attire, titles, and practices while in office). Fonseca, on the other hand, arrogated the title "Provisional Dictator" and "Generalissimo," placed many military men and relatives in important government posts, promoted all civilian members of his cabinet to the rank of "honorary general," and took a salary 20 percent higher than that of the U.S. Harrison. He also doubled the size of the armed forces, raised their pay 40 percent, and set about revising military training to ensure soldiers a more active political role in the new regime. The regime passed wide-ranging legislation by decree without consulting anyone outside of the cabinet and enforced a rigid censorship law that made the press open to charges of military sedition for defamation of character or disturbing the public order. Most troubling of all, the dictator announced that elections for a constituent congress would not be held until September, and the new body would first convene a full year after the fall of the Empire. Then it would merely consider a document already drafted by the cabinet of the Provisional Dictatorship.[52] One of the Provisional Dictatorship's severest critics, Eduardo Prado, ridiculed this transformation of Brazil: "It is no longer possible to describe the sort of measures that daily occur in Brazil. That [regime] is no longer militarism nor dictatorship nor republic. Its name is Carnival."[53] Many American observers took the actions of Brazil's military government less good naturedly. Deodoro's rule smacked of a typical South American military dictatorship.

The U.S. press was divided in its appraisal of the new regime. Dom Pedro had been very popular and was believed to be a unifying factor. There was fear that Brazil would fall prey to civil war and petty despots without him. The *New Orleans States* complained bitterly that "a great change, probably for the worse, has taken place in that country" because "Dom Pedro was dethroned, not by the people, for there is really no people in Brazil, in the sense that term is understood in enlightened and free countries, but by a mercenary army. That the present government of Brazil is a mere mongrel military despotism there is little doubt."[54] Many racists agreed that the removal of a European sovereign (though actually born in Brazil) by a Brazilian "mongrel" would cause Brazil to shed its veneer of civilization and lapse into barbarism. The race of the ruler was more important than the form of government. The *Washington Star* took a more populist stand; the paper felt it improper for the United States to recognize "a government which the people of Brazil [had] not yet had the opportunity of approving or disapproving." The *Cleveland Leader and Herald* concurred that "the voice of the people of Brazil [had] not yet been heard in this matter," and the *Kansas City Journal* objected to the fact that "at present Brazil is substantially in the hands of a dictator."[55] Somewhat surprisingly, the wait-and-see attitude was mainly expressed by the presumably expansionist Republican press. (Their views of Brazil may well have been affected by domestic political considerations: Republicans were seeking to pass the "force bill" to enfranchise black—and presumably Republican—voters in the South.)

On the other hand, Democrats tried to appeal to antimonarchist and anti-British sentiment by calling for immediate recognition to increase U.S. influence in Latin America's largest country and prevent restoration of the monarchy. The Democratic Senator John Tyler Morgan had presented a resolution to that effect in the Committee on Foreign Relations. The *Milwaukee Evening Wisconsin* lamented:

> The actions of the Government at Washington in this matter is enough to make every patriotic American hang his head with shame. If the Republic in Brazil falls, it will be because the United States withholds its recognition. . . . What an electric thrill the presence of half a dozen American men-of-war in the harbor of Rio [de] Janeiro at this moment would give to republicans and democrats all around the globe![56]

Four years later they would get their "electric thrill" when U.S. gunboats intervened in a naval revolt in Rio's Guanabara Bay, but even now, influential Brazilian politicians welcomed the idea of American gunboats.

Speedy recognition by the United States was of great importance to the young Brazilian Republic. Fear of European restorationist movement was also great because Brazil's new regime commanded weak support at home. The Empire had fallen, after all, at precisely the moment that it had had the greatest international standing because of its booming economy and greatest domestic popularity because of the abolition of slavery. When the emperor's son-in-law, the Conde d'Eu, visited Bahia a few weeks before the coup, large enthusiastic crowds of freedmen had greeted him. But when the militant republican Antonio da Silva Jardim landed at the same time to organize a demonstration against the Conde, the same Bahians chased and beat the Republican activist. Similarly, Dom Pedro's return from Europe in late 1888 and his trip to Minas Gerais in 1889 were met by delirious crowds (though planters were conspicuously absent from the gatherings). In elections as late as October 1889 the monarchist Liberal Party's reform platform was resoundingly endorsed, while republicans received little support. At such a juncture, it should not be difficult to understand that it was much easier for the republicans to seize power than it was for them to win the hearts and minds of the population. The public was at best apathetic about the new regime.

"No revolution of such a magnitude was ever effected with so little excitement," snickered the London *Economist* when soldiers in Rio de Janeiro's Campo de Sant'Anna brought down the Empire.[57] The revolution, which some of its most radical defenders compared to the French Revolution, was actually a palace coup. One of the republican leaders later recalled: "There was almost no collaboration of the civilian element, [people] stood by stupidly, beastlike, astonished, surprised, without knowing what was happening. Many of them sincerely believed that they were witnessing a parade."[58] The *South American Journal* reported that the revolution occurred "without bloodshed and with very little more excitement than is customary in the streets during Carnival."[59] Newspapers throughout Brazil noted the restraint with which the Brazilian people greeted the Republic.[60]

The Empire crumbled because of lack of support rather than because of strong opposition. Paulistas wished for regional autonomy and aid to immigration; Paraíba Valley planters were angered by the uncompensated loss of their slaves; soldiers were led into revolt by inadequate salaries and promotions; and clerics were disturbed by the lack of imperial patronage. Most important was that the royal family refused to organize opposition to the Republic, and almost every influential imperial politician quickly sided with the new regime.

As the Barão de Rio Branco so aptly put it, the choice was not "between monarchy and republic, but between republic and anarchy."[61] The Visconde de Sinambu pled for support for the Republic to prevent military revolts from attacking "the integrity of our country," while Senator Paulo de Souza Dantas argued that it was necessary to align with the Republic to safeguard the integrity of property, Brazil's foreign credit, and the public order.[62] It is not that they loved the Republic better; they feared the alternative worse.

Republicans enjoyed little internal cohesion and less national support. Even in the republican strongholds in the Southeast, the parties (for there was no one true national party) were in the minority.[63] Moreover, they were divided between radical reformers such as Antonio de Silva Jardin and conservative ex–slave owners such as Manoel Ferraz de Campos Sales. While followers of the former dreamed of a more industrialized, urban Brazil, many of the members of the conservative wing mainly wanted to ensure greater local autonomy and prevent land reform. Outside of the Center-South, republicanism was an even weaker political force. It was virtually nonexistent in the Northeast, which still held over 40 percent of Brazil's population. The *Jornal de Noticias* of Bahia reported in May 1890 that "The inscription on the old banner is changed, the men in power are unalterably the same." It went on to explain that "adherence to the Republic does not imply a complete change on their [Bahia's] part. They are Republicans because they yielded to the force of circumstances, they are, and will continue to be, ambitious."[64] Many observers believed that Brazil would break in half with the Northeast preferring a monarchy and the Southeast a republic.

The armed forces responsible for the Empire's overthrow were also too weak and fractured to institute praetorian rule. The army only had some 17,000 troops in Brazil. Equally important, the officer corps was divided between younger politicized junior officers and more compliant senior officers who opposed change. Military revolts intended to restore the monarchy on November 18, 1889, and January 14, 1890, underlined the threat.[65] Professional jealousies between army and navy also created discord so serious that the navy ultimately would revolt in 1893.[66] To exacerbate the situation even further, the one man who held the military together, Marshal Deodoro, was gravely ill, and the health of the intellectual author of the military revolt, General Benjamin Constant Magalhães, was also failing.[67]

The new regime's lack of domestic support made it particularly suspicious of European designs. There was fear that the Portuguese would aid the restoration of the monarchy because of ties of blood between members of the House of Braganza (Pedro's father, sister, and nephews had ruled Portugal for virtually the entire nineteenth century), because so many Portuguese financiers and merchants had prospered under the monarchy, and because Portugal so depended on remissions from Brazil. As early as 1878 a Portuguese economist, J. P. Oliveira Martins, marveled that the funds coming from Brazil were no longer just immigrant remissions, but also "the capital of Portuguese or Brazilians resident in America [Brazil]." Capital from Brazil bought up most of the Portuguese government's bonds. Oliveira Martins noted Portugal's ironic situation caused by its "unusual form of exploiting a foreign country and remaining among the league of colonial nations despite having lost the region politically."[68] Portugal had become a virtual colony of Brazil.

When the exiled Dom Pedro II arrived in Lisbon's port after being dethroned, a Brazilian lieutenant on board the ship attempted to run up the new republican flag, but the Portuguese government refused permission because the new regime had not been recognized.[69] This symbolic act, combined with rumors flying around Europe of royal assistance to the emperor from various courts, did little to calm the worries of Brazilian republicans. The rumors certainly seemed believable. After all, Dom Pedro's mother was a Belgian princess, and his wife was the daughter of the King of Naples. Dom Pedro's son-in-law, the Conde d'Eu, was the grandson of King Louis Phillipe of France. The British, fearing that the Republic represented an opening for their rival the United States, also had good diplomatic and economic reasons to oppose it.

Brazil faced other international pressure from its Latin American neighbor Argentina. The two nations had long disputed territory in the area known as Missiones. Although little populated, the area comprised some 11,500 square miles of fertile land—more than three times the size of Portugal—and was a point of national honor. Brazil and Argentina had often been enemies. Spain and Portugal had fought numerous wars in the eighteenth and early nineteenth centuries over the area, adjacent to Missiones, that became Uruguay in 1828. Brazil had also joined with disgruntled Argentines to overthrow Argentina's most powerful leader, Juan Manuel Rosas, in 1852. Relations between the two countries remained fragile. Earlier attempts in 1759, 1789, and 1857 to settle the Missiones boundary had failed. Finally in 1885 the two countries agreed to appoint a joint survey team and resolve the issue. In September 1889, after the area had been mapped, Argentina and Brazil signed a pact agreeing to reach a settlement within 90 days or else submit the question for arbitration to the president of the

United States. The republican revolution broke out before the 90-day period had elapsed. Thus when Brazil's minister, Salvador de Mendonça, began campaigning for U.S. recognition, he believed that friendship with the United States might influence the outcome of the territorial settlement between Brazil and Argentina.[70]

Brazil also had territorial disputes with France, England, Colombia, Peru, and Bolivia. The most serious was with France over a small stretch of land between Amapá and French Guyana called Counani. The rubber boom of the late nineteenth century made this inhospitable, torrid region of less than 1,000 residents suddenly valuable. A group of Frenchmen had attempted to convince France to annex the area and then attempted to create an independent state there in the late 1880's, a situation that was still unresolved.[71]

Under these circumstances, it is not surprising that the minister of foreign affairs of the Republic's provisional government, Quintino Bocayuva, urged Brazil's representatives in the United States to gain U.S. recognition quickly and enter into a secret "intimate treaty" of alliance. Bocayuva was busily signing pacts with Argentina, Uruguay, Peru, and Bolivia, while offering to arbitrate the country's northern boundary with France to protect Brazil from foreign attack.[72]

His efforts in the United States were graced with success when Harrison accepted the credentials of the Brazilian minister to the United States, J. G. Amaral Valente, on January 30, 1890. Harrison noted in accepting the credentials that he sought to "increase personal intercourse and enlarge the commercial exchanges between the two republics." Nothing was said of the lack of democratic elections that had prevented earlier recognition by the United States.[73] Yet the Provisional Dictatorship had done nothing in the two months since it took power to enhance democratic government. So why had Harrison changed his mind? Harrison later explained to Congress that he had established diplomatic relations but would not "completely recognize" the regime until the government had "popular approval and support."[74] That was splitting hairs. The U.S. press and the Brazilian government took the reception of the republican minister as diplomatic recognition.[75]

A number of factors combined to persuade Harrison to recognize Brazil before any European power had done so. The *New York World* attributed the change of position to the fact that "public sentiment has so plainly asserted itself."[76] Certainly Americans began to pay much more attention to Brazil as trade talks and the booming Brazilian stock market whetted appetites already piqued by Flint's propaganda campaigns.[77] It is also true that the young regime appeared to some to grow more stable. Marshal Deodoro's health improved, and leading monarchists accepted the Republic and had foresworn a restorationist attempt.[78] On the other hand, several regiments revolted in Rio on January 14 with more than 100 casualties. The government responded by executing 21 noncommissioned officers and enlisted men and arresting several prominent Imperial politicians.[79] Conditions were also very unsettled in the strategic state of Rio Grande do Sul.

Despite continuing concerns about the stability and autocratic nature of the new republican regime in Brazil, Harrison and Blaine were willing to recognize Marshal Deodoro's government because it offered a strategically important alliance and a trade agreement. Brazil's assistance was vital in the Pan American Conference, then in full swing. Blaine was having difficulty convincing Latin American delegates to agree to a customs union or even to bilateral reciprocal treaties. Argentina's and Chile's representatives were the most difficult. Since Latin Americans' endorsement of commercial agreements was the linchpin of Blaine's publicity campaign to sell reciprocity to Congress, the intransigence of those countries threatened to doom the secretary of state's trade initiative. He looked to Brazil for help.

Brazil was the one country most receptive to Blaine's position.[80] Particularly key was the Brazilian delegate Salvador de Mendonça. The Brazilian diplomat would play an exceptionally large role in U.S.-Brazilian relations for most of the 1890's because of his personal ties to influential Americans. Usually in Latin America, foreign policy was made and treaties negotiated by the president and the minister of finance; the minister of foreign relations was left on the margins. Under Mendonça, however, the Brazilian foreign office and its representative in Washington exercised a surprisingly large degree of authority. Salvador de Mendonça was especially friendly with Blaine; he was the member of the Brazilian delegation who took the most active part in negotiating the trade treaty. Mendonça, who had lived in New York for some fifteen years as the Brazilian consul and had married an American, was intimately familiar with American ways and perspectives.[81] Indeed, he well may have had business arrangements with Flint and other U.S. businessmen. Mendonça's successor as consul general in New York claimed that Mendonça had lent Flint Brazilian funds that were supposed to be used to purchase silver. Instead, Flint used the money to speculate and transform his commercial house into one of the most important in the market.[82]

Mendonça's experience with both U.S. and Latin American approaches, and his friendship with Flint, allowed him to serve as Blaine's translator or press agent. He and Blaine often conversed on morning walks after which Mendonça presented Blaine's position to his fellow Latin American diplomats at the conference. The Brazilian representative also busily issued eloquent articles advocating reciprocity in U.S. newspapers. His importance to Blaine was underlined when he was appointed the chief of the Brazilian mission to the Pan American Conference a week after the birth of the Republic.[83] Mendonça's promotion was probably a concession to Blaine (and very useful for the minister's friend, Flint, who barely knew Mendonça's predecessor).[84] Mendonça's personal role in negotiations would be further accentuated when instead of being named minister to Switzerland as the Provisional Government originally intended, at the end of 1890 he was appointed Brazil's minister to the United States, where he would remain for eight years.[85] Mendonça and Brazil would continue to be the most loyal allies of the United States in the conference and subsequently in Pan American affairs, as well as strong advocates of reciprocity.

Harrison also found recognition of the Republic expedient because he and fellow Republicans worried about the possible political reverberations in the United States of a loudly rumored European intervention to restore the monarchy. The Democrats had quickly taken on the cause of the Brazilian Republic. Consequently, if the monarchy were allowed to return—and with it a British diplomatic victory—Republicans could be badly damaged in the approaching congressional elections.

A third, less important, source of pressure arguing for the resumption of diplomatic relations was Flint, who served as a virtual representative of Brazil in the United States—just as he had been previously for Chile, Costa Rica, and Nicaragua—since he had long been a buying agent for the Brazilian government. Indeed, in the first days after the fall of the Republic major New York newspapers such as the *Times* relied on Flint's telegraphic correspondence with Brazil for information on the latest events, and Flint's opinions were eagerly solicited. Flint lobbied forcefully for recognition of the Republic.[86]

He had personal reasons to be concerned with the new regime's friendship. Flint was gravely concerned when the state government of Pará awarded a monopoly concession on rubber exports to the Brazilian Companhia Mercantil. As the world's leading rubber importer and finding himself in the potentially embarrassing position of holding only a two-week stock of crude rubber, Flint stood to suffer greatly from this turn of events. He pushed Undersecretary of State Wharton to intercede with the Brazilian federal government to annul the concession.[87] Flint was also apparently interested in investing in tram lines, a flour mill, a bank, and an insurance company and was a stockholder in the U.S. and Brazil Mail Steamship Company, which was seeking a subsidy from the Brazilian government. Government concessions and goodwill were therefore important to him.[88]

These various pressures combined to produce a pact that was much more than a simple mutual recognition of legitimacy and exchange of diplomatic representatives. To be sure, the agreement called for rapid U.S. recognition, but it also called for broadly defined American friendship. Blaine supposedly promised Mendonça the same sort of support in the case of European intervention that the United States had provided Mexico against Maximilian. Physical evidence of this came soon as the U.S. Navy's most modern ships, known as the "squadron of evolution," visited Rio, where they were greeted by thundering cannons, a "great blaze of illumination" from rockets and colored lights, cheering crowds, and a "pronounced ovation."[89] Moreover, according to Mexico's minister in Washington, Blaine had sent Marshal Deodoro two million dollars to "win the support of various military chiefs, provincial presidents and members of the press."[90] Blaine also hinted that he favored the Brazilian case in the Missiones dispute. In exchange, Blaine wanted Brazil's support at the Pan American Conference and the assurance that Brazil would enter into no treaties with European powers relative to their colonies or borders. He also wanted a trade treaty. It is thus small wonder that Brazil became the first country to sign a commercial pact under the reciprocity provisions of the McKinley Tariff a year later, and that the treaty was negotiated by Mendonça and Blaine with considerable assistance by Flint.[91]

The Provisional Dictatorship

The events of 1890 increased the republican regime's desire for a commercial treaty. Europeans remained unfriendly to the new government. Foreign investors ended their mad rush to purchase Brazilian entities. European capital markets refused to extend the government loans as well. As a consequence, Brazil's balance of payments turned negative, the milreis began a long downward slide, and prices inflated. The collapse was exacerbated by events in Argentina where the government's failure to service the debt in April 1890, a revolt in July, and the near collapse of the House of Baring in November frightened European investors away from all South American issues.[92]

Equally troubling to Marshal Deodoro da Fonseca were internal political clashes. Deodoro, who governed between November 15, 1889, and November 24, 1891, quickly broke with the Republican Party members of his government. The feud was almost inevitable. The *Rio News* observed in Deodoro's obituary in 1892, "A plain, indifferently-educated soldier, he was led, after over forty years of service to the monarchy, into a political movement with which he had never been personally connected and for which he apparently felt little sympathy."[93] Quintino Bocayuva, the head of the national Republican Party in 1889, later reminisced that Deodoro "was almost completely unfamiliar with the republican group."[94] Indeed, the marshal had not set out on November 15 to install the Republic. Pulled from his sick bed by republican plotters, he believed that his troops were merely forcing a change in ministry. He never mentioned a republic as his troops stood down the imperial guard in the Campo de Sant'Anna. Rather, civilians in front of Rio's city hall proclaimed the Republic and unfurled its new flag.[95]

Consequently, Deodoro's objectives differed sharply from those of the republicans. He sought to continue imperial policy but not the Empire's political system. Rather, the Provisional Dictator essentially established military rule. He lectured the Brazilian Congress, declaring, "To the army and navy belongs the glory of having affected the Revolution of November 15."[96] Having brought the Republic into existence, many members of the military believed that the nation had entrusted its welfare to them. Lt.

Lauro Sodré, a deputy to the Constituent Congress in 1890 and later governor of Pará, clearly expressed this view: "The historic mission of embodying the summation of national aspirations is reserved to the armed forces."[97] Admiral Custódio de Mello, a bitter critic of military rule, protested that the military "convinced themselves that the Republic was entirely their doing and therefore it was up to them to occupy the principal administrative and political positions in the country."[98]

Deodoro put this thought into practice. He humbly professed to be "only competent to command the troops,"[99] so he treated Congress and the nation as if they were his troops. While Provisional Dictator from November 1889 to February 1891, he ruled by decree. To make himself comfortable with his cabinet, he promoted all of them to honorary general, even though only two ministers were even in the armed forces. These "generals," particularly Provisional Vice President Rui Barbosa, also governed as petty despots answerable only to Deodoro. In the arbitrary award of government contracts, allocation of revenue, proclamation of states of siege, censorship of critics, and removal of opponents from political office, Deodoro was more autocratic than Dom Pedro had been.

Military predominance was also evident on the state level. In 1890 ten officers served as state governors, ruling half of the states in the country. They governed some of the largest: Rio Grande do Sul, Bahia, Pernambuco, Ceará, and Pará. This is not surprising because prior to the drafting of republican state constitutions Deodoro appointed the majority of governors.[100] Even in states governed by civilians, such as São Paulo, Deodoro installed men loyal to himself rather than entrusting the selection of the governor to the local republican party.

Deodoro's autocratic and militaristic style alienated republicans. Among their principal goals had been decentralization of power from the executive to the legislature and, more important, from the central government to the states. Some republicans were placated, and enriched, by the Provisional Dictatorship's generous issue of concessions, expansion of the money supply, and loosening of incorporation and stock restrictions. In 1890 alone, the minister of agriculture, Francisco Glycerio, committed the government to 700,000 contos in colonization contracts, the equivalent of the entire federal budget for four years, and distributed vast land grants greater than the size of Italy to companies and individuals. He also contracted for the building of 15,000 kilometers of track at a time when the entire national system reached only 9,000 kilometers.[101] But too often for republican tastes, the beneficiaries of these grants were the same men who had flourished under the Empire: monarchist financiers.

Given the muted public enthusiasm that greeted the republican revolution, the narrow, divided political base of the republicans and the military, and the conservative predisposition of Marshal Fonseca, it is not surprising that Deodoro's government did not break sharply with imperial policy. The first republican government's economic program was motivated primarily by the need to buy friends for the regime among the imperial ruling class, not to reward a newly ascendent republican planter class. The most important sector of the imperial elite was the bankers and financiers who designed and profited from the Encilhamento stock spree. These men were granted unprecedented concessions and even lent substantial Treasury sums. The architect of this policy, Minister of Finance Rui Barbosa, consciously turned away from the laissez-faire policies advocated by Brazilian Historic Republicans (the originators of the Brazilian republican movement) and British liberals to a program of corporate liberalism similar to that followed by the U.S. Republicans during the Gilded Age. Barbosa's speeches cited the examples of Alexander Hamilton's effort to create a national bank in the United States and the great banks that were transforming the face of Germany. His critics accused him of seeking to create a "mercantile republic" in which "a small fraction of society is constituted into a privileged group so that the personal fortune of a small number of citizens grows in detriment to the collective welfare."[102] The French consul in Rio reported that Barbosa "wants to inaugurate the republican era with the establishment of a state socialism" that favored financiers.[103]

The second fraction of the imperial elite courted by Deodoro were Northeastern planters. He appealed to them out of personal proclivity and political necessity. Deodoro was himself from the Northeast as were a majority of army officers, particularly the most politicized. Of the 40 soldiers who came to serve in Congress, 68 percent were born in the Northeast or North, and 45 percent of them represented states from the North or Northeast. São Paulo and Minas Gerais, the center of republicanism, were the only two states to have no military representatives.[104] Deodoro manifested his sympathy for Northeasterners when he was able to replace his first cabinet in January 1891. The Provisional Dictator replaced the Historic Republicans who had been included in the first cabinet because of their participation in the Empire's overthrow with Northeasterners who, just as Deodoro, had risen in national politics under the Empire. Eight of the nine cabinet ministers in the new cabinet were from the Northeast or the North, and most had been conservatives.[105] The monarchist Joaquim Nabuco gloated that this was the end of republican influence in the marshal's government.[106]

Harrison, Blaine, and the U.S. press chose to ignore Deodoro's marginalization of republicans. The Blaine-Mendonça Accord proceeded unimpeded; indeed, as we will see, it became a vehicle for Deodoro to thwart the Historic Republicans and a major political battleground. However, the transformation of the essence of the cabinet away from republicanism was not even commented on in the official correspondence between Blaine and Mendonça. Realpolitik, not sympathy for Brazilian republicanism, guided U.S. foreign policy.

Political exigencies dictated Deodoro's alliance with Northeasterners. Having alienated republicans from the Southeast because of his authoritarian, centralizing tendencies, the marshal needed a counterforce. Northeasterners, who had been more receptive to imperial centralization and were not enthusiastic about the proclamation of the Republic, made natural allies against the Southeastern republicans.

Northeastern support for a centralized regime resulted from the region's relative economic decline in the nineteenth century. In the colonial period Brazil's most prosperous and populous area, the Northeast continued to be the principal exporting area because of the success of sugar. Only in 1831 had coffee, grown in the Southeast, become the principal export. Thereafter the Northeastern economy went into steady decline. Between 1860 and 1890 real agricultural wages fell by two-thirds, and the absolute literate population declined. It has been estimated that by the end of the Empire the Southeast had three times as much per capita wealth as the Northeast.[107] In fact the very last years of the monarchy were some of the century's worst because a serious drought parched the backlands of Bahia and Alagoas and banditry grew. Nonetheless, republicanism did not prosper.[108]

It seems counterintuitive that the Northeast's impoverishment would make it more loyal to the monarchy's central government than the prosperous Southeast, but that is what happened. By the 1880's, regional autonomy, for which Northeasterners had strongly fought earlier in the century, was much less attractive. Northeasterners would only control their own empty treasuries. Instead, the Northeastern elite turned its attention to control of the central government and its resource-extracting apparatus (which taxed the prosperous Southeast, particularly São Paulo, disproportionately) as well as its ability to borrow abroad. Even though its economy stagnated, the Northeast's hold on national office remained constant. In the Empire's last decade, 70 percent of the prime ministers came from the Northeast and none from São Paulo.[109] It was this sort of skewed representation that so angered planters from São Paulo and turned them toward republicanism.

Northeastern planters were less inclined to republicanism than their southern countrymen because they were not alienated by the abolition of slavery to the same extent as Southeastern planters. As coffee surpassed sugar, coffee fazendeiros (planters) in the Southeast purchased the slaves from Northeastern planters. The result was that the Northeast, which had half the slave population as late as 1864, had only one-quarter in 1883. By the end of the era of slavery, slaves were much less essential to the growing of sugar than they were to coffee production.[110] In fact the Northeastern state of Ceará abolished slavery on its own years before the monarchy decreed emancipation nationally.

But Northeastern monarchical sympathy could not necessarily be translated into support for Deodoro in his struggle against Southeastern republicans. After all, the marshal had overthrown the monarchy and replaced the local elite with military officers in the states. He needed a carrot to offer the Northeastern elite, and he found a sweet one in the U.S. sugar market.

Sugar had long been the mainstay of the Northeastern economy. Indeed, in the late sixteenth and early seventeenth centuries Brazil was the world's greatest and most sophisticated producer. Caribbean producers then took over world leadership in sugar, but it continued as Brazil's main agricultural export until shortly after independence when coffee became king and sugar's fortunes plummeted. Sugar dropped from 48 percent of national exports in 1828 to 5 percent by 1889. Even the absolute value of sugar exports was no higher in 1889 than it had been in 1840.[111]

Brazilian sugar had stagnated initially because of European colonialism. The French and British had restricted their purchases to their own colonies. World demand for sugar had grown spectacularly before 1800 (British demand alone swelled 2,500 percent in 150 years), and European continental powers, except France, did not have sugar-producing colonies of their own.[112] There was thus still room for Brazilian cane sugar.

The nineteenth century saw a much greater and more threatening transformation of the world sugar market. The British continental blockade of Napoleon stimulated the development of the sugar beet, a tuber that grew in temperate climates. Although still an insignificant source of sugar at midcentury, generous tax incentives by the German government encouraged great biological and technical strides. With government tax drawbacks (a practice that the Austrians and French also followed) and increased productivity, the sugar beet began to replace cane. Not only did Germany cease importing sugar, but its exports grew 32-fold between 1875 and 1884. Other continental nations such as Austria-Hungary, France, and Russia also became sugar exporters rather than importers. Even England, where the world price for sugar was set, turned to beet sugar at the expense of its own colonies.[113]

Brazil found itself shut out of the European sugar market. Great Britain had been the principal destination for Brazilian sugar. In the mid-1870's more than three-quarters of Brazil's exports went through England, but the beet invasion marginalized Brazilian sugar. By the late 1880's less than half went to Great Britain, and the total was dropping steadily.[114] The continental European powers had come to control the world sugar market. They used sugar exports as an arm of diplomacy, engaging in cut-throat competition. They protected their home markets and gave tax drawbacks to encourage exports. The price had fallen so low that the competing countries attempted to reach an agreement and stabilize the market. Meetings were held six times between 1864 and 1887 but to no avail.[115] The revealing aspects of these meetings for Brazil and the United States were not only the admission that states should manipulate the world market for a key commodity, but also the fact that neither American country, one a leading producer and the other a leading consumer, was invited to any of the meetings. It would be a European solution to the world sugar market.[116]

With these world market conditions and European disdain for American participants, the attractiveness of the U.S. sugar market is easy to understand. American sugar consumption rose prodigiously in the nineteenth century because of the country's swelling population, rising wealth, and development of a national sweet tooth. Between 1850 and 1889 American imports of sugar grew thirteenfold. By 1889 the United States had almost overtaken the British as the world's largest sugar market.[117]

Equally important, only about 10 percent of American demand was met by domestic production, and the United States still had no sugar-producing colonies. Hawaii, though drawn ever closer to the United States and exporting ever more sugar, was still an independent kingdom and met a small share of the U.S. demand. The Blaine-Mendonça agreement appeared to provide Brazil with a favored position in that market. The prospect of exporting to the United States was not only appealing on economic grounds, but diplomatically the gesture assured Brazil of an important place in the American system.

CHAPTER 4

Brazil Debates the Treaty

The Blaine-Mendonça pact was not greeted kindly in Brazil. Just as in the debate over reciprocity in the United States, the reactions to the accord in Brazil were conditioned mostly by brewing internal political feuds, not international diplomatic concerns. The trade agreement became trapped in the crossfire between Marshal Deodoro and Congress, between former monarchists and Historic Republicans, between Northeasterners and Southerners, and between centralists and federalists. Ironically, the agreement that was supposed to realign republican Brazil with its fellow republican powers was opposed by the principal republican parties; exmonarchists who had often favored friendship with Great Britain became the pact's defenders. The Blaine-Mendonça treaty was caught in the middle of a dispute that would eventually lead first to a presidential coup by Marshal Deodoro and then a countercoup that would overthrow him within the year. Certainly such turbulence over a fairly innocuous commercial agreement had not been anticipated in Washington, but the treaty looked very different from Rio.

The Pact's Charms

Deodoro da Fonseca used his powers as Provisional Dictator of Brazil to sign the Blaine-Mendonça Accord in the name of the Brazilian government.[1] The provisional government—soldiers, republicans, Northeasterners, and Southeasterners alike—agreed to the commercial treaty with the United

States mainly on the basis of the politically sensitive arguments presented by the treaty's most ardent supporter: Salvador de Mendonça.

Diplomatically, the accord was deemed necessary because it constituted a fundamental part of the "intimate alliance" between Brazil and the United States that promised U.S. recognition of the Republic, American naval support, and a favorable interpretation in the Missiones dispute. If the trade treaty were not approved by the provisional government, Mendonça hinted darkly, the United States might withdraw its recognition of the Republic and sever the friendship.[2]

Close relations with the United States had become even more pressing by the beginning of 1891. The Missiones settlement engineered the year before by the provisional government had unraveled. When news of it leaked out, the Brazilian population became enraged by the proposed cession to Argentina of land they believed was rightfully Brazilian. Now the dispute would have to be settled by international arbitration. Consequently, Brazil wanted, in the words of the Portuguese minister, to "sweeten the mouth of the future judge"—the president of the United States.[3]

Other events made the promise of American military support more enticing. The French minister in Rio reported that tensions were so high over Missiones that any insignificant act could lead to war with Argentina. At the same time, Uruguayan troops were massing on the Brazilian border because of political unrest within the province of Rio Grande do Sul.[4]

Events in Chile had more symbolic importance. In January 1891 parliamentary forces revolted against nationalist president Balmaceda.[5] Balmaceda had incurred the hatred of the landed oligarchy and foreign investors through his centralizing, developmental policies and his anti-British stand. The Congress revolted against the president. It was not difficult for Deodoro to put himself in Balmaceda's place, especially when the Chilean congressionalists, after receiving congratulations from Brazil's Chamber of Deputies, in turn unanimously resolved to extend to Brazil's Congress "sympathy for its defense of its institutions" against Deodoro's power.[6] The marshal was comforted when the U.S. Navy sided with Balmaceda by capturing rebel ships, and American businessmen—most prominently Charles Flint—provided Balmaceda's forces with munitions.[7] Less reassuring was the fact that the parliamentary troops, possibly aided by the British, ultimately overthrew Balmaceda.

The Chilean revolt struck a responsive cord in Brazil because Deodoro's authoritarian habits drove him ever farther from the republicans and Congress. After the Historic Republicans in his first cabinet resigned in January 1891, he replaced them with men of the monarchy and the Northeast. The new ministers viewed Congress as if it were still the Empire's parliament that could be dismissed at the executive's pleasure rather than an independent legislature.

Deodoro's subsequent election to the presidency in February 1891 cemented the rift. Fraud played a large part in his victory. The constituent deputies who were to vote for the president had their own victories verified by electoral boards appointed by Deodoro; they were often chosen for their loyalty to the marshal. As a further incentive to vote for Deodoro, bankers and stockholders, enriched by the provisional government's concessions, bribed deputies. If Mexican intelligence was accurate, Blaine also provided Deodoro with funds for bribes. Finally, the Provisional Dictator threatened a military coup if he were not confirmed. The marshal brought the fifteenth infantry battalion from Belem to strengthen his hand and put the Rio garrisons on alert the day of the election, while his nephew warned Congress in a newspaper article to "obey [the] dictatorship [or be] turned out at the point of the bayonet and trampled under the horses' hoofs."[8] These tactics worked.

Electoral totals revealed that Fonseca had won more through coercion than popularity. Even though he was confirmed 129 to 97, the deputies expressed their indignation at his tactics by defeating his running mate. Fifty-six electors who had voted for Deodoro split the ticket, and sixteen abstained altogether. Marshal Floriano Peixoto, the opposition candidate for the vice presidency, won a resounding 165 to 54 victory. When, shortly after the vote, Generalissimo Deodoro triumphantly strode into the luxurious salon of the former imperial palace in the Quinta de Boa Vista where the Constituent Congress was meeting, he was greeted by lukewarm applause that was soon hushed down. The new president faced a room silent except for a dozen clapping hands. Vice President Floriano Peixoto then entered the salon; it exploded with applause. One observer recalled that the crowd was "delirious," waving handkerchiefs and tossing flowers.[9] Deodoro, who had been the hero of the republican revolution (Floriano's role had been simply not to resist the coup), must have been deeply offended by this display of partiality to the opposition candidate.

Chagrined at what he rightfully perceived as a personal insult, President Deodoro responded in kind. He singled out São Paulo, the stronghold of republicanism, for retribution. The president replaced the republican governor of São Paulo with one of his own supporters and appointed loyal followers to all important posts in the state. In response, leaders of the Paulista republicans, Prudente de Morais and Francisco Glycério, began organizing opposition in the states. Strained relations between the president and Paulista leaders also fed mounting congressional hostility to the executive.[10]

Under these conditions, Deodoro could not reveal to Congress the nature of the "intimate alliance" with the United States as a justification for the trade pact. Congress would likely see the implicit promise of naval support by the United States as a weapon the executive could turn against the legislature and the states as had just occurred in Chile. The alliance may also have been kept secret to prevent the Argentinês from discovering its extent and withdrawing from the Missiones arbitration. As a result, Mendonça had to base his official justification for the tariff agreement on economic grounds.

Sugar Sweetens the Accord

Although some historians have suggested that the accord was negotiated to aid coffee, Mendonça maintained that the agreement's principal
benefit would be a privileged position in the vast U.S. market for Northeast
Brazilian sugar.[11] The pact also promised duty exemptions to exports from
other regions of the country: Southeastern coffee and Southern hides, but
these were really side-benefits. Mendonça reasoned that Brazil had nothing
to fear from a U.S. tariff on coffee. Since Brazil already supplied two-thirds
of the American market and over half of the world's coffee, the three-cents-
a-pound increase in coffee duties that the McKinley Tariff threatened if
Brazil failed to grant U.S. goods reciprocal duty reductions would not significantly affect exports. There simply was no other coffee producer large
enough to take up the Brazilian slack. Consequently, if the rate on Brazilian
coffee were raised, the level of all coffee prices would increase, and American consumers would cry out for lower duties.[12] Hides, which the United
States produced itself in abundance, could also bear additional duties since
they could simply be redirected to an eager European market. Besides, exports of hides had never been important to Brazil. Sugar, however, the final
item on which the McKinley Tariff would raise duties, could not bear the
burden of a 52 to 72 percent ad valorum increase. Brazil would not be able to
compete successfully with the Spanish-American territories of Cuba and
Puerto Rico for the rich U.S. market. Nor could Brazilian planters look
to Europe because of the thriving sugar beet industries of Germany and
Austria-Hungary.[13]

Tristao de Alencar Araripe, at the time minister of the treasury, was
convinced by Mendonça's argument: "I refer especially to sugar because
upon this article were always directed all of the arguments in favor of the
celebration of the treaty."[14] Alcindo Guanabara, a member of Congress during Deodoro's administration, concurred.[15] So did Justo Chermont, minister
of foreign relations under Deodoro, who acknowledged that "the intentions
of the government when it made the accord with such a sacrifice was only
to protect its saccharin industry."[16] Finally, we have the testimony of the
Barão de Lucena, the guiding force in Deodoro's government after the Historic Republicans resigned en mass in January 1891, who noted the geopolitical significance of the health of sugar: "Very precarious would become
the fate of the states of northern Brazil if the treaty were not signed."[17]

The agreement seemed so vital to Northeastern sugar because, according to Mendonça, it promised Brazil a virtual monopoly of the U.S. market.
Mendonça maintained that Blaine had promised him that no reciprocal
treaties would be signed with any other major sugar producer. He specifically excluded the possibility of an agreement with Spain on behalf of its
Cuban colony or Great Britain for its West Indian colonies. Brazil's minister
asserted that Spain could not enter into a treaty with the United States

because the colonial power had treaty obligations with England and Germany that precluded a reciprocal pact with the United States. Moreover, he claimed that Blaine had told him that the United States wanted to "reduce Cuba and Puerto Rico to poverty and create there a state of permanent revolution that would result in independence of those Spanish colonies and their annexation as states to the United States."[18] Mendonça believed that Anglophobia would prevent an agreement with Great Britain. No other Latin American producer was in a position to compete with Brazil, and, reasoned Mendonça, no European sugar producer would be willing to offer the United States reciprocal privileges because their "most favored nation" clause agreements would automatically confer the same privileges on competitors of the United States.[19] Members of the provisional government such as Rui Barbosa, Justo Chermont, and Cesario Alvim all later testified that they had based their approval of the agreement solely on the understanding that it promised a virtual Brazilian monopoly of the U.S. sugar market.[20]

At first glance, Mendonça's argument sounds convincing. Certainly the United States long coveted Cuba, and President Harrison and his secretary of state had expressed interest in annexing the island. In August 1891 Blaine wrote Harrison a prescient note: "I think there are only three places there of value enough to be taken, that are not continental. One is Hawaii and the others are Cuba and Puerto Rico."[21] During the Pan American Congress he had vehemently objected to renouncing America's right of conquest.[22] Moreover, Blaine had opposed a reciprocal treaty with Spain in favor of Cuba when the Arthur administration proposed it in 1883.

It was certainly true that relations between the United States and Great Britain were particularly strained at the time because of a controversy over Bering Straits fishing rights. This led to strong sentiment against what would have been the most important and obvious partner for reciprocity: Canada. Canada's isolation was underlined when it was left off Cleveland's guest list for the Pan American Conference. The chances of a reciprocal treaty with the much poorer and more sparsely populated British West Indian colonies were even more remote.

Hawaii was removed from competition in the short run because its queen rejected the demanding U.S. terms for a reciprocal treaty, a blueprint for the 1901 Platt amendment in Cuba: a base at Pearl Harbor, prior consultation with U.S. officials on foreign affairs, and permission for U.S. troops to invade to restore order.[23] (It is revealing how much harsher the U.S. terms were for a small, dependent country like Hawaii than for a large autonomous nation like Brazil. Harrison was following a two-track foreign policy that already envisioned the eventual annexation of Hawaii.)

The *Washington Post*'s reception of the treaty could also have led the Brazilian government to expect to dominate the North American sugar market:

The fact that the production of sugar in Brazil is languishing was another important factor in the negotiations. It is believed now that under the stimulating influence of free imports Brazil will send this year at least 200,000 tons, next year 500,000 tons and that within three years, or five at the furthest, Brazil will furnish, if necessary, every pound of sugar used in the United States. . . . The result will be a marked reduction in the price of sugar for every consumer in this country.[24]

The True Sugar Agreement

In fact, Brazil had no guarantee of the U.S. market. Within three months of the signing of the Blaine-Mendonça treaty, the United States signed a treaty with Spain; it later added Great Britain and even European sugar producers. The U.S.-Brazilian pact had never proscribed reciprocal treaties with other major sugar producers. Brazil's provisional government assumed that the prohibition had been hidden in a "reserve clause," a secret agreement that could not be disclosed for fear of alienating the European powers. Mendonça had led them to believe that such was the case. But there was no reserve clause.[25] What had gone wrong?

Mendonça maintained that Blaine promised him special consideration in order to secure the first major reciprocal treaty. The Brazilian minister argued that the U.S. secretary of state was playing off Brazil against the other sugar competitors. Another Brazilian diplomat, Oliveira Lima, as well as the respected American weekly *The Nation*, concurred.[26] There was certainly some truth to this version. John Foster, who negotiated the U.S. side of the agreements, later recalled the relationship between them:

> In my conference with Mr. Blaine at his residence the next morning [after signing the treaty with Brazil] we congratulated ourselves that our work was auspiciously begun but we had one more step to take before we could be assured of full success. Until we could bring the large sugar-producing island of Cuba into the arrangement, we could hardly expect the other sugar-exporting countries to accede to our terms for commercial reciprocity. I felt, however, that the agreement with Brazil would make the sugar planters of Cuba the more anxious to preserve a free market in the United States for their production.[27]

The treaty with Brazil was the first step because, given the Republic's need for U.S. political and armed support, it would be the easiest to secure. That, in turn, was to be used to open the Cuban market, which was in fact much greater for American agricultural products. Even Cuba was something of a pawn.

The treaty with Cuba was used to secure agreements for the much larger markets of Germany and Austria-Hungary. These two countries had anticipated Upton Sinclair's scathing indictment of the meat industry by decades when in 1880 they banned American pork imports because of inadequate

American meat inspection. They were able to sign reciprocal agreements in 1891 (and France entered into negotiations) because they were able to satisfy U.S. demands for reciprocity by lifting the prohibitions on U.S. pork in exchange for free access to the U.S. sugar market. Since Germany and Austria-Hungary lifted health restrictions rather than lowering duties, their other trade partners could not claim similar advantages under the most favored nation clause.[28] Thus Blaine's Latin American policy was intimately linked to his European designs. Even though the Blaine-Mendonça treaty was part of a larger strategy, however, this does not mean that Blaine lied to the Brazilian representative. Evidence suggests that he did not.

If Mendonça had followed the congressional debates over the McKinley Tariff closely, he would have realized that there never was a serious suggestion that Brazil or any other country should have a monopoly of the sugar market. Amaral Valente, Brazil's minister in Washington at the time but who was not involved in the negotiations, reported two months before the trade treaty was promulgated that Brazilian sugar would have no special privileges.[29] Yes, Blaine had earlier testified to the House Ways and Means Committee that a reciprocal treaty with Spain was unlikely, but he had already changed his mind by late July 1890.[30] It is also true that in the early stages of tariff debate in the Senate, the Hale amendment had been proposed, which would have refused reciprocity to any European country or European colony. This had been defeated, however, well before negotiations were concluded on the Blaine-Mendonça Accord.[31]

Instead, Republicans and Democrats alike wanted to lower the price of sugar and customs receipts on imported sugar. This meant that reciprocal treaties had to be signed with producers sufficiently large that they could meet almost all of the huge U.S. demand. Otherwise, much sugar would be imported under the McKinley Tariff's harsh punitive schedule, which would both raise the price of sugar to consumers several cents a pound and increase the Treasury's fiscal surplus.[32] Even the wildly optimistic report in the *Washington Post* (which appears to have been written by Mendonça) admitted that Brazilian growers, who in 1889–90 provided under 4 percent of America's sugar, would require three to five years before they could produce enough to satisfy demand. Because of the backwardness of the Brazilian sugar industry, the U.S. Congress had never considered a Brazilian monopoly to be feasible.[33]

Blaine had always intended to obtain an agreement with Cuba. In July 1890, six months before the treaty between the United States and Brazil was signed, Blaine wrote Harrison that he was contemplating a treaty with Spain. Five months later Harrison informed Congress that Cuba had a "peculiar importance" to U.S. trade. He added, "It is not doubted that a special arrangement in regard to commerce, based upon the reciprocity provision of the recent tariff act, would operate most beneficially for both governments. This subject is now receiving attention."[34] The day the *Wash-*

ington Post triumphantly announced the Blaine-Mendonça treaty, it also mentioned in the same article that "It is understood that similar agreements with Cuba and Venezuela are also being negotiated."[35] That same day Rio's *Jornal do Commércio* reported that North Americans had opened negotiations in Madrid with the Spanish government.[36] In fact, congressmen had demanded that Blaine not only engage in negotiations with Spain but England as well to ensure sufficient duty-free sugar. The French consul in Rio ridiculed Mendonça's interpretation of the McKinley Tariff. Clearly, the consul remonstrated, article three stated that no country would receive special privileges.[37]

Mendonça deflected the blame for the U.S. agreement with Spain from himself and Blaine to European diplomats and the Brazilian Congress. He blamed European pressures and the hostile reception that the treaty had received in Rio, which had placed into doubt Brazil's ability to supply duty-free sugar.[38] The Brazilian minister to the United States explained to his outraged government that the United States could enter into a treaty with Cuba despite the understanding with Brazil because Brazil's sugar monopoly "never was a condition of the tariff accord." Therefore, Mendonça had "worked to prevent a treaty with Spain."[39]

Mendonça's apparent misrepresentation of the treaty was important in securing its approval. Indeed, Minister of Finance Rui Barbosa complained that he had been tricked and therefore would not "accept the paternity of the American treaty."[40] He blamed Mendonça. Other observers believed that the fault lay with James G. Blaine for misleading Mendonça. The Brazilian minister was suffering from glaucoma at the time; had he been simply unable to read published reports of the political wranglings?[41] The evidence suggests that in fact Mendonça was not deceived.

After the United States signed its Spanish treaty, Mendonça reported that although Blaine had indeed promised not to engage the Spanish, the secretary of state had not first gained Harrison's approval. Harrison wanted to embarrass Blaine who, he feared, was becoming too popular politically and independent, so he broke Blaine's promise. Harrison was free to do this because, due to Bocayuva's concerns with Argentina and the Missiones treaty, Brazil had not actually entered into the intimate alliance that would have forbade the United States from entering into a treaty with a Spanish American colony.[42] In fact, knowing that Brazil had no guaranteed monopoly of the U.S. sugar market, Mendonça and Blaine, with the aid of Charles Flint, worked—not to prevent a treaty with Spain—but rather to delay its discovery by Brazil's Congress. Two months after the treaty's promulgation Flint wrote Blaine:

> Congress will be in session at Rio de Janeiro from May 1 to September first. I am satisfied that our Brazilian treaty will be accepted in Brazil and by that time the opposition will be so tired out that the making of a treaty with the Spanish by the United States will not seriously affect the Reciprocity ar-

rangement with Brazil. Mendonça has handled the matter very ably, but the possibility of an exclusive right to enter our sugar market free of duty should, in my judgement, be continued until after the adjournment of the Brazilian Congress.[43]

Salvador de Mendonça

Why did the Brazilian minister join in this conspiracy to delude his government? A quick sketch of Mendonça's background might provide some clues. Salvador de Mendonça, "a slight man of middle age" with hair "streaked with gray," had been born in 1841 to a coffee fazendeiro family in Rio de Janeiro state. Well educated in Rio city, he became a member of the urban professional elite, working first as a journalist and then as a teacher at the prestigious Colegio Dom Pedro II. While there, he fell in with the group that was to form the Historic Republicans. Mendonça was one of the signers of the Republican Manifesto of 1870, the official beginning of the movement. He became a member of the party's central committee, associate director of the republican newspaper, and organizer of the Clube Republicano, the first republican club in the city of Rio. Hence, the man mainly responsible for a treaty that supposedly mostly benefited Northeastern sugar was closely tied to coffee and Southeastern interests.[44]

Mendonça, albeit iconoclastic, had long been an important diplomatic agent for the Empire. Since 1875 he had been Brazilian consul in the single most important port for Brazilian exports in the world, New York. There his "quiet and suave" manner as well as his stylish attire and "excellent English" served him well.[45] In 1883 he had been a representative to the International Exposition in New Orleans at which he helped to obtain higher prices for coffee.[46] In 1887 Mendonça had negotiated the abortive trade treaty with President Cleveland, and of course in 1889 he had been one of the Brazilian representatives to the first Pan American Conference where he consistently sided with the United States.

Despite his long service for the Empire, the republican provisional government had no doubt about where Mendonça's loyalty lay. Upon the overthrow of the Empire, not only was he retained as a Brazilian representative at the Pan American Conference, but he was put in charge of the delegation. He was also promoted from consul general to minister plenipotentiary within a year. The allegation, made by some critics at the time, that Mendonça entered into the trade treaty to harm the Republic because of secret monarchical sympathies does not withstand scrutiny. Certainly the Brazilian foreign service did not question Mendonça's allegiance; he remained Brazil's minister to the United States until 1898.

Mendonça was a sincere admirer of the United States and Pan-Americanism. In a fourth of July speech he described Pan-Americanism as the "only obstacle" to the possible "existence of some new Egypt [in the Americas] governed and liquidated by English bankers."[47] He promoted the

American political system, made a wide network of friends, and married an American. So concerned was he with American friendship that in his work *A situação internacional* the minister went to great lengths to demonstrate the cordial relations that prevailed and the esteem of U.S. officials he commanded. In his opinion, at least, it was he, not the Barão de Rio Branco, who sowed the seeds of friendship with the United States that only would yield a bountiful harvest in the next century.[48] The Blaine-Mendonça Accord, the first ever between Brazil and the United States and the only commercial treaty that Brazil signed in more than 50 years, was the capstone of Mendonça's diplomatic career. He proclaimed the accord "the beginning of a new era . . . because it not only places us at the right hand of the powerful North American Union . . . but it also guarantees us the virtual monopoly of this great market for our principal products."[49] He might have been willing to win Brazilian acceptance, even at the cost of misrepresentation, to win broader U.S. friendship for Brazil and increase his own prestige in Washington. On a more personal level, Mendonça was quite flattered at the special attentions that Blaine paid him, which, he thought, prompted jealousy among his Spanish American counterparts. He worked hard to sustain this special relationship.

A second personal motive may have been Mendonça's business dealings with Charles Flint. The two men had become friends earlier. Flint was a major exporter to Brazil. Already in 1873 he had delivered 63 Baldwin locomotives, at the time the largest such shipment in Brazilian history. He continued to be the principal exporter of "miscellaneous manufactured goods," and he was also busily engaged in cornering the Brazilian rubber market. Flint, who entertained lavishly and lobbied energetically, had won over Mendonça.[50] Together they had crafted solutions to impasses at the Pan American Conference, orchestrated the U.S. recognition for Brazil, and negotiated the Blaine-Mendonça treaty. Indeed, Flint often operated virtually as Brazil's minister to the United States. When Mendonça was ill, the New York merchant negotiated in his stead with Blaine.[51] Flint clearly stood to benefit from greater trade between the two countries. If Mendonça had a business understanding with Flint, as one of the minister's enemies alleged, the minister also stood to profit from increased commerce between the two countries. The minister's successor as Brazilian consul general at New York claimed that Mendonça received sufficient funds from Blaine for entering into the trade pact that he soon thereafter built a large country home in New York. As we will see, there is good evidence that Mendonça profited handsomely three years later from close U.S.-Brazilian relations.[52]

Brazilian Objections

Whatever Mendonça's true motives, the treaty's negative reception in Brazil did not hinge solely on the lack of a monopoly in the U.S. sugar market. Objections to the treaty in Brazil preceded U.S. negotiations with Cuba. From the beginning the Congress had objected to the treaty. The *Rio News*, an avid supporter of the agreement, was forced to conclude that because "the discussions in the past week, both in Congress and in the press, have shown so bitter a feeling . . . against the treaty" the newspaper had no choice but to be "heartily in favor of its repeal."[53] The *Jornal do Commércio* estimated that a majority of Congress opposed the treaty. The U.S. consul general concluded dejectedly that "there seemed to be very few people with the knowledge, the courage, or the desire, to defend the so-called treaty," a sentiment with which the Portuguese minister concurred.[54]

Some of the objections sprang from the McKinley Tariff's free sugar provision. Although Mendonça and all other ministers spoke of "free sugar" imports, in fact the tariff freed from duties only sugars above Dutch 16 or more commonly known as raw sugar. The American Sugar Refining trust, which supposedly "had a hand in drafting the McKinley Bill," wanted to import the raw material more cheaply while continuing to be protected from the competition of foreign refiners.[55] This constituted a serious blow to Brazil's sugar modernization program. Brazilians had been aware of the backwardness of their sugar sector for decades and had complained loudly. Everything—credit, transportation, cultivation technique, and refining—required improvement if the country was going to keep step with the falling prices caused by increased productivity in Europe, Cuba, Hawaii, and even Louisiana.[56]

In its last decade the imperial state had begun to take the complaints seriously. Railroad concessions were granted and agricultural banks established in the sugar area. Most importantly, the central and provincial government passed a series of laws awarding central sugar mills guarantees of profit and bonuses for greater productivity. Some British and French investors were attracted and built modern efficient sugar mills in the Northeast. The hope was that by lowering production costs and increasing quality, Brazil could step up its exports. The Barão de Lucena, effectively the leader of Deodoro's government in 1891, directed the sugar modernization drive while governor of Pernambuco in 1874 and again as governor in 1890. The Republic had radically boosted aid to sugar mills,[57] but now the commercial treaty threatened to abort the promising modernization program by promoting the export of the raw material.[58]

The treaty's potential damage to Brazilian industrial interests, sugar, and other sectors, was one of the principal targets of criticism. Antao de Faria, one of the most influential men in Congress, later a minister in Floriano Peixoto's cabinet, and an advocate of industrialization, pointed out the central flaw in the Blaine-Mendonça treaty: it was unequal because the United States only granted privileges on raw materials that did not compete with domestic interests while exporting finished goods such as wheat, lard, and textiles that did compete with important Brazilian industries.[59]

Industry in Brazil

That the first republican regime would agree to a diplomatic initiative that undercut industry is startling in light of the government's reputation as one of the most bourgeois and developmentalist in the first 100 years of Brazilian statehood.[60] The Empire in its last years had already begun evincing interest in fomenting and protecting industry. A protective tariff in 1887 had a "lei dos similares" provision that prohibited duty exemptions on imports of any good that was already produced in Brazil "with a view of favoring certain industries which urgently need the assistance of the state."[61] Further concern was demonstrated in 1889 when, to compensate for the unusually strong milreis, a mobile schedule was enacted. It raised the tax rate when the milreis appreciated to keep domestic goods competitive with imports.[62]

The Republic's first minister of finance, Rui Barbosa, has been called the "minister of Brazilian economic independence" and "one of the most active leaders of the nascent industrial bourgeoisie."[63] His successor, the Barão de Lucena, who had been instrumental in the Pernambuco sugar industry, also worked to develop other industries. He sought a protective tariff, though he was removed from office before it could be enacted.[64] These hardly seem the men to sell out industry, especially since factories were springing up all over Brazil.

The late 1880's and the early 1890's in Brazil witnessed a fevered industrialization drive. The greatest expansion was in the country's heartland, Rio de Janeiro, São Paulo, and Minas Gerais, but the boom extended from north to south. In Pará the German consul reported the falling off of the import trade because of domestic production. He cited beer, matches, linen, cheap dress fabrics, prepared chemicals, furniture, pins, and boots. In Pernambuco the British consul noted "the industrial evolution of the last five years has been very great."[65] He discussed not only Pernambuco, but also Alagoas, Rio Grande do Sul, and Paraíba. Although he emphasized cotton textile factories, he also noted the establishment of a nail factory, a soap work, a cottonseed oil mill, four large rum distilleries, two factories for making wine, two hydraulic presses for bailing cotton, a match factory, a gunpowder factory, and finally a large sugar refinery.

The national extent of manufacturing was illustrated in the 1889 national exposition. Of the 274 manufacturing representatives, 107 came from the Northeast and nineteen from the South with the rest from the Southeast.[66] Still at an early and relatively unsophisticated stage of industrialization, Brazilian manufactured goods had a very large raw material component and small value added. Consequently, planters and farmers were often also involved in industry. The list of industries that Francisco de Paula Rodrigues Alves, former governor of São Paulo, planter, and future president, wanted protected illustrates the symbiotic relationship between agriculture and industry: hats, mostly produced in São Paulo, lard, shoes, and salted meat from Rio Grande do Sul, rice from Maranhão, the butter of Minas Gerais, and ceramics produced chiefly in Minas Gerais, São Paulo, and Rio de Janeiro state. Pine lumber from Paraná and textiles in Maranhão and Pernambuco also had their champions.[67] Industrial production, then, was a national concern.

Mendonça was aware of the rise of an industrial spirit and lobby in Brazil. Brazilian industry would not be harmed, he promised. Mendonça pointed out that although it appeared that Brazil had conceded the United States a great advantage because of the extensive list of goods that were reduced either 25 percent or 100 percent, this was illusory. Many of the U.S. goods exempted had already been duty free for all nations before the treaty. Others that received 25 percent duty reductions were not consumed much in Brazil. Consequently, the privileges advanced to American goods by the treaty were insufficient to enable them to overcome European or Brazilian competition: "The North American industries are not, for the most part, in a position to compete with their European counterparts. Except for the growth of wheat flour, United States exports to Brazil will not increase."[68] After all, American producers believed that they needed tariff protection to compete in their home market because domestic production costs were superior to European costs. They certainly could not compete in Brazil where they had no credit arrangements, few representatives, and poor transportation connections. Since European imports, often taxed at higher rates, would continue to dominate the trade, Brazil's treasury would lose no customs income. (Since customs duties provided two-thirds of the central government's revenues, this was a major consideration.) Since American producers could not compete with Brazilians, there would be no increase in imports, a constant concern because of Brazil's balance-of-payments deficit and depreciating currency.[69]

Mendonça presented a battery of figures and estimates to demonstrate that Brazil benefited disproportionately from the treaty. The United States stood to lose $10 million from coffee revenue, $1.5 million from hides, and $5 million from sugar by exempting them from duties, but Brazil only faced a loss of $992,941.64, merely 6 percent of the projected American loss. Furthermore, the treaty opened a rich market of 63 million people to Brazilian products while facilitating United States entry into a modest market of only 14 million.[70]

However, there is reason to doubt the sincerity of Mendonça's argument on the effects of the treaty. He was a free trader who believed that Brazil's interests lay in exporting much rather than substituting imports, and he was not overly concerned with the fate of industry. He revealed this bias in his self-defense that he wrote to Itamaraty in 1891: "We are still in a period of agricultural industry and, as in all evolutionary processes, one cannot leap ahead." He felt it would be "many years" before Brazil moved ahead.[71]

In his newspaper articles in the United States, the minister drew a very different picture from the one he had painted for the Brazilian audience. In the United States he contended that the treaty would allow U.S. exports to Brazil to grow impressively.

Certainly industrial representatives in Brazil's Congress were not swayed by Mendonça's arguments. One deputy protested that the treaty "struck deeply at individual initiative as well as at nascent industries, incontestably in a period of substantial development."[72] Interests in Amazonas, Alagoas, and São Paulo also objected to the treaty's duty reductions. The main focus of opposition was the state of Rio Grande do Sul. The state's legislature strongly denounced the pact. It noted that benefits accrued only to states that exported sugar, coffee, or hides, for these states would reap larger export taxes. But Rio Grande do Sul did not produce the first two and could not compete internationally in hides. Instead, the state's producers depended on domestic markets. Reductions in the duty schedule for American lard and bacon, two of the state's main products, were viewed with alarm.[73]

Nationalism

It should be pointed out that the thrust of the industrial lobby's objections was not anti-American, but rather, pro-Brazilian. One of the treaty's most outspoken critics was a leader of Brazil's incipient workers' movement, Augusto Vinhaes. He urged that Congress aid domestic industry and "put aside the suggestions of European capitalists who are interested in maintaining the subservience of Brazil to the industries of England and other countries."[74] His preoccupation with European producers was mirrored by other nationalists. It is somewhat ironic that this concern manifested itself in opposition to the Blaine-Mendonça agreement since the original purpose of a Brazilian alliance with the United States was to free Brazil from British influence.

Nationalism and Pan-Americanism were not contradictory in the early Republic. The provisional government and the first constitutional regime passed some daring nationalist legislation, but they also embraced Pan-Americanism. In March 1890 the Provisional Dictatorship decreed that all people residing in Brazil on November 15, 1889, were considered Brazilian citizens unless they renounced their Brazilian citizenship within six months.[75] A year later Brazilian coastal shipping was nationalized.[76] At the end of 1891 there were even calls for revising the constitution to allow the nationalization of the retail trade.[77] Treasury deposit requirements of foreign corporations petitioning to operate in Brazil were also dramatically increased.[78]

At the same time, Brazil, of all participants at the Pan American Conference, most embraced the principles of Pan-Americanism. Brazil contributed funds to the preliminary surveys of the intercontinental railroad and to the International Bureau of American States.[79] Even more significantly, in October 1891 the Chamber of Deputies approved the Washington treaty for obligatory arbitration that had grown out of the Pan American Conference.[80] The Brazilian government also committed itself to building a pavilion at the forthcoming Columbian Exposition in Chicago, to creating its own international fair in São Paulo, and to funding increased steamship commerce between the United States and Brazil.[81]

European Reactions

Although Brazil's industrial representatives did not oppose the Blaine-Mendonça Accord because of anti-Americanism, the reactions of the European powers to the pact did reflect their growing rivalry with the United States. European appreciation of the accord also belied Mendonça's dismissal of trade concessions to the United States as insignificant. The publication of the agreement in France alarmed industrialists and merchants who petitioned their government for the same privileges in Brazil. The Portuguese minister believed the pact would harm Portuguese interests, while the *Economist* predicted that Great Britain and Canada would suffer. The Russians were so concerned that they sent an agent of their finance ministry to South America to study the treaty's possible effects. He concluded that it would help U.S. trade, especially textiles, "substantially" while being "very prejudicial" to nascent Russian trade with Brazil.[82]

U.S. consuls in Rio, Bahia, Recife, and Belem all reported strong opposition to the treaty among foreign merchants, particularly the British. The consuls believed that the British were actively subverting the treaty by creating financial havoc that would be blamed on the treaty and by bribing Brazilian politicians.[83] Lawrence Hill, in his study of U.S.-Brazilian relations, concluded that foreign influences were mainly responsible for the Brazilian press's hostility to the treaty.[84] However, Hill based his conclusion exclusively on a reading of U.S. consular dispatches. It is doubtless true that foreign merchants opposed the treaty. It is also true that foreign merchants were very powerful. An estimate made in 1897 concluded that 11,486 of the 14,486 businessmen in Rio were foreigners. Indeed, a French observer commented in the 1880's that Rio was so dominated by foreign interests that chiefly concerned themselves with making money that a republican revolution in the city was precluded.[85] Obviously he—and the U.S. consuls—had overestimated the power of foreigners. This is not to deny that foreign financiers enjoyed great influence both before and after the rise of the Republic, but they were mostly Portuguese, not British, and had no special stake in British trade.[86] There is no need to posit a foreign conspiracy to understand the Brazilian displeasure with the treaty. Brazilians thought for themselves and found plenty of homegrown reasons for opposition.

Congressional Hostility

Concern for the health of the budding industrial sector has already been discussed. Much opposition also derived from the manner in which the treaty was enacted. Deodoro signed the pact without congressional approval. As already discussed, Deodoro's autocratic bearing had alienated many deputies long before the agreement with the United States was brought to the chamber. As a man who believed that he was "chosen by fate, or Providence, for the realization of a work of grandeur and sacrifice," Deodoro was not interested in the give-and-take of politics.[87] Rather than learning the delicate art of compromise, the marshal wanted (but the constitution denied him) the sledgehammer of the veto. Just reading the preface to the treaty was sufficiently irritating to inspire congressional opposition: "Marshal Manoel Deodoro da Fonseca, head of the Provisional Government established by the Army and Navy, in the name of the Nation . . . decrees . . . "[88]

At the time of its promulgation, legislative authority lay in the Provisional Dictatorship's executive. The Constituent Congress was in the act of drafting the constitution that was only finished on February 24, 1891. Since they had been elected only for that purpose, they had delegated "pro tempore" to Deodoro "all the attributes concerning the public administration of the country until the approval of the constitution and the election of the first president."[89] Whether "public administration" included treaties with foreign nations was disputed. Many members of the Constituent Congress asserted that Deodoro in fact did not have the authority to deal with foreign nations without congressional consent. Quintino Bocayuva, who as minister of foreign relations had initiated the treaty's negotiations, declared that "the treaty was made *ad referendum* for the Constituent Congress, with a clause that only was valid after the approval [of Congress]; therefore the treaty will have neither value nor effect."[90] Mendonça seems to have had the same understanding.[91] However, Prudente de Morais, presiding president of the Constituent Convention and a leading Paulista Historic Republican, ruled that since the sole purpose of the convention was to approve a constitution, not to legislate, the treaty was law without congressional consent.[92] This was a peculiar position for Prudente to take since he was a leader of the opposition to Deodoro, but he was also a candidate for the presidency in the election that would take place at the end of the month. The Paulista probably wanted to assuage Deodoro's reservations about the possibility of civilian rule so that the marshal would allow Prudente to serve if he were elected. (His gesture apparently fell on deaf ears since Deodoro nonetheless threatened a coup at election time.) Despite Prudente's ruling, defenders of the legislature's prerogative barely failed to convince a majority of Congress to direct the executive to secure congressional approval for the treaty.[93] The treaty became law, but it left a bitter taste in the mouths of many congressmen who were rankled by this apparent executive usurpation of legislative prerogative.

The controversy over the treaty's validity resurfaced under the constitutional government. The constituent congressmen declared themselves the first constitutional deputies and senators in an obvious legislative coup aimed at preventing Deodoro from replacing them with men loyal to himself. By the time they convened in June the U.S. treaty with Spain on Cuba had become known; opposition heated up.

Deodoro and his minister of foreign relations, Justo Chermont, were also upset by the American agreement with Spain on Cuba and sought means of placating Congress. They considered raising duties on U.S. goods or raising the general level of the tariff that Mendonça advised them was permissible under the terms of the agreement.[94] Lucena began crafting a new tariff. The administration also undertook a new diplomatic initiative. The French minister noticed a change in the Brazilian foreign minister's attitude after news of the Cuban treaty. Chermont made three "quasi-overtures" regarding a treaty with France and also approached Portugal.

It is not clear, however, whether these gestures were sincere efforts to win European trade and friendship or rather were bargaining chips for Mendonça, still in Washington desperately attempting to induce the modification of the agreement with Spain. Conde Paço d'Arco, Portugal's minister to Brazil, thought it quite possible that Brazil never really meant to sign treaties with the Europeans. (No treaties were enacted, but a preliminary agreement was signed with Portugal.) Even the French minister, A. Gerard, recognized that

> There is no doubt that the Brazilian government, deceived by Washington, is not showing itself any more deferential to Europe; at the same time, the unanimity with which the European powers have been outraged by the treaty concluded with the United States proves to them [the Brazilian government] the price that Europe attaches to the maintenance of commercial relations with Brazil.[95]

Lucena's overtures did not sufficiently satisfy Congress, which was bent on modifying the Blaine-Mendonça Accord. The conflict came to a head in September.

The timing of the explosion is intriguing. Deodoro was taken ill at the end of July. Observers believed him near death, so politicians began planning a new government.[96] The Congress returned to debating the commercial pact at precisely the same time that the Historic Republicans were seeking three cabinet positions in the prospective new government. It would appear that the republicans were attempting to threaten one of Deodoro's favorite achievements to gain negotiating leverage.[97] To forestall such action, Mendonça was recalled to Rio to mollify Congress in September 1891. Mendonça had hoped to avoid this confrontation. He asked Blaine in May to delay the publication of the treaty with Spain until after the

Brazilian Congress had approved its pact with the United States. In fact, the Spanish government did not approve the treaty until mid-July, but the text of the agreement was published earlier in an attempt to force Germany into an agreement.[98] Now faced by a hostile Congress, Mendonça summoned his full oratorical and diplomatic skills in defense of his pact. He argued that even without a monopoly of the U.S. sugar market, the agreement should not be renounced. If it were, he darkly predicted, there would be "a disruption of relations with this country [by the United States], a withdrawal of the American minister within twenty-four hours and a tariff war in which we can do nothing but lose, together with the commercial advantages which at the present are certain, the friendship of a country which has always treated us with respect."[99]

The appeal failed. Congress continued to clamor for renunciation. This was perceived by Deodoro, who returned to office the beginning of October, as a personal attack, and, indeed, it was. Congressmen began to suggest that all acts of the provisional government should be rejected "beginning with the commercial treaty."[100] Opinion in Congress on the treaty split on regional lines very similar to the topography of Deodoro's support. Of the ten deputies who vocally defended the agreement, six were from the Northeast. On the other hand, 80 percent of the 53 proclaimed antagonists to the pact were from the Southeast or South.[101] Other measures of the Lucena government, particularly the concession of large privileges to a few bankers, aroused even greater fury. Deodoro finally seized the power the constitution had denied him and closed Congress on November 3, 1891. Prominent among the reasons for the presidential coup was defense of the commercial agreement.[102] Twenty days after Marshal Fonseca expelled Congress, a naval and army revolt removed him from office. He was replaced by Marshal Floriano Peixoto, a man who had opposed the Blaine-Mendonça Accord from the beginning.

Fig. 1. James G. Blaine, leading Republican strategist. As U.S. Secretary of State (1881 and 1889–92), he fathered the first Pan American Conference and reciprocity. Photo courtesy of the Library of Congress (hereafter LC).

Fig. 2. Salvador de Mendonça, Brazil's minister to the United States and representative at the Pan American Conference. He was an architect of the Blaine-Mendonça Accord and co-organizer of Flint's Fleet. Courtesy of LC.

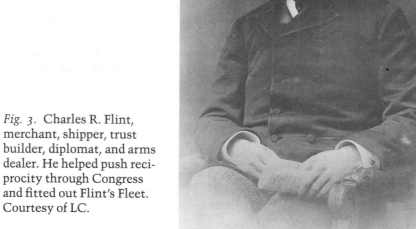

Fig. 3. Charles R. Flint, merchant, shipper, trust builder, diplomat, and arms dealer. He helped push reciprocity through Congress and fitted out Flint's Fleet. Courtesy of LC.

Fig. 4. Floriano Peixoto, vice president and then leader of Brazil, 1891–94. He supported industrialization but also cemented Brazil's friendship with the United States during the naval revolt. From Luiz Jose Pereira da Silva, *Floriano Peixoto: tracos biographicos* (Rio de Janeiro: Fauchon, 1894).

Fig. 5. William McKinley, U.S. congressman from Ohio. He engineered the McKinley tariff and later, as president (1897–1901), became one of reciprocity's strongest champions. Courtesy of LC.

Fig. 6. Benjamin Harrison, president of the United States (1889–93). He oversaw the most activist and one of the most expansionist administrations of the nineteenth century. Courtesy of LC.

Fig. 7. José Custódio de Mello, admiral and secretary of the Brazilian navy under Floriano Peixoto. He initiated and led the naval revolt (1893–94), hoping to gain power. From José Custódio de Mello, *O governo provisório e a revolução de 1893.*

Fig. 8. Saldanha da Gama, Brazilian admiral and head of the
naval academy. He joined the naval revolt and compromised
it when he appeared to call for a return to monarchy. From
Pedro Lafayette, *Saldanha da Gama* (Rio de Janeiro: Editora
Souza, 1959).

Fig. 9. The teeming harbor of Rio de Janeiro's Guanabara Bay before the outbreak of the revolt. The naturally protected harbor hosted the largest ports in Latin America, and indeed one of the largest outside Europe and North America. From Gilberto Ferrez, *A marinha.*

Fig. 10. Destruction in Rio caused by the naval revolt. The six-month-long rebellion between September 1893 and March 1894 caused much destruction to Rio's business area and to its commerce. Photo courtesy of the Department of Special Collections, University Research Library, University of California, Los Angeles (UCLA).

Fig. 11. Niterói, the capital of Rio de Janeiro state, across the bay from the city of Rio de Janeiro. It was badly damaged by insurgents during the naval revolt. Photo courtesy of the Department of Special Collections, University Research Library, UCLA.

Fig. 12. Cartoon of Charles R. Flint. The armsmonger with his toy fleet was the object of great interest and some derision in the U.S. press at the end of 1894. Reprinted from *The New York World.*

'BRAZIL'S WAR UP TO DATE.

Fig. 13. Cartoon of admirals Benham and da Gama. Caricatured as blustering bad aims in the American press, the Brazilian insurgent leaders were dismissed in the early stages of the revolt as characters in a comic opera. Reprinted from *The New York World*, which had reprinted it from *The Philadelphia Press*.

Fig. 14. Cartoon of Admiral Benham. The U.S. commander of the South Atlantic Fleet was lionized in the American press for asserting U.S. naval might and the Monroe Doctrine in ending the naval revolt. Reprinted from *The New York World*.

HANDS OFF!

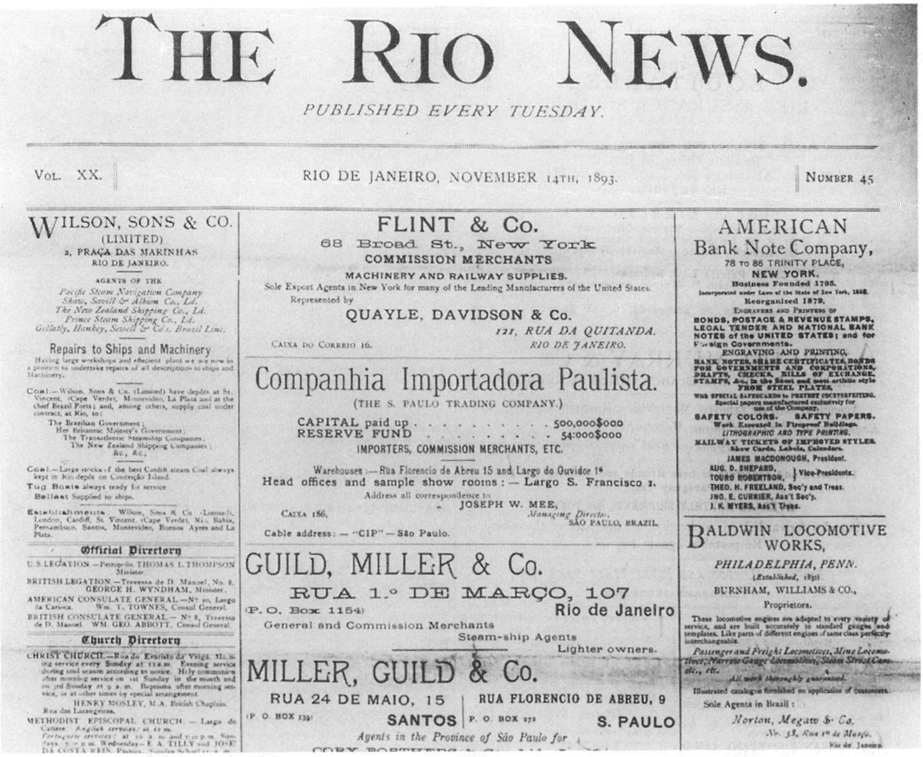

THE RIO NEWS.

PUBLISHED EVERY TUESDAY.

VOL. XX. | RIO DE JANEIRO, NOVEMBER 14TH, 1893. | NUMBER 45

WILSON, SONS & CO.
(LIMITED)
2, PRAÇA DAS MARINHAS
RIO DE JANEIRO.

AGENTS OF THE
Pacific Steam Navigation Company
Shaw, Savill & Albion Co., Ld.
The New Zealand Shipping Co., Ld.
Prince Steam Shipping Co., Ld.
Gellatly, Hankey, Sewell & Co's. Brazil Line.

Repairs to Ships and Machinery

Having large workshops and effecient plant we are now in a position to undertake repairs of all descriptions to ships and Machinery.

Coal.—Wilson, Sons & Co. (Limited) have depôts at St. Vincent, (Cape Verde), Montevideo, La Plata and at the chief Brazil Ports; and, among others, supply coal under contract, at Rio, to:
The Brazilian Government;
Her Britannic Majesty's Government;
The Transatlantic Steamship Companies,
The New Zealand Shipping Companies;
&c., &c.,

Coal.—Large stocks of the best Cardiff steam Coal always kept in Rio depôt on Conceição Island.

Tug Boats always ready for service

Ballast Supplied to ships.

Establishments: Wilson, Sons & Co. (Limited), London, Cardiff, St. Vincent, (Cape Verde), Rio, Bahia, Pernambuco, Santos, Montevideo, Buenos Ayres and La Plata.

Official Directory

U.S. LEGATION.—Petropolis. THOMAS L. THOMPSON Minister.

BRITISH LEGATION.—Travessa de D. Manoel, No. 8. GEORGE H. WYNDHAM, Minister.

AMERICAN CONSULATE GENERAL.—No 20, Largo da Carioca. Wm. T. TOWNES, Consul General.

BRITISH CONSULATE GENERAL.—No 8, Travessa de D. Manoel. WM. GEO. ABBOTT, Consul General.

Church Directory

CHRIST CHURCH.—Rua do Evaristo da Veiga. Morning service every Sunday at 11 a.m. Evening service during cool season according to notice. Holy communion after morning service on 1st Sunday in the month and on 3rd Sunday at 9 a.m. Baptisms after morning service, or at other times by special arrangement.
HENRY MOSLEY, M.A. British Chaplain.
Rua das Larangeiras.

METHODIST EPISCOPAL CHURCH.—Largo do Cattete. *English services:* at 11 m. *Portuguese services:* at 10 a. m. and 7.30 p.m. Sundays. 7.30 p.m. Wednesday.—F. A. TILLY and JOSE DA COSTA REIS, Pastors. ...

FLINT & Co.
68 Broad St., New York
COMMISSION MERCHANTS
MACHINERY AND RAILWAY SUPPLIES.
Sole Export Agents in New York for many of the Leading Manufacturers of the United States.
Represented by
QUAYLE, DAVIDSON & Co.
121, RUA DA QUITANDA.
CAIXA DO CORREIO 16. *RIO DE JANEIRO.*

Companhia Importadora Paulista.
(THE S. PAULO TRADING COMPANY.)
CAPITAL paid up . . . . 500,000$000
RESERVE FUND . . . . 54:000$000
IMPORTERS, COMMISSION MERCHANTS, ETC.
Warehouses:—Rua Florencio de Abreu 15 and Largo do Ouvidor 1a
Head offices and sample show rooms:—Largo S. Francisco 1.
Address all correspondence to
JOSEPH W. MEE,
Managing Director.
CAIXA 186, SÃO PAULO, BRAZIL.
Cable address:—"CIP"—São Paulo.

GUILD, MILLER & Co.
RUA 1.° DE MARÇO, 107
(P. O. Box 1154) Rio de Janeiro
General and Commission Merchants
Steam-ship Agents
Lighter owners.

MILLER, GUILD & Co.
RUA 24 DE MAIO, 15 (P. O. BOX 139) SANTOS
RUA FLORENCIO DE ABREU, 9 (P. O. BOX 272) S. PAULO
Agents in the Province of São Paulo for
CORY BROTHERS ...

AMERICAN
Bank Note Company,
78 TO 86 TRINITY PLACE,
NEW YORK.
Business Founded 1795.
Incorporated under Laws of the State of New York, 1858.
Reorganized 1879.
ENGRAVERS AND PRINTERS OF
BONDS, POSTAGE & REVENUE STAMPS, LEGAL TENDER AND NATIONAL BANK NOTES of the UNITED STATES; and for Foreign Governments.
ENGRAVING AND PRINTING,
BANK NOTES, SHARE CERTIFICATES, BONDS FOR GOVERNMENTS AND CORPORATIONS, DRAFTS, CHECKS, BILLS OF EXCHANGE, STAMPS, &c., in the finest and most artistic style FROM STEEL PLATES,
With SPECIAL SAFEGUARDS to PREVENT COUNTERFEITING.
Special papers manufactured exclusively for use of the Company.
SAFETY COLORS. SAFETY PAPERS.
Work Executed in Fireproof Buildings.
LITHOGRAPHIC AND TYPE PRINTING.
RAILWAY TICKETS OF IMPROVED STYLES.
Show Cards, Labels, Calendars.
JAMES MACDONOUGH, President.
AUG. D. SHEPARD, TOURO ROBERTSON, Vice-Presidents.
THEO. H. FREELAND, Sec'y and Treas.
JNO. E. CURRIER, Ass't Sec'y.
J. K. MYERS, Ass't Treas.

BALDWIN LOCOMOTIVE WORKS,
PHILADELPHIA, PENN.
(*Established,* 1831)
BURNHAM, WILLIAMS & CO.,
Proprietors.
These locomotive engines are adapted to every variety of service, and are built accurately to standard gauges and templates. Like parts of different engines of same class perfectly interchangeable.
Passenger and Freight Locomotives, Mine Locomotives, Narrow Gauge Locomotives, Steam Street Cars, etc., etc.
All work thoroughly guaranteed.
Illustrated catalogue furnished on application of customers.
Sole Agents in Brazil:
Norton, Megaw & Co.
No. 58, Rua 1° de Março,
Rio de Janeiro.

Fig. 15. Front page of *The Rio News.* Flint and Company had a central place on page one of the leading English-language newspaper in Rio de Janeiro and in the diplomatic dealings between the United States and Brazil. Reprinted from *The Rio News.*

Fig. 16. The cruiser *Nichteroy.* Transformed from Huntington's luxury liner *El Cid* into Flint's Fleet's most potent weapon with the addition of a dynamite gun, the cruiser helped to end Brazil's naval revolt. Four years later it fought on the U.S. side in the Spanish-American War as the USS *New York.* From Ferrez, *A marinha.*

Fig. 17. The battleship *Aquibadan.* This modern, iron-clad battleship was the jewel of the Brazilian navy. Seized by Admiral Custódio de Mello, it became the flagship of the insurgents during the naval revolt until it was torpedoed by Flint's Fleet. From Ferrez, *A marinha.*

CHAPTER 5

The Iron Marshal and the Northern Giant

Vice President Marshal Floriano Peixoto, the man who re-placed Deodoro da Fonseca as leader of Brazil on Novem-ber 24, 1891, was in many ways a paradoxical figure and an improbable hero. Although he had dedicated his military career to defend-ing the monarchy, he became known as the savior of the Republic. A thin, wiry, sickly man with a drooping mustache and morose disposition, he inspired his most militant followers, known as "Florianistas," to a state of near frenzy. An authoritarian, iron-fisted centralizing leader known to his admirers as "the Iron Marshal," he became the ally of the civilian federalists from São Paulo and Rio Grande do Sul. He was the son of a modest sugar planter in the Northeastern state of Alagoas and the adopted son (after his father died) of a wealthy, powerful planter in the same state. Yet Floriano became the defender of industry and the patron saint of a petite bourgeois and working-class nationalist movement known as the Jacobins centered in the Federal District. The vice president's alliance with Historic Republi-cans, industrialists, and nationalists—all of whom had opposed the Blaine-Mendonça treaty—led his followers to expect the xenophobic and chauvin-ist Iron Marshal to abrogate the pact and retreat from Deodoro's informal alliance with the United States. But Floriano was a survivor, not an ideo-logue. The perilous situation in which he soon found himself trapped per-suaded him not just to maintain relations with the United States, but to strengthen them.

History and historiography have been kind to Floriano Peixoto since he left power, but the three years (November 1891 to November 1894) he commanded the country through a virtual military dictatorship were tormented by conspiracies, civil wars, and foreign intrigues. During his administration opinion was bitterly divided. His supporters idolized the Iron Marshal, finding virtue in his taciturn personality and his suspicious and vengeful nature. To them, Floriano was a self-sacrificing spartan general training his wrath on the former ruling class, the enemies of the Republic. Floriano was the savior of the Patria and the legal order. The Florianistas pledged their loyalty, and even their lives, to the Iron Marshal.

His enemies, who were many, accused Floriano of being a cruel tyrant, an ignorant, power-hungry dictator worse than Deodoro. He was likened to the Argentine caudillo Rosas and the Paraguayan autocrat Francia.[1] He was subverting the Republic rather than consolidating it. They plotted the overthrow of this enigmatic "caboclo."

So ambiguous was Floriano's legacy that both the "tenentes" (lieutenants) who in 1930 attempted to usher in a more broadly based democratic regime by overthrowing the oligarchic Republic and the leaders of the military coup of 1964 that replaced a popular, social democratic regime with a right-wing dictatorship could trace their lineage to him.

Certainly Floriano Peixoto was very much a man of his times, shaped and pushed by the tumultuous, chaotic events of the early 1890's. He inherited a deeply troubled economy. Despite the prosperity of the export sector, the financial policies of Deodoro's administrations had driven the milreis to less than half its former value in just two years. Foreign investment virtually ceased after the near collapse of the British banking house of Baring in November 1891.[2] Before the world economy could recover from this shock, it would plunge into the deepest, longest depression of the century between 1893 and 1896. In Brazil the Encilhamento was fizzling. The glamour and unimaginable profits of the first two years had dimmed by late 1891. Giant conglomerates such as the Companhia Geral de Estradas de Ferro and the Companhia Geral de Obras Publicas crashed during Floriano's tenure, devastating the stock market.[3] At the same time, consumer prices rose over 50 percent in one year.[4] A Frenchman complained that Rio had become much more expensive than Paris. The Rio chief of police alarmedly described the "growing statistic of crimes against property and individuals recently committed in this capital; the audacity of their authors; the vertiginous rapidity with which the class of trouble makers and vagrants grows; the enormous avalanche of heterogenous elements which compose the growing population of this capital."[5]

In these dark circumstances, Floriano seized power.[6] He faced not only grave economic and social problems, but also a very serious political crisis. His predecessor, Marshal Deodoro, had continued to enjoy substantial support down to the end. All governors but one (all of whom the Provisional Dictator had appointed) had applauded his closure of Congress, and the army and navy had initially supported the act as well.[7] Deodoro relented in the face of a revolt by elements in the army and navy combined with a railroad strike, but not necessarily because the balance of forces was against him. Old and sick, Deodoro was concerned more with posterity's judgment of this proclaimer of the Republic than with retaining his office, so he acquiesced to Floriano's forces. Deodora may have "invited" Floriano to assume power by "spontaneously resigning," but Deodoro's supporters remained numerous and powerful even after his overthrow.[8]

Deodoro's supporters continued to plague Floriano's rule. The end of November and December 1891 were shaken by revolts in many states aimed at overthrowing the governors who had favored Deodoro. In Pernambuco the revolt cost as many as 300 lives.[9] In January 1892, 160 prisoners at the Rio fort of Santa Cruz seized it and two others demanding Deodoro's reinstatement before being subdued. In the next month, revolts overthrew the governors of Ceará and Mato Grosso but failed in Pernambuco and Rio de Janeiro state, while the southern part of Minas Gerais attempted to create a separate state. The *New York Times* lamented, "All the signs . . . have pointed to the disintegration of the enormous Empire over which he [Dom Pedro] ruled."[10] In March a revolt broke out in the southern state of Rio Grande do Sul; there was talk of the state separating from Brazil to join Uruguay in a "Cisplatine Republic." Bloody fighting would continue in the south for three years. In April, the state legislature of Mato Grosso declared independence for the republic of "Transatlantica," which comprised one-fifth of Brazil's national territory. It would take federal gunboats and hundreds of troops four months to suppress the revolt.[11] The struggle returned to the Federal District in April when plots to restore Deodoro on April 1 and again on April 10 failed.[12] It had become clear to everyone that the overthrow of the Empire had unleashed a tiger, or better, many tigers, that were ripping away at the nation.

To contain the fury of the opposition, Marshal Floriano Peixoto was forced to alter the nature of the power block that undergirded his rule. While Floriano initially attracted the support of all of Deodoro's opponents, he came to base his power on politicized junior officers and militant republican members of the urban middle class. This would seem to put him on a collision course with the United States. His civilian followers were centered in Rio de Janeiro, the country's largest city and its economic, financial, cultural, and political capital. Floriano's three years in office witnessed policies consciously directed at fostering industrialization and improving the economic standing of the urban middle and working classes. He also displayed a virulent xenophobia.

The vice president was able to forge this unprecedented power base because he also struck alliances with the Historic Republicans of the Southeast. The Southeast was much better represented in Floriano's cabinet than it had been under Deodoro; nine of the seventeen ministers he appointed came from there. Only two of the men who served him had been conservatives under the Empire, while four had long been republicans. Another six ministers were military men. Floriano's appointees were twenty to thirty

years younger than Deodoro's and had not been entrenched in imperial politics. Almost all of them owed their political rise to the birth of the Republic.[13] Hence, while Deodoro had counted on the "conservative classes"
to defend him in his 1891 coup, Floriano turned to the newly enfranchised
such as students, young officers, and bureaucrats, as well as the republican
parties for support.[14]

The Military in Politics

Marshal Floriano succeeded in neutralizing the opposition of the rural
oligarchy to his reform program by allying with their governments in the
states to allow himself freedom of action in the center. Long before President Campos Sales (1898–1902), Floriano instituted a "politics of governors." The military held the balance of power in Brazil's disordered political
system and was instrumental in most of the coups that removed Deodoro's
friends from governorships. In São Paulo, Minas Gerais, and Rio Grande do
Sul, Floriano won the backing of the Republican parties by throwing the
army behind them. He cemented his agreement with the Paulistas by ap-
pointing influential members of the Partido Republicano Paulista (PRP) to
key positions. For example, Francisco de Paula Rodrigues Alves served as
minister of finance and Francisco Glycério as head of the government party
in Congress. In a number of Northeastern states such as Maranhão, Mato
Grosso, Ceará, and Rio Grande do Norte, Floriano attracted the friendship
of an important segment of the oligarchy by lending them the military force
with which they threw out Deodorista governments. The army not only
won the vice president allies, it delivered political shock troops to keep the
new-found friends loyal.

Further bolstering military autonomy, many officers held office themselves. In addition to the important cabinet positions they held, another 40
army and navy officers served as deputies in the Constituent Congress (of a
total of 269 members), and by 1893, 174 additional officers exercised administrative and political functions in the federal government. In the states
their presence was even more impressive. By 1893 over half of the states had
soldier-governors.[15]

Marshal Floriano seized on the opportunity that his independent martial power and political alliances had presented to institute policies favored
by the young, militant, republican element of the officer corps and the politicized urban middle and working classes. His reasons for such a choice are
not obvious. Like his predecessor, Floriano was a career soldier who had received training only in the martial arts and then worked his way up through
the ranks under the Empire. He was very much a product of the Empire's
social and political systems. The son of a modest sugar planter, he inherited
late in life a sizable plantation and even considered abandoning his military
career to become a "senhor de engenho." Within the military he rose because of his gifts in battle, displayed in heroic leadership during the Par-

aguayan War (1865–70), and his avoidance of controversy in peacetime. Unlike many fellow officers, Floriano had not manifested sympathies for republicanism. As adjutant general, he was in command of the troops at the Campo de Sant'Anna on November 15 charged by the Empire with subduing the republican revolution. Instead, Floriano bowed to circumstances and allowed the coup to succeed, claiming he would not fire on countrymen (a surprising concern in light of the subsequent vicious struggle he waged against revolters in Rio de Janeiro and Rio Grande do Sul). Floriano had been appointed to the ministry of war in the provisional government because he seemed to be an obedient bureaucrat, much less dangerous than the militant republican ideologue, Benjamin Constant de Magalhães, whom he replaced in that position. The republicans and other opponents of Deodoro rallied behind Floriano as their vice-presidential candidate because he commanded the loyalty of many troops and, perhaps more important, he seemed easy to manipulate. As vice president, Floriano rarely made pronouncements and never presided over the Senate (which was his constitutional obligation). He preferred to allow the Paulista Prudente de Morais to run the Senate in his absence. His transformation into the Iron Marshal upon replacing Deodoro was quite a shock for Paulistas.

The explanation for the alliances Floriano chose to make and the positions he took is to be found in his view of the military's proper role, not in his concept of republicanism.[16] Two years before the end of the monarchy Floriano had written a friend that the Empire was mistreating the armed forces, which demonstrated "the rottenness that this country is experiencing and therefore the necessity of a military dictatorship to cleanse it. As the liberal that I am, I cannot wish for my country a government of the sword. But no one is unaware . . . that there exist individuals who know how to purify the blood of the social body [corpo social], which, like ours, is corrupted."[17] Once Deodoro offered himself as the "man on horseback" to end the country's corruption, Floriano revised his own liberalism and his view of the military's appropriate place. Since the Republic was the creation of the military, the army had to steer it through its first dangerous, uncertain years. Only a strong military hand at the helm could guide the country through the shoals of monarchist restoration, chaotic civilian internecine struggles, and regional separatism.

Floriano's praetorian view of governance alienated most senior officers who had been schooled by the Empire to abstain from politics. They believed that politicization would open fissures within the military corporation that would subject it to outside pressures and weaken its internal unity and resolve. Barely two months after the Marshal's victory over Deodoro, the fort of Santa Cruz in Rio revolted to pressure Floriano to step down. Other officers clamored for Floriano to call for presidential elections that they hoped would replace him with a civilian.[18] Thirteen generals issued a manifesto in April 1892 calling on him to retire from office.[19] Instead, Floriano retired the protesting officers.

The intramilitary conflict drove Floriano to depend on junior officers who believed, as Lieutenant Lauro Sodré grandiloquently announced, "the historic mission of embodying the summation of national aspirations is reserved to the armed forces."[20] Floriano's regime, then, was not a typical caudillo-style dictatorship, but rather a Nassarist movement in which, according to Joaquim Nabuco, he "gave preponderance to the lowest ranks over the highest . . . which is to say that he inverted the hierarchy of posts from top to bottom."[21]

The political outlook of junior officers clashed with that of their superior officers and the rural oligarchy because of their differences in social background and education. Younger soldiers—especially the post–Paraguayan War generation—joined the military less because they aspired to martial glory as had their superior officers, than because it represented one of the few avenues of upward mobility for Brazil's middle and lower classes. The military provided a free college-level technical education that equaled or surpassed civilian learning. An analysis of the backgrounds of the generals reveals growing middle-class influence in the army. The most outspoken and politically active of the Florianistas all came from middle-class backgrounds.[22]

Equally important, Floriano's military supporters found themselves in the middle class in terms of the pay they received because they were junior officers. Important politicized officers such as Tasso Fragoso, Felipe Schmidt, August Vinhaes, José Bevilacqua, José Freire Bezerril Fontenele, Lauro Sodré, Lauro Muller, and Alexandre José Barbosa Lima, all of whom served as congressmen or governors, were lieutenants or majors in 1889.[23] The composition of the military contingent in Congress between 1890 and 1894 demonstrates the youth and low rank of politicized officers. Of the 38 military congressmen whose age is known, 22 were in their twenties or thirties and nine in their forties; in the same group 25 were majors or below.[24] Cadets in the military schools also were ardent Florianistas. As low-ranking officers in an army not noted for its high pay and during a time of high inflation, Florianistas identified with the economic plight of the middle and working classes. They turned against the traditional European-oriented export economy.

Frustrated by the Empire's slow promotion rate and poor pay as well as its conservative economic order, militant young officers had looked to the founding of the Republic as the dawn of a new era. Positivism, with its doctrine of scientific progress, organic corporatism, and hierarchical order greatly influenced many junior officers. One-quarter of the soldiers in Congress were self-professed positivists—almost all of them Florianistas—and many others leaned toward the ideology; it was particularly strong in the military academies.[25] Viewing the imperial ruling class as a feudalistic drag on the nation's progress, a hindrance to social mobility, and a barrier to military modernization, many Florianistas called for military rule with a new social content. Themselves well educated, the officers sought a society in which skill rather than birth dictated success.[26]

The young officers' middle-class, urban upbringing, technical education, concern with military infrastructure, and advocacy of scientific progress brought them to champion industrialization. Floriano's military supporters in Congress often backed public works projects and, more important, duty-free importation of industrial inputs and increased tariff protection for threatened Brazilian products.[27]

Jacobins and Other Civilian Allies

The social background of Florianista officers and Floriano's power struggle with the former imperial elite led the vice president to curry the favor of the urban middle and working classes. Although they were small in number, their political importance outweighed their size because of the small size of political society and the disorganization of the traditional ruling elite. The 85 percent of the national population living in the countryside were politically inert, subjects of their local bosses. It was in the cities, where the rich and powerful generally resided and where the important political and economic decisions were made, that the national-level political struggles were fought out. Militant Florianista Raul Pompeia complained in 1895, "All of the Republic's difficulties can be boiled down to this: the capital's permanent state of revolt against the nation."[28] Rio de Janeiro, the Federal District, loomed over all other cities. In 1890 its population equaled that of the country's next seven largest cities combined. Not only was it by far the nation's largest city; it also enjoyed the distinction of being the nation's leading commercial entrepôt, industrial center, banking capital, and the seat of government. Most of the country's most important people lived in Rio at one time or another.[29]

The middle class constituted an appreciable portion of Rio's population. In 1890, 8 percent of the *carioca* (residents of Rio de Janeiro city) economically active population were white-collar workers (e.g., engineers, architects, doctors, bookkeepers). If shopkeepers are included, the middle class reaches about one-quarter of the total.[30] This was to a considerable degree a dependent class since one-third of the middle class was in the government's employ. From the government's point of view, this made them dependable allies.[31]

Workers' numbers also mounted in the late nineteenth century. Although industry remained small and artisanal, it expanded to meet new consumer demands. Workers were even more important in the export infrastructure as stevedores and railroad workers. Many of these laborers were also on the government payroll as employees of the federally owned Central do Brasil railroad or the docks and customs houses. Industrial and transportation workers constituted 29 percent of Rio's work force in 1890.[32]

These people (overwhelmingly male) had become increasingly vocal and politicized in the Empire's last two decades. Most significant was the abolitionist movement that brought substantial crowds into the fray. Battles between republicans and monarchists also mobilized the urban middle class for the first time since the beginning of Dom Pedro II's reign.[33] A national worker's party founded chapters in the states of Rio, Ceará, Bahia, Paraná, São Paulo, Rio Grande do Norte, and Pernambuco in 1890 and 1891. The country's first Brazilian Socialist Congress met in Rio in 1892.[34]

Members of these groups joined together in the first mass-based nationalistic movement in Brazil's history, the Jacobins. Organized only on the local level in clubs, the Jacobins commanded a national constituency by virtue of a common ideology and vocal nativist press rather than a national organization. The Jacobins' nationalist zeal and their campaign in favor of greater opportunities for native Brazilians attracted adherents from cities all over the country, but their center of popularity and influence was in the Federal District.[35] So important did they become that the monarchist Joaquim Nabuco decried "the revolutionary danger heightened by the preponderance and ascendancy of an element that calls itself Jacobin," and the Portuguese ambassador feared their power.[36] Nabuco accused them of conducting a reign of terror with the police becoming "an agency of spies and butchers" who were aided by "a revolutionary army of security" with "battalions of political fanatics specially charged with suspects and arrests" who "deliver justice with their own hands."[37]

The republican revolution delivered an unprecedented opportunity for political activism for these formerly marginalized classes, but the former ruling class held on to much of its earlier prominence. Rio's delegation to the Constituent Congress mirrored the growing complexity and strains of urban politics. The delegation included traditional representatives of the imperial financial elite: Francisco Mayrink and the Conde de Figueiredo, the militant abolitionist and republican polemicist José Lopes Trovão, the leading labor leader Augusto Vinhaes, and one of the most outspoken Jacobins, João Batista Sampaio Ferraz.

Jacobin Ideology

These nationalist allies of Floriano believed that the republican revolution was of great consequence. Rio's *Echo Popular* announced a few months afterwards that it was "a universal revolution [which] changed the face of civilization."[38] Bahia's *Voz do Operario* considered the advent of the Republic "the conquest of liberty and democracy" as well as the precursor of "social and material progress."[39] Militant republicans were strongly antimonarchist because they believed that the Empire had been a feudal system in which the people had been nothing more than "beasts of burden without any rights," while the aristocracy had the "privilege of position and the benefit of remunerative sinecures as a birth-right."[40] Indeed they borrowed their name from the French Revolution precisely because they believed, as Florianista deputy Barbosa Lima proclaimed, that in Brazil, as in France, "the bourgeoisie [was] courageously rising up against the feudal lords."[41]

The analogy with France made some sense. Brazil's precapitalist economic form, slavery, had been abolished in 1888. The Republic proclaimed the end of the aristocracy (which had only been honorific anyway), the separation of church and state, and the end of monarchy. A new definition of citizenship was confirmed in which corporate privileges such as property requirements for the franchise and different categories of electors as well as a vital national guard were ended or phased out. Many political positions became elective rather than appointive. The new Brazilian Republic also adopted the symbolic trappings of the French Revolution. The official salutation was "citizen" and the closing "health and fraternity." The 14th of July was widely celebrated, and the *Marseillaise* sung.[42]

In order to consolidate the newly won gains and develop the nation, Florianistas and Jacobins (not always coterminous) called for a strong central government that only the military could provide.[43] But the sword alone could not defeat the planter elite. Jacobins also espoused a new economic system that would allow Brazil to transform its supposedly feudal social structure. It needed to industrialize to undercut the power of the coffee and sugar barons. Lieutenant Colonel Inocencio Serzedello Corrêa, Floriano's minister of finance and later president of Brazil's largest industrial association, explained that the problem was greater. Brazil was an economic colony because of its dependence on coffee exports. The foreign commercial community held Brazil in thrall. Foreigners dominated 85 percent of the value of commerce and sent their profits abroad. They also drove down the currency through speculation, gouged consumers with exorbitant prices, and monopolized commercial employment. Only the development of domestic industry could remedy this woeful situation. Native industry would undercut the profits and influence of foreign importers, exporters, and financial institutions that all flourished largely because of their connections with producers in Europe.[44]

This argument, which was widely endorsed, cleverly placed industrialization at the center of Florianista concerns. Just as in Peru, where Paul Gootenberg has shown the strength of the industrial lobby in the midst of a liberal export-oriented regime, industry had strong support in the first years of the Brazilian coffee republic.[45] The call for industry became more than just one item on a menu of political demands. It became central to the world view of the militant republicans and Floriano's cabinet.[46] Even Jacobins, who were most concerned with consumer issues such as high food prices, the lack of good jobs, and costly rents, became converted to industrialism. They formed a transitional movement between the consumer-oriented, rather spontaneous direct actions and appeals to authority of the ancien regime and the modern, organized, and more autonomous movements. The Jacobins began a broader structural analysis of society's ills without abandoning the traditional xenophobia and scapegoating.[47] They directly blamed Portuguese merchants and speculators for these ills and indirectly the cosmopolitan and stagnant nature of the export economy. Hence, industrialization was the remedy.

Since the monarchy and the export economy were inextricably linked in the minds of Florianistas, the groups that supported the export economy must naturally support a monarchist restoration. Foreign merchants were singled out. *O Republicano* of Forteleza, for instance, vowed to "defend the Republic and fight with all means possible [against] those associated with the monarchist club and with the support of foreigners."[48] Portuguese worked against the Republic for cultural as well as economic reasons: they were Catholic. *O Nacional* of Belem feared that Brazil would become another Vendée in which clerics worked for the restoration of the monarchy. The Portuguese served as the clerics' "advance guards," trying to "make religion the weapon for propagating the regressive system of monarchist government."[49] The British also were viewed by the nationalists as enemies of the Republic, but for economic reasons. They wanted to maintain Brazil's dependence. *O Nativista* of São Paulo reported that there were benefits for the British in "discrediting" the Republic and attempting restoration in order to gain "great profits."[50] Both Deodoro and Floriano shared this view of the British.[51] There was also some concern that the French, because of Dom Pedro's son-in-law, and the Germans, because of their own monarchy, favored restoration.

Jacobin Pan-Americanism

Given Marshal Floriano's alliance with a nationalist group committed to promoting industrialism and ending the hegemony of the export oligarchy, one would expect him to oppose the Blaine-Mendonça Accord that had been signed to aid sugar exporters. However, Jacobins did not urge him to end the agreement. Perhaps surprisingly, the United States was the only major power that was not accused of subverting the Republic and undermining its development policy. Nativists considered the United States to be different from the European powers because it was also American, an ex-colony, and a republic. As a fellow American state, the United States could help in fending off the menacing political and economic influence of Europe. *O Jacobino*, the largest Jacobin newspaper, tied Pan-Americanism into nationalism: its masthead read, "Brazil for Brazilians and America for Americans." It was the Europeans who had established Brazil's export economy and benefited from it; Europeans favored the monarchy and Brazil's neocolonial status. In response, the Americans had to join together to protect themselves and establish independent economies. Hence the Monroe Doctrine appeared to *O Nativista* "the sublime theory of the great and eminent statesman James Monroe."[52]

Of a different opinion, the monarchist Eduardo Prado, scion of one of São Paulo's richest and most influential families, published a diatribe against the United States entitled *A illusão americana* (The American Illusion) precisely because he believed republicans too enamored of the United States at the expense of Brazil's true friend, Great Britain. He protested that it "was time to react against the insanity of the absolute fraternization that they intend to impose between Brazil and the great Anglo-Saxon republic."[53] The book was banned under Floriano.

Ironically, one of the main reasons that the North American giant was so warmly regarded by many of Floriano's civilian and military followers was that while the United States was extremely successful in developing its own internal economy, in Brazil its citizens were failures. There were virtually no U.S. traders in Brazil. In fact in the whole country there were only about 1,500 Americans, most of whom were farmers, with some dentists and professional people. U.S. manufacturers, with only a few exceptions, did not have representatives abroad either.[54] Nor were there any American-owned banks, railroads, or public utility companies. Indeed, there was little U.S. investment of any kind in Brazil. Moreover, American factories did not threaten Brazilian manufacturers because they exported relatively little to Brazil, though the trade treaty was supposed to change this. Brazilian preference for British and other European goods meant that Brazil exported to the United States six times as much as it imported. In addition, the filibustering and expansionism of American slavocrats was long dead and the Spanish American War as well as the self-appointment by the United States as "Policeman of the Caribbean" were still several years in the future. The United States appeared a benign, anticolonialist power. After all, it had been the first major power to recognize and promise to help defend the new republic, and President Harrison had gently advised Deodoro to renounce his coup after he had closed Congress. Hence Florianistas looked on their northern neighbor as a fellow excolony rather than as an imperialist threat.[55]

Floriano and the Blaine-Mendonça Accord

Floriano faced a dilemma with the Blaine-Mendonça agreement, however. As a nationalist, he opposed all commercial treaties as dangerous entanglements. The Portuguese minister lamented that "the majority of republicans . . . absolutely disdain other nations, distrusting them all . . . and therefore don't want to be obliged by treaties."[56] In fact, so suspicious and disdainful was Floriano of diplomacy that he met the diplomatic community only once in his first two years in office and refused to extend them the minimal civilities of diplomatic protocol. Weary of this treatment, the French minister became enraged when Floriano refused to receive him at the end of the minister's term in Rio. Unwilling to give up, the Frenchman sought him out uninvited in the vice president's modest suburban residence. There, the minister felt insulted when he was met at the door by a maid nursing a child. Floriano still refused to see him then, sending instead a note calling for a meeting the next day, which the marshal missed.[57]

It comes as little surprise, then, that Floriano refused the entreaties of the major European powers and several South American neighbors for commercial agreements.[58] Nor is it cause for wonder that he objected to the Blaine-Mendonça pact. The marshal had opposed the accord when it was signed in 1891 because he feared that it would undercut Brazilian industry that was important for the country's development and dear to many of his supporters.[59] The French minister thought the Blaine-Mendonça agreement dead once the vice president assumed power.[60]

The pact was not terminated, however. Floriano desperately needed American friendship to protect the Republic from the perceived monarchist restorationist movement; Jacobins also sought close relations with the fellow republic. Floriano had alienated not only Deodoro's friends and many apolitical senior officers. His reform program, which won him the admiration of many among the middle and working classes, deeply antagonized much of the ruling class, especially the powerful financiers. Floriano took the position of the Jacobin editor Anníbal Mascarenhas, who denounced stock market plungers for attempting to "prostrate the Republic, and with its fall, work to transform this great fatherland into a European trading post."[61] The vice president first turned down a handsome bribe from the banker Conde de Leopoldina; then he attacked the financiers on all fronts. He ended most banks' concessions for currency issues, resuming Treasury emissions, merged the two largest banks in the country and placed them under a government appointee, arrested several directors of important companies, and exiled several major financiers.[62] (This policy had the happy side-benefit of pleasing the Paulistas because most of the financiers under attack were headquartered in Rio and had attempted to control the Paulista economy.) The financiers had close business relations with Europe and, it was believed, sympathies for the monarchy; they attempted to bring some European powers onto the side of restoration.

U.S. friendship was now more important than ever. Mendonça, whom Floriano kept as Brazil's representative to Washington after an initial hesitency, stressed the regime's dire situation. He wrote Blaine, "The republican and monarchical forces in Brazil are now in a balance." Some of the governors who had recently taken office could "hardly be counted on in case of armed conflict" with monarchists, and he thought such a conflict likely.[63] To aid the Florianista forces, the minister requested a statement of support by the U.S. Congress: "An expression through diplomatic channels to the courts of Europe of the adherence of the United States to the principles of the Monroe Doctrine . . . and that any interference in the support of a monarchical restoration in Brazil would be construed as an act inconsistent in the maintenance of said doctrine" and the presence of the American Navy in Brazilian ports.[64] In return, he could offer Brazil's continued adherence to the Blaine-Mendonça pact.

As a result of these contradictory impulses and threats, Floriano maintained the Blaine-Mendonça treaty, but modified it to protect native industry. One of his first actions in office was to change the tariff structure to protect domestic manufacturers and negate American trade advantages. His revisions were similar to those recommended in 1891 by Antao de Faria, now a cabinet minister. Brazil's most important industry—cotton textiles—received the shelter of a 60 percent duty increase. The bill also levied a 10 percent "port" charge on all duty-exempt goods that struck directly at the items the Blaine-Mendonça treaty had exempted. In addition, Floriano reduced the official rate of exchange for the milreis from 24 to 12 British pence, thereby doubling the milreis duties that imports had to pay.[65]

This was not in fact as dramatic an act as it sounds, though it won the approval of nationalists and has been offered subsequently by historians as evidence of Floriano's industrial policy. Duty protection had in fact fallen fairly sharply since the 1887 tariff because of the devaluation of the milreis. Brazilian duties were only ad valorem in theory. Every several years goods were evaluated and the duty established. For example, hypothetically, all cotton blankets would pay a 10 milreis duty that in theory was 50 percent because cotton blankets were evaluated at 20 milreis, no matter what their actual cost-insurance-freight (c.i.f.) price. As the milreis devalued, the market price of the blanket rose to 40 milreis, but the duty was still 10, now only a 25 percent tax. This depreciation cost the Treasury a good deal since the real value of its customs receipts was depreciating. That is why the duty schedule was revised,[66] but even the new tariff was lower in real terms than its 1887 predecessor.[67]

The United States accepted most of the reform with equanimity. The American minister, Edwin Conger, reported calmly that Congress had raised duties because it had ended the requirement that duties be paid in gold. Instead they could be paid in depreciated milreis. To compensate, taxes were raised. (The French minister believed that the new tariff raised duties 15 to 25 percent even once the abolition of gold duties was taken into account.) The relative position of the United States was still superior because of the 25 percent duty reduction. The one revision that was protested was the 10 percent port tax. Blaine and Conger pushed for, and finally attained, its abolition and the refund of the fees already levied under its jurisdiction.[68]

The United States accepted this alteration because, according to Mendonça, tariff revisions had always been permitted by the treaty and because the United States was itself already considering revising its own tariff. The elections of 1890 had cost the Republicans their majority in the House, and the 1892 elections gave the Democrats the Senate and the presidency as well. One of their major campaign planks had been revising the tariff to reduce duties and encourage exports.[69]

CHAPTER 6

The Democrats Take Over

Bby the time Marshal Floriano began tampering with the Blaine-Mendonça Accord, the political landscape in the United States had changed dramatically from the Republicans' halcyon days of 1889 and early 1890. Just months after the triumphant passage of the McKinley Tariff, the 1890 congressional elections subjected the Republicans to their greatest slaughter ever at the polls. Many of the recently legislated programs, including reciprocity, were endangered by the changes in Congress, but Harrison remained firmly committed to the Republican program of protectionism and active government that had been so disastrously defeated in the congressional elections. However, Blaine did convince him to begin to focus his upcoming presidential campaign on the virtues of reciprocity. The Indiana general, stymied at home by an unfriendly Congress, turned to foreign policy where he became more aggressive.

Harrison's bravado could not secure him reelection in 1892, however. His opponent was again Grover Cleveland, and the battle was fought on already well-trodden terrain with the tariff still the single most compelling issue. Agrarian unrest, rising consumer prices, and distrust of activist government combined to squeeze Cleveland into office and award the Democratic candidate—for the first time since the Civil War—with a Democratically controlled Congress.

Although both Democrats and Republicans had come to recognize the importance of foreign markets, Democrats chose quite different means for opening those markets; they stressed freer trade. Cleveland pledged the party to tariff reform. A new tariff that would jeopardize the Blaine-Mendonça agreement was expected. Cleveland retreated from other activist measures Harrison had initiated at home and sought to disengage from Republican foreign policy initiatives. He found, however, that domestic political considerations brought on by the economic depression and the rising tide of expansionism that Harrison had encouraged eventually forced him to become a forceful supporter of the Monroe Doctrine. These conflicting and conspiring pressures would play themselves out in Brazil and transform the nature of the U.S.-Brazilian alliance.

The Election of 1890

Republicans lost their congressional majority in the 1890 elections in good part because of their pietistic domestic policies that carried over from the party's reformist origins and reconstruction. Immigrants in the Midwest were upset with Republican laws to enforce English-language teaching in the schools—private as well as public. Laws to restrict Sunday drinking and other threats to inebriation also convinced many voters that Republicans wanted to interfere in private areas the government should stay out of.[1] In the South and border areas, growing government reform was manifested in the federal election bill, known by Democrats as the "Force Bill." Harrison's party wanted federal officials to prevent the use of Jim Crow laws to disenfranchise black (and presumably Republican) voters.[2]

The new Republican ideal of strong state economic promotion also came under fierce attack. The Fifty-first Congress, considered by some historians one of the most progressive in United States history, was jeered by Democrats as the "Billion Dollar Congress." The passage of the Sherman Antitrust Act, the Sherman Silver Purchase Act, and attempts at a merchant marine subsidy and federal election and education laws upset many people. More pointed was the expansion of federal pensions and government jobs. The crystallization of the activist state, with its centralized control, mounting taxes, and favors for special interests, was to be found in the McKinley Tariff.

Passed just months before the 1890 election, it really had no time to demonstrate its consequences. Nonetheless, Democrats preached jeremiads against its sins. They also set out to fulfill their own prophecies. The prices on some goods rose because of the McKinley Tariff's higher duties or because merchants profiteered by raising prices across the board, even on goods unaffected by the new rates. In other cases Democrats jumped in, not trusting the whims of the market or the greed of merchants. In a number of midwestern states thousands of Democratic drummers were released to go door-to-door offering tin goods at twice the prevailing price. Republicans responded by boasting that the new tariff protected wool and offering inflated prices for sheep. The Republicans wound up with many costly sheep, and the Democrats wound up with many unsold tin goods; but the Democrats also scared up many votes.

The heart of the battle was joined in William McKinley's Ohio congressional district. Each party threw its most eloquent, fiery orators and its most energetic and inventive campaigners into the fray. President Harrison made five visits to the district himself. In the end, McKinley—as well as most of his fellow Republican congressmen—lost. Little did it matter that McKinley had been defeated in part because the Democratic-controlled state legislature had gerrymandered his district or that elsewhere local issues outside the federal government's purview had cost the party votes.

When the votes were counted, the Republicans had fallen to their lowest minority in the House in their history, only 88 seats to 235 for the Democrats. Republicans barely held on to their majority in the Senate. In an equally ominous development, the Farmers' Alliance won ten congressional seats, six governorships, and a majority in eight state legislatures, reflecting the depth of farmers' despair. Although historians such as Richard Jensen and Paul Kleppner have concluded that local issues played perhaps a decisive role in the landslide, at the time the vote was taken as a referendum on national issues.[3] The *North American Review* concluded, for instance, "There has scarcely, if ever, been a Congressional campaign in this country in which purely local questions were so little discussed, or in which local party or personal dissensions had so little influence as the one just closed."[4]

Most newspapers, Republican, Democratic, and independent alike, agreed that the tariff and the elections bill were the two key issues of the election.[5] Foreign policy had not played a significant role in the congressional outcomes. Blaine urged Harrison to make international relations a key electoral issue for the first time in the upcoming presidential contest.

Harrison's Last Two Years

Without a working majority, Harrison's last two years in office were pale imitations of the frenetic and productive first two years. The president mostly bode his time and sought a formula for turning around the vote in the forthcoming presidential election. He made it clear in his presidential message the month after his party's disastrous defeat that he would not retreat on his domestic program.[6] Nonetheless, he turned his attention from domestic issues, where he was stymied, to foreign affairs where the executive had greater freedom to maneuver and where he hoped to pick up additional votes. Rivalry with the European Great Powers, particularly the British, was a central element in his foreign policy and an issue he hoped would play well with the American voting public.

Reciprocal trade treaties became one of Harrison's most cherished issues. The president had initially opposed reciprocity. Indeed, as late as February 1891 the *New York Times* was reporting that reciprocity was doomed, and two months later—*after* the promulgation of the Blaine-Mendonça treaty—the *Times* believed that Harrison still opposed reciprocity.[7] But he was slowly becoming a convert. That same April he wrote a friend, "I am one of those who believes that a home market is necessarily the best market for the producer" because of cheaper transportation. Harrison recognized, however, that "the extraordinary development of the productions of agriculture which has taken place in a recent period in this country . . . very naturally has called attention to the value and, indeed, necessity of larger markets." The president pointed to reciprocity as the wedge for opening those markets.[8]

The favorable reception that greeted the Blaine-Mendonça agreement in the United States (in contrast to the hostility it provoked in Brazil) no doubt warmed Harrison's regard for reciprocity. The *New York Times* congratulated Harrison and called it a good political move that "undoubtedly strengthens the republic with just those classes in which there was a lingering reactionary feeling."[9] The *New York Tribune* concluded that the treaty "does incalculably increase the prospective and potential market for the products of American industry."[10] In even more resounding language, the *Engineering and Mining Journal* applauded the treaty as "the most important step taken in behalf of commercial development of this country for many years."[11] The *Chicago Inter-Ocean* thought it "among the most important diplomatic achievements of the State Department from Washington to Harrison," and the *Pittsburgh Times* said it was "the first ray in the dawn of the new era in the foreign trade of the United States."[12]

Equally satisfying, the British press received news of the Blaine-Mendonça treaty with alarm. London's *Economist* reported the worries of Britain's vice consul in Rio Grande do Sul that "the treaty cannot fail to have a very injurious effect." The journal concluded that the treaty's "concessions will favour United States trade to the detriment of exports to Brazil from this country and from British North America."[13] The *Financial Times* feared that "a vast industry may be seriously injured if the current of its trade is not permanently diverted."[14]

The reception of the Blaine-Mendonça Accord convinced Harrison to proceed with pacts with Spain (for Cuba and Puerto Rico), Great Britain (for the British West Indies), France, Germany, Austria-Hungary, as well as several Latin American countries. Harrison set a precedent for active state efforts to open foreign markets.

Commercial designs that gave birth to reciprocity were also wedded with the imperial imperative in Hawaii. Hawaii had a tradition of trade with the United States and a small but influential group of American residents. An 1876 reciprocity treaty and the establishment of steamship lines aimed at bringing the islands closer into the U.S. sphere. Blaine had demonstrated his interest when Hawaii was invited to participate in the Pan American Conference. The secretary of state was also responding to a perception among Americans in Hawaii that they were losing influence in the kingdom to the British. Blaine sent a new consul, his friend from Maine, John Stevens, to oversee U.S. interests. When the McKinley Tariff passed with its free sugar provision, it further worried American planters. Hawaii's sugar, which had previously entered the U.S. duty free while other imported sugar was taxed, lost its privileged position in the one market where it sold 99 percent of its production. Worse, King Kalakaua and later Queen Liliuo-kalani (who ascended to the throne after her father died in 1891) would not agree to reciprocity conditions: the rights to build a harbor at the mouth of the Pearl River and Hawaii's becoming a virtual U.S. protectorate. Now Hawaiian sugar was taxed while competitors were not.

The obvious solution to the American planters on the island was annex-ation by the United States. Then not only would sugar exports be free of duty, but the planters would receive the same sugar bounty as Louisiana planters. The head of the Annexationist Club in Honolulu, Lorrin A. Thurs-ton, explained to Blaine that "the reasons why annexation is favored by the foreign investors of capital, are mainly because of the changed conditions brought about by the McKinley Tariff bill."[15] Thus the same reciprocity clause that was intended to tighten relations between the United States and Brazil and Cuba initially strained relations with Hawaii.

Eventually the tariff provoked the annexation of the islands. Consul Stevens worked with the annexationists who were upset when the queen sought to restore royal prerogatives. He sent ashore 70 armed marines and sailors, supposedly to protect American property; the next day the planter clique staged a virtually bloodless coup. Stevens quickly declared a protec-torate, arguing that the British would intervene otherwise.[16] Without con-sulting the people of Hawaii, Harrison quickly referred the annexation mea-sure to Congress, though he left office before annexation could be approved.

The president also emboldened some of the other half-hearted foreign policy initiatives that he had inherited, using them to play to the Anglo-phobic voters. Closest to home, Harrison became embroiled in a contro-versy with the British over sealing rights in the Bering Straits. A monopoly on sealing on islands off the coast of Alaska had been awarded to a commer-cial company partly owned by Stephen Elkins (Blaine's 1884 campaign man-ager). When British ships began seizing American fishing boats off the At-lantic coast in 1886, the United States responded by seizing seven British sealing ships in the Bering Straits—outside the three mile limit—on the grounds that they were doing irreparable damage to the seal herd. Cleve-land, in his first administration, had returned the ships and sent the issue to negotiations that were broken off shortly before Harrison took office. Harrison immediately had six more British ships seized. After some half-hearted war threats on both sides, an agreement was reached that banned all sealing for the next two years and sent the question to arbitration.[17] The British were made aware that the United States would now challenge their hegemony over the sea.

In the South Pacific Harrison was yet more aggressive. The United

States had signed a treaty with tiny, far-off Samoa in 1878 to intercede with third parties in return for coaling rights. When the Germans threatened to take over the island kingdom in the late 1880's through a puppet king, the United States responded by sending warships. Ultimately, the two powers, along with the British, reached the unusual solution of a tripartite protectorate over the islands, committing the United States, for the first time ever, to governing an overseas people.[18]

The Republican president also involved the United States in Latin American affairs. Backing Chile's President Balmaceda against a joint parliamentary-naval revolt in early 1891, he sent a cruiser to interdict an insurgent Chilean ship picking up war supplies in California. The revolters were viewed in the United States as allies of the British. Unfortunately for Harrison, Balmaceda was defeated, straining U.S. relations with the new rebel government. As discussed earlier, the United States reached the brink of war with the new regime over a perceived affront to American sailors.[19]

Harrison also intervened in a civil war in Haiti, again taking sides against a European power. The United States backed General Hyppolite against French-supported General Légitime in return for an apparent promise of a reciprocal trade treaty and possible use of Mole St. Nicolas as a naval base. In the end, Hyppolite's forces won but refused to award Blaine the treaty.[20]

On commercial grounds Harrison also took an important initiative in Nicaragua. Buoyed by the bankruptcy and scandal of the French Panamanian canal company, the president attempted to replace the French venture with an American canal. To succeed, he also had to overcome British influence in Central America by modifying or ignoring the Clayton-Bulwer treaty that pledged the United States and Great Britain to a joint isthmian canal. Instead, he relied on a U.S. treaty with only Nicaragua. In 1887 the Maritime Canal Company was organized and building was under way (Cornelius Bliss and Andrew Carnegie were major shareholders, and former Nicaraguan consul, Charles Flint, apparently served as a go-between). Four years later Harrison proposed that the U.S. government guarantee the bonds of the private company to ensure an American canal.[21]

All of these foreign policy initiatives demanded either a larger navy or merchant marine. Harrison was sensitive to both. The U.S. Navy had fallen into utter disrepair when Chester Arthur initiated the New Navy in 1883 by authorizing three small unarmored steel cruisers and opening the Naval War College. Under Cleveland, nine more steel warships were authorized. Even halfway through his term, the United States remained so vulnerable to sea attack that many observers worried that if it declared war on Chile, the Chilean fleet would destroy San Francisco. Harrison appointed the activist Benjamin Franklin Tracy secretary of the navy and proceeded to build up the modern navy, pushing the construction of battleships, armored cruisers, rapid fire guns, and torpedoes. He set out not only to build up the navy's destructive capacity, but also to launch the U.S. maritime weapons industry. Among those who benefited from the building program was Carnegie, who received the contract for nickel-plating the ships. Tracy made clear the relationship between naval construction and trade expansion in 1889 when he called the New Navy "a practical business question of insuring our property and our trade."[22] This position was later elevated into military doctrine in Alfred T. Mahan's seminal *The Influence of Sea Power upon History*. Usually left unsaid was the concern that a modern navy would be necessary in the—probable—event of war with Great Britain.[23]

A trade war also loomed. To join it, the United States needed a merchant marine. Subsidies for American bottoms ended after Reconstruction and with them the international fleet virtually disappeared from the seas. To rectify this sorry state of affairs the Republicans proposed a mail subsidy law and a bill to subsidize shipbuilding in the United States.

The Election of 1892

Despite the impressive achievements of the Harrison administration, it was not at all clear that the incumbent would be his party's candidate in 1892. The devastating congressional losses in 1890 had led most observers to expect Blaine to replace Harrison. The consensus was that Republicans had lost because of the McKinley Tariff. Only Blaine could blunt public opposition to the tariff. The *St. Louis Globe-Democrat* explained, "Mr. Blaine, on the tariff question, stands for the opposite theory to that represented by the Reed and McKinley school. He is the pioneer as well as the ablest and most conspicuous champion of the movement to broaden the circle of the country's commercial activities."[24] Thus reciprocity seemed to offer Blaine one more chance to become president and confirmed his intuition that trade expansion was a powerful electoral platform.

His popularity held into 1892. A straw vote in the New York state Republican delegation found 639 votes for Blaine and only 16 for Harrison; a similar outcome was reported with the Massachusetts delegation. However, observers were unclear if Blaine wanted to run despite the support for his candidacy. Sick and heartbroken by the death of two of his children within a month of each other in 1890 and then a third in 1892, Blaine had declared in February 1892 that he would not be a candidate, but he continued to act like a candidate. Harrison was so upset with this challenge that in June he gave Blaine an ultimatum: either publicly decline the nomination again or resign his post at the State Department. Blaine chose the latter course, creating quite a sensation and stirring hope in his supporters. In Minneapolis, 6,000 Blaine supporters staged the largest parade of the Republican convention. Their hopes were dashed, however, when Blaine refused to run. Harrison won the nomination on the first ballot.

Harrison realized that he was the Republican candidate not because of his own popularity or the popularity of his program, but because of Blaine's infirmity (Blaine died four months later).[25] Harrison responded by running a campaign on Blaine's positions, particularly reciprocity. Harrison's letter of acceptance of the presidential nomination in September 1892 devoted two pages to discussing reciprocity and six more defending the McKinley Tariff. Indeed, only seven of the text's eighteen pages did not discuss reciprocity, foreign trade, or the tariff.[26] Harrison spoke out himself and used some of the publicity machine that Blaine had so effectively manipulated in the battle for reciprocity. The Bureau of the American Republics issued hundreds of reports on the successes and prospects of Latin American trade brought by reciprocity, while the American Protective League, presided over by Cornelius Bliss, made weekly copy for 3,500 newspapers in favor of the tariff and expanded trade.[27] They emphasized that trade with Brazil and Cuba had grown while British trade with Latin America fell.[28] Unfortunately, Blaine was able to give only one speech in the campaign due to his illness.

The Republican platform of 1892 demonstrated the importance that foreign trade and foreign affairs had come to occupy in party thinking. After "reaffirming the American doctrine of protection" the platform pointed to "the success of the Republican policy of reciprocity, under which our export trade has vastly increased and new and enlarge markets have been opened for the products of our farms and workshops." It went on to assert that "our present law will eventually give us control of the trade of the world." Then turning to support for a federal election bill, bimetallism, and an international silver conference, the document spoke in favor of "the extension of our foreign commerce, the restoration of our mercantile marine by home-built ships and the creation of a navy for the protection of our National interests and the honor of our flag." It also championed a Nicaraguan canal that "should be controlled by the United States government." Finally, the Republicans reaffirmed "approval of the Monroe doctrine," and their belief "in the achievement of the manifest destiny of the Republic in its broadest sense."[29] Expansionism and state activism were the two faces of the same Republican coin. Grover Cleveland would find that while he could retard the latter, the former's momentum would prove difficult to halt. But initially he tried.

Cleveland was again the Democrats' standard-bearer. Again, he employed the same arguments that had lost in 1888 but had fared well two years later. Cleveland's basic principles were lower taxes for a smaller, more honest government. Staunchly opposed to free silver, yet recognizing the growing strength of the free silver wing of the party, Cleveland returned to the tariff as "the only issue upon which there is the least hope of carrying the country."[30] He sought tariff reform but did not want to go as far as the party platform's bold advocacy of replacing protectionism with a tariff "for revenue only." Cleveland favored lower duties because, he argued, they would expand trade and reduce domestic prices, but he denounced reciprocity as a "sham," which juggles with the people's desire for enlarged foreign markets and freer exchanges by pretending to establish closer trade relations for a country whose articles of export are almost exclusively agricultural products with other countries that are also agricultural, while erecting a customhouse barrier of prohibitive tariff taxes against the richest countries of the world that stand ready to take our entire surplus of products and to exchange therefore commodities which are necessaries and comforts of life among our own people.[31]

The Democrats pointed out that some of the richest countries in Latin America such as Argentina, Chile, Mexico, and Uruguay had refused to sign reciprocal agreements. They had no interest in lower duties on coffee, sugar, hides, molasses, and cocoa, none of which they exported in any volume. Negotiations with Canada also proved fruitless because of disagreement over duties on manufactures.[32] Moreover, reciprocity had created enmity when Harrison enforced the punitive provision of the McKinley Tariff to raise duties on Colombia and Venezuela for refusing to agree to reciprocity treaties. Even in the two major cases where reciprocal treaties had stimulated increased trade, Brazil and Cuba, U.S. exports grew about $8 million but imports allegedly exploded $69 million, increasing the American trade deficit.[33] The heart of the Democratic argument was that reciprocity was not substantially increasing exports to the agricultural countries it targeted, while the protective duties of the McKinley Tariff, which was the father of reciprocity, prevented exports to European markets where there was much greater demand for U.S. products.[34]

The Democratic denunciation of reciprocity derived from their faith in free markets and small government. Many historians of the Gilded Age's foreign policy tend to chart a consistently expansionist position between 1880 and 1898 as if the twentieth-century practice of a bipartisan foreign policy applied to that era.[35] In fact, Cleveland sought a sharp break with his Republican predecessor, and not simply because of his own "moralistic aversion" to "anything akin to imperialism" as has been suggested.[36] Democratic party leaders had a consistent and well-thought-out program that extended their trust in decentralization and small government to the international sphere. Their inability to fully enact their program revealed more about contradictory domestic interests and the nature of the international imperialist regime than Democratic lack of intellectual rigor. Most Democrats held that the government should not take a direct role in trade promotion. The Nicaraguan canal should be private with the U.S. government's only role to protect it from "foreign control." Nothing was said of the merchant marine. Instead of the Monroe Doctrine and manifest destiny, the Democrats viewed "with alarm the tendency to a policy of irritation and bluster, which is liable at any time to confront us with the alternative of humiliation or war."[37]

The voters' alternatives were not restricted to only the Republicans and

Democrats in the election of 1892. They also were appealed to by the most successful third party of the nineteenth century, the People's Party (known as the Populists), which wedded the Republican vision of an activist state with Democratic concerns over the influence of special interests. Joining together angry farmers and workmen, Populists posed a great threat to the two established parties, particularly the Republicans, forcing them to reconstruct some of their campaign rhetoric. The Populist platform, one of the most radical and articulate of the century, concentrated on domestic ills and solutions. Its chief panacea was free and unlimited coinage of silver. The existing currency was responsible for "falling prices, the formation of combines and rings, the impoverishment of the producing class." Thus silver, not foreign markets, would solve the rural crises. Indeed, Populists violently denounced the tariff debate of the two established parties: "They propose to drown the outcries of a plundered people with the uproar of a sham battle over the tariff, so that capitalists, corporations, national banks, rings, trusts, watered stock, the demonetarization of silver, and the oppression of the usurers may all be lost sight of. They propose to sacrifice our homes, lives, and children on the altar of mammon."[38]

Unlike the Democrats, the Populists did not oppose state activism even though they opposed the protective tariff. In fact the Populists demanded that "the powers of the Government—in other words of the people—should be expanded." First, however, the government that currently "destroys the multitude in order to secure corruption funds from the millionaires" had to be restored "to the hands of the 'plain people.'" The issue was not what the state should do, but who should benefit from its actions. They called for land reform, state ownership of railroads, telegraphs, telephone systems, and postal banks. The Nicaraguan canal should be constructed and controlled by the U.S. government.[39]

While seeking a stronger public sector, Populists opposed all "government subsidies and aid to private corporations for any purpose," as well as tariff protection for special interests.[40] This same fear had led many voters to balk at the Billion Dollar Congress's maritime subsidies or enlarged bureaucracy. They were not concerned so much that the public sphere grew, but that public monies had been privatized by small, wealthy cliques. The party's presidential candidate, General Weaver, pointedly stated the central message of the Populist campaign: "Equal rights for all and special privileges for none."[41] Much of the opposition to Harrison's initiatives should be read as antitrust sentiment, not opposition to a strong state or expansion.

Cleveland tapped this populist hostility toward special interests in a call to moralistic reform, though his popularity in a time of rural despair seems puzzling. The beefy candidate was so aloof to the problems of the farmer that he reminded one Farmers' Alliance leader of "the man who was so tall he never knew when his feet were cold."[42] Despite his seeming indifference to the cold political landscape of the farmer during the period,

Cleveland was able to carry the election by proclaiming support for lower taxes and civil service reform while denouncing machine politics, the force bill, and pietistic legislation on drinking.[43]

The election should not be interpreted—as it was—as a repudiation of Harrison's active state and expansionism, however. Support for state activism and expansion was still strong. Certainly everyone agreed that the tariff was a central issue, but stupid tactics, such as the brutality of management in the Homestead Strike and Harrison's treatment of the Coeur d'Alene strike, as well as chance—Blaine's inability to campaign because of illness—cost many votes.[44] Frustration with pietistic-inspired local reforms hurt Republican national candidates in the Midwest and Great Plains again as they had in 1890. The Democrats successfully played to racist prejudice by opposing the federal election law and opposing Chinese immigration in California. The hemorrhaging of votes because of the appeal of the Populists also hurt Harrison.[45] There is no reason to think that Harrison's foreign policy cost him the election, a lesson that Cleveland soon learned. Indeed, many political observers thought reciprocity helped narrow the margin of defeat.

The defeat was very narrow indeed. Cleveland's popular vote in 1892 was only 14,000 (0.25 percent) greater than in 1888. The difference was the marginal decline of the Republicans that cost them key swing states such as New York, Illinois, Indiana (a testimony to Harrison's lack of personal appeal), and Wisconsin.[46] Cleveland would soon learn how fragile his support was and the large bastion of support that Republican expansionism continued to hold.

Cleveland in Office

Cleveland had become only the second man in U.S. history to win a plurality of the presidential vote three times. His personal image of honesty and strength had allowed the fractured Democrats to control the presidency and both houses of Congress for the first time since the Civil War. He had campaigned on tariff reform and announced in his inaugural address that "tariff reform is still our purpose."[47] The tariff should have been the first order of business, but, as he had already learned in 1887 when the party had failed to bring about significant change, Cleveland faced a monumental task in forging a coherent tariff reform out of the conflicting local interests Democrats represented.[48] Now Cleveland faced additional burdens. He had alienated some of the most powerful men in the Democratic party through his campaigns against machine politics and his vetoes of what he considered pork barrel bills (he had vetoed three times as many bills in his first term as all preceding presidents combined).[49] Cleveland's appointment of Walter Gresham—a former Republican cabinet member and presidential candidate—to the powerful post of secretary of state, in the words of Congressman Champ Clark, "slapped every Democrat betwixt the two seas squarely in the face."[50] To add to the brewing personal enmity, Cleveland was "not in harmony with his party upon the principal issues of the present time"—the tariff and the silver standard.[51]

Cleveland had used the tariff to divert attention from the differences within his party over the coinage of silver. Unfortunately, ominous signs of the depression of 1893 began to appear shortly after he took office. A strong gold man, Cleveland was convinced that the Sherman Silver Purchase Act was reducing the money supply. To rectify the situation, Cleveland cashed in his political IOUs and pressed his personal prestige into repealing the act. By the time he had succeeded, the president had little ammunition left to push through tariff reform.

The result was the mongrel Wilson-Gorman Act that pleased no one and reformed little. Cleveland found himself caught in "all sorts of tangles among the private and local interests of our party."[52] The president was unwilling to propose a free trade tariff "for revenue only" as the Democratic platform had promised, but he did want to lower rates and increase the free list. Secretary of State Gresham, whom the Populists had hoped to make their presidential candidate in 1892, became concerned about the "growing symptoms of revolution" throughout the country.[53] The cause of unrest was the fact that "our mills and factories can supply the home demand by running six or seven months in the year," which meant "enforced idleness for the balance of the year." The solution, in addition to "a more equitable division of the joint product of capital and labor," was free raw materials for manufacturers, which "would lower the cost of the manufactured article and enable our people to compete in foreign markets with Great Britain."[54]

The Democrats enjoyed a considerable majority in the House so they were able to pass easily the Wilson bill, which prescribed a long free list including sugar and an average rate reduction of 15 percent. In the Senate, however, where their majority was slender, the bill ran into great difficulties. Each senator bargained for his vote. Senator Gorman (cousin of the Pan American Conference's Henry Gassaway Davis) accepted all 634 amendments, gutting the heart of reform. Key items such as iron ore, coal, and sugar were no longer free.

Free sugar, which had been an important issue for representatives of the farm states, was defeated by a combination of Louisiana senators defending their local planters and the lobbyists of the American Refining Company who defended their monopoly from the competition of imported sugar. The fact that a number of senators were speculating in sugar futures also undermined free sugar.[55] Frank Taussig, one of the nation's leading contemporary students of the tariff, concluded, "The trust had conquered."[56] Cleveland tried to put the best face on this defeat. The Wilson-Gorman Act represented a "vast improvement" because it would "lighten many tariff burdens" and provide "a barrier against the return of mad protection." Still, he could hardly see the free list of molasses, coffee, tea, hides, and raw wool as important free raw materials that he believed were "necessary" to "unshackle American enterprise and ingenuity and . . . open the doors of foreign markets to the reception of our wares."[57] Ultimately Cleveland allowed the tariff to become law without his signature because there were "provisions in this bill which are not in line with honest tariff reform."[58]

The passage of the Wilson-Gorman Act put the reciprocal trade treaties signed under the authority of the McKinley Tariff into doubt. Although he had proposed a customs union with Brazil, Cleveland had long opposed partial reciprocal treaties. In his first term he had opposed the reciprocal treaties with Mexico, Cuba, and the Dominican Republic negotiated under his predecessor.[59] In his 1892 campaign the Democrat had denounced reciprocity as a Band-Aid for protection. Shortly after taking office he had Gresham make an inquiry into the legal and economic ramifications of abrogation of the treaty.

They concluded that the United States could end the treaty within three months without Brazilian consent. In fact, in what the Brazilian government could only take as a slap in the face, Gresham argued that "the so-called treaties or agreements that were entered into, based upon the third section of the McKinley bill, were not treaties binding upon the two governments."[60] But should they? They had evidence of growing support for reciprocity in the House Ways and Means Committee's 1892 survey of manufacturers, commercial associations, and farm groups. John Foster noted that the survey found "a remarkable unanimity of sentiment expressed concerning the value and results of reciprocity arrangements negotiated with certain countries and the disastrous effects of their repeal."[61] Many commercial and trade associations as well as farmer organizations petitioned Congress in favor of reciprocity. Populist leaders such as Tom Watson, who had concentrated on free silver and government regulation in 1892 to solve the farmer's problems, had become impressed by the depression that "the most striking fact about the whole thing is that the number of our people today wholly dependent on foreign markets is larger than the number of those employed in the protected industries."[62]

Reciprocity was integral to protection and therefore anathema to the Democrats, however, and Democratic congressmen vehemently objected to the executive authority under which the reciprocity treaties were negotiated: "We do not believe the Congress can rightly vest in the President of the United States any authority or power to impose or release taxes on our people."[63]

Moreover, they were able to marshall impressive figures that refuted the accomplishments of reciprocity. Although they conceded that total trade with treaty countries had indeed grown substantially in the two years of reciprocity, Democrats pointed out that in many countries trade actually fell. In the cases where trade showed its most impressive growth—Brazil, Cuba, and the West Indies—imports far outstripped exports causing the trade deficit to swell. The commercial deficit, in turn, forced an outflow of species that further reduced the U.S. money supply. More serious to the Democrats, reciprocity was based on protective duties against European imports that closed the much more attractive European markets to American exports. Cleveland decided to terminate the treaty with Brazil but had to wait a year and a half, to the end of 1894, before the Wilson-Gorman Act finally passed through Congress to replace the McKinley Tariff.[64]

Cleveland's retreat from the Republicans' aggressive state promotion of trade expansion was only a part of a broader program to reduce public economic initiatives. He had already demonstrated his narrow view of the state in his first administration when he had vetoed a congressional act to send seed to drought-stricken Texas farmers on the grounds that "the people support the Government, Government should not support the people."[65] Now he set about dismantling the achievements of the Fifty-first Congress. The Sherman Silver Purchase Act was repealed, the Sherman Antitrust Act virtually ignored. Aggressive measures that had derived from the Pan American Conference were set aside. The Pan American railroad, still in the planning stages, was abandoned, as were the Inter-American Bank and subsidies to American steamship builders.[66]

In foreign affairs observers also noted a strong effort to heed the Democratic platform's caution against "entangling alliances" and the Republican policy of "irritation and bluster."[67] Cleveland had earlier opposed the Frelinghusen-Zavala treaty on the Nicaraguan canal because it would make Nicaragua a virtual protectorate of the United States and had objected to U.S. participation in the 1884 Berlin Convention because the United States had no role in Africa. In his second term he sought a way out of U.S. participation in the protectorate over Samoa and slowed down the expansion of the New Navy, even threatening to close the Naval War College.[68] Most spectacularly, he refused to annex Hawaii.

Cleveland and Gresham initially not only stymied the Republican annexation effort, they sought to undo the planter coup that had overthrown Queen Liliuokalani on the grounds that it was achieved through the intervention of American troops to support an illegal seizure of power by a tiny planter minority.[69] The president and his secretary of state were motivated by both a republican disdain for colonialism and a distrust of the islands' racial composition. Gresham feared "If we enter upon a career of acquisition of distant territory, governing it as Great Britain and other European powers govern their dependencies, our republic will not long endure. Should we acquire the Hawaiian Islands with their population, we will have a hotbed of corruption."[70]

They were also motivated by U.S. sugar refiners who feared competition from Hawaiian refineries were the islands annexed. At the same time, some American workers worried that Hawaii, which depended on Chinese and Portuguese immigrants, would set a precedent for importing cheap workers to "degrade American labor and lessen the wages" as the Democratic platform had warned.[71]

Gresham, however, was unable to convince Sanford Dole, president of Hawaii's provisional republican government, to return constitutional power to the queen, partly because she insisted on having the heads of all conspirators if returned to the throne. Thus Hawaii remained an independent republic—but one that was drawn more closely into the American commercial sphere. Where the McKinley Tariff's free sugar had negated the Hawaiian advantages of their 1887 reciprocal trade treaty and caused them to refuse to honor it, the Wilson-Gorman Tariff's return to sugar duties encouraged Hawaii to abide by the 1887 agreement. The United States retained continued economic mastery and the right to build a harbor on the Pearl River.

The Hawaiian affair highlighted the nature of Cleveland's foreign policy. Historians of the foreign policy of this era have tended to look for the roots of the Spanish-American war and American empire. "Imperialism" and "expansion" are generally taken as synonomous with "annexation" and "colonialism." Yet most politicians of the time very clearly distinguished between the two groups of concepts. Cleveland and Gresham, although opposed to annexation and a large navy, came to recognize as the depression of 1893 took its toll the importance of foreign markets. Gresham was particularly eloquent in disengaging commercial expansion from political expansion.[72]

But Cleveland discovered that the search for foreign markets carried with it an unwanted side effect: political obligations. He would discover that in the Age of Empire, simple laissez-faire free trade alone could not gain American goods admittance to the world's lucrative markets. Doors were more easily opened—or kept open—by twenty-inch guns.

Cleveland was also backed into a more forceful foreign policy than he would have wanted by Republican accusations of his Anglophilia. Cleveland had been badly hurt in the 1888 election when the British minister to the United States wrote a letter assuring that Cleveland was friendly to Great Britain. The Republicans combined this with the Democrats' supposed free trade preference to argue that Cleveland favored British interests over native ones.[73] His resistance to the Nicaraguan canal because it contravened the Clayton-Bulwer treaty provided nationalists with further ammunition. Most important, his spearheading the repeal of the Sherman Silver Purchase Act and later reliance on the British-American House of Morgan to borrow gold in London for the depleted Treasury opened Cleveland to attack at a time that Anglophobia was cresting. By late 1893 the president was feeling particularly embattled. The depression and his problems with his own party were magnified when many Republicans replaced Democratic incumbents in the 1893 gubernatorial elections. Most frightening, the embodiment of Republican protectionism, William McKinley, won election in Ohio. Sensing the shift of political winds, Cleveland quickly sought issues to divert public attention from the domestic chaos created by the depression. Commercial expansion and rivalry with the British became solutions. They would push Cleveland into taking a much more aggressive role in Brazil than he preferred, a role that was an important step toward cementing U.S. hegemony in the Americas.

CHAPTER 7

Of Revolts and Gunboats

Floriano adhered to the Blaine-Mendonça Accord even with the Democrats in power in the United States because the commercial treaty no longer seemed very damaging and, more important, the intimate alliance shifted to a military rather than a commercial basis. Wracked by revolts and conspiracies throughout the country, the Rio government—despite its nationalist and even nativist rhetoric—desperately needed foreign assistance. European unfriendliness and Jacobin Pan-Americanism made the United States the logical candidate. However, Cleveland's reluctance to become entangled in foreign quarrels that he demonstrated in Hawaii cast doubt on the U.S. commitment to the alliance with Brazil.

Fortunately for Floriano, a confluence of American commercial interests, political considerations, desire to test the New Navy, and resentment of the role of the Great Powers—particularly the British in Guanabara Bay—led Cleveland to take a fatal step on the path to an imperialist foreign policy. Although constantly remaining neutral in word, the American president became aggressive in deed. As Walter LaFeber and William Appleman Williams have noted, the actions in Rio Bay—which witnessed the greatest concentration of U.S. gunboats in American history to that point—led directly to the expansionist policy that would continue the buildup of the New Navy, yield the Olney Doctrine in Venezuela, and lead to the Spanish-American War.[1]

The event that would engage the Americans' attention and change their perceptions was the revolt of the Brazilian navy between September 1893 and March 1894. Initially, the insurrection that was played out before Rio's docks struck foreign observers as comic. Within five months, however, it became clear that the script actually called for a tragic civil war costing thousands of lives. The British in particular stopped smirking as they found themselves diplomatically supplanted by the United States in the largest of the Latin American countries.[2] The U.S. Navy and Yankee traders, especially Charles Flint, played a large role in setting this course.

The naval revolt has been the subject of a number of articles in the United States and books in Brazil.[3] Many of the works are fine accounts of the events but from the limited perspective of single nationalities. They have consequently tended to denigrate or misrepresent the contribution of the other nationalities to the conflict. None have joined the international dimension of the U.S. debate on expansionism and its rivalry with the Great Powers to the internal dynamics of the civil war within Brazil (which itself has been poorly studied). That is the task of the next two chapters.

Brazil in 1893

Floriano could well afford to maintain the Blaine-Mendonça Accord despite the passage of the Wilson-Gorman Act in the United States. Early data showed that Brazil fared well. In the treaty's first twenty months, exports to the United States more than doubled over the previous period, while U.S. trade benefited little.[4] At the same time, the internal and international threat to Floriano's regime grew, making American friendship more important than ever. One year after the Iron Marshal came to power the country was in chaos. The alarmed Portuguese minister reported a catalog of horrors: governors in most states were overthrown, revolution broke out in the state of Mato Grosso, civil war erupted in the state of Rio Grande do Sul, the Santa Cruz garrison across the bay from Rio revolted, Sebastianists (monarchist restorationists), anarchists, and socialists loudly organized, Jacobins demonstrated in the streets attacking "enemies" of the regime, and war with Argentina loomed because of the Missiones dispute. At the same time, the minister reported somewhat hysterically, 15,000 troops from Uruguay invaded Rio Grande do Sul to attack Floriano's allies there. In order to defend Brazil from these external threats, the minister of the navy, Admiral Custódio de Mello, requested and received from Congress 10,000 contos (approximately $2 million) to modernize the navy.[5] Ironically, of this encyclopedia of political turmoil, it was Floriano's own navy that proved the most threatening to his regime.

Civil War in Rio Grande do Sul

The theater of the bloodiest fighting was Rio Grande do Sul (see Map 1). There the local dispute eventually provoked an international crisis. Bordering on Argentina and Uruguay, the state had a separatist, martial culture

Map 1. Brazil during the Civil War of the 1890's.

and pastoral vocation more resembling its southern neighbors than its fellow countrymen to the north. Landowners in Rio Grande do Sul, Uruguay, and Argentina had ranches and political allies on both sides of the poorly patrolled borders.[6] Local disputes threatened to become international war.

Under the Empire, Rio Grande do Sul had been the political fief of Counselor Gaspar de Silveira Martins, one of the monarchy's most popular figures. The republican revolution had been initiated in large part because Deodoro had wanted to prevent Silveira Martins from becoming prime minister. Victorious, Deodoro ordered Silveira Martins arrested and exiled. Rio Grande do Sul then fell to the Partido Republicano Riograndense (PRR) led by Julio Castilhos. Castilhos designed a constitution for the state, much admired by radical Florianistas and Jacobins, that called for a strong president to replace the parliamentary form of government Silveira Martins supported. While the dispute between Castilhos's and Silveira Martins's forces was in fact mostly over power, the struggle over forms of government invested it with great symbolic importance. Castilhos represented republicanism, and the federalist Silveira Martins's forces were accused of monarchist pretensions.[7] It was this dimension that caused the civil war to become eventually embroiled in international intrigues. The historian José Maria Bello eloquently evoked Rio Grande do Sul's significance: "Proclaimed in a bloodless coup, in an atmosphere of vague indifference in a large, neglected and lazy cosmopolitan city of businessmen, the Republic would prove here [in Rio Grande do Sul] whether or not it could survive."[8]

The Federalists relentlessly waged war against the PRR. In February 1893 5,000 Brazilians, Argentines, and Uruguayans invaded from Uruguay to oust the PRR. They were led by Gumercindo Saraiva, who embodied the transnational nature of the struggle. Born in Brazil, he had been raised in Uruguay. His preferred language was Spanish, and his brother and co-leader would later become the leader of the Blancos, one of Uruguay's two major parties.[9] Gumercindo's initial invasion was defeated by a combination of state police, irregulars, and federal troops. Some of his defeated Federalists returned to Uruguay, while a segment under Saraiva began to move northward. To this point the rebellion was a local one, but with broader implications.[10]

In July this changed. The revolt took on a national character focused on Floriano's rule. Admiral Wandenkolk, who had been defeated by Floriano for the office of vice president in the 1891 election and then had been one of the thirteen "generals" forced to retire for demanding new elections, attempted a naval revolt in Rio Grande do Sul hoping to link up with Saraiva's ground forces.[11] His goal was to remove not only Castilhos, but Floriano as well.

Although Wandenkolk's rebellion also failed, it revealed the sharp divisions that Floriano confronted. In Congress an attempt was made to impeach Floriano on several grounds: he was illegally engaging federal troops in a state affair, he had retired officers illegally, and he had merged the major banks and stripped them of their right to issue currency. The issues of impeachment presented in crystallized form Floriano's adversaries and their resentments: supporters of states' rights, civil libertarians, senior apolitical army officers, the navy, and financiers. The impeachment effort failed, but more than one-third of Congress voted for it.[12]

The Alienation of the Navy

At the same time, a new threat to Floriano was rising that would make the crisis an international affair, one that would demand American help. The armed forces had long suffered a deep split. The navy, which had attracted the children of aristocrats, had been the favorite of the Empire. Sailors had received disproportionately more funds and prestige. Dom Pedro II himself had dressed in a naval uniform on formal state occasions.[13] To its resentment, the more plebian army was neglected by the monarchy.[14]

The dawn of the Republic changed the relative standing of the two services as the army took for itself the bulk of the increase in military funding. Promotions and pay raises along with a 50 percent increase in the size of the army and soldiers' appointments to important political positions angered naval officers, causing them to unify against Floriano. The first political evidence of this split had come when Marshal Floriano defeated Admiral Wandenkolk for the office of vice president in early 1891. Then in November of that year when Deodoro was overthrown, principally by the naval revolt led by Admiral Custódio de Mello, de Mello was not rewarded. He did not share in the power that he so craved and believed he deserved because Floriano refused to call new elections. Adding to these insults, the engagement of federal troops in the Rio Grande do Sul civil war appeared to naval officers as further evidence of the army's superiority in national politics. In protest, Admiral de Mello resigned his post as minister of the navy in late April 1893. When Wandenkolk revolted three months later, members of the Naval Club in Rio, leaving no doubt as to their sympathies, elected the rebel their president.

The Navy Revolts

Although events began to reveal the serious fissures in the Brazilian body politic, foreign observers refused initially to take them seriously. When the navy finally revolted on September 6, 1893, the foreign press described it figuratively as comic opera.

Attending the legitimate opera, *Hueguenottes*, in Rio de Janeiro with other members of the military command and high government officials, Admiral de Mello left the theater early and slipped out to the largest ship in the Brazilian navy, the *Aquibadan*, to orchestrate the coup. De Mello hoped to replicate his act of two years earlier when a mere show of force and a few cannon shots combined with a strike on Rio's principal railroad had convinced Marshal Deodoro to resign the presidency. Now the admiral's fifteen warships and the nine merchantmen he seized easily dominated the bay (though sabotaging of four railway stations failed to block the Central Railroad).[15] The famous French actress Sarah Bernhardt, who was in the bay in the first days of the revolt, enthused over the excitement of the pyrotechnics: "I never before had such an experience. It was a marvel—a scene of a lifetime. . . . The display was superb but nobody apparently shot to kill. Not a shot, as far as I saw or heard, hit or hurt anything. It seemed as if they had created a splendid spectacle to frighten each other and were doing their best to make the greatest possible noise without injuring anybody." In Rio, she continued, "business was going on as usual." In the afternoons the ladies were out "driving and calling as if nothing was happening, and in the evening the places of amusement were as full as ever." She concluded that "from what I heard, I gathered that the existing state of things could not last much longer. Probably it will end with the victory of Admiral Mello and the surrender of the city to him."[16] Bernhardt's cheerful account of the revolt was echoed in the foreign press.[17] Many shared her optimism about the brevity of the conflict and de Mello's victory.[18]

Few observers expected Marshal Floriano to ignite an intramilitary civil war by resisting the insurrection. An unhealthy man, having spent most of the second half of the 1880's on sick leave, he had refused to train the guns of his 2,000 troops on Deodoro's 600 revolters in the Campo de Sant'Anna to defend the monarchy on November 15, 1889. Nor had violence been necessary when he himself took office; Deodoro had voluntarily stepped down rather than permit a bloodbath. Indeed, according to de Mello, Deodoro's overthrow had been entirely the work of the navy since Floriano had been afraid to commit troops against the president.[19] It was expected that Floriano would also shrink from the navy's guns. De Mello was said to have boasted while breakfasting on the battleship *Aquibadan* that he would dine that night in the presidential palace.

The Rebels Strengthen Their Position

The insurgents certainly held a good hand. Although they had only some 1,500 men to the government's 7,000 to 8,000 troops (5,000 of them regular soldiers), de Mello used surprise and swift action to seize the munitions depot quickly as well as the large Ilha do Governador, an island at the back of the bay. The admiral controlled one of the world's larger and more modern navies. Since 1883 Brazil had begun purchasing the latest iron- and steel-clad ships. De Mello commanded a 5,000-ton battleship built in 1885, and two protected cruisers, a steel gunboat, and four torpedo boats, all built in Europe since 1890. The two new cruisers, according to the *New York Times*, "in general fighting efficiency have no superiors probably in their class in the world."[20] When the battleship *Aquibadan* had paid a visit to the United States in 1890, American naval experts studied it admiringly. The

Brazilian armed cruiser *Riachuelo* served as the model for the ill-fated American battleship *Maine*.[21] Only seven countries in the world had more protected cruisers than Brazil.[22] True, the government held all but one of the forts that surrounded the bay, but their guns were outmoded, so they inflicted little damage to the rebel fleet.

De Mello's ships could dominate the seas and harass other ports once they demonstrated the ability to slip past the hail of cannon fire that erupted from the forts at the mouth of Guanabara Bay; the legal forces commanded no navy to speak of. Two of the largest government ships were in France undergoing repairs; the loyalty of their crews was suspect, so they would sit out the war in Toulon. The few other ships that did not side with the insurgents were old, small, and slow.[23]

Control of the seas was particularly important in Brazil because the vast majority of its population lived within 200 miles of its 4,600-mile-long coastline. No roads or railroads connected the country's far-flung regions. Ships were the arteries that carried the nation's lifeblood. In addition to crippling domestic commerce, the naval revolt tied down soldiers defending the ports that were now all at risk of naval attack and prevented troop movements from one region to another.[24] Not only did the insurgents control Brazil's waters, but in the beginning it was widely believed in the foreign press and in foreign capitals that they had the support of a large share of the population, which may well have been true.[25]

Their cause was described as a righteous blow against dictatorship. Somewhat disingenuously, de Mello explained to the Brazilian people that he revolted to defend the constitution and civilian government against militarism.[26] He claimed that his action was precipitated by Floriano's veto of a bill that would have ordered the president to step down in November 1894 without an opportunity for reelection. The veto, de Mello proclaimed, was evidence of the marshal's intention to maintain an army dictatorship. Floriano, in his own defense, had argued that the bill was unconstitutional.[27] This exchange between a dictator and a rebel over who better defended the constitution did not strike most Brazilians as absurd.[28] In fact, however, the direct result of the uprising was a declaration of martial law, arrests of hundreds of suspected rebel sympathizers, censorship of the press and telegrams, the imposition of internal passports, and suspension of the planned October congressional elections.[29] The March presidential elections were also cast into doubt. De Mello had created a self-fulfilling prophecy.

Anatomy of the Revolt

The true aims of the insurgents and the nature of their followers was debated at the time, though subsequently historians have not given the revolt close attention. Part of the difficulty stems from the fact that de Mello's own aims were vague and his followers diverse.[30] His movement was embraced by people with very different goals and grievances united only in their opposition to President Floriano Peixoto. Floriano quickly characterized the revolt as an attempt to restore the monarchy. Certainly many monarchists did support the rebellion, but so did republicans. In part the insurrection was an interservice feud over the distribution of privilege, prestige, and perquisites. But this explanation is too simple. Many members of the army leaned to the rebels and many sailors refused to join the revolt.[31] De Mello also attracted disgruntled provincial politicians who had been shunted aside by Florianistas and members of the elite and middle class concerned with military rule, the sanctity of the constitution, and civil rights.[32]

This was not simply a factional feud. Forces tended to align according to their subjective social class. Florianistas certainly appealed to class allegiances. They argued that de Mello wanted to reestablish the hegemony of the feudal elite while Floriano was defending the progressive middle and working classes.[33]

There is some evidence to support their contention. In his two years in power Floriano had made friends with the urban population of Rio by providing low-cost meat and open-air markets, closing down tenements, and denouncing profiteering merchants. He also increased the size of the government bureaucracy and awarded pay raises. His own simple lifestyle also won him friends among the masses: Floriano would leave his office in the Itamaraty palace at night unaccompanied and take a streetcar to his simple residence in the suburbs.[34] Many students were attracted by the marshal's fervent nationalism. Students, workers, and government employees demonstrated their support for the government during the rebellion by enlisting by the thousands in "patriotic battalions" and the national guard to defend both the coastline and the interior. Hundreds of them fell in the fighting. On the other hand, very few of Rio's citizens joined or aided the rebels.[35]

It is also true that Floriano had enraged some of the country's plutocrats with his stock market and banking reforms. Some of the most important of these men, such as Francisco de Paula Mayrink, the Visconde de Figueiredo, and the Conde de Leopoldina, seem to have supplied funds, munitions, and even merchant ships to the rebels. There was some evidence that Mayrink funded the naval rebels, and his company even provided the ship that Admiral Wandenkolk used to sail to Rio Grande do Sul in his attempted coup. It was reported that one optimistic banker (probably Figueiredo) lent de Mello "a large sum" that was to be repaid in eight days, by which time the revolt was expected to be victorious.[36] Commercial speculators in Rio, who were profiting from the jump in prices caused by the naval blockade, also seem to have lent the rebels funds.[37]

Some of the naval officers had good reasons to support the financiers as well. One of the revolt's eventual leaders, Admiral Saldanha da Gama, was a good friend of Mayrink, while de Mello was a confidant of Figueiredo. Several leaders of the Rio conspiracy, as well as leaders of the rebellion in the south of the country, had important positions in Mayrink companies, while the minister of the navy, Admiral Wandenkolk, had been president of a major company owned by Figueiredo.[38] The business ties between naval officers and bankers were not in themselves enough to launch a revolt, since many army officers also shared in the spoils of the Encilhamento. But when added to the interservice feud and Floriano's campaign against "speculators," this volatile mixture exploded.

Financiers not only lent their own funds to the insurgents but also undertook financial missions to Europe to secure further funds for the rebellion.[39] The close ties of the Brazilian and Portuguese financiers to European money markets tied the naval rebels to European capitalists. Floriano played upon this theme to feed popular indignation against the insurgents and their traitorous supporters. This also proved a popular argument in garnering support in the United States where animosity against European bankers was high.

The Iron Marshal was aided in his project of linking the insurgents to European capitalists by the loud support given to the revolters by Rio's main French and English expatriate newspapers as well as the European press. Floriano ultimately closed down the *Rio News* and the *Echo du Brèsil*, leading papers of the foreign commercial community, because of their vocal advocacy of the rebellion. He also incarcerated some of their readers. Joaquim Nabuco complained that when the police began arresting hundreds of suspected rebel sympathizers (the *London Times* claimed that the number reached 1,500, and the editor of *Echo du Brèsil* maintained there were 5,000 political prisoners), they imprisoned "among the finest in Rio de Janeiro society."[40] Floriano claimed in his 1894 message to Congress that among his enemies were "cosmopolitans" and "stock market speculators."[41] The marshal's perception of his enemies was realistic. When Admiral da Gama entered the revolt, he claimed to be fighting with the support of "all of the conservative classes" and implicitly against Jacobins whom he accused of "sedition, riots and disorder." A second manifesto swore "Death to the Jacobins."[42]

Yet we must be careful to not draw too sharply the class lines dividing the combatants. Lt. August Vinhaes, the preeminent labor leader in the country, sided with the revolt as did Inocencio Serzedello Corrêa, one of the stanchest defenders of the Republic and industrialization. Rui Barbosa, later enshrined by historians as the guardian angel of Brazil's middle class and a "modernizer," was a spokesman for the revolt and a contender for its leadership. On the other side, the Paulista Republican Party, surely the central committee for an important fraction of the country's national bourgeoisie and the loudest advocates of federalism, never wavered in its support for the government.

These unexpected alignments only complicate rather than contradict the class nature of the rebellion. For these men, class considerations were overshadowed by political exigencies. Barbosa had been the virtual partner of the financier class, especially Mayrink, under attack by Floriano. He had risen to great national importance the first time as Deodoro's minister of finance through his support of military privilege and the coup of November 15. He probably hoped to regain his former prominence under a de Mello administration. Vinhaes, similarly, was a political opportunist who used labor to bolster his own prestige; he was a friend of the embattled banker Conde de Mattosinhos. Serzedello Corrêa, who later became president of an insurance company and spokesman for the Paulista president Campos Sales, had no commitment to Floriano's radical populism.[43]

On the other side, Paulistas received from Floriano important cabinet posts, autonomy in their state, and the soon-to-be-realized hope that the marshal would eventually relinquish the presidency to a Paulista. They also harbored no fond memories of the monarchy, which had neglected them, nor of Deodoro, who had imposed his own governor in São Paulo. In addition, they objected to de Mello's attempts to blockade their port of Santos. They were not disturbed by Floriano's campaign against Rio financiers and Portuguese and English businessmen since, if anything, it helped free São Paulo from Rio's commercial yoke.[44]

The International Perspective

Although the revolt was rooted in domestic disputes, international issues played a part in provoking and shaping it. The suggestion by Williams and LaFeber that the Blaine-Mendonça Accord played a part in aligning Brazilian forces is hard to sustain.[45] After all, Rui Barbosa and other Deodoristas who were now in revolt had negotiated and signed the treaty. The opposition to it had centered in the states' rights coalition headed by the Paulistas and represented by Floriano who now sustained the pact. On the other hand, it is possible that the treaty convinced the British to side with the rebels as the U.S. Minister Thomas Thompson suggested: "It cannot be denied that it [the Blaine-Mendonça agreement] has given to our merchants a leverage of which all Europeans are extremely jealous and it is possible they hope for its abrogation upon the overthrow of the present Government."[46] It is certainly true that interest in the Brazilian market ultimately helped induce Cleveland to take a more aggressive role than he would have preferred.

Although differences over the trade agreement did not incite the revolt, the United States would come to play an instrumental role in dictating its course. Indeed, U.S. actions during the rebellion would be of greater importance in sealing an unofficial U.S.-Brazilian alliance than the trade pact had been. Initially, however, U.S. policy followed the British lead; Cleveland was reluctant to carve out an aggressive, independent position. As the insurgency progressed, he was drawn in through a complex and serpentine process.

When the revolt erupted, the United States was in no position to assert itself, for there were no American warships in Guanabara Bay.[47] Three British, one Portuguese, one Italian, and one French man-of-war oversaw the bay and defended the foreign merchant fleet loading and unloading there.[48] For the first three to four months of the revolt the Europeans dictated the foreign response to circumstances in Guanabara Bay.

Foreigners were not supposed to play any role at all. De Mello's initial plan was to scare Floriano into a quick capitulation. He was so sure that history would repeat itself that he made no long-term strategic plans.[49] When it became apparent that the marshal was not going to resign, however, de Mello decided to seek belligerency status from the foreign naval commanders in the bay. As a recognized belligerent, his ships could blockade Rio's port, thereby denying the government customs revenues, necessary imports, and military materiel.

The foreign diplomatic community met and agreed to maintain strict neutrality. Yet they differed on the definition of "neutrality." The Latin American and German diplomats argued that the revolt was an internal affair; foreign countries should not become involved. Indeed, the Germans rarely met with the other foreign commanders and maintained an independent policy. It is unclear whether their noninterference should be construed as a moral stand against imperialist intervention or as support of the rebels through tacit acceptance of their blockade. U.S. Captain Picking reported a conversation with the German Commander Schmidt who asked what the U.S. response would be if the people of Brazil wanted monarchy. When Picking replied that the United States would acquiesce to the will of the Brazilian people but not to monarchy imposed by de Mello, Schmidt asked what would be the response if a European government imposed monarchy? There were also reports of German financial aid to the rebels.[50]

The British, French, Italians, Portuguese, and U.S. representatives, on the other hand, believed that they should intervene. The *London Times* noted quite candidly that

> Humanity, however, is not the ground on which they base their intervention. Primarily the struggle between President Peixoto and Admiral de Mello is no concern of theirs. . . . All of them, and more particularly Great Britain, have interests of a more or less substantial order in the city of Rio, and it is intolerable that those interests should be wantonly sacrificed to enable one Brazilian politician to put pressure on another.[51]

The newspaper made its imperial view of the world even clearer when it disdainfully discussed what it considered the childish and ridiculous pageant being played out by Brazilians whose cannon accuracy was so poor that they hit their target only once a week and whose population treated the spectacle as "pantomime." However, the paper went on, the irresponsible Brazilians did not realize that

> Pantomime, however, though the whole business is from the military point of view, it has its very serious side for foreigners and its very tragic inci-

dents for Brazilians. . . . All serious transactions are necessarily at a stand-
still. . . . Foreign creditors, to whom the industrial development of the
country *is entirely due* must look on while the rival factions are destroying
their property [emphasis added].[52]

This is much the same language that Europeans had used in the rest of
Latin America throughout the nineteenth century. Now that Brazil was no
longer ruled by the European house of Braganza, they believed that it had
become another irresponsible South American mestizo country where en-
demic (congenital) fighting between caudillos impeded material progress.
Europeans and, to a much lesser extent Americans, were the only serious,
responsible people engaged in building up the countries.

However, Brazil was in an important regard different from most of its
Latin American neighbors, requiring an even sterner international response
than usual. The German-American coffee exporter Herman Sielcken explained that the revolutions in Central and South America "offer abundant
proof of the instability of the respective Governments," but in those countries "not yet claiming or practicing the methods of advanced civilization,"
foreigners were aware of the risks and were on their own. "But when a rebellion occurs in one of the principal gateways of maritime intercourse like
the Bay of Rio de Janeiro, offering a menace to international ocean commerce . . . it is a different matter altogether."[53] Rio was too important to be
left to the Brazilians. This was the Age of Empire after all. The Great Powers
felt it their duty and right to defend their commerce and citizens (most of
whom were engaged in trade and business). The real business of Rio was
business, which should be maintained at all costs. Politics was a nuisance
that threatened to impede business and should be controlled by the capitalist policemen. The establishment or defense of democracy was certainly
not at issue. Initially, the United States followed its decades-long practice of
joining the European powers (except, in this case, Germany) in defending
foreign property rather than taking sides in the Brazilian dispute.[54]

This policy has been referred to by many students of the revolt as one of
neutrality.[55] Cleveland, himself, to the end asserted the neutrality of the
United States position. To the extent that the Great Powers actually were
neutral they only refrained from siding with one of the combatants. They
certainly were not unaligned. They stood clearly and emphatically for foreign property. A foreign armada of eighteen men-of-war representing eight
nations in the bay of Brazil's political and commercial capital could not help
but affect the course of events.

The Foreign Policemen

Harboring an imperious and imperialist view, the European and American members of the diplomatic community took the unusual and impolitic
step of refusing to meet with Floriano when he called them for discussions

at the outbreak of the rebellion. At the same time, they refused to offer belligerency status to the rebels though they did confer with the rebel leader. They would not recognize the blockade, and they would protect foreign property on all ships and lighters flying the flags of the powers. To defend the foreign community, the commanders of the foreign naval forces informed de Mello that they "would oppose with force all his undertakings against the city of Rio de Janeiro."[56] The threat convinced the admiral to agree not to fire on Rio (a promise he frequently broke).

In exchange, the commanders secured a pledge from Floriano that he would not place guns on Rio's hilltops, thereby avoiding a pretext for further bombardments by de Mello's forces. The foreign captains also prohibited the landing of arms and munitions for government forces in Rio. Since Brazil imported almost all of its war materiel, new supplies would have to be landed at Santos. From there they had to be brought to Rio by train because the rebels prevented Brazilian munitions ships from entering Rio and the British would not allow Floriano to lease British ships for that purpose.[57] Thus the foreign powers acted "neutrally" by imposing conditions on both sides of the conflict, radically reshaping the terms of the conflict. To underline the fact that their purpose was the protection of foreign property and foreign lives, not a more global humanitarianism, the city of Niterói (capital of the state of Rio de Janeiro) that lay across the bay from Rio was deemed a fair target. (See Map 2.) Naval guns and invading troops "resulted in practically the demolition of the business and principal residence portion of the place" and forced the transfer of Rio state's capital to Petrópolis without protest from the foreign commanders or diplomats.[58]

The defense of the merchant marine was left to the foreign commanders who came to play a central role in the revolt. Although initially their combined war fleet was smaller than that of de Mello, the European ships were more modern and powerful.[59] The foreign commanders extended their policing powers to the shore when they made contingency plans to land 750 marines and sailors in Rio if foreigners became threatened by either naval bombardment or an outbreak of unrest in the city.[60] It was clear that diplomatic right derived from naval might as the diplomatic corps of Latin American countries, which had no gunboats in Guanabara harbor but many citizens at risk in Rio, were not even consulted by the armed powers. No action was taken when the rebels seized an Argentine steamer.[61] The captains in the bay were in essence unilaterally extending rights of extraterritoriality to all European citizens in Rio.

Stripped of his navy, Floriano had no choice but to cede policing powers for the bay to the foreign commanders, which he deeply resented. But he drew the line at the shore. He threatened the foreign naval commanders that if they in fact did land hundreds of marines, they would be met "by bullets."[62] Then he quickly moved to reduce his dependence by erecting batteries on the shore and hillsides while reinforcing the men and armaments in the forts despite his promise to leave them undefended. In his

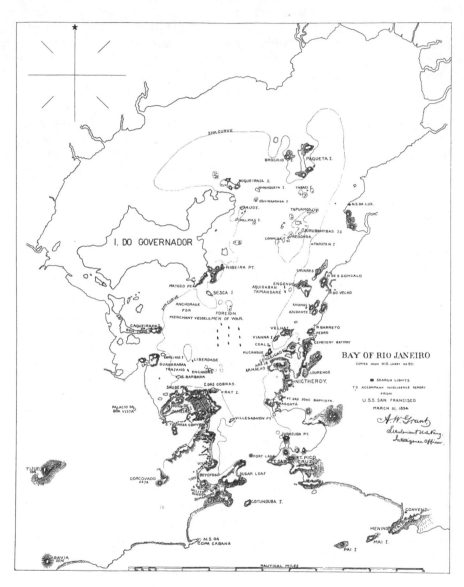

Map 2. Guanabara Bay, 1894. Labeled "Bay of Rio de Janeiro," this map was drawn by U.S. navy intelligence officer Lt. A. W. Grant on March 31, 1894. Note the proximity of the foreign men-of-war to the anchorage for foreign vessels. Reproduced with modifications from Lt. C. C. Rogers, "The Revolt in Brazil" Office of Naval Intelligence, *Notes on the Year's Naval Progress* (Washington, D.C.: Government Printing Office, 1894), p. 416.

anguish, the marshal entertained the most extravagant proposals. He went so far as to attempt to build a balloon to drop dynamite on the rebels, which naturally made the foreign commanders uncomfortable "about the idea of having a dynamite-laden balloon floating above their ships with Mello's sharpshooters firing at it in an endeavor to bring it down anywhere but upon their own heads."[63] An attempt to assassinate de Mello with a hollowed-out copy of the *Rules and Regulations of the Argentine Republic* stuffed with a bomb was equally ill-fated as was a plan to stretch explosives on an underwater cable.[64] Floriano did not cease mobilizing his defenses, however. The Iron Marshal would not trust his fate to foreign commanders or diplomats.

Floriano and his followers, already suspicious of British and Portuguese aims, quickly concluded that the European ships were favoring the rebels. Florianistas, given their authoritarian temperament and deep conviction of righteousness, did not understand how a policy of "strict neutrality" between the legal defender of the nation and rebel pirates could be neutral at all. They believed that by not supporting the legal forces, the foreign commanders were establishing the legitimacy of an illegitimate movement. The reporting in the European and the Rio expatriate press favorable to the rebels and their predictions of a quick rebel victory seemed to confirm Florianista apprehensions.[65]

In fairness, it should be noted that rebel sympathizers believed that the foreign men-of-war prevented an insurgent victory by giving Floriano time to arm and organize troops and eventually a navy.[66] The powers were neutral in the sense that they offended both sides, or at least gave both sides an excuse for military failures.

The Initial U.S. Response

The United States initially endorsed the stand of the European powers.[67] Much official consular opinion was ill disposed toward Brazil and its government.[68] Secretary of State Gresham wired the U.S. minister in Brazil, Thomas Thompson, that U.S. goods could be landed but "must respect military prohibitions when duly notified."[69] This allowed de Mello virtually to put a halt to unloading since his ships frequently fired on the merchant ships and occasionally seized the goods on lighters. Cleveland and Gresham did not back Floriano more overtly because they were afraid of committing the same error their predecessors had in Chile in 1891 when Harrison and Blaine had sided with President Balmaceda against a victorious naval-parliamentary revolt backed by the British.[70]

To prevent the U.S. government from staking out a strong stand favoring the legal forces, rebel sympathizers in Buenos Aires, Montevideo, Lisbon, and London waged a campaign of insurgent propaganda and distortions aimed at the American reading public. Most of the reports appearing in U.S. newspapers had non-Brazilian datelines because Floriano greatly restricted and censored Brazilian internal and international telegraphic communications.[71] Some of the most spectacular reports issued from the pen of Rui Barbosa (called the "recognized mouthpiece of Brazil's insurgent forces on land" by the *New York Herald* and "Rui Verbosa" by the *New York Times*), who fled first to Buenos Aires and later Lisbon and London to build international support for the uprising. Common were stories such as the one the *New York Herald* reprinted that announced that "the Diplomatic Corps is in favor of Peixoto withdrawing from Rio," that "streets are unsafe and homes are not secure against Peixoto's armed bands," and that "the unanimous sentiment is bitter against the President."[72] The *New York Times* reprinted a story of Floriano's "reign of terror."[73] Ironically, now that the civilian Barbosa was actually fighting in a war—albeit with his pen—Marshal Floriano stripped him of the honorary generalship Deodoro had conferred upon him.[74]

Warfare Intensifies

By the end of September, the aquatic "opera" being performed in Guanabara Bay had ceased to be comic, and the threat to Floriano's regime had become very serious indeed. The insurgents occasionally bombarded Rio and the largest city of Rio de Janeiro state across the bay, Niterói. Already an estimated 100,000 people fled the city: "One viewed the most painful spectacle at the central [train] station. Men, women, the elderly, children swarmed barefoot, exhausted, threw themselves against the doors . . . fell on the benches or gathered on the platforms, to leave with no particular destination, just to find refuge."[75] At the same time, one of the rebels' most modern ships had steamed south, first attempting to blockade the port of Santos, then attacking other smaller ports such as Angra dos Reis, and finally linking up with rebels in Santa Catarina who had taken over much of the state. There on October 23 a provisional government on the island of Desterro was set up, and Captain Frederico Lorena (a man of no national stature) became provisional president. Now the rebels could stake their claim for belligerency status on control of not only the seas but also a fairly large, though sparsely populated, state. Meanwhile Federalists from Rio Grande do Sul, having joined with dissenters in Santa Catarina, began coordinating their efforts with the naval rebels and started their march on Paraná with Rio de Janeiro their final destination. To add to the disaster in the south, strong anti-Florianista sentiment emerged in Bahia, and an unsuccessful revolt broke out in Pernambuco.[76]

De Mello appealed to the United States and to European countries for belligerency status on the grounds of this martial success but was turned down. Gresham concluded that control of Desterro (a "Robinson Crusoe island" as one critic sneered) did not constitute sufficient territory to warrant belligerency status according to international law. This has been cited by historians as evidence of his strict legalism and anti-expansionism.[77]

Actually, concern for international law was not a major motive. The

United States, with its own experience in its civil war, as a rule refused to award rebels belligerency status. (Gresham must have felt this principle strongly since he had been a union general in the Civil War.) This latter consideration and the friendship between Floriana's administration and the United States were actually far more important in denying the rebels' requests for belligerency status than international law, which was the public justification. If control of area were the actual criterion, surely the insurgents would have been recognized once they seized control of the state of Paraná in January. By then the rebels effectively controlled an area ten times larger than Portugal, much larger than England, and equal to the size of Italy, but Gresham continued to ignore rebel requests and rebuffed Europeans wanting to recognize them.

Boynton the Dynamiter

American assertiveness was not initially evident. In the early phase of the Brazilian civil war only one incident could be interpreted as an American action in favor of Floriano, and it was disowned by the U.S. government. At the end of September an American mercenary named George Boynton was apprehended by the British on a launch flying the Union Jack and towing a twelve-foot-long torpedo packed with 500 pounds of dynamite. Both de Mello and Floriano had sought Boynton's services before the outbreak of the revolt. De Mello wanted him to scuttle the armed cruiser *República*, which was suspected of loyalty to Floriano, but Floriano's offer of $600,000 to destroy the jewel of the Brazilian navy, the 5,000-ton iron-clad battleship *Aquibadan*, was more attractive. Unfortunately for Boynton, de Mello's spies tipped off the British who arrested Boynton as a pirate for flying the British flag, this despite the fact that Floriano had commissioned him as a colonel in the Brazilian army and, as Boynton explained to his British captors, "You are not now on the high seas. An act of the British Parliament is of no effect within another country, and if you will consult your charts, you will find that you are in the enclosed waters of Brazil."[78] The British Captain Lang was exceeding his orders, since Boynton's plot in no way affected British shipping. Afraid to act unilaterally, he delivered the dynamiter to U.S. Captain Picking. Although Boynton had broken no U.S. law, the dynamiter was transferred to a U.S. ship where he remained for two months before being sent back secretly to the United States to prevent Floriano from attempting to free him. Boynton claimed that the U.S. captain acted out of an affection for de Mello and his cause.[79]

What makes this incident particularly intriguing is Boynton's previous history. A lifelong naval mercenary, he had commanded a blockade runner during the Civil War, a French ship in the Franco-Prussian War, landed weapons on Cuba during its Ten Years' War, and delivered rifles to Venezuelan strongman Guzman Blanco. During the War of the Pacific, he had aided the Peruvians just like Charles Flint, by shipping in rifles. Flint's involvement in the Brazilian incident is unclear. Perhaps relevant was the report that Boynton was introduced to Floriano by a "prominent American" residing in Rio.[80] In any case, Flint's participation would soon become unquestionable as he acted as "a sort of brevet Secretary of the Navy."[81]

The New Navy Looks On

Flint first had to overcome considerable reluctance in American official circles for backing Floriano. Certainly officials in the U.S. Navy were not supporting the Brazilian government. In fact, initially they were not doing much of anything. The navy's performance in the first months of the revolt was slow and confused. The *New York Times* proclaimed in its front-page headline "Uncle Sam is Embarrassed."[82] The Guanabara adventure started badly as a proving ground for the New Navy. The *Charleston*, the *Detroit*, and the *Newark* were ordered to Rio "to protect [U.S.] commercial interests and American citizens."[83] However, the *Charleston* found that its steering gear was faulty, the brand-new *Detroit* required a shake-down cruise before the government took possession of her, and the *Newark* was delayed in leaving Norfolk, Virginia. The *Charleston* was the first to arrive when it finally steamed into Rio on September 26, almost three weeks after the rebellion had begun.[84]

The actions of the American navy became even more embarrassing when the *Newark*, flying the flag of Rear Admiral Stanton, finally reached Guanabara Bay on October 19. Despite the strenuous efforts of the U.S. State Department to refuse belligerency status or any implicit recognition of the rebels, Stanton returned the cannon salute given him by de Mello's fleet. Before meeting with Floriano, the American admiral entertained de Mello aboard his ship and introduced the insurgent chief to the U.S. minister. This implicit recognition outraged the Brazilian government.[85] Mendonça rushed to report the incident to Gresham. Gresham and the U.S. press were upset by the gesture, which the *Philadelphia North American* called a "foolish blunder."[86] When Cleveland heard of his action, Stanton was replaced in an interim capacity by Captain Henry F. Picking who was advised to maintain neutrality. The secretary of the navy accused Stanton of "a grave error of judgement." Stanton's removal was interpreted by the legal government as support for their cause.[87]

Da Gama Enters the Fray

The United States role in Guanabara Bay became more complicated after December 9, when Admiral Saldanha da Gama, who had remained neutral since September 6, declared for the rebellion. A direct descendant of the Portuguese explorer Vasco da Gama, he was the most popular man in the navy. He was, as described by one of his students at the naval academy, "robust, erect, elegant, with a bearing of authority, replete with nobility, pride, and dignity."[88] An internationally experienced polyglot of learning and refinement, he much impressed the foreign commanders in the bay. He had many friends in the American navy as well. Da Gama had visited the United States in 1886 when he brought Prince Augusto on a state visit and a tour of military and naval bases.[89] (One of the high points had been a trip up the Hudson on Flint's yacht.) Three years later he represented Brazil at an international maritime conference in New York and stayed on to study at Annapolis while he was attached to the Brazilian legation.[90] In Rio, according to Consul General Thompson, the foreign commanders "abandoned the position taken with Mello"; "the commercial control of the bay" was "given over to Admiral da Gama."[91]

Da Gama brought not only his popularity and standing with the foreign commanders to the revolt, but also the 280 men of the naval academy on Enxadas Island, and Cobras Island which he had controlled.[92] He also further divided the rebel command since he and de Mello were rivals rather than friends, while provisional president Lorena in Desterro was jealous of the authority of both admirals.[93] At the beginning of December de Mello steamed south to link up with the Federalists while da Gama took over command of Guanabara Bay and prosecuted the blockade more violently.

The war was now going very badly for Florianista forces. Indeed, by mid-December Gresham was under pressure from the British and other European powers to grant the rebels belligerency status. In an interview with Mendonça, the secretary of state noted that the rebel navy had held the bay for three months and was effectively preventing the unloading of commerce. The rebels held several forts, as well as control over the sea. Moreover, since establishing a provisional government in Desterro, they organized a local national guard there and controlled the state.[94] De Mello's squadron had also taken Paraná's main port at Paranagua and attacked its capital, Curitiba, while Federalists were holding important parts of Rio Grande do Sul and one wing was marching into Santa Catarina and Paraná. There were reports from around Brazil of lack of support for Floriano. If, right under his watchful eye, the municipal council in Niterói could support the insurgents, even greater was support for the rebels in the more distant South and Northeast.

Gresham now thought that these developments constituted grounds for recognition of belligerency status.[95] Unnamed "persons connected with government circles" reported that the Cleveland administration saw Floriano's chances of victory declining daily.[96] The Navy Department began to believe that "Mello will eventually overthrow the Peixoto government."[97] The administration did not want the United States to repeat the mistake it made with Chile's President Balmaceda in 1891 when the United States backed the losing side by refusing to offer the rebelling navy belligerency status.

Mendonça could not argue with Gresham about the success of the blockade. Despite the fact that the port was legally "open" and the rebels had agreed not to fire on the ships, they continued their attacks on the coast. The powers had advised their men-of-war not to protect merchantmen that passed through the line of fire so shipping was greatly reduced. The French minister estimated that shipping was at less than half the normal level because of the blockade. He calculated that the French had lost between September 6 and January 18 some 6.5 million francs because of the naval action.[98] Another report noted that coffee exports from Rio dropped 35 percent in the first twenty days of December.[99] The problem was that once da Gama joined the revolt, the Ilha de Cobras also went over to the rebels, permitting them to fire easily on the customs house on the Ilha Fiscal and the nearby wharves.[100]

The French and U.S. commanders continued to protect their ships, but the British admiral refused on the grounds that assistance was too dangerous. Dangerous it was. Several English sailors and marines were killed or wounded, though in some cases their demise came while they were busy aiding the rebels rather than helping British shippers. The commander of the U.S. fleet, Captain Picking, also ignored Minister Thompson's admonitions and the State Department's instructions to defend American ships; he too cited the danger.[101] Like the British commander, Picking was known to be friendly with de Mello.[102]

Secretary of the Navy Hilary Herbert refused to order Picking to exert the New Navy in a more aggressive defense of U.S. shipping. Herbert, who as a Confederate colonel during the Civil War may have felt more sympathy for the Brazilian rebels than did Gresham, was asserting a foreign policy somewhat independently of the State Department. Although Herbert believed that "a nation's navy is the right arm of its diplomacy," he also subscribed to the opinion of Assistant Secretary of the Navy William McAdoo: "The captain of a warship exercises kingly authority as compared with military command on land, subject only to the President of the United States, speaking through the Secretary of the Navy."[103] The State Department was not in the chain of command. Indeed the navy had a long history of considering their ships "floating embassies."[104] According to one study, Annapolis graduates "resented all civilian control."[105]

In Rio, Captain Picking fought Minister Thompson and Consul General Townes in the diplomatic traffic and in the press, each side accusing the other of ignorance and insubordination. The naval commander's position was strengthened by the fact that Minister Thompson chose to sit out much of the revolt in the mountain city of Petrôpolis, "quite out of range of Mello's longest-ranged gun." This left the captain, floating in the bay, as the principal person involved in negotiations and Washington's main source of information.[106] Picking decided that the powerful new American cruisers would not accompany U.S. freighters to the wharves under fire, although the fears of danger that purportedly paralyzed Picking and the British commander may have been groundless: little damage was done to the French men-of-war that escorted compatriot freighters to the wharves in the subsequent month. However little the insurgents damaged foreign freighters, the decisions of the British and American commanders certainly damaged trade.[107]

Even conceding the injury done to commerce, Mendonça had more compelling political arguments for why the United States should deny the rebels belligerency status. The Brazilian minister warned Gresham that if the United States recognized the rebels, he would be "falling into a trap artfully constructed by the British."[108] According to Mendonça, the British were playing a card game with marked cards in Guanabara Bay. The British knew in advance what actions the rebels would take and were assisting them in maintaining the blockade. The British hoped thereby to convince the United States to recognize the rebels. They sought American compliance because the Europeans had de facto acknowledged the special role of the United States in inter-American affairs and agreed they should not act without U.S. concurrence. Mendonça explained that the Europeans hoped to restore the monarchy by awarding the insurgents belligerent status.

Monarchists and Rebels

Mendonça's case was strengthened by Saldanha da Gama's manifesto issued December 9. The rebel leader pronounced against Floriano's militarism, "sectarianism," and "radicalism" and concluded that "Logic and the justice of the matter authorize me to seek by force of arms to return the government to the position it occupied on November 15, 1889, when in a moment of surprise and national stupefaction it was overcome by a military revolt of which the present government is only a continuation."[109] He called for a national plebiscite on the appropriate form of government for Brazil. This was the first time that any leader of either the naval revolt or the rebellion in Rio Grande do Sul had apparently openly endorsed restoration.

In fact, it is not clear that da Gama actually was proclaiming for the monarchy. He supposedly was protesting only the military origins of the Republic and argued in another manifesto, sent out under his name several days later, that he was calling for a plebiscite on the form the Republic should take (congressional or parliamentary), not on the possibility of a return to monarchy. Certainly some of his followers did not believe that da Gama was a monarchist,[110] but Florianista censorship and propaganda prevented wide distribution of da Gama's clarification and pounded away at the restorationist theme of the first manifesto. The rebels thus became associated with monarchy. Even de Mello's ingenious decision to decorate his vessels on November 15 in honor of the Republic did not stanch the hemorrhaging of support for the rebels caused by da Gama's manifesto.[111]

Da Gama's first manifesto allowed Mendonça to deliver his most telling argument to Gresham. Referring to the Cleveland administration's early refusal to recognize the republic that overthrew Hawaii's Queen Liliuokalani, the Brazilian minister asked rhetorically, "Do you not think that two attempts to restore monarchies are too many for one Democratic administration?" He suggested that the way to defeat the British plot was for the United States to break the blockade. The British would have no choice but to follow, since they would not "want to watch with arms crossed as only North American ships freely unload in Rio."[112]

The British in Guanabara

Whether the British actually were plotting Floriano's overthrow is controversial. Historian Joseph Smith maintains that they never had any interest in aiding the rebels, and Richard Graham concurs.[113] Yet the information that Gresham received from his minister in Rio convinced him that the British were indeed aiding the revolt. Three days before his conversation with Mendonça he received a telegram from Thompson advising him that the Brazilian minister of foreign affairs had shown him a confidential affidavit alleging that the British naval commandant had offered the rebels munitions. The secretary of state also received reports that the British were refusing the landing of munitions and other war materiel to the legal forces while denying protection to merchant ships.[114] Thompson also reported, "It is known that the English people here are in sympathy with the insurgents."[115] In February, Thompson wrote in exasperation, "Nowhere else has there ever occurred what is now taking place in the Harbor of Rio de Janeiro, where the Insurgent ships keep in daily communication with the ships of the foreign powers, and moreover, avail themselves of their presence in order to escape the hostility of the legal Government."[116]

There was other alleged evidence of British complicity. Mendonça reported receiving a petition from August Belmont, Jr., the London Rothschilds' U.S. representative, supporting the rebel cause. Other European bankers allegedly offered da Gama loans at usurious terms, though they were loath to make outright contributions. After the end of the revolt a Brazilian commission studied the question and concluded, "It has been clearly proven to us, and our judgement is that English subjects placed themselves since the beginning of the struggle on the side of Brazilians who, by law, were considered pirates."[117] They accused the British of fraternizing with the rebels, supplying them with munitions, staffing their hospital with two doctors, and aiding their retreat from Guanabara Bay. The committee concluded pointedly that the British furnished the insurgents with "gunners, engineers, and some supplies."[118] Mendonça presented the essence of this report to Gresham who concluded in a confidential letter that "While there may be inaccuracies in these statements . . . I think in the main they are correct."[119]

There is little doubt that some "British subjects," as the report put it, helped the insurgents. Certainly officers of the British navy sympathized with their counterparts in the Brazilian navy and many merchants objected to Floriano's ruthless tactics. The antipathy of the commercial community grew during the revolt as they became subject to searches, seizures, internal passports, and summary expulsions.[120] They were also angered by the losses caused by the drawn-out siege.[121] In England, newspapers revealed a preference for the insurgents.[122] But did the British government support the rebels and, if so, did it hope to restore the monarchy as Floriano maintained?

Smith makes a strong case that the British Foreign Office did in fact wish to remain aloof from the fight. It did not want to defy the United States in this area of modest importance to the United Kingdom.[123] The British were spread out all over the globe and faced serious problems in Africa where they almost came to war with the French in the Sudan and where the Boer War threatened.

The British minister in Rio, however, took a much stronger, partisan position than did diplomats in London. Minister Hugh Wyndham wired London recommending belligerency status late in January, and, indeed, the Foreign Office had a committee seriously considering the action.[124]

It is probably safe to conclude that the British Foreign Office, like the Rothschilds and other investors, simply wanted stability in Brazil.[125] They disdained the Republic because of its constant riots, revolts, and revolutions. However, there is little reason to believe that there was a strong sentiment in favor of reestablishing the monarchy for the sake of principle. The British had prospered under Brazil's Empire, but they had been even more successful in republican Argentina and the United States, while they had little success with Maximilian's monarchy in Mexico. Business was business, political systems were fairly irrelevant. Even Gresham did not think the British foreign office sought to restore the monarchy.[126]

Besides, there was little chance for monarchist restoration once Dom Pedro died in December 1891. His daughter was politically inept and "completely in the dark" as to da Gama's proclamation.[127] Her husband was unpopular. Equally important, the Brazilian royal family made few efforts to encourage the monarchists and apparently none to finance them. The secretary of the Brazilian legation in Paris, A. N. Feitosa, denied that the royal consort, the Conde d'Eu, was aiding de Mello because "all the Orleans dukes are skinflints."[128] The royal family's strongest statement came in November when the Conde d'Eu's political advisor claimed that while remaining aloof from politics, "should the Brazilian nation, however, at any time call upon the imperial family to resume the reins of government, I do not doubt that the Princess and her husband would do their duty."[129] Despite many rumors that Princess Isabel's sons were interested in restoring the crown, their only action was an ill-fated return that was aborted before the prince could step foot on Brazil. The monarchists in Brazil were simply too disorganized to "call on the imperial family to resume the reins of government." An elitist group with disdain for the masses, they were unable or unwilling to attract a popular following.[130] Thus they could not promise foreign investors and traders a government more stable than Floriano's.

In hindsight we can see British acquiesence to the American lead and their indifference to the restoration of monarchy in Brazil; at the time, however, Gresham was quite worried about the British rivalry. His wife remembered later that "The sympathy of the British shipping interests at Rio, the activity of monarchists in Lisbon, London, and Paris . . . made it a question of much concern to our government."[131]

Many Americans were angry with the British in the mid-1890's. Not only did the diplomatic controversies of the Bering Straits sealing rights and rights over a Nicaraguan canal arouse bitter feelings, but the severe depression the country had just entered was blamed by many on the English plutocrats who controlled the world's gold.[132] Gresham, who had almost been put up by the Populists as their 1892 presidential candidate but was also an advocate of the gold standard, was sensitive to the national temper and the domestic political implications of a foreign policy that could be characterized as pro-British.[133] Cleveland, too, was worried about his reputation as an Anglophile. A member of the British legation in Washington wrote in 1893, "Cleveland is bound to show that he was *not* elected by British gold by being as disagreeable to us as possible."[134] Thus both the president and his secretary of state were particularly susceptible to Mendonça's charge of British collusion with the naval rebels. Gresham decided after his conversation with Mendonça in late December to take the minister's advice and break the blockade.[135] He prevailed upon Cleveland, who in turn ordered Admiral Benham to steam the *San Francisco* to Rio and take over operations there.

The Publicity Campaign in the United States

Gresham was swayed by more than just the force of Mendonça's argument hammered home in daily meetings between the men, though the Brazilian minister, who was among Gresham's "special friends," made a powerful impression.[136] Since October a pro-Floriano propaganda campaign was being waged in the U.S. press. Its chief architect was Flint, working closely with Mendonça. He launched a three-pronged attack. First, American newspapers began printing many articles, some by Mendonça and Flint, hailing the strength of Floriano's forces and the weakness of the rebels. Second, frequent pieces appeared claiming that the rebels were monarchists and that monarchists in Europe, particularly the British, were supplying them with funds and arms. Third, and most spectacularly, Floriano contracted to outfit a fleet of seven cruisers, monitors, and torpedo boats in the United States, which he undertook with great fanfare and hyperbole. This bizarre, little-known episode in U.S. foreign relations will be detailed in the next chapter.

Although the press campaign fired American support for Floriano and influenced the Cleveland administration,[137] the precise reasons that the president, secretary of state, and secretary of the navy had a change of heart are open to debate. The Brazilian minister and foreign minister both believed that strategic concerns and the Great Power rivalry together with domestic political considerations within the United States most motivated the change. LaFeber, on the other hand, has argued that immediate economic considerations mobilized the secretary of state.[138] He notes that William Rockefeller, W. S. Crossman, and Isidor Straus, all influential businessmen, wrote to Gresham pleading for naval intervention.[139] In addition to transitory concerns over the difficulty of unloading ships, LaFeber suggests that some petitioners feared that the rebels would terminate the Blaine-Mendonça agreement.

What is striking about this list of petitioners, however, is that all but Rockefeller were importers, not exporters. They were not concerned with maintaining access to the Brazilian market through reciprocity. Straus, in fact, was an archfoe of the McKinley Tariff. Even Rockefeller, who was concerned about landing a $5,000 load of kerosene, had not benefited from reciprocity because kerosene was not covered by the trade agreement.[140] Moreover, Gresham's responses to these businessmen were not particularly solicitous. He explained that all necessary precautions had already been taken; only an attempt by the Europeans to reestablish the monarchy would occasion a change in U.S. policy.[141] This is unsurprising since Gresham, as well as Herbert, was hostile to men he perceived as plutocrats and to government protection of special interests.[142] Broader structural concerns, which did indeed turn on commercial expansion, motivated them. Gresham sought to expand American business interests generally, not protect special interests.

Herman Sielcken, a partner of the important coffee-importing house of W. S. Crossman and the man who would engineer Brazil's coffee valorization program twelve years later, presented what was becoming an increasingly common position and one that Gresham probably and Herbert certainly found more comfortable than protecting particular business interests. Sielcken observed that although the Pan American Conference and the reciprocity treaties were welcomed attempts at increasing trade to the south, so far only the South American countries had benefited from the pacts. A different course was necessary. Rather than looking at U.S. participation in the naval revolt in Rio as a necessary protection for the Blaine-Mendonça pact, he saw it as "an opportunity to the United States to stimulate its own commerce on the same lines adopted by the European powers." He wanted the American navy, not commercial agreements, to open Brazilian markets to U.S. goods. It was time, he continued, for "the United States to assume the direction of all salutary measures for the protection of property of its citizens and regulation of difficulties."[143] The navy was creating a diplomatic dynamic of its own.

The New Navy as Big Business

The U.S. Navy was becoming more than just a servant of foreign policy and overseas economic expansion; it was becoming a vested interest in the emerging industrial society. To reawaken political support for the continued expansion of the navy's fleet, which had slackened under the parsimonious Cleveland, the usefulness of the new ships had to be demonstrated. Brazil appeared, serendipitously, as a proving ground.

Congress had appropriated the then astounding amount of $244 million dollars for the New Navy between 1883 and 1893.[144] The new ships were just beginning to roll out of the shipyards, lifting the United States from the nineteenth largest navy in the world to the seventh. Important for national defense and foreign policy, these ships also represented big business. After the Civil War the arms industry had fallen into decline. Many famous American arms producers such as the Hotchkiss, Colt, and Gatling companies had had to move to Europe to find buyers, and others such as the Ericcson Company went into decline. Now Congress used the naval initiative to strengthen the domestic arms and steel industries. All the new ships were required by law to be built in the United States and, as much as possible, employ American plans and parts. The New Navy was the Star Wars initiative of the 1890's, spurring the imagination and greed of a wide array of industries and promising to bail out the troubled steel industry.[145] Harrison had already noted in his presidential message at the end of 1891 that "the officers of the Navy and the proprietors and engineers of our grand private shops have responded with wonderful intelligence and professional zeal to the confidence expressed by Congress in its liberal legislation."[146] It was not merely by chance that proprietors and engineers were mentioned together. Many Annapolis men left the service to go into industry.[147] As Benjamin Franklin Cooling notes, "a military-industrial complex [was] born."[148]

It is worth pointing out that this industry was not separate from American commercial interests. The U.S. delegates to the Pan American Conference, for instance, who were to be privileged beneficiaries of Harrison's commercial expansion initiatives, were also involved in the war industry. Carnegie's steel company was one of two major suppliers of steel plating, a Bliss company supplied torpedoes, and Flint was a partner in a torpedo company, a director of the American Ordnance Company which supplied steel projectiles, and a major exporter of Hotchkiss ordnance.[149]

The U.S. Navy Arrives in Guanabara Bay

Naval men around the world focused their attention on Guanabara Bay because the first major naval battle in 30 years seemed to be shaping up, the first ever using many of the new technologies embodied in the New Navy.[150] The success of the American fleet could accelerate the pace of naval building, which had stagnated since Cleveland took office.

Admiral Andrew Benham arrived aboard the *San Francisco* in early January.[151] He joined the *Charleston*, the *Detroit*, the *Newark*, and the *New York*—five-sixths of the entire U.S. South Atlantic squadron. The recently swollen size of the U.S. squadron was indicative of the importance laid on the Brazilian revolt. The navy was probably less preoccupied with Brazilian friendship than with the potential challenge to the Monroe Doctrine that the presence of the European fleet in Guanabara Bay embodied. This was the first time that the United States had a navy sufficiently powerful to rise to such a challenge. As Hammett points out, "hardly a month went by during Herbert's term when an American warship was not anchored off at least one of the 'banana republics' to protect American interests during revolutionary upheavals."[152]

This was something different, however. Brazil was not, as Sielcken had explained, a banana republic. The U.S. squadron was not only by far the largest fleet in Guanabara Bay, it was, according to Assistant Secretary of the Navy McAdoo, "the most powerful fleet which ever represented our flag abroad."[153] The *New York*, later renamed the *Saratoga*, was one of the newest, largest ships in the New Navy with six eight-inch guns, 8,000-ton displacement, and a top speed of 21 knots. It became the flagship for Admiral Sampson during the Spanish-American War. The *San Francisco* and *Newark* were 4,000-ton protected cruisers with twelve six-inch rifles, ten rapid-fire guns, and three Hotchkiss cannons; the *Charleston* was a 4,000-ton protected cruiser with two eight-inch guns, two six-inch rifles, and eighteen secondary pieces, while the *Detroit* was a 2,000-ton cruiser with ten five-inch rifles and ten secondary pieces.[154] The Portuguese commander, Augusto Castilho, noted with envy that they were "five of the largest, most modern and most powerful cruisers" then afloat. He also observed that they "were interested in affirming their decisive action in favor of the government of the Marshal [Floriano]."[155] Benham's ships enjoyed far greater firepower and maneuverability than the rebels and than any single squadron of the other foreign powers. The American admiral also commanded more sailors than the rebels had troops in Rio. (At the time there were only five rebel ships of any size and eleven British, Italian, German, Portuguese, French, and Austrio-Hungarian men-of-war in the bay. This order of battle demonstrated how internationally important the rebellion had become.)

Commanding such firepower encouraged Benham to follow an aggressive policy. The American admiral was not eager to float on the sidelines with more than one-third of the total tonnage of the U.S. Navy under his command in Guanabara Bay and the other powers willing to follow his lead. The fact that Cleveland and Herbert had committed such an arsenal to Brazil also belied their claims of moderation and neutrality.[156]

Almost immediately on arriving at Rio, Benham began forging his own foreign policy. Not at all a creation of the New Navy—Benham had begun his naval service with sailing ships thirteen years before the outbreak of the Civil War—the rear admiral was quick to adapt old navy techniques to the navy's new diplomatic mission once presented with sufficient firepower and opportunity. He probably did not worry about the somewhat ironic position he found himself in as a blockade breaker—ironic because Benham had first made his name during the Civil War by imposing a blockade on the western Gulf of Mexico.[157] Now he was given general orders to use his "wise discretion" to protect American shipping.[158] Without contradicting his orders from Herbert and Gresham, Benham seems to have used substantial personal discretion as he assumed command of the foreign fleets in the bay and attempted to negotiate a settlement.[159] He came to assert American predominance and the Monroe Doctrine.

His new duty contrasted poignantly with the charge he had recently fulfilled escorting across the Atlantic reproductions of the *Nina*, the *Pinta*, and the *Santa Maria*. Their voyage commemorated the four-hundredth anniversary of Columbus's "discovery" of the New World in a celebration of the European contribution to the Americas.[160] Now he would escort North American ships to Rio's wharves under the protection of his readied guns in a much shorter, but no less significant voyage that undertook to control the European force in American waters. The reciprocity treaties had been the forerunners of dollar diplomacy. Now Benham signaled the course for gunboat diplomacy. Although the U.S. Navy had actively protected commerce in the early days of the republic, this function had diminished by the 1890's.[161] The experience in Rio would reawaken it.

Benham's use of force in breaking the rebel blockade has been well studied and will be examined later.[162] What is less known is the admiral's attempts at diplomacy prior to his confrontation with rebel ships. Rather than simply concern himself with the protection of foreign property and lives, Benham set out to negotiate an end to the revolt. He wrote Herbert: "I have spoken to a friend of the Brazilian President and to Da Gama and informed them I would be glad to do anything to restore peace, but cannot do anything officially without special authority from my government."[163] In his capacity as an ostensibly private individual, the admiral attempted to serve as a go-between to da Gama, de Mello, and Floriano. The extent of his success is unclear. Da Gama and de Mello thought him partial to the legal government but were willing to talk.[164] Floriano believed that the United States joined other Latin American nations "united in an American policy of neutrality and nonintercourse with the insurgents," while the European favored the rebels.[165] Benham passed notes between the parties. (Perhaps reflecting his ties to international financiers, da Gama's representative to Benham was the "exceedingly mysterious" G. M. Rollins, a Wall Street banker.)[166]

Benham's efforts to settle the conflict seem to have been important in changing the political direction of Brazil. When da Gama demanded as a condition of surrender that Floriano step down and a civilian president be freely elected before he quit the rebellion, Benham, apparently possessing privileged information, responded that Floriano would announce the next day that his successor would be a civilian.[167] According to Mendonça and several newspaper accounts, Floriano then in fact did offer to resign the presidency, restricting himself to the military prosecution of the war as head of the army. This was reportedly turned down by the civilian who would have assumed the office, the Paulista Prudente de Morais, because he would have only served until Floriano's term ended in November and then have been ineligible for the next term.[168] Instead, a decision was made to hold presidential elections on March 1, despite the fact that a war was still raging. The state of siege was ended on February 25 to allow four days for campaigning. More time was not necessary, since Prudente's election was assured, though two other candidates had the temerity to run.

This momentous decision brought Brazil's first elected civilian president to office. It was one of the first times (if not the first) in Latin American history that a general-president called civilian elections and then voluntarily stepped down. Yet surprisingly, it has been very little studied. The election was particularly noteworthy because Floriano had gained office through an armed coup and had exercised office under a state of siege for much of his term. The timing of the election has been attributed to the constitution, which called for the March 1 date. However, Floriano had already postponed the congressional elections three times because of the fighting, so he was under no obligation to respect the presidential deadline. One could assume that the revolt was sufficiently contained that free elections could now be held, except that in fact presidential elections were not held in the three southernmost states because of warfare. Moreover, if Floriano thought the revolt was almost extinguished, why, after suspending for only four days the state of siege that prevailed in Rio and São Paulo, did he not only reinstate it but impose the much more draconian martial law, now over the entire country, not just the theaters of combat? He also expanded the size of the army.[169]

Floriano was clearly acting under duress when he agreed to the election. He opposed the candidacy of Prudente and seems to have contemplated preventing the Paulista from taking office down to November 15 when Prudente assumed the presidency.[170] The election was held in states under Floriano's control, and returns came back in record time announcing the election of Prudente by one of the smallest electorates in Brazilian history. Washington had already received on March 4 the results of the presidential elections held on March 1, an impossibly fast result for a country with poor transport and communications. Washington, in fact, seems to have received the results before most of Brazil. They were only published four days later in São Paulo.[171] Da Gama then (in reciprocation?) sought to take his fleet out of Rio Bay. He failed to do so only because the rebel battleship *Aquibadan* did not aid him in getting past the government's forts at the mouth of the bay.[172]

The evidence that Benham negotiated the election of Brazil's first civilian president and da Gama's aborted departure from Guanabara is circumstantial. None of the participants made that claim. Given the amour propre of the participants, however, it stands to reason that Floriano would not admit to calling elections under duress or da Gama the need for American intercession. Benham's correspondence with Secretary of the Navy Herbert is opaque on the issue because during the days that these negotiations would have been taking place, all of Benham's messages to Washington are in code. This is the only moment in the correspondence that is entirely in code and no translations accompany it. This is certainly not conclusive proof. Since neither I nor the reference researchers at the National Archives were able to break the code, the correspondence will remain for the moment unintelligible. But removing the translations at precisely this point in the archive is suspicious. It is extremely rare for such exchanges to be so secretive.[173]

Even if we assume Benham did force Floriano into holding the presidential elections, the American admiral could not alone convince the Brazilian marshal. No doubt the additional threat of European recognition of the rebels' belligerency status and the pressure of his Paulista allies to return to civilian rule weighed in the decision.[174] On February 5 da Gama announced he would begin to blockade Rio two days later.[175] On February 7, the European diplomatic corps in Rio counseled their governments to recognize the rebels. This was only headed off when the United States responded that Washington not only refused to recognize the belligerents but would destroy the blockading ships, and it implicitly threatened the European gunboats if they came to the insurgents' aid.[176]

It is doubtful that the timing of the American response and Floriano's decision to hold elections were coincidental. The Americans seem to have been involved in the decision to call the election. The election decree was issued on the same day of the American response to the insurgents, February 7, and one day after a meeting between Floriano and Minister Thompson. (Floriano had been refusing to meet with Thompson for five months.)[177] There is no evidence that other Brazilians were aware that the decision was imminent, but some Americans knew of the date of the presidential elections before most Brazilians because the president held an interview with the *New York World* announcing the decision.[178] The reporter noted that Floriano authorized elections in order to "remove all cause for continuing the war."[179] Da Gama had agreed to end the blockade if Prudente were made president, the exact conditions Benham had secured. On February 9, the Iron Marshal entertained Minister Thompson and Admiral Benham at the presidential mansion. As the U.S. representatives made their way from the American consulate to the mansion, escorted by a company of lancers ("an unprecedented act of courtesy and compliment" according to the *World*), crowds along the way gave them ovations.[180] Thompson made clear his view of the events in a letter to Benham on February 9:

> Politically it has been apparent for some time that it would be necessary for Uncle Sam to call the bluff of Mr. Bull and I expected it would be done on the Venezuela trick. I agree with you [Benham] that it was time to take a stand on the Monroe Doctrine and let the European nations generally know that we would maintain it even at the deplorable cost of war. Without the issue that has been made encroachment would have continued until it was demonstrated, as has been so often proclaimed, that there was nothing in the doctrine. Now I imagine that all Europe will recognize that it is not a dead

issue and that we are able to stand on our own now and fight the world if necessary in support of the principle.[181]

Benham's powerful squadron had been placed in Rio not only to protect American commerce from the insurgents but to impose the will of the United States on the other Great Powers.

June Hahner has argued that Paulista troops defending that state's southern border from Federalist soldiers, not American gunboats, convinced Floriano to acquiesce to the election by threatening to withhold their support if Prudente were not elected. It is revealing, however, that rebel accounts of General Saraiva's actions on the Paulista border do not discuss any concern with Paulista troops. The Federalists were more concerned with the American presence.[182] In fact, the Paulistas did not have a strong force to throw against the rebels at that point. At the end of January Florianista forces in Paraná had been routed with thousands of people fleeing to São Paulo. With popular revolts breaking out in Paraná, the newly ascendant Paulista republicans must have feared losing their grip on the state. After all, São Paulo had suffered "perturbations" the year before to the extent that martial law had been declared. Floriano continued to include the state in his martial law decrees because he believed it unstable.[183] The last government holdout, Lapa, was about to fall, freeing the insurgents to march north.

Yet the Paulistas had not yet organized much of a resistance. Governor Bernardino de Campos wrote to Floriano on February 3: "The resources that have arrived are incomplete and insufficient to impede the sacrifice of the existing small garrisons if they are not quickly reinforced with battle ready troops."[184] Three days later, on the day that Floriano announced the presidential elections, Campos was still pleading for arms from the minister of war, for otherwise he would "have people for the fight without being able to use them."[185] At the end of February Campos Sales was still worried about the arrival of reinforcements and arms and a possible Federalist victory.[186]

Although it is certainly true that Paulistas were grouping on their border to resist the rebels, many of their men were unarmed and untrained. The U.S. consul in Santos, Henry C. Smith, reported at the end of February that "over two-thirds of the 'new made army' here so far as I have been able to learn, are against the government in sentiment, as well, also, as are the people of Santos."[187] Indeed, Smith reported a plot to take over the fort protecting Santos for the rebels that involved the president of the city's municipal council. The Paulistas were begging for federal aid to defend themselves rather than threatening to withhold their aid from Floriano if he did not accede to their demands for a civilian president. They also depended on the U.S. Navy and the mercenary fleet that Flint had assembled to prevent the rebels from landing on the Paulista coast.[188]

Certainly Benham had given the rebels reason to fear American action. When, upon arrival, the rear admiral proclaimed his intention to escort American ships to the docks, he was at first left alone. Recognizing that

Benham's unilateral action was destroying the blockade, da Gama warned that his ships would fire upon any ships approaching the wharves and did in fact fire upon several merchantmen. The rebels apparently found a solution to the impasse by offering the free use of tugs to unload the American merchant barks if they refrained from landing at the wharf. But Benham was in no mood for compromises. He informed the captains of the U.S. freighters that although they "had changed their minds, the Commander in Chief of the US Naval Force had not changed his intentions, and the *Detroit* was in there to see that no American merchant vessel was prevented from going to the wharf."[189]

When Benham disregarded the rebel warning on January 28, 1894, by escorting two American ships to the docks, one of da Gama's ships (the *Trajano*) fired a blank shell across the bow of a U.S. merchant ship. The *Detroit* responded with a live shell within six feet of the stem of the rebel ship and the warning "I will sink you" if the rebels returned fire. Another insurgent ship, the *Guanabara*, then fired at the merchant ship and received in return a musket shot in its rudder. The only casualty was the *Detroit*'s assistant paymaster who shot himself in the leg. (To increase the importance of the American role, the Florianista newspaper *O Tempo* reported that the *Detroit* had actually fired eleven shots and hit the *Trajano* with seven of them.)[190] Da Gama not only withdrew, but according to several reports, including that of the *Detroit*'s captain, he wanted to offer Benham his sword until junior officers convinced him to continue the fight. Benham (perhaps hoping to defend da Gama's honor) denied this.[191] It seems likely that in fact da Gama had offered to quit but Benham was reluctant to accept such a dramatic act given the opposition of the European commanders and Cleveland's desire to appear neutral.

Studies of this incident have taken the *Detroit*'s single shot as the cause of da Gama's withdrawal. This makes the incident seem much more trivial, even opéra bouffe, than it actually was. The accounts ignore the fact that Benham had his other four cruisers lined up broadside to the rest of Gama's fleet and sent the crews to battle stations. The 8,000-ton *New York*, the newest, largest, and most powerful ship in the New Navy, trained its guns on the jewel of the Brazilian navy, the 5,000-ton battleship *Aquibadan*. An armed response to the *Detroit* probably would have led to the sinking of the entire rebel fleet.[192] The rebel ship had no choice but to withdraw from the confrontation. The New Navy had proven sufficiently menacing to carry the day and end the blockade without demonstrating the thunder of its guns. Although naval observers were disappointed that the New Navy's weapons were not tested against Brazilian steel and bone—and the historic importance given to the incident was much diminished by the absence of bloodshed—Benham had made his point. The Europeans tacitly acknowledged American supremacy in Brazilian matters. U.S. cruisers began aiding ships flying the flags of many nations in part because the British persisted in refusing to escort their countrymen to the docks.[193]

Benham's aggressive defense of American commerce was joyously celebrated in the U.S. press by Democratic and Republican papers alike; the rear
admiral was lionized. The *New York Times* congratulated the "plucky"
admiral who "restored our prestige in the eyes of foreign nations and effectively interrupted the harassing interference with our merchant ships."[194]
The *Boston Advertiser* believed that Benham had "acted with consummate
bravery, discretion and good sense," the *Omaha Bee* agreed that the admiral
was the "type of naval commander of which all Americans may feel proud,"
and the *Cincinnati Enquirer* toasted "all honor to the President and the
Secretary of the Navy and to Rear Admiral Benham, of the Navy, for this
assertion of American rights." The *New York Journal of Commerce* put the
incident in its broader context:

> Several newspapers in this country are anxious to have the Navy abolished
> and habitually represent our naval officers as swashbucklers, who sail from
> port to port trying to involve us in hostilities with foreign powers. There
> are, happily, very few Americans who are not glad that we had a Navy, and
> that a sufficient portion of it, under an efficient commander, was in the port
> of Rio when Da Gama fired on an American merchantman.[195]

No complaints of American imperialism were heard in the United States.
Benham's family, then in Paris, was feted and toasted by the émigré community in France. The European press, however, was much less pleased by this
assertion of American independence.[196]

The U.S. fleet's blow against the revolt has been viewed as a key incident in transforming the United States into an imperialist power. William
Appleman Williams views it as one of nine crucial events that "consolidated the expansionist outlook" of the United States in the years between
1892 and 1895, and LaFeber sees it as setting an important precedent.[197] Put
in different terms, John W. Foster, former secretary of state, saw the U.S.
role in the naval revolt as one of the most important "assertions of the
Monroe Doctrine" of the nineteenth century.[198]

Cleveland and Gresham maintained to the end that they were acting
neutrally. This was more rhetoric for domestic consumption, however, not
reality. When U.S. Consul in Santos Henry C. Smith announced that the
key port of Santos had been spared a rebel invasion because of the aggressive
action of the USS *Detroit* and the threat of Flint's Fleet, Consul General
Thomas Thompson admonished him that he should not make such public
statements because the official U.S. position was neutrality. Thompson did
not argue with the facts, just the label.[199] Cleveland played the same game.
He sent in many of the largest, newest ships of the New Navy and for six
months prevented the European powers from recognizing the belligerency
status of the rebels all the while claiming to be neutral. The U.S. Navy
knew better.

Benham's actions in Guanabara Bay were an important first step in
asserting American supremacy over the British in Latin America. To be sure

there had been earlier attempts, but the efforts in Peru in 1878 and Chile in 1891 had failed. This time the British acquiesced to the will of the United States. After the admiral's success, he was sent directly to Nicaragua to challenge the British claim to the Mosquito Coast. The next year Cleveland asserted the right of the United States to interfere in British negotiations with Venezuela under the Olney Doctrine.[200]

The *Detroit*'s shot across the bow of the *Trajano* also won the New Navy new friends in the United States. Assistant Secretary of the Navy McAdoo pointed out that one of the lessons of the revolt was the inability of Brazilian forts to impede the movement of the insurgent warships. He counseled that the United States, which had traditionally depended upon forts and smaller ships for coastal defense, should use the navy, and implicitly large cruisers, as the first line of defense.[201] The stagnation in shipbuilding of the first years of the Cleveland administration ceased, and the threat to extinguish the Navy War College was averted.[202]

But for all of Benham's success in bequeathing an expansionist legacy, his squadron did not entirely solve the problem it was assigned. Most American studies of the naval revolt assume that Benham's bravado put an end to the Brazilian rebellion.[203] In fact, the heaviest fighting of the naval revolt came a week *after* Benham's action, and the civil war in the south continued on for more than a year. As noted, the British continued to consider the possibility of recognizing the insurgents after the incident.[204] This is not to say that the participation of the United States was unimportant in determining the outcome of the rebellion, but students of U.S.-Brazilian relations have missed what may have been the most significant, and surely the most bizarre chapter of the affair: Flint's Fleet.

CHAPTER 8

Flint's Fleet

The twelve-ship flotilla that Charles Flint assembled primarily in the United States to defend the government of Marshal Floriano has been swallowed up by history, leaving hardly a trace. During Brazil's civil war it was known as the "legal," "Florianista," or "Jeronymo's" squadron. Subsequently, detractors ridiculed it as an imaginary "cardboard squadron," while Flint boastfully christened it the "dynamite squadron."[1] Here it is called the more appropriate "Flint's Fleet."

Although modern historians give the fleet no credit for affecting the outcome of the civil war, for the six months between October 1893 and May 1894 Flint's Fleet became the last hope of Floriano, and the nightmare of the naval rebels.[2] It grabbed headlines in the United States and piqued European interest. The mercenary fleet illustrated how in the age of corporate liberalism private U.S. interests could conduct foreign policy with only the occasional assistance or acquiesence of the U.S. government.[3] This curious and quixotic episode also revealed the marriage of interest of the U.S. commercial, financial, military, industrial, and journalistic communities. Most important, however, Flint's Fleet may well have been the decisive factor in saving Floriano's government and cementing U.S.-Brazilian friendship.

When the navy revolted at the beginning of September, Floriano scrambled to concoct another fleet loyal to his government. His makeshift navy was supposed to assure the allegiance of the northern part of Brazil and break the blockade in Rio. When efforts to purchase ships from Argentina failed, he commissioned Mendonça to seek gunboats in the United States,

but Cleveland refused to sell him warships. The United States, just beginning to rebuild its long-neglected navy, had none to spare.[4]

Mendonça then faced an important decision. Should he follow the advice of Admiral J. Maurity? The naval officer, then posted as a Brazilian
representative at the Columbian Exposition in Chicago, suggested that instead of wasting money cobbling together an expensive and probably worth-
less squadron in the United States, Mendonça should just wait until Brazil's
two modern cruisers in construction in Toulon, France, were ready. Mendonça decided to ignore the admiral. Instead, he proceeded to outfit a squadron in the United States, in part because the ships in Toulon would take too
long to prepare and time was pressing.

However, the minister's argument is somewhat suspect. The two ships
in France were in fact repaired before Flint's Fleet was put into battle.[5]
Mendonça's true motivation in assembling an American squadron was
probably the diplomatic and publicity value of spending a great deal of
money (ultimately more than $1.5 million) for a dramatic gesture in the
United States. After Floriano approved Mendonça's plan, the minister further demonstrated his Yankeephilia by again ignoring the advice of Brazilian naval experts and, instead, organizing a technical advisory staff made
up exclusively of current or former members of the U.S. Navy.[6] These men
would prove invaluable in securing the assistance of influential members of
the Cleveland administration. Mendonça probably also refused to heed Admiral Maurity's advice because the admiral was a monarchist and a friend of
de Mello. Maurity had originally been slated to command Flint's Fleet, but
he and the entire Brazilian navy were marginalized from the squadron's
refitting and initial command. Instead, Charles Flint took over.[7] Flint's loyalty to the bottom line was more trustworthy than Maurity's fidelity to the
Republic.

Charles Flint, Brazilian Agent

That Floriano turned to the United States is testimony to the warm
diplomatic relations that drew the two countries together; military and
economic pragmatism would have dictated European ships. In the early
1890's U.S. naval architects had no experience in designing modern heavy
warships, nor did American manufacturers have practice in building them.[8]
Given the political nature of the decision, however, it made sense for Mendonça to call upon his friend and ally Flint for assistance.

Flint was a natural for the assignment. As the *Brooklyn Daily Eagle*
revealed, "How real and great a power he really is in all the South American
republics is a subject little known except in Washington and the capitals of
the countries situated around the equator."[9] Not only did he have a vested
interest in U.S.-Brazilian relations and commerce, but he had long experience in shipping and the arms trade. His father and uncle were two of the
largest shipbuilders in Maine and later in Brooklyn, and Charles himself

had chartered freighters for the Grace company, owned a shipping company, and was an important stockholder in the U.S. and Brazil Mail Steamship Company.[10]

He also stood out in the shadowy world of international arms and mercenaries. In 1869 Flint had helped Peru fit out two monitors and three transport ships. Then, when war broke out between Peru and Chile seven years later, he sent torpedoes to Peru. This was more than a simple business transaction; Peru served as a testing ground for the Lay Torpedo Company, which the trader partly owned.[11] As he later recalled, "We tried out a lot of new ideas in that war."[12] Flint also provided state-of-the-art underwater dynamite torpedoes that could be fired from merchant ships, an experience that would serve him well more than two decades later when he converted freighters into gunboats for Brazil. In the meantime, he sent munitions to Brazil in the 1880's and, in 1891, secured arms for Chile when its president unsuccessfully struggled to put down a naval revolt.[13]

More important, Flint had considerable standing in the United States. His influence at the Pan American Congress and behind the campaign for reciprocity have already been discussed. The merchant also demonstrated his pull with the State Department in 1891. He had tipped off Blaine that his former partners, the Graces, were supplying arms to the Chilean rebels aboard the ship *Itata* and convinced the secretary of state to send a navy cruiser to seize the cargo. In the meantime, Flint himself armed Chile's legal government.[14] (Ironically, the *Los Angeles Times* would later refer to Flint's Fleet as "Another Itata" not realizing that Flint had helped intercept the original *Itata*.)[15]

Flint had his own publicity organ. His close ties to the New York press and to the Pan American Union's publicity director, William Curtis, have already been mentioned.[16] In 1893 he took control more directly of an important news vehicle when he led a syndicate that bought the ailing *New York Times*. Flint made it clear that this was only secondly a business venture. He wanted the paper in order to bend it to pet causes such as the gold standard and Floriano's regime. Typical of Flint's behind-the-scenes maneuvering, he hid his reorganization of the *Times* from the public to the extent that the newspaper's own seventy-fifth anniversary edition neglected to mention him by name. However, Iphigine Ochs Sulzberger, daughter of Adolf S. Ochs and wife of Arthur Hayes Sulzberger who together ran the paper between 1896 and 1935, remembered years later, "My one childhood recollection was overhearing some talk about an 'angel' named Charles Flint." She was later disappointed to find him "just a short man with a pointed beard and no wings at all."[17]

Although, sadly, he had no wings, the New York trader enjoyed powerful international political connections that helped him get this undertaking off the ground. Flint's ties to Latin America began in his early years as a partner in the New York–Peruvian trading company of W. R. Grace and perhaps reached back to his own family's involvement in the Caribbean shipping trade. He had been consul for Costa Rica and Nicaragua, served as an agent for the Peruvian government, and was named consul general for Chile to the United States under President Balmaceda in 1891. His brother Wallace was consul for Uruguay.[18]

In addition to being a politically well-connected arms dealer with sympathies for Brazil's Republic, Flint was an important financier with close ties to high finance. He was a business associate of Jacob Schiff, August Belmont, and J. P. Morgan and had often gone hunting in Maine with one of the principals of the British financial house of Baring, the U.S. Navy's overseas financial agent for materiel purchases.[19]

Flint took advantage of these ties to finance the Brazilian fleet. Because he could not easily procure American credit in those days of deep depression, he had to seek a loan in Europe. The Barings were still reeling from their Argentine misadventures, so Flint, with the mediation of August Belmont, turned to another British financial empire to fund the dynamite squadron—the Rothschilds.[20] This was rather a natural source since N. M. Rothschilds had been the Brazilian government's sole financial agent for more than 40 years. It is only surprising in light of Brazilian republicans' suspicions that the Rothschilds were actively working to overthrow the Republic and Mendonça's allegation that Belmont had presented him a petition from financiers favoring the restoration of the monarchy.[21] Of course, this was not necessarily a contradiction. If the London bankers were in fact aiding the rebels, it would not have been the first time that a company sought to profit from both sides of a conflict.

The Rothschilds not only served as a plentiful source of credit, but they also helped Flint extend his private diplomatic network. When Mendonça wanted to know the British government's candid opinion of the naval rebellion, he queried Flint who asked Belmont who in turn questioned the Rothschilds who sounded out the British government.[22] Mendonça apparently thought that this was a more reliable channel for information than going directly to the British ambassador in Washington.

Flint Assembles a Fleet

Unable to purchase warships from governments, and with too little time to construct new ones, Flint sought out Collis P. Huntington, who owned a large merchant fleet. According to Flint, he outsmarted the unknowing Huntington. According to his account, Flint realized that the price would go up if Huntington discovered the real purpose of the ship; therefore Flint implied he was intending to employ it in commerce. Flint told a reporter years later that he and Huntington laughed about the incident afterwards; the shipping tycoon told Flint "he would have held [Flint] up right there if he had known that he was fitting out a revolution."[23] Flint then, according to his memoirs, purchased the 400-foot-long 4,600-ton passenger liner El Cid for U.S.$600,000. (In fact, the contract shows that the price was

$475,000 with an extra $25,000 commission for Flint.) Although the price was attacked as excessive in the press, it was essentially the price Huntington had paid for the freighter, which had only been christened two months before.[24]

It is possible, but unlikely, that this sale was a straightforward business deal as Flint claims in his memoirs. There are reasons to believe that Huntington gladly sold Flint his newest, fastest steamliner at cost because he hoped to win favor with Floriano's government to benefit two of the tycoon's companies. Flint and Huntington were not the distant business acquaintances he implied. Both had been involved in the U.S. and Brazil Mail Steamship Company, of which Huntington was vice president, and the two men apparently had other dealings.[25] The steamship company, which had a major subsidy from the Brazilian government, went into receivership in March 1893 after the failure of its president's attempt to obtain a lucrative concession in Brazil.[26] There was still hope of resurrecting the company.

The shipping magnate was not the only connection between Flint's Fleet and the USBMSCo. Its president, William Ivins, had been a boyhood friend of Flint's, a partner with him in the Grace Company, and a stockholder in Flint's commercial company. He was in charge of the propaganda campaign for the mercenary fleet.[27] G. A. Burt, an important official of the shipping firm, served as Flint's recruiter and sailed to Brazil as his troubleshooter.[28] The captain of the converted *El Cid*, H. Baker, had skippered ships for the steamship company.[29] Other USBMSCo. employees served as navigators, accountants and surgeon for Flint's Fleet.[30] The dynamite fleet was converted to war use at the Morgan shipyard, which had belonged to the founder of the steamship line, John Roach. Ingratiating themselves with Floriano's regime should have appealed to Huntington and employees of the shipping company who stood to gain from the marshal's reciprocal gratitude.

Moreover, Flint and Huntington had another common interest in Brazil. At almost the same time that he was purchasing the ship from Huntington, Flint was proposing that the two men join with several other "leading express-men of this city" to extend "the express business of the United States into South and Central America." Flint reassured Huntington that "with certain governments I think I could exert considerable influence in securing desirable concessions."[31] These business dealings may have cautioned Flint to announce publicly Huntington's ignorance of the mercenary purposes to which he intended to convert the *El Cid*.

If the negotiations for the purchase of the *El Cid* were in fact circumspect, the rest of the fleet was brought together with great fanfare. Flint intentionally made purchases and overtures that would spark the public imagination. Not only Flint's *New York Times*, but newspapers all over the country breathlessly rumor-mongered that Flint would purchase some of the biggest, fastest, most advanced, and most luxurious ships in the United States. Flint made it his "custom" to feed this speculative frenzy by refusing "to deny or confirm any of these reports."[32] The *Times* boasted that "in the opinion of many naval officers in New York" the *El Cid*, after being fitted out for war, "will be the superior to any vessel in the United States Navy of her tonnage class."[33] The paper also boasted that not only was the *El Cid* "the fastest American-built merchant steamer afloat," but she was "also the fastest vessel of her class in the world" capable of nineteen knots. No ships of the New Navy could match its speed.[34] The *New York Herald* chimed in that once armed, the converted freighter would have "a battery that may make her a match for the whole naval force commanded by the Brazilian insurgent, Admiral Mello," an evaluation carried by the *San Francisco Chronicle* as well.[35] The second cruiser Flint purchased, the 275-foot, 2,600-ton, three-year-old *Britannia*, was, according to the *New York Herald*, the fastest, largest, and most luxurious ship ever built in Norway: "There are few more elegantly fitted up passenger ships afloat." Flint paid $225,000 for this floating hotel that he converted into a cruiser.[36]

The *Destroyer* had a more appropriately fierce appellation. This 130-foot warship was built by the same Ericcson company that had built the *Monitor* of Civil War fame and another monitor that Flint had sent to Peru two decades earlier. Based on the same principle, the *Destroyer* had a single revolving cannon in its turret and could almost fully submerge to fire its experimental underwater torpedoes. Built originally for the U.S. Navy, the torpedo ship cost Brazil $30,000.[37] The *Feiseen*, a new seventeen-ton wooden yacht that would be converted into a torpedo boat, had set a speed record of 27 knots and supposedly cost $30,000. Flint added a new 60-ton Yarrow torpedo boat and the 30-ton yacht *Javelin*, which had been his own personal pleasure craft, and purchased five new torpedo boats from the German Schichau company.[38]

Flint maximized press coverage while mounting his fleet by making overtures to many other steamship companies and private individuals. Flint took out options on five other ships (that formerly had belonged to the U.S. and Brazil Mail Steamship Company) now belonging to Huntington and Charles Pratt of Standard Oil.[39] Reports circulated that Flint was negotiating for the private yachts of James Stillman of National City Bank, Jay Gould of railroad fame, and J. P. Morgan.[40] None of these were bought. Instead, Flint used the opportunity to sell his personal yacht, the *Javelin*, to Brazil. This was the same boat he had used to escort Admiral da Gama up the Hudson to West Point in 1889. Flint replaced it with another, faster vessel, the *Nada*, which he originally purchased for Brazil.[41]

The mercenary squadron also won public attention by arming its ships with some of the most sophisticated and, in some cases, experimental weapons in existence. Flint went to the length of taking the long train ride to Chicago to buy a dozen Hotchkiss rapid-fire guns off the showroom floor of the Columbian Exposition where the latest military technology was on display. He also purchased Howell torpedoes, and an invention of Thomas Edison, the Sims-Edison submarine electrical fish torpedo, as well as a submarine gun. None of these had ever been tested in actual warfare.[42]

The most spectacular acquisition was the pneumatic gun, known as the dynamite gun. The dynamite gun fired dynamite projectiles as large as 980 pounds; with smaller shells, it had a three-mile range. Developed by a naval gunner, Captain E. L. Zalinski, the gun had been undergoing tests for years. Naval gun trials in the 1890's were similar to rocket launches in the 1960's; they attracted large crowds and much press attention. Americans knew about the amazing new gun, and it also aroused international interest. The German, Italian, Russian, Spanish, and French governments considered purchasing pneumatic guns. The U.S. Navy had built one experimental ship, the *Vesuvius*, to carry dynamite guns and had ordered twelve guns for coastal defense. So far, trials had proven inconclusive aboard ship; the gun was not consistently accurate. Further tests had been canceled by the navy because of budget constraints brought on by a swelling economic depression. Naval experts were anxious to test it in live combat and welcomed the opportunity to arm Flint's Fleet. The *New York Herald* reported that if the gun proved to be a success in actual battle it would have the effect of revolutionizing naval warfare and the construction of warships all over the world.[43] Or, as the more circumspect *Baltimore News* reflected, "The result will be highly interesting to persons at a safe distance."[44] Flint bought a dynamite gun and shells for about $90,000.[45]

Mendonça and Flint were attacked in the United States and Brazil for their extravagance, and they were accused of war profiteering.[46] This was apparently not the case, at least not for Flint, though his was certainly not charity work. On December 22, 1893, Flint wrote to Mendonça:

Now that the business of fitting out the vessels for Brazil has been concluded, so that which I can offer can have no bearing or influence in such transactions I have the pleasure in handing you an agreement with my firm to pay to such person as you may designate three quarters of all our profits in this business. Considering the urgency of the business and the special facilities experience and influence required and the necessity of my giving all my time for this work at the sacrifice of all my other interests I do not think anyone would consider our profits excessive. At all events, I can truly say that they are not as large proportionate to the effort as received by me in the two last pieces of work on which I concentrated my entire time and facilities, viz, the organization of the United States Rubber Company and the Mechanical Rubber Company. I make this explanation so that you may clearly understand that what profits I have secured I consider I have fairly earned and that in handing you the enclosed agreement after the business has been practically closed that I do so out of personal consideration and realizing that I have many money making opportunities while you have none owing to the necessity of your concentrating all your efforts on the work of the Legation.[47]

It is likely that Mendonça did in fact receive three-quarters of the profits. There is a contract to that effect in the Flint papers, but suspiciously, the name of the beneficiary has been torn out of the document.[48] The Brazilian consul general at New York, Fontoura Xavier, asserted that Mendonça bought a "palace" in Washington, D.C., with the profits from Flint's Fleet.[49] There were also reports that Mendonça was receiving bonuses from some merchants for purchasing arms from them.[50] If the total cost of fitting out Flint's Fleet was the alleged $1.5 million and the commissions were, as on the *El Cid*, 5 percent plus the apparent 20 percent markup, total profits could have been as much as $312,000, a very substantial sum given that Mendonça's annual salary as minister for Brazil was under $10,000. Profits might even have been higher if the reported 130 percent markup on the German torpedo ships was indicative of other transactions.[51] On the other hand, Mendonça denied receiving any income outside of his government salary. He attributed his fine art collection and summer house to personal savings from his salary.[52]

Whether profit was a strong motive or not, certainly the urge to maximize publicity drove many of the purchases. Said Flint, "It was important that the new fleet should have prestige. I hoped that it would have so much prestige that no one would want to fight it."[53] The fleet was purchased and converted for war between the end of October and early December, precisely the time that Gresham and Cleveland were having second thoughts about recognizing the naval rebels. The object of this fleet was as much to interest the American public in general and weapons manufacturers in particular in the fate of Floriano's government as to build a first-rate fighting force.

Flint established a literary bureau to publish propaganda favorable to the squadron. It was headed by the American William Ivins, a law partner of former Secretary of the Navy Benjamin Tracy and an important figure in New York politics, as well as head of the USBMSCo. Flint gloated years later, "As there was censorship of all cables, we controlled the news from Brazil and Ivins fed out the news in the proportion of about one inch of news for six inches of propaganda describing the dynamite squadron."[54] Mendonça at the same time published numerous articles in U.S. newspapers appealing to the adventurous and explaining the patriotic goals of defending the Monroe Doctrine involved.[55]

The conversion of the *El Cid* at the Morgan shipyard, where three shifts worked around the clock, attracted hundreds of onlookers. The circus atmosphere created such a crush that the police had to intervene. Journalists became so enamored of the project that Flint delightedly recalled a decade and a half later, "I could have manned the ships with newspaper men and put a literary battery behind the guns, so anxious were the knights of the press to accompany an expedition that so appealed to their sense of humor."[56] Reporters from the *New York Herald*, the *New York World*, and the Associated Press did in fact ship out with the fleet.[57]

Contracts were dangled before various U.S. companies to build a constituency. The *London Times* reported that "large orders for arms and ammunition for the contending forces in Brazil have been placed in the United States, giving work to various New England factories."[58] As mentioned, the

Hotchkiss, Pneumatic Gun, Sims-Edison, and Howell companies benefited. Dupont won a substantial contract for dynamite and guncotton and Winchester for ammunition. Mendonça had many other industrial suitors including a big western iron company.[59] The Morgan shipyard also profited. While these firms did not constitute the powerful military-industrial lobby that they became during World War I and afterwards, they did have the ear of influential men in Congress and in the navy.

In fact, impressing the U.S. Navy's high command with the seriousness of this expedition was probably one of Flint's primary goals. By rapidly converting merchantmen to gunboats and fitting out the ships with the most advanced experimental weapons, Flint was providing the U.S. Navy with combat trials. This was a time of great innovation in weaponry, but the United States lagged far behind the Europeans in experimentation. They generally waited for Europeans to conduct trials, and there had been no major naval engagements to battle-test equipment since Austria fought Italy and the U.S. Civil War almost 30 years earlier.[60] The mercenary squadron's impending engagement was anxiously awaited. The *Scientific American* observed that "the preparing, equipping and arming of this fleet has excited much interest, and especially among naval men."[61] The *New York Times* reported, "The State and Navy Department people have read with much interest the reports in the *New York Times* of the preparations being made by the Brazilian agents in New York for substantial warfare against the Mello Insurgents."[62]

Mendonça recognized the U.S. Navy's "scientific" interest in his enterprise from the outset. That is why he chose a technical staff composed of Commodore J. H. Gillis, Captain Charles H. Loring, the ex-chief of United States Naval Construction John C. Kafer, and the designer of the dynamite gun Captain E. L. Zalinski.[63] These men were able to convince the navy to allow Flint to purchase gunpowder, torpedoes, and even the dynamite gun, which all had been contracted originally by the navy. As Mendonça noted, military hardware "is not for sale like a commodity and ordinarily is only manufactured on the orders and at the expense of governments."[64] Only the "goodwill" of the U.S. government allowed Brazil to assemble Flint's Fleet quickly. Indeed, the navy's assistance went beyond redirecting war materiel to Flint. Secretary of the Navy Herbert also allowed Brazil to purchase the *Destroyer*, which had been commissioned by the navy and was undergoing final tests before being incorporated into the U.S. fleet.[65]

The United States went yet further in aiding Floriano's cause when it allowed Flint to recruit sailors for his squadron in New York. With grand promises of high pay (sailors received a $500 signing bonus plus $100 per month, while officers received $5,000 per three months), the arms merchant was able to attract over 1,000 eager applicants competing for the 400 positions.[66] It is no surprise that Flint's offer proved so seductive. The average *annual* income of a textile worker in 1890 was $332. His U.S. and Brazil steamship line had paid sailors only five dollars a month.[67] Flint attracted a capable crew. Nearly one-half of the *El Cid*'s crew and many of the men on other ships had reportedly served in the U.S. Navy. Indeed, the *New York Times* boasted that this Brazilian squadron had a greater percentage of Americans in its crew than any ship in the U.S. Navy since the Civil War. While it is clear that there were also many non-Americans on board, the claim is still possible since at the time more than one-third of the crews on U.S. naval vessels were foreigners.[68]

Some of the men in Flint's Fleet had high standing in the navy. The *El Cid*'s chief of gunners, E. C. Millen, had three times won the award as the best gunner in the North Atlantic Squadron. The *Destroyer* had a technical expert, Nils de Foch, friend and colleague of Ericcson, in charge of the submarine cannon.[69] To add luster to the expedition, the captains of the ships and many of the officers were Annapolis men. Some had inherited influence such as W. A. Russel, who was nephew to Rear Admiral Russel, and Lt. Craven, son of Admiral Craven. Others had personal influence such as the dynamite gun inventor Zalinski who, because of illness, could not sign on for the voyage to Brazil, but did accompany the *El Cid* for initial gunnery practice, supposedly at the exorbitant pay of $15,000 for one month's service. Others were famous for their bravery. Josh Slocum, an early-day, seafaring Charles Lindbergh who had already crossed the Atlantic single-handedly and would later be the first man to circumnavigate the world alone, was first officer and navigator of the *Destroyer*.[70] Flint also attempted to hire Commodore Gillis (only retired one year from naval service) to command the squadron, but the U.S. Navy prohibited this.[71]

The presence of fellow navy men on Flint's Fleet helped win over members of the U.S. Navy who to that point tended to be partial to the Brazilian naval rebels in their battle against the army. As the *New York Times* observed, "Their [the Annapolis men] performances at Rio will be closely watched by their friends in the United States Navy."[72] The *St. Louis Post-Dispatch* saw Flint's Fleet as a precursor of a sort of Latin American minor leagues where American sailors were battle-tested in the constant disputes that broke out there:

> The young American seamen who receive their baptism of fire in Brazilian waters may be useful in Uncle Sam's wars that are to come. The South American and Central American republics will perhaps be utilized more in future as training schools for our soldiers and sailors. As patrons of our ship dealers and arms and ammunition manufacturers, as well as tutors of our fighters, they may gradually become indispensable to us."[73]

The hiring of American sailors to serve on Brazilian warships was probably illegal and certainly, as Flint recognized, a breach of international custom. U.S. government officials, though very much aware of the recruiting, ignored its legal implications until two men brought suit against Flint and Mendonça in New York. They charged that the hirings were in violation of U.S. neutrality laws that forbade the recruitment of people for war against a country with which the United States was at peace.[74] Certainly such a construction of the law was reasonable. Given Cleveland's protests of neutrality and his reputation for seeking to avoid an aggressive foreign policy, one would have expected an American court to prevent Flint's undertaking. As we have seen, however, Cleveland was not in fact neutral. The New York district attorney ruled that there was no violation of law and refused to prosecute the case. (It probably did not hurt Flint's cause that his head of publicity, William Ivins, had recently been advocate general of New York state and was a partner in the law firm of Thomas Platt, one of the two most important politicians in New York.)

Turned down in New York, the two men appealed to Cleveland. His cabinet met and decided to take no action. They probably accepted Mendonça's argument that the men being hired were employees of Flint & Company whose only duty was to bring the ships to Brazil where they would turn them over to Brazilians.[75] The minister was not asked to explain why, if they were not expected to enter combat, over half the crew had man-of-war experience, why gunners were hired, and why Zalinski and Foch trained the crew in use of the dynamite gun and the underwater cannon. The cabinet secretaries were probably also unaware that Mendonça promised the crew of the *Destroyer* $60,000 if they destroyed a rebel cruiser.[76] They apparently also paid little attention to the newspapers where an Associated Press interview with the "well-known steamship engineer" James P. Satchell clearly reported, "When we enlist, we have to give up all allegiance to the United States and swear allegiance to Brazil. When we arrive at Brazil we are supposed to have an option whether or not we enter government service."[77]

Although Flint had averted a test in the courts, he remained curious about the strangers who had attempted to block his recruiting for the fleet. He hired Pinkerton detectives to follow them around and discovered them consorting with the Brazilian consul in Montreal, José Custodio de Alves Lima, who obviously was sympathetic to the rebels.[78] Flint then sent a Major W. J. C. Gadsby of the Canadian army to trace the activities of Lima and the two other men. Gadsby discovered that they had sought to charter vessels in Halifax, apparently to send a regiment to the rebels from Canada or the United States, and had sought to purchase arms. Gadsby was instructed by Flint to seek action from Canada's premier. The premier met with the major and assured him that neither of the men "nor any other parties could raise or equip men for Brazil in Canada" and instructed the deputy minister of marine to enforce this command.[79] The U.S. government followed a similar principle, preventing de Mello's agents from purchasing arms or recruiting in the United States. Indeed, according to Mendonça, the United States had secret police follow suspected agents of de Mello and report to the Brazilian minister.[80]

At the same time, Captain Julius Rhodes of Elmira, New York, claimed to have a commission from Floriano to recruit troops in the United States.

Adjutant General Ruggles did not find this a violation of neutrality laws, and, claimed Rhodes, Secretary Gresham approved the plan. Rhodes attracted some 800 troops from six East Coast cities (mostly unemployed men with no soldiering experience) with "flattering wages." Unfortunately, Rhodes's Sharpshooters were apparently a scam. Rhodes had taken advantage of the public interest in Flint's Fleet and the perception that the Brazilian government was flush with money to float this make-believe regiment. He convinced some of the recruits to advance him money for their uniforms. Mendonça exposed the plot, and the regiment disbanded.[81]

Flint's Fleet Departs for Brazil

Flint's Fleet was gathered, the ships converted, and the crews hired in record time. Two months after Flint began this adventure, the mercenary squadron was ready to leave New York. Now it was time to christen the ships. Years later Flint recalled the quixotic edge of this ceremony presided over by Brazil's minister, conducted by Mrs. Flint, and attended by hundreds of onlookers, "The only odd feature was that there was not a man aboard the ship who had ever seen the flag before, or who could speak the language of the country for which he was faring forth so gallantly to fight."[82] Indeed, later the new recruits offered much heartier cheers for the Stars and Stripes than for the Brazilian green and yellow, a fact that baffled neighboring ships unaware of the mercenary nature of the apparently Brazilian ship.[83] The dynamite crew steeled themselves with ditties that boasted of their bravery and confessed their ignorance:

> Mello Mello, where are you, old fellow?
> A Yankee ship and a Yankee crew is out to the sea to look for you.
> To knock you all to hell-o.
> We fly a flag of orange and green, Sir,
> the likes of which we've never seen, Sir.
> Our good ship's name, we cannot tell it.
> We haven't had time to learn to spell it.
> But what has a flag and a name to do
> With a Yankee ship and a Yankee crew that's out on the sea to look
>   for you
> To knock you all to hell-o.[84]

The crew stumbled over their ships' names because the originals were converted to more fitting Brazilian ones, mostly of indigenous origins (demonstrating Florianista lusophobia). The *Destroyer* became the *Piritinin*, the Yarrow boat became the *Moxoto*, the *Javelin* the *Poty*. More symbolically, the *Britannia* was changed first to the *America*, as the United States linguistically, at least, eclipsed the British. Once in Brazil it was changed again to the *Andrada*, presumably in honor of a hero of Brazilian independence. The *El Cid* was renamed the *Nictheroy*. The new name not only commemorated the capital city of Rio de Janeiro state, so badly battered by the naval rebels, it also recalled another mercenary fleet that had helped Brazil at a time of crisis.[85]

That other mercenary fleet had come to Brazil's aid shortly after it declared its independence in 1822. The Portuguese had sent a huge convoy of thirteen warships and about 70 transports and merchant ships carrying some 5,000 troops and vast stores of military materiel to the ex-colonial capital of Bahia to recapture the excolony. Before arriving, this impressive fleet received news that the English mercenary Lord Cochrane, who had already won impressive battles against the Spanish off the coast of Chile and Peru, was now commanding a Brazilian squadron that was sailing to engage it. The Portuguese fled for Lisbon rather than land their men. Cochrane's reputation inspired such fear that the Portuguese commanders did not pause to observe that the Englishman was chasing them with a motley squadron of just nine ships. During the crossing, three-quarters of the Portuguese fleet was sunk by the mercenaries, the last four ships being burned at the mouth of the river Tagus by a Brazilian ship commanded by another English captain, John Taylor. The name of his ship was the *Nictheroy*.[86]

Now Floriano was hoping that another mercenary fleet, formed by another mercenary who had helped wage naval warfare in Chile and Peru, could compensate for its small size and numbers by the reputation of its crew and its exotic weapons of destruction. To the marshal's mind, the naval rebels represented the Portuguese, trying to restore an exhausted political regime, while Flint was a latter-day Cochrane (the procurer of weapons becoming as important as the noble warrior). In the sequel to Cochrane's successful raid, the Americans replaced the British as the defenders of Brazilian sovereignty.[87]

Misadventures on the Road to Rio

Flint's Fleet had to traverse the South Atlantic and join the battle while rumors raged of de Mello's plots to intercept the fleet on the high seas. Fear of attack and sabotage shadowed the voyage south. There had already been numerous reports of rebel efforts to thwart the departure of the mercenary squadron.[88] A journalist on board reported that the "officers and men expected Mello at every moment. Every bay and inlet was watched with suspicion. Quarters were sounded every time a sail was sighted on the horizon."[89] To prevent disaster, the armed cruiser *New York* received secret orders to accompany the mercenaries on their trip.[90] Because the loyalty of Pernambuco was in doubt, the *Nictheroy* first landed in the northern state of Ceará before ascertaining the safety of Pernambuco.[91]

The assembling and staffing of the fleet had proved much easier and faster than would readying the men and bringing the ships into the theater of battle. Almost three months passed from that rousing day when Mendonça baptized the *Nictheroy* before the dynamite squadron faced da Gama's men across Guanabara Bay. What took so long?

The particulars are clear enough. Some of the fleet, the *Andrada* (ex-*Britannia*) and the *Piritinin* (ex-*Destroyer*), had mechanical trouble in the crossing. The *Andrada* had to put into port at Martinique for repairs, while the *Piritinin* limped into Pernambuco, Brazil, to be fixed. The ships also had discipline trouble with the crews. When the *Nictheroy* arrived in Recife, some 60 of its crew were in irons.[92] Crews of other ships proved even more truculent.

What caused the damages and disturbances? Mendonça claimed that rebels had placed agents among the mercenary crews. These agents had sabotaged the ships and aroused unrest among the men.[93] The crews' version was somewhat different. They blamed their revolt on overly harsh treatment by the officers and insufficient pay and the ships' mechanical failures on the rushed preparations to wartime use.[94] Predictably, the officers accused the crew of drunkenness and insubordination. Said Lt. Conway of the *Nictheroy*, "They [the crew] were more or less mutinous while on the ship, and since leaving it they have been almost continually drunk and disorderly."[95]

Who should be believed? None of the returning sailors or their officers spoke of rebel agents among the original crew. Neither did the reporters who accompanied the voyage nor the United States consul in Pernambuco who interviewed them.[96] The one piece of evidence that corroborates Mendonça's accusation of sabotage comes from a questionable source. A U.S. engineer who resided for a number of years in Brazil, Jeff Ross, claimed in a letter to a friend that he had served as a secret agent for both Floriano and the rebels. In that capacity he had both hired sailors and paid some to commit sabotage. His veracity is somewhat suspect, however, because he also asserted that he had assembled Flint's Fleet.[97]

The reporters and consul did agree both that treatment had been harsh and that a number of the sailors were trouble-making drunks. The amount of trouble varied by ship. Although the *Nictheroy* had an unusually large number of insubordinates, the men of the *America* were much worse. In a long, baleful letter Consul Burke bitterly protested that "A very large number of the crew since they landed here [January 1] have been drunk and disorderly on and about the streets disgracing themselves, fighting amongst themselves and a reproach and a shame and a scandal to our country and to American citizens residing here."[98]

Although the mercenaries had been contracted in the name of the Brazilian government, the responsibility for the men who refused to reenlist or who were rejected in Recife fell to Consul Burke (demonstrating again the role of the American government in this purported private, commercial transaction). He spent two full weeks tending to the men's complaints—when they were sober enough to be comprehensible—of uncomfortable quarters in the naval arsenal and of being robbed by Brazilian soldiers while thcy slept. Others he had to bail out of jail. Despite his disgust at the behavior of the mercenaries and his anger at having to look after the men who decided to return to the United States, Burke did not blame the men. Instead, he blamed Flint and Mendonça for giving them "cruel, almost inhuman" treatment and poorly organizing the enterprise.[99] The consul at Recife sent Mendonça a bill for the services he rendered the seamen and a plea to the assistant secretary of state, "I most sincerely hope no other expedition of a like character will be allowed to come to this country in such an irresponsible and badly conducted manner."[100] Consul Burke also reported that the *Destroyer* arrived in such bad condition that the Brazilian government refused to accept it without prior repairs. He did not blame saboteurs, however: "Evidently . . . the Brazilian government has not been treated with perfect fairness in the purchase of this steamship."[101]

It is certain that many of the mercenary crew became disillusioned with this adventure and declined to sign into the Brazilian navy to enter combat. This was true for about sixty of the *Nictheroy's* men. Some of the dissidents distrusted the ships; others despised the Annapolis officers. Yet others desisted because they refused to be subject to the Brazilian officers who boarded in Recife. The discharged crew members were given passage back to New York by the Brazilian government where some tried, unsuccessfully, to reclaim wages they believed Flint's office owed them.[102] Apparently the sailors' reputations were not entirely sullied, though their enthusiasm was. On the return trip to New York, an agent for de Mello attempted to hire the disaffected men to fight for the rebels. He failed.[103]

It is also clear that Floriano was unhappy with many of the New York recruits and refused their services. He took on none of the *America's* sailors and only one of the *Piritinin's*.[104] Brazil's president found himself in a difficult position, however. Nationalist resentment of foreign sailors encouraged him to seek Brazilians,[105] but distrust of his own navy left him with few alternatives. He reportedly could find no volunteers in Recife, so his recruiters were consigned to "forcibly enter houses and take them."[106] He resorted to army officers to complement the remaining Annapolis graduates and the few Brazilian naval officers willing to serve him. The crew that was shanghaied consisted of clerks, artisans, farmers, and longshoremen.[107]

Despite Floriano's dismay at the disorderliness of some of the recruits from New York, it should be noted that on the most important ship, the *Nictheroy*, 170 of the original crew, including all but one of the officers, signed on to the Brazilian navy. Captain Baker continued to command the ship.[108] The Americans were useful not only because they were difficult to replace with trustworthy Brazilians and because of the interest they engendered in the United States, but because they had been trained in the use of the dynamite gun. In particular, Captain Baker was retained because he was a close friend of Admiral da Gama who respected the ability of the *Nictheroy's* skipper.[109]

The *Nictheroy* arrived in Recife on December 14, but it had a long wait for the *America* to make port and for the *Piritinin* to be repaired. By the middle of January all of Flint's Fleet had gathered in Recife, Pernambuco. They were joined there by five German torpedo ships, with German captains and crew who were replaced by Brazilians. Naval experts were surprised that the small boats were able to cross the heavy Atlantic seas they encountered.[110] Floriano found no active admiral sufficiently trustworthy to direct this expedition. Instead, he had to turn to a 59-year-old retired Brazilian commandant, Jeronymo Gonçalves. Gonçalves, who had never commanded anything larger than a small river expedition, had been retired ten years earlier for insubordination and a slow promotion rate. (Jacobins claimed that he was retired for his republicanism.)[111] He now brought a ragtag squadron of seven small monitors, corvettes, torpedo boats, and gunboats together with three merchantmen, joined it to Flint's Fleet, and took over command of the entire, now legal, fleet.

Despite many false starts, the squadron remained in Recife until the middle of February. The apparent reluctance to join the battle in the south was in part explained by the fact that Recife was more than just a convenient rendezvous point. Flint's Fleet had been dispatched there in part to prevent rebels from taking the Northeast. Flint remembered later that "it was vital that the importance of the new navy should be known at once in the northern provinces of Brazil."[112]

This populous region had never embraced the Republic. Pernambuco's elite seemed to favor the naval rebels, while the masses remained apathetic. In early October 1893 three of the five daily newspapers in Recife supported the revolt. In the middle of November, a leading politician, José Mariano, issued a proclamation in favor of the rebels that was warmly greeted by a leading newspaper and university students. In response, Pernambuco became the only state in the Northeast to suffer martial law, the police broke up public demonstrations, newspapers were closed down, and many prominent citizens were arrested. By November 22, Consul Burke could report that "Restoration of monarchy is very strongly talked of privately among a very large class of Brazilians in this city."[113] Two weeks later, there were rumors of unrest in the countryside and reports that de Mello was headed to Recife. Burke wrote worriedly, "The feeling for restoration grows."[114] As the *Nictheroy* arrived in port fifteen Brazilian sailors revolted and were set before a firing line of marines. The marines revealed their sympathies by refusing to shoot the ten rebels who survived the first volley.[115] A rebel conspirator with dynamite presumably destined for the *Nictheroy* was discovered and executed in the middle of January as rumors of plots continued throughout the month, amplified by reports that de Mello was approaching aboard the mighty *Aquibadan*.[116]

Consul Burke had called repeatedly since November for a U.S. gunboat to visit Recife and protect the small contingent of Americans there. The *San Francisco* had made a call, but had left for Rio on January 3.[117] The *Nic-*

theroy's sojourn in Recife then filled the double strategic purpose of protecting Americans and defending against the rebels.

Flint's Fleet delayed its departure for more pragmatic reasons as well. Until the reenlisting Americans reached terms and the Brazilian government paid for the ships, they were not going south.[118] For the mercenaries war was a business; they would not fight unless paid first. This, together with enlisting or impressing Brazilians to replace the undesirable mercenaries, took more than a month. Although the *Nictheroy* had been accepted the day after it arrived in port, the *Piritinin* and the *America* had to be modified in Recife before the Brazilian government would accept them.

Even once the fleet was brought together, paid for, and staffed with relatively reliable crews, its departure was delayed. When the *Nictheroy* finally steamed south, it delivered some 300 cadets and troops to the beach outside Guanabara Bay on February 18 and returned for Pernambuco without firing its heralded dynamite gun.[119] Not until February 21 did the entire fleet reach Bahia, another center of monarchist sentiment. The apparent lethargy of Flint's Fleet was puzzling and frustrating to Floriano, whose regime hung in the balance.

Despite Flint's whimsical treatment of his fleet, it was not a comic or irrelevant sideshow in Brazil. The opinion of American historians notwithstanding, Admiral Benham had not broken the naval revolt with his gunboats at the end of January. He had only broken the blockade. The Federalists' overrunning of the southern state of Paraná at about the same time created "an indescribable panic" in Rio and frightened Paulistas who stood on Paraná's border.[120] Even da Gama believed that 5,000 Federalist troops were about to attack the São Paulo frontier. At the beginning of February, Colonel Jardim of the army wrote Floriano alarmed that if the legal squadron did not arrive soon, the Federalists would attack the government's weakly fortified positions by sea as well as land.[121] In mid-January a U.S. officer had inspected the insurgent *Tamandere* and found it "abundantly supplied with ammo" as well as with "plenty of food."[122] Five weeks later the *New York Times* reported that the naval rebels in Guanabara Bay had sufficient food and arms to last for months, while as late as February 19 the *Baltimore Herald* editorialized that "there is no longer any doubt that the cause of the Brazilian insurgents is strong and may ultimately triumph."[123] Members of Floriano's national guard were slowly changing sides, and important officers were plotting to join the insurgents.[124] The largest battle of the revolt took place on February 9 when 500 rebels landed in the city of Niterói that they controlled for a time. Although finally driven out, the insurgents demonstrated the threat they posed if they could be joined up with land troops.

It was in preventing the naval rebels and the Federalists from joining forces that Flint's Fleet, despite its mishaps and tardiness, played a crucial role. Already back in December, when de Mello had sailed for Desterro,

Santa Catarina, in order to bring back reinforcements for da Gama in Rio, he had returned empty-handed, because, he claimed, he feared encountering the *Nictheroy*.[125] When in January, de Mello heard of the troubles Admiral Jcronymo was having with Flint's Fleet in the Northeast, he sent the only two modern ships left to him, the *República* and the *Aquibadan*, north to intercept the legal forces.[126] The *República* reportedly lost its steering a few hours out of Rio Bay and had to retreat for the rebel-held port of Paranagua for repairs. The *Aquibadan*, hearing that Flint's Fleet was finally headed south (the destination was unclear), then also retreated to Paranagua, supposedly to protect the *República*.[127] By this act, de Mello, always jealous of da Gama's control of the situation in Rio, effectively abandoned the revolt in Guanabara Bay.

Although de Mello and other participants in the revolt such as Admiral Alexandrino Alencar argued that they had avoided clashing with the fleet out of strategic considerations, in fact, fear of the *Nictheroy*'s dynamite gun was probably their greatest concern. For all the deprecation of Flint's Fleet and its crew, the fact remained that the *Nictheroy* was almost as large as the *Aquibadan*, and, more important, it was faster. This was even truer now that the *Aquibadan* had been crippled, for the rebels had not held onto any major navy yards. Their fleet gradually deteriorated.[128]

The insurgents were well aware of the dynamite gun. Da Gama learned of the new weapon when he toured U.S. naval installations in 1889. He had predicted that the gun was "destined to revolutionize modern naval warfare" and had recommended that Brazil purchase two of them.[129] De Mello was apparently also in awe of the pneumatic cannon.

The "incomprehensible inaction" of the insurgent navy, which so troubled admirals da Gama, Villar, and many others, can be explained by fear.[130] De Mello did not attempt to intercept Flint's Fleet on the high seas, did not take advantage of the mercenary fleet's disorganization in January, and did not seek it out, despite orders, in February. Several months later, de Mello would again demonstrate his reluctance to engage this fleet that Villar (then a rebel in Guanabara Bay) later ridiculed as a "force of bizarre composition, curious heterogeneity and limited military power."[131] Clearly Flint's Fleet, paper tiger or no, lost in retrospect some of the awful threat it possessed during the fighting. Men on the sidelines scoffed. Those who had to face its terrible guns and torpedoes shrank from becoming targets for the newfangled "secret weapons."[132] Even people on shore "were out of their wits as long as the *Nictheroy* was in their midst," and complained of insomnia and even retreated from the shoreline.[133]

Ironically, Flint's Fleet inspired fear even while floundering with difficulties. It was fortunate that no rebel agents were on hand when the dynamite gun was first tested in Pernambuco, for "when the first shot was fired there came out of the gun not the expected steel, but an old hat and a pair of socks. The look of surprise on the Brazilian Admiral's [Gonçalves] face was worth coming all the way to Pernambuco to look at."[134] Flint's Fleet continued to be plagued by machine and weapon breakdowns. The *Nictheroy*'s dynamite gun was temporarily out of service when the ship arrived the first time off Rio. The German torpedo boats suffered from the violent storms they had encountered in crossing the Atlantic.

When the fleet headed south in February, problems continued. The *Piritinin*, damaged by its towship, was brought into a Bahian shipyard for work. Nils de Foch, the only Ericcson representative still with the ship, complained of the lack of good will in Bahia; no one was interested in repairing the torpedo ship. The Yarrow boat (*Moxoto*) was ruined when, overladen, it was dropped as it was being hoisted to the deck of the *Nictheroy*.[135] Two of the German torpedo boats were lost on their first attempt to head south, one in a collision with another member of the fleet. The remaining torpedo boats had to return to Pernambuco to regroup.[136]

Critics of the fleet blamed the mishaps on the ships' unseaworthiness, while American seamen complained of the inability of the Brazilian crews, some of whom were accused of sabotage.[137] Given the extraordinary number of delays and accidents as well as the strong prorebel sentiment in Recife and Bahia where the Brazilians were recruited, sabotage on this leg of the journey was certainly possible.[138] Consul General Thompson obviously believed in "disloyalty among the crews" and noted that some of the commanding officers "refused to fight against their brothers of the Navy."[139] The naval expert who, after reading all the official reports and interviewing participants, wrote his own analysis concluded that "insurgent emissaries seem to have been in every one of these craft, and to have seized all opportunities for surreptitiously damaging the machinery, and even for imperilling the existence of the vessels."[140] Officers of the *America* agreed with this conclusion, while the surgeon of the *Nictheroy* believed that Admiral Gonçalves "was in sympathy with Mello" and attempting to impede Flint's Fleet. So fearful was Floriano of treason that he arrested the commanders of the government men-of-war *Bahia* and *Tiradentes* as well as the commandant of Fort Santa Cruz.[141]

Because of these impediments, the fleet only headed toward Rio at the beginning of March. In a remarkable coincidence, the fleet embarked on the same day Floriano conducted the national election for his presidential successor. It is unclear the extent to which the fleet's departure depended upon the election, but certainly conducting it while the southern part of the country was still in revolt was unusual. The extended delays of the mercenary squadron are also difficult to explain if the ships' timetables were unrelated to the election.

When the squadron arrived off Rio de Janeiro on March 10, 1894, the naval revolt had ebbed. In retrospect, participants realized that the revolt had been doomed since February when the land assault was brutally repulsed with hundreds of casualties.[142] At the time, however, the fate of the revolt was still cloudy, so much so that Joaquim Nabuco wrote to a friend the day the squadron steamed into Guanabara Bay that although he had long thought that Floriano would be victorious, he now believed that the rebels would win.[143]

The arrival of Flint's Fleet convinced Floriano to attempt to put an end to the naval revolt. The day after the fleet arrived, Floriano informed the rebels that he would begin bombarding them with the full force of his batteries, which had been considerably strengthened in the preceding months. He recommended to the inhabitants of Rio that they flee or take other precautions. The foreign commanders, afraid of errant shots by the land guns and particularly worried about the accuracy of the dynamite gun, demanded that before he readied his cannons, Floriano post a large bond to cover damages to foreign property.[144] But the foreign commanders had little influence once an outbreak of yellow fever reduced the foreign contingent in the bay to just three ships. Not surprisingly, now that the marshal's military position was so overwhelming, he ignored the demand. The foreign commanders discovered they no longer had a say in the course of the war, nor the means to determine the outcome.

Critics afterward sneered that the final act of the naval rebellion in Rio resembled comic opera much as had its outbreak. In fact, the citizens of Rio expected an enormous and bloody battle. One witness breathlessly recalled, "The exodus of the population assumed indescribable proportions."[145] Another recounted, "Street cars became loaded with women, babies and bedding. Lines of mule carts, loaded in like fashion, passed through the streets, while men, with huge bundles on their heads and followed by their families, were seen everywhere in the main thoroughfares."[146] The government erected sheds along the Central do Brasil railroad, and provided free train fare to the suburbs as well as food for the poor. In an act calculated to outrage the supposed monarchist rebels, Floriano also opened the Isabel Palace and built barracks in the former royal estate of the Quinta de Boa Vista to house refugees from the impending battle.[147] Everyone either fled to the temporary housing that the government had built out of harm's way or to the mountains surrounding the bay for a view of the impending pyrotechnical display.

The dynamite fleet, which Rio residents had been hearing about since November and whose arrival had been rumored since January, aroused great curiosity and even greater expectations. When the fleet anchored outside of Guanabara Bay on March 10, crowds of *cariocas* crammed the streetcars to go out and see it. Two days later, in a demonstration test, the dynamite gun successfully hit a target two miles away, impressing onlookers. When the fleet finally entered the bay at 4:00 P.M. on April 13, it was greeted by a 21-gun salute and wild cheers. "It was a moment of true delirium."[148]

Flint's Fleet set out with the objective of firing three dynamite projectiles, 2,600 pounds of dynamite, at the rebel-held fort at Villagaignon. The threat of the dynamite gun, which had demonstrated its capacity in Pernambuco, was sufficient to induce da Gama and his forces to surrender. According to the surgeon aboard the *Nictheroy*, Floriano ordered that the gun not be fired for fear that its "projectiles would result in great destruction and loss of life in Rio."[149] Five-hundred-thirty-two rebels quit ships and forts to seek refuge aboard two Portuguese cruisers escorted out of the bay by British men-of-war. This act outraged Floriano who would accept nothing short of unconditional surrender. He broke relations with Portugal and resented the British intrusion. Eventually, the rebels were carried to Argentina or Portugal from which some of them rejoined the fight. But the naval revolt was broken.[150]

The news of the defeat of the naval revolt had great repercussions. Paulistas celebrated the victory of the 13th. Meanwhile, the Federalist forces led by Gumercindo Saraiva that were poised on the Paraná border to launch an attack on São Paulo retreated when news arrived that the naval revolt had been crushed.[151] They estimated that the revolt had tied down some 10,000 soldiers in Rio. With these free to march on São Paulo, since the government once again had a fleet and controlled the seas, the rebels returned to Rio Grande do Sul.[152]

In Rio, Captain Baker and the American crew retired from the *Nictheroy* with only one casualty among the original recruits—a soldier killed in a Rio brawl three days after the insurgents surrendered.[153] This was not to be the end of the contribution of the mercenary fleet, however. After several weeks' respite, the fleet left Rio for the capital of the rebel provisional government, Desterro. There they netted de Mello's largest ship, the *Aquibadan*, which lay crippled. The *Nictheroy* fired the dynamite gun two times to test it and frighten the crew of the *Aquibadan*, but Floriano did not want the rebel battleship (soon to become a government battleship once again) blown up. Instead, torpedoes tore a hole in its hull, and the *Aquibadan*'s crew along with its captain abandoned ship.[154] Government troops then disembarked at Desterro and initiated a campaign of terror.[155] Further to the south, de Mello heard that Flint's Fleet, triumphant in Rio, had now headed south. Afraid of encountering the *Nictheroy*, de Mello abandoned over 2,000 troops who were attempting to take the key port city of Rio Grande do Sul. With the government back in control of the ports of Rio, Paranagua, and Desterro, he had nowhere to go in Brazil, so he steamed his remaining ships to Uruguay, to surrender and quit the war.[156] Although guerrilla fighting continued in Rio Grande do Sul for another year, the struggle receded from a national to a local one. The threat to Floriano's regime had ended.

Flint's Fleet Is Feted

When Flint's Fleet returned to Rio, it was greeted with jubilation. The 23d of June was declared a national holiday in the fleet's honor as Floriano, a congressional commission, generals, and the municipal council of Rio turned out to fete the returning heroes.[157] Floriano credited the fleet with ending the revolt in his speech to Congress on May 7, 1894, "It is appropriate that the national navy [mostly composed of Flint's Fleet], so tarnished by some of its members, should give the final blow to this revolt."[158] (However, neither Floriano nor any of the Florianista historians of the naval revolt gave Flint or any Americans credit for the squadron.)[159] The insurgent Frederico Villar lamented, "History repeats itself": as in previous revolts, "without control of the seas" rebels could not win.[160]

It is difficult to ascertain the fighting capacity of Flint's Fleet since its mettle was never tried. The *Scientific American* had mused as the squadron set off from New York that because of the untested experimental nature of so much of the weaponry, "No fleet ever sailed with more chances for and against its success than this provisional squadron."[161] The problems with machinery and weapons lent credence to critics' denunciation of the fleet's shoddy workmanship. As mentioned, however, rebel sabotage probably also played a part. It is worth noting that most of the ships Flint purchased for Brazil remained in the Brazilian navy for more than a decade, proof of their seaworthiness.

That the fleet did not militarily defeat the rebels, except to disable the *Aquibadan*, does not indicate failure. It fulfilled its propaganda role wonderfully. American public opinion was swayed to the side of Floriano, and American naval men were compelled by the success of the fleet.[162] Europeans interpreted Cleveland's tacit support for the adventure as U.S. backing for the Brazilian government that undercut efforts to recognize the rebels.[163] Da Gama surrendered without a fight in part because he was well aware of the destructive power of the dynamite gun; and de Mello, aboard the *República*, and Alexandrinho Alencar, the captain of the *Aquibadan*, so feared the mercenaries that they refused to pursue them in the Northeast and fled when the fleet tracked them.

Flint's Fleet, combined with Benham's aggressiveness, had established the U.S. commitment to the Monroe Doctrine and demonstrated the myriad of ways it could be enforced. Private entrepreneurs and mercenaries, working with tacit and sometimes active federal support, had played a significant role. Moreover, the adventure demonstrated an expansion of the Monroe Doctrine; not only was the United States opposed to European recolonization, but also to European involvement in Latin American affairs. Indeed, even a domestically inspired attempt to return to what Americans perceived as a European form of government, monarchy, now came under the doctrine's aegis.[164]

This episode further cemented the bonds between the United States and Brazil. In 1894, Floriano, previously so aloof, sent a cavalry troop and a representative to the U.S. minister on Washington's Birthday to pay respects. The Fourth of July was decreed a national Brazilian holiday, and immense fireworks displays commemorated the day. Ironically, some of the fireworks left over from that celebration were fired for the inauguration of President Prudente de Morais on November 15. The new Brazilian president was greeted by the confused spectacle of a grand, aquatic pyrotechnic exposition featuring the Goddess of Liberty with the Brazilian flag in one hand and the Stars and Stripes of the United States in the other. That same day, the cornerstone to a monument to James Monroe and the Monroe Doctrine was laid in Rio.[165] Given the possibility that Admiral Benham had brokered Prudente's election, the display and the monument were appropriate for the inauguration. Brazil's Congress also ordered a medal struck with Cleveland on one side and Floriano on the other, and municipalities in Amazonas and Santa Catarina were named "Clevelandia."[166]

These medals, honors, and celebrations testified to the success of the American naval effort in Brazil and the warming friendship between the two countries. But could the victories of Benham and Flint be redeemed in the Brazilian market? After all, Cleveland, Gresham, Herbert, and Flint (just as Harrison and Blaine before them) really had envisioned dominating Brazil's trade. Despite the new cordiality, the United States abrogated the McKinley Tariff and the Blaine-Mendonça treaty effective October 1894. Brazil followed suit on January 1, 1895. Had reciprocity and the diplomatic rapprochement increased commerce?

CHAPTER 9

Yankee Traders in Brazil

The American business community had welcomed the Blaine-Mendonça Accord with bright predictions of a large-scale commercial invasion of Brazil. Industrialists and agriculturalists both envisioned the Brazilian market to be a veritable bonanza for American commerce.[1] Requests for commercial information flooded U.S. consulates in Brazil.[2] Did such an enthusiastic response betoken sincere interest in foreign markets on the part of U.S. producers, and did the Blaine-Mendonça agreement ignite American trade expansion? Too often the optimism and wishfulness of Yankee traders would be crushed by the realities of the inadequate American commercial infrastructure in the underdeveloped Brazilian market and the reluctance of the U.S. Congress to provide necessary aid.

Walter LaFeber argues that one of the principal aims of American foreign policy during the 1890's was to open new markets to industrial goods. As already noted, he claims that increasingly sophisticated technology in the United States brought with it surpluses of industrial and agricultural goods that in turn forced shutdowns and declines in profitability. Foreign markets were seen as an outlet for the surplus and the remedy for the ills brought on by the new stage of industrial development. Reciprocity treaties represented one manifestation of the growing U.S. interest in foreign commerce.[3]

The earlier discussion here of the McKinley Tariff pointed to a limited interest by Congress in promoting exports. Internal political considerations such as the agricultural vote and concern with maintaining protection took precedence over foreign market promotion. Reciprocity appeared to be an afterthought. Its advantages for American commerce in those few countries that accepted reciprocal arrangements were open to question. Mendonça, after all, had predicted that the treaty offered American producers insufficient privileges to overcome lower European wages, credit, and transportation costs.[4] This chapter examines the American commercial response to the opening provided by the Blaine-Mendonça Accord.

The Commercial Balance Sheet

Trade statistics in the United States and Brazil revealed that the Blaine-Mendonça pact had an ambiguous effect on gross U.S. exports to Brazil. The treaty became effective in the last two months of fiscal 1891 (April 1, 1891) and ended almost three or seven months into fiscal 1895, depending if one uses the U.S. or Brazilian termination date (August 27, 1894, for the United States and January 1, 1895, for Brazil). The U.S. Tariff Commission studying reciprocal treaties used 1891–94 as the treaty period for the purpose of analysis, in part because news of the impending treaty inspired more trade already well before the April 1 starting date. American exports to Brazil between 1891 and 1894 were about 45 percent above the average for the preceding three years. It is evident that reciprocity facilitated the movement of U.S. goods into the Brazilian market. Products receiving special favors from the Blaine-Mendonça treaty grew (except in 1893) from one-third to two-thirds more than nonfavored goods.[5] On the other hand, as Table 1 demonstrates, U.S. exports to Brazil did not rise steadily; after reaching a high point in 1892, they declined. Ironically, they climbed again after the treaty's termination in 1895 and 1896, though dropping thereafter. Average U.S. exports to Brazil under the treaty were $13,515,334, while the average for the three following years was $13,955,444.[6]

Brazilians fared better in entering the U.S. market, which caused the trade deficit with Brazil to grow. A study Floriano presented to the Brazilian Congress in mid-1893 found that Brazil reaped $40 million more than the United States from the treaty.[7] The first two years were particularly notable as Brazilian exports jumped 50 percent. Thereafter, however, they leveled off, but still remained one-third above the average of the three most recent pretreaty years.

Unfortunately, there is a problem in ascertaining the exact effect of the treaty on Brazilian exports because of an important error in the data. The Manager of Trade Statistics in Washington, Worthington C. Ford, explained in 1893, "It appears that free imports such as coffee, sugar, etc. from Brazil have been valued at the 'par value' of their currency, although this has been much depreciated. By this arrangement the trade with Brazil under the McKinley Act (and reciprocity) appears nearly double what it actually is."[8] The Treasury Department adjusted for this error in the 1893 data and thereafter changed the accounting procedure. But the 1892 figure remained greatly inflated. Even if we apply the same procedure used by the Treasury

TABLE I

U.S.-Brazilian Commerce, 1888–97
(in thousands of current U.S. dollars)

Fiscal Year	U.S. Imports from Brazil	U.S. Exports to Brazil
1888	53,710.2	7,137.0
1889	60,323.5	9,276.5
1890	59,318.8	11,902.5
1891	83,161.8	14,049.3
1892	118,633.6	14,240.0
1893	76,222.1	12,388.1
1894	79,360.2	13,866.0
1895	78,831.5	15,165.1
1896	71,060.0	14,258.2
1897	69,039.4	12,441.1

SOURCE: *Statistical Abstract of the United States, 1897* (Washington, D.C.: Treasury Dept., Bureau of Statistics, 1897), p. 94.

TABLE 2

Brazilian Exports of Cane Sugar to the United States,
1888–97, and Index of Trade with the United States,
1888–97[a]

Fiscal Year	Brazilian Sugar Exports	Brazilian Exports (total)	U.S. Exports (total)
1888	$6,752,000	93	60
1889	4,838,000	105	78
1890	1,659,000	100	100
1891	*5,142,000*	*144*	*118*
1892	*4,468,000*	*206*	*119*
1893	*2,922,000*	*132*	*103*
1894	*5,689,000*	*138*	*116*
1895	2,701,000	137	128
1896	3,776,000	123	120
1897	2,137,000	119	104

SOURCE: *Statistical Abstract of the United States, 1897*, p. 195, and Brazil, *Boletim Commemorativo da Exposiçao Nacional de 1908* (Rio: DGE, 1908), p. 101.

[a]Sugar exports are for cane sugar affected by the Blaine-Mendonça Accord (between Dutch 13 and 16), in U.S. dollars. For the index of exports, 1890 = 100. The years affected by the trade agreement are in italic type.

to adjust the 1892 amount, however, average exports for the treaty years still were about 40 percent greater than in the prior period.[9]

Even with this error in its favor, most Brazilian exports did not show impressive gains except in 1892 (though export data were notably unreliable once the states became responsible in 1891 for collecting statistics and transferring them to the federal government).[10] Sugar, for instance, did not live up to the hopes of Deodoro's government (see Table 2). The sudden

TABLE 3
U.S. Sugar Imports, 1888–97[a]

Fiscal Year	Total	Percent from Brazil	Percent Duty Free
1888	$74,200,000	9.0%	0%
1889	88,500,000	5.4	0
1890	96,100,000	1.7	0
1891	*105,700,000*	*4.8*	*32.6*
1892	*104,400,000*	*4.3*	*91.8*
1893	*116,300,000*	*2.5*	*87.8*
1894	*126,900,000*	*4.5*	*85.7*
1895	76,500,000	3.5	36.7
1896	89,200,000	4.3	12.8
1897	99,100,000	2.1	13.3

SOURCE: *Statistical Abstract of the United States, 1897*, p. 195.
[a]Sugar exports are in U.S. dollars. The years affected by the trade agreement are in italic type.

increase in sugar exports in 1891 and 1892 resulted from the lack of competition. Sugar from the British possessions did not become duty free until February 1, 1892, while Spanish-Cuban sugar did not enjoy free status until September 1, 1891. Thus, for two months in fiscal 1891 and two months in fiscal 1892, Brazil did have a monopoly on free sugar to the United States.[11] The higher mark in 1894 is probably attributable to the growth of the U.S. sugar market. Free sugar meant lower prices that, in turn, invited greater consumption (see Table 3). Even so, Brazil's greatest sugar export total under the treaty was lower than the totals prior to the pact. Brazil never supplied as much as 5 percent of U.S. sugar imports. The growing U.S. demand was met by Cuba and Hawaii and by the domestic sugar industry of Louisiana, which received 30 million dollars in sugar bounties under the McKinley Tariff.[12]

Other Brazilian exports, such as cotton, tobacco, hides, or piassava, which already faced stiff international competition or were little known abroad, were harmed by the Republic's new fiscal system. Suddenly the states rather than the central government set and collected export taxes. Some were greedy and set the ad valorum rates as high as 25 percent, which effectively shut them out of foreign markets.[13]

Consequently, the growth in Brazilian exports came almost entirely from burgeoning coffee and rubber exports during the treaty years. Since these goods received no special concessions from the trade agreement, their growth was due simply to market forces. In 1892 Brazilian coffee registered its greatest gains in the U.S. market. That year lower coffee prices also stimulated especially large coffee shipments to France and Germany with whom Brazil had made no tariff agreement. A similar phenomenon occurred in the three years after the treaty's end when a precipitous fall in the price of coffee encouraged a jump of almost 50 percent in coffee tonnage exported to the United States.[14]

Benefits from the Treaty

Although trade between the United States and Brazil grew, it did not meet the optimistic expectations that the treaty had aroused (see Table 4). The problem stemmed in part from the fact that expectations were always unrealistic. Also, as Salvador de Mendonça had argued to his government, the treaty in fact offered U.S. producers few real advantages.

In fact, Secretary of State Blaine's defense of the trade agreement had been somewhat contrived. He painted pictures of glorious riches that were illusory. He had estimated, for example, that in 1889 Brazil imported $38,631,242 worth of goods that would, under the treaty, be placed on the free list for the United States. They included such goods as wheat flour, coal, agricultural and industrial machinery, and railway construction material. Before the pact, only about 5 percent of these had come from the United States. If all of the reduced duty goods were added to that total, Brazil imported $58,635,182 worth of goods referred to by the treaty, and only $5,430,532 of them had been produced in the United States. Hence, argued Blaine, the treaty allowed the United States to tap a large market that already existed and in which U.S. producers had ample space to grow.[15] Blaine ignored an important fact, however. The free entry that the treaty awarded to agricultural, mining, and industrial machinery, railroad cars, and locomotives would not rectify the existing trade imbalance because Brazilian industrial exemptions granted in 1890 freed these imports of duties regardless of their nationality. U.S. producers had no special privilege.[16]

The rest of the free list was less impressive yet because Brazil had no market for many of the goods enumerated. For instance, Brazilians did not consume rye, rye flour, buckwheat, barley, or oats. They imported little corn, cornmeal, beans, peas, lumber, or rosin.[17] Indeed, the only American goods that the *Rio News* expected would make inroads were wheat flour, potatoes, vegetables, furniture, and perhaps a small increase in vehicles and agricultural machinery.[18] Brazilian producers of pork fat and textiles also felt threatened by the treaty, but the 1892 Brazilian tariff put an end to their fears by providing additional protection.[19]

The 1892 law, which raised the duties on most goods 50 to 60 percent, further undermined the advantages of the Blaine-Mendonça agreement.[20] Although passed primarily to aid the impoverished national treasury, the new Brazilian tariff demonstrated the growing importance of domestic industry and the government's support of it. The sudden duty increase must have shaken American confidence in the Brazilian government's commitment to freer trade between the two countries. In addition to raising duties in general, the government levied a new tax called the *expediente*. It served to pay for port and customs costs and applied to all free goods. In effect, they were charged a 10 percent duty. Considering that the prevailing duty rate was 5 percent on wheat, coal, agricultural tools, and railway materials and

TABLE 4
Brazilian Imports in Constant Milreis,
1889–1895[a]

Fiscal Year	Brazilian Imports in Current Milreis	Brazilian Imports in Constant Milreis
1889	217,800	217,800
1890	255,520	217,977
1891	413,680	231,995
1892	527,104	238,696
1893	546,144	237,892
1894	649,402	246,345
1895	709,018	265,093

SOURCE: Calculated from FIBGE, *Séries estatísticas retrospectivas*, vol. 1, p. 68.
[a]Constant milreis calculated by dividing 1889 milreis exchange rate (compared to the £) by that of each subsequent year.

15 percent on wheat flour, potatoes, corn, rye, barley, rosin, tar, and turpentine (all of which were free items under the treaty), the *expediente* essentially negated the treaty's advantages.[21] Thus, disregarding semantic sleight-of-hand, American goods guaranteed free entry were no longer free only a half year after the initiation of the agreement. The *expediente* was eventually rescinded and the fees returned, but that only happened as the pact was nearing its end.

Although the trade agreement's provisions were not as generous to American exporters as they initially appeared, the pact should not be dismissed as simply a political ploy on Blaine's part. European exporters were quite alarmed by the pact and demanded that their governments secure similar concessions from Brazil.[22] Although the French, British, and Portuguese ministers pressed to acquire similar privileges, they failed. The French minister attributed his inability to "nativist and protectionist sentiment" in Brazil.[23] The concessions that Blaine won may have been limited, but given the few reciprocal privileges the U.S. Congress had allowed him to offer in exchange, and the growing strength of Brazilian domestic industry and nativism, the secretary of state did very well to grasp any special advantages over the European competition.

Brazilian Trade in the Early 1890's

The American commercial advance was slowed more by market conditions within Brazil than by diplomatic failure. Although at first glance it appears that the Brazilian market for imports grew enormously during the early 1890s, tripling between 1889 and 1894, that apparent growth was actually an artifact of the depreciation of the milreis. In those years the milreis lost almost 60 percent of its value in gold. Consequently, the value of Brazil's imports in pounds sterling, rather than enjoying dizzying growth was rather flat. This confused contemporary observers who were unfamiliar with the mechanisms of inflation. To that point Brazil had enjoyed Latin America's most steady currency. The sudden inflation made it more difficult to recognize the true size of the market. As Table 4 demonstrates, total real Brazilian imports during the treaty years grew only 6 percent. The market presented a "zero-sum" game. The principal means for United States exporters to make gains in this situation was to replace someone else's trade, a considerably more difficult prospect than taking part of an expanding trade. The nature of the import market, then, was such that even if the treaty did provide the United States with the privileges British and French competitors believed it did, chances for success were not great.

The stagnation of imports was less a sign of bad faith on the part of the Brazilian trade negotiators than of a level capacity to import caused by internal problems that dampened booming coffee exports. True, part of the imports' problems resulted from a somewhat conscious import substitution policy. Public policy awarded factories cheap credit, a more accessible stock market, some tax breaks, and an apparently higher tariff,[24] though as I have shown elsewhere, industrial development was primarily a side effect of policies more concerned with buying political friends for the new republican regime than with restructuring Brazil's economy.[25]

As a British merchant wrote to Brazil's finance minister in 1892, the reason for the slowdown in imports was not the higher duties of 1892, but rather the low value of exchange, restricted credit, and lack of confidence caused by the debacle of the Encilhamento's collapse.[26] The milreis fell from 27 pence in 1889 to 10 pence by 1894, driving up the milreis price of imported goods 170 percent. Wages did not keep up so workers could consume less imports. By one estimate, real wages plummeted 50 percent between 1890 and 1891 alone.[27] Financial disorder caused by the Encilhamento made the credit market unattractive. With exchange rates changing daily, state banks emitting unbacked paper that was often nonnegotiable, and mounting inflation, normal commercial risks were greatly amplified. In the interior, commerce had deteriorated to the point that, according to one observer, "business has become almost impossible [because of] the uncertainty connected with the validity of the currency."[28] Small purchases were discouraged by a scarcity of low-denomination coins.[29]

Brazilian instability was more than just economic. The young Republic constantly struggled to stay alive and quell internal disorder. The numerous revolts that erupted, or threatened to erupt, cast doubt on the government's ability to sustain itself and, in turn, brought into question not only the effectiveness of the Blaine-Mendonça Accord but the economy as well. Discord within the government also served to deter new commercial ventures. The roar of congressional disapproval that greeted the treaty in Brazil, for instance, caused numerous American mercantile houses to delay exports to Brazil until the status of the treaty was clarified.[30] The treaty's future remained in doubt because of, first, the strong and vocal opposition to Deodoro, and then questions about Floriano's commitment to international trade. Imports, then, fell because of a *failure* of Brazilian government policy and process, not because of a consciously autarkic program.

If Brazil's recession and disarray after 1891 did not deter the Yankee trader, structural impediments and inadequate infrastructure gave pause to even the most ambitious and energetic of exporters trying to break into the Brazilian market. The *Rio News*, a newspaper mainly concerned with commerce, was always pessimistic about the treaty. In response to the optimistic predictions Americans at home were making, the newspaper's American editor confessed, "We who have lived in Brazil for a term of years, know that such a belief is absurd."[31] C. C. Andrews, U.S. consul general to Brazil in the late 1880's, believed that "while we may hope for a gradual increase of American exports to Brazil, any high expectations in that direction are not likely to be realized."[32]

The structure of the Brazilian economy provoked such pessimism. Many of the problems that beset the Americans, such as inefficiency of customs houses, were faced by all importing merchants. However, the impact of the hindrances was much larger on the invading commercial power than on entrenched ones. Merchants and producers new to Brazil found the language and laws strange; they had no influential contacts to defend them. More important, the success of their venture was only hypothetical, while British, French, and German merchants knew, through experience, that after dealing with government regulations they would turn a profit. Moreover, because of Brazilian unfamiliarity with American products, U.S. merchants and manufacturers undertook a greater risk once they overcame the difficulties. Thus the more economic and governmental obstacles and the more uncertainly confronted, the less the likelihood that U.S. merchants and exporters would find the Brazilian market inviting.

Shipping and Communications

The problem began in the ports of North America. Freight rates from New York were higher than from London, even though New York was 25 percent closer to Rio than was London. American steamships were 25 to 50 percent more expensive to operate than their European competitors because of higher ship construction costs in the United States, higher sailor wages, and greater coal consumption.[33] Steamers were so expensive that during the treaty years four times as much cargo was carried in American sailing ships as in its steamers. The ratio was almost the reverse for European ships clearing New York and Baltimore for Brazil.[34]

Moreover, the much greater export trade of European countries to Brazil and Argentina (ships in route to or from Buenos Aires often put in at Rio) meant that many ships crossed the Atlantic southward with near full capacity, allowing a relatively low freight rate per unit. To take advantage of this trade, there were five regular British lines, three French, two Italian, two

Austro-Hungarian, and two German companies.[35] Twenty steamships a month arrived in Rio from Europe but only one from the United States. The ratio was far worse in Argentina, where in 1885 1,153 British steamers arrived but no U.S. ships. These ships competed for return cargos to Europe, driving down the fares un the northward leg. They also were willing to carry Brazilian exports to the United States. Consequently there were five regular lines and many tramp steamers that made the Brazil to U.S. run, but only one company, the U.S. and Brazil Mail Steamship Company, that regularly left the United States for Brazil, and it only sent two ships a month.[36] The result was that not only did European exporters pay substantially less than American traders for freight from their home countries to Brazil, but the freight tariff from New York to Rio was four times the rate of the return trip, encouraging a U.S. trade deficit with Brazil.[37]

The U.S. merchant marine had fallen into obsolescence after the Civil War. Despite the founding of the U.S. and Brazil Mail Steamship Company (USBMSCo.) in 1883, complaints from consuls were constant and vituperative.[38] Noting that only 8.2 percent of U.S. imports and 15.5 percent of its exports were carried in American bottoms, U.S. Minister Thomas Thompson concluded that "to extend the commerce of the U.S. a merchant marine is absolutely necessary."[39] The Brazilian government did award the USBMSCo. a $105,000-a-year subsidy in the late 1880's, but the U.S. Congress refused to provide more than a nominal sum of $11,743. The company's British competitor received £109,653 ($531,817) from Her Majesty's exchequer.[40] Moreover, the Brazilian subsidy was not to encourage international trade between Brazil and the United States. Rather, the American shipping line was paid to carry coastal freight in Brazil, forcing its ships to make stops in Pará, Recife, and Bahia.[41]

Despite the hearty advocacy of Harrison and Blaine, strong political resistance from the South and the Midwest prevented the Merchant Marine Act of 1891 from providing adequate subsidies.[42] Consequently, the USBMSCo., one of the few companies covered by the 1891 act, had to charge higher rates to cover its expenses and could not afford to expand its service to reduce unit costs and make itself more attractive to exporters. The company purchased two new American ships for $450,000 each in anticipation of large subsidies since the new law required the use of American-built ships. When the funds were not forthcoming, the line that had survived for eight years *before* the reciprocity treaty went bankrupt under the treaty in mid-1893.[43]

In reflecting on this episode, John Hutchins, a student of the merchant marine, concluded, "Only strong, state-supported carriers or government-owned shipping could hope to achieve a firm position in many such liner trades. It seems, therefore, that the policy of comparative laissez-faire followed by the United States played into the hands of such established organizations and tended to freeze the existing situation."[44] As a result, the percentage of the Brazilian trade carried in American ships did not increase.

Before the treaty in 1889, 21.8 percent of the trade was carried in U.S. bottoms; in 1892 the figure was 22.8 percent; and in 1897, after the treaty expired, U.S. ships carried only 5 percent of the commerce between the two nations. By the turn of the century, there was no regular shipping line between the United States and Brazil.[45]

The failure of the shipping initiative should not be viewed simply as a lack of congressional resolve, disinterest in foreign markets, or ideological blinders. The subsidy act had been seen from the start as pork barrel for special friends of the administration rather than a more general developmental program. The *New York Times* had warned that when the Blaine-Mendonça treaty was passed it would unleash a herd of steamship subsidy hunters.[46] The U.S. consul in Belém, J. Kerby, voiced a common complaint. After rejoicing at the initial news of the postal subsidy bill, "The first application of the new law as exemplified by the United States and Brazil Mail Steamship Company caused a very great disappointment to the people and leaves the impression that the law was solely and only enacted in the interests of this one American steamship company that reaches Brazilian ports at irregular intervals with its five slow class ships."[47]

There was much opposition to awarding privileges on a given route to a single company not only because its stockholders would reap special benefits, but also because the company's service was directed to a particular, limited clientele. Owned by major New York merchants, the USBMSCo. gave lower freight rates to these merchants' companies. This awarded individuals such as stockholder Charles Flint special consideration. Perhaps this explains why at the banquet of the Hispanic-American Commercial Union of New York held on December 20, 1889, the only speaker to support steamship subsidies was William Ivins—president of the USBMSCo. and business partner of Flint.[48]

Regional jealousies also spurred opposition to the steamship subsidy. The company sought to strengthen New York's dominance of the Rio trade that it had wrested from Baltimore since the Civil War. Congressmen from the Midwest and the South resented subsidies that would further strengthen the city's commercial advantage.[49] In a bit of commercial propaganda, the head of the Bureau of American Republics (and confidant of Flint), William Curtis, published a study to prove that the USBMSCo. actually aided many parts of the country. Analyzing the manifest of one USBMSCo. ship, Curtis found products from 25 states. However, New York contributed 28 percent and together with Pennsylvania and Massachusetts supplied half of the cargo. On another steamer he found goods from 36 states, but, again, New York provided one-quarter and with three other Middle Atlantic states half the cargo.[50] If the shipments had been broken down by location of exporter rather than producer, the benefits to New York merchants would have been much more pronounced. Thus U.S. shipping failed to expand under reciprocity not so much because of provincialism or antistatism as because the subsidy bill was too often viewed as a tool of political corruption and narrow interests rather than as a vehicle for economic expansion.

It should be pointed out that one key weapon in the arsenal for commercial invasion had been developed: the telegraph. The French minister in Rio believed that Brazil's orientation toward Europe rather than the Americas was attributable to the "few and weak links" of steamships and telegraph.[51] However, since the late 1880's three telegraph lines had been completed that tied Brazil to the United States through Buenos Aires and the west coast of South America, Central America, and Texas, through the Caribbean to Florida, or across the Atlantic to Senegal up through Europe and back to New York. These added to the first line that had connected Brazil with Portugal and back across the Atlantic. The two companies that linked Brazil to the United States through western South America and the Caribbean were American, and the other two were British. This competition caused telegraph rates to the United States to fall by at least one-half, linking closely the markets of New York and Rio.[52] Telegraphs were successful because they did not depend on government aid. Due to the great U.S. interest in the Brazilian coffee and rubber markets, private companies could turn a commercial profit without government subsidies.

Doing Business in Brazil

After overcoming the Atlantic barrier, American exporters encountered the first obstacle in Brazil's ports. Despite the country's dependence on international trade, the ports were antiquated and terribly inefficient. The docks at Santos were enlarged beginning in 1891, and Rio Grande do Sul was also under expansion but the civil war there retarded progress. Bahia and Rio were also slowly improving services, but they remained poor. Ships had to be unloaded in the port by lighters rather than at dockside. The larger shipping companies had their own lighter fleets, but American merchant ships were often tramp steamers and had no such infrastructure awaiting them. Lighters were in short supply, which meant that ships might have to wait in ports such as Santos and Rio de Janeiro for three to four months before discharging their cargo. Freight backed up so badly that at one point there were 74 vessels in Rio waiting to be unloaded.[53] The very real threat of yellow fever—a terrible epidemic seized Rio in the first months of 1894—made such delays all the more disconcerting.[54] The Maryland Line of steamships, which ran ships between Baltimore and Rio for six months in 1891, went bankrupt because of such problems with long delays and yellow fever.[55]

Once the goods made their way to the customs house, they faced another long wait. The American consul at Belém reported that "nothing can be 'dispatched' through a Brazilian Alfandega in less than thirty days." In fact, sometimes it "might be six months," the duration depending largely "on the amount of cash advanced to the dispatcher."[56] Here, again, the commercial newcomer who did not have his own private *dispachante* (dispatcher) or a relationship with the government officials was at a disadvantage.

Yet further obstacles lurked at the customs house. Between May 1890 and October 1891 all duties had to be paid in gold so that revenues would not decrease with the milreis's decline. Because there was a shortage of available gold, most importers had to purchase it from the government at 14$500 per gold sovereign. When paying duties, however, the government only accorded 8$890 per sovereign. Hence importers lost 5$610 on each sovereign, a de facto duty increase of 63 percent.[57] U.S. exporters were unfamiliar with other intricacies of the tariff such as the fact that heavy packing boxes used by Yankee merchants were made to pay the same customs rate as the merchandise inside. The British circumvented this by packing in light, durable material.[58]

Once importers fought their way through the *alfandega*, they encountered new difficulties. Goods might have to wait months to be loaded on a train. Railroad service to the major ports had not grown with trade. In addition to normal delays, the civil war in the south suspended much train service as did the naval revolt and strikes in Rio. Those goods that finally overcame this bottleneck often arrived damaged or were sent to the wrong depot because of negligence in transit.[59]

A problem that affected American shipping alone during the period of the treaty was brought on by a cholera scare caused by reports of some cases of the disease on the eastern seaboard of the United States. In response, the Brazilian government required all ships arriving from the United States first to undergo a quarantine in a station near Rio de Janeiro. Besides the time wasted in the 30-day delay, the requirement constituted a serious detour for ships sailing to the Northeast of Brazil; they had to travel via Rio. The quarantine lasted from the middle of 1892 until the middle of 1893.[60]

The structure and limited size of the market hindered American commercial expansion. Approximately 85 percent of Brazil's fifteen million people lived in rural areas. The rural aristocracy and gentry constituted no more than 5 percent of the population, and few places in the country had an independent farmer class. Most people in the countryside were either self-sufficient squatters or workers who received over half their compensation in nonmonetary forms. Many agricultural workers, then, were barely in the money economy. They earned on average some 35 cents a day plus room and board and often had to buy from the company store.[61] When rural workers did buy merchandise, they usually purchased domestically produced goods.[62] Moreover, agricultural production itself required few machine inputs, and tools were generally rudimentary and domestically produced. Only luxury products for the rural rich provided much of a market for imports, and this market was severely restricted.

Urban consumers were more import oriented because almost all major Brazilian cities either were ports or were close to one. Even the urban poor depended on imported textiles and foodstuffs.[63] There was also a middle class that had a greater capacity to import. The Encilhamento, how-ever, seriously squeezed their purchasing power by the time the Blaine-Mendonça Accord went into effect.

American Competitiveness

Although U.S. exporters confronted barriers in the Brazilian market, they surpassed all major European exporters in the short 1886/89 to 1890/93 period for the most part preceding the Blaine-Mendonça agreement. In these years U.S. exports to Brazil grew 73 percent, while German exports expanded 56 percent, French 38 percent, and British 30 percent.[64] One would expect American exporters to react vigorously to the possibilities provided by the treaty, at least at the outset, because of such promising recent experience. Did they, in fact, react only to be stymied by the obstacles posed by the Brazilian economy?

The increase in imports from the United States in the years preceding the treaty suggests Brazilians were willing to purchase American merchandise. C. C. Andrews, former U.S. consul general to Brazil, maintained that "American manufactures generally have a good name in Brazil."[65] E. H. Conger, minister to Brazil, said: "So popular, indeed are the products of our skill, and labor, that many European manufacturers mark their goods with American brands to facilitate their sales."[66] Consul General O. K. Dockery asserted that "under reciprocity . . . we could, other things being equal, soon control a respectable portion of this valuable trade."[67] The French and Portuguese ministers and many British merchants also believed that the Blaine-Mendonça Accord promised to expand U.S. trade.

The depression of 1893 might have made U.S. goods even more competitive. The prices of U.S. products tumbled,[68] but Yankee traders could not fully take advantage of lowered prices to wedge open the Brazilian market because of the general decline in European export prices also caused by the depression. Nonetheless, the prices of American industrial goods declined faster than did their British counterparts.[69]

Marketing U.S. Goods

The *Rio News* laid the blame for American commercial failure at the feet of American merchants, rather than U.S. manufacturers or shippers. One year after the Blaine-Mendonça Accord went into effect, it concluded, "There has been an increased importation of American goods, of course, and in some respects the new trade has come here to stay; but in the absence of American commercial entrepreneurs and the feeble efforts made to study the market and introduce goods suited to its requirements it must be confessed that there is no slight occasion for disappointment on their part."[70]

U.S. merchandise was sold by non-U.S. houses because there were practically no American merchants.[71] Very few U.S. manufacturers had their own representatives in Brazil, nor were there many traveling salesmen, though a number of companies did send down representatives on exploratory trips after the trade agreement was signed. The lack of sales representatives was a marked disadvantage. As one of the partners in W. R. Grace wrote in 1888, "It seems to me that the era of consigning goods is rapidly passing away; the whole tendency of trade is in the direction of bringing producer and consumer in actual contact and avoiding religiously the interposition of middlemen."[72] Europeans had a wide network of agents, merchants, and traveling salesmen who reached the secondary cities. "All of these agents speak Portuguese and are retained in the trade year after year and are not only familiar with the markets and credit but become acclimatized."[73] Even though the United States purchased most of Brazil's exports, coffee was mostly exported by European houses; few Yankees had ever gone south to set up shop.

Even when they had a hand in the export trade, Americans did not get involved in imports. In Belém, prosperous from selling rubber to the United States, the American consul complained, "The American capital here is in no way interested in developing trade from our country with the valley. They are here to purchase rubber for cash only."[74] William R. Grace, one of the most important American exporters in the Amazon, wrote his agent of "the absolute necessity of a Manaus connection." Yet Grace warned him to offer only little credit to sell U.S. goods because he did not "want to extend our moneyed responsibilities in Pará."[75] The presence of numerous British, German, and Portuguese merchants attested to the rich market in the area.[76] The Americans, however, were only in Pará to buy rubber, which was shipped to New York (usually on British ships) for sale to manufacturers. Buyers were middlemen who had no hand in selling goods in return partly because they represented no manufacturing interests.[77] Although Charles Flint was in the process of bringing together rubber exporters and manufacturers as he formed the U.S. Rubber Company, this did not alter the business practices of exporters.[78]

Lack of interest rather than lack of opportunity prevented U.S. exports to the Amazon valley. Consul Jack Kerby found leather shoes in Belém selling for nine dollars that were produced in New England for less than $3.50 and shirts selling for two and a half times New York prices.[79] Not only did the buyers not introduce American goods, they bought rubber with drafts on British banks because there were no U.S. credit sources in Brazil.[80]

Yankee merchants' lack of credit in Brazil was disastrous. Most of the large importers at this time were foreigners who used the credit extended by the manufacturer to market goods. With commercial bank loans rare, manufacturer credit was critical to mercantile success. Since there were very few American-owned commercial outlets, American exporters had to rely on the merchants of other nationalities. To introduce new merchandise into the market one had to be willing to take a temporary loss as inducement to consignment merchants.[81] Otherwise, British and French merchants would sell goods from their country since it was from there that they derived their credit.[82]

Unfortunately, American business practices precluded the possibility of working extensively through foreign firms. A special congressional agent, Lincoln Hutchinson, explained that "The unwillingness of American exporters to extend credits as freely as their trans-Atlantic competitors drives many orders to Europe."[83] Such an attitude stemmed, in part, from unfamiliarity with Brazilian businesses. American businessmen did not know which were good risks and would have difficulty recovering loans.[84] American reluctance also derived from a lack of great concern with the Brazilian market. Hutchinson concluded that "American exporters have not met with greater success largely because they have not made a sufficiently persistent effort."[85]

It is surprising that there were no U.S. banks or credit agencies in Brazil until 1915 considering that half of all Brazilian exports went to the United States.[86] The Germans and French opened banks in 1889 and 1890 in Rio and the British opened a second one at the same time, while Portuguese merchants played an important role in the founding of numerous banks in the first years of the Republic.

This situation came about because throughout the nineteenth century, Brazil's export trade was dominated by European firms. Hence, there was practically no American commercial paper in the market. In 1895, of $94,060,000 worth of business between the United States and Brazil, only $395,600 did not go through a foreign middleman.[87] Since the foreign banks charged 1.5 percent interest to discount the notes, the absence of a commercial infrastructure cost the United States over $1 million a year in finance charges.[88] Even the U.S. government paid its consuls with drafts on London. That was not always easy to do. The American consul at Bahia communicated his efforts at cashing a $172 draft: "I notified the London and Brazil Bank, through which the draft was negotiated, of the circumstances of the case, but the President was not satisfied to have the risk of having them dishonored and refuses to accept future drafts from me pending instructions from London."[89] The Inter-American Bank that Flint had pushed through the Pan American Conference and convinced Harrison and Blaine to recommend to Congress was designed to resolve precisely these problems, but congressional suspicion and resentment of financiers, monopolies, and special interests doomed his bank and blunted the American commercial advance on Brazil.[90]

In addition to a lack of credit facilities, a poor merchant marine, and reluctance to exploit the position of the United States as the leading importer of Brazilian goods by establishing a commercial infrastructure in Brazil, those merchants who did attempt to compete often failed to conform to the necessities of the Brazilian market. Because they were inexperienced in the trade and had no representatives in Brazil, they were unaware of the rough treatment goods received in Brazil and consequently did not compensate for it with sturdier packing.[91] Butter, cheese, meal, and fish were packed inadequately for the tropical climate. Goods often were not properly waterproofed, so they were damaged in transit or during the long stay at the customs house.[92] There were incidents of American bacon and butter being bought by British merchants, shipped to Great Britain, repacked there, and then sold in Brazil where the reexport was preferred to the goods imported directly from the United States.[93]

In textiles, American merchants did not provide the sizes and patterns requested. One U.S. consul complained in an exasperated tone, "All attempts have failed so far to import prints, which are so vastly consumed. The American manufacturers have been doing all they can do to be kept from this market as they will not accommodate themselves to its requirements."[94]

U.S. Consular Service

Merchants were not wholly to blame for their problems in the Brazilian market. They got little help from the U.S. consular service, which was still quite amateurish. American businessmen complained that positions were doled out as rewards for political favors within the United States regardless of the nominee's experience in diplomacy or trade. A biographical study of high-level foreign service appointments in the 1890's found that close to half of the 226 men (there were no women) were lawyers or government officials and only one-fourth were businessmen or farmers.[95] The State Department began to use civil service rules in 1890, but further attempts in 1894, 1895, and 1896 to reform the service pushed by the Boston Merchants Association and the National Association of Manufacturers failed because of the overwhelming political pressure for political spoils.[96]

Still, there was a concerted effort by Blaine to place people in Brazil who could help Americans interested in the Brazilian market. Interestingly, one of his most notable acts was to forbid in October 1890 people "in the business of exporting to the United States" from consular or vice-consular positions.[97] Previously exporters such as Grace had placed their agents in consular positions, but this led to situations such as in Rio and São Paulo where U.S. coffee exporters complained of the negligence of the consuls. Both consuls headed mercantile houses and attended to consular duties at their leisure.[98] Apparently Blaine believed that exporter-consuls would not work hard at finding buyers for U.S. goods in Brazil. So adamant was he about this restriction that he preferred Europeans to American exporters as viceconsuls. In some cases Europeans were chosen—even though they had served in the consular service of another power—simply because there were so few Americans in Brazil that there was no alternative.[99]

On the other hand, some consuls were chosen with the intention that they expand U.S. sales in Brazil. William T. Townes was appointed consul general in Rio in 1893 because of the endorsement of Virginia and North Carolina tobacco growers who hoped to export to Brazil under the Blaine-

Mendonça treaty. Townes was a tobacco expert from Virginia who later represented the American Tobacco Company in the Caribbean.[100] Blaine sent Jack Kerby to the rubber district of Belém, Pará, because, as he told the consul, "You are a telegrapher and a practical electrician, and we want to know something about the rubber insulation in this electrical age in its relation to reciprocity." Kerby was also a journalist and was supposed to "write of the possibilities for business of American merchants."[101] He later continued as a commercial boomer reporting for the *Bulletin* of the International Bureau of American Republics and the *Daily Consular and Trade Reports.*[102]

While the State Department tried to bend the consular service to commercial ends, the fact remained that the quality of its appointments left much to be desired. Kerby himself complained that few people in Washington knew anything about Brazil; most thought that Spanish was the national language. He railed in his memoirs that "One of the absurdities of the former consular service consists in the sending out of persons like myself to represent our commercial and industrial interests who had gained no knowledge of the language of the country to which they are accredited."[103] Kerby had been forced to look in an atlas to discover where Pará was.

A good part of the problem in finding suitable consuls and vice-consuls in the secondary cities was that they were very poorly paid. If coming from the United States, they had to pay their own fare to Brazil. Once there they received just $1,000 to $2,000 a year salary, supposedly one-quarter of what British consuls earned. American consuls constantly complained that their expenses exceeded their pay. A consul in Belém was so strapped by his four-year duty that he had to borrow money for the return passage to the United States.[104]

The American diplomatic representatives in Brazil were disheartened by their low pay and thus begrudged special services to U.S. manufacturers or exporters seeking market information. While all the consuls reported receiving a "mass of correspondence" of commercial inquires, they did not answer unless paid by the correspondent. Said the consul general at Rio, "We have no time to investigate the peculiarities of trade and finance which I conceive to be the principal feature to the United States at this point."[105] Consul General O. K. Dockery put consular exasperation most poignantly: "Perhaps it is best to abandon the field at once, for half-paid public officials in this distant land can be of no service to their own country."[106] Despite Blaine's pronouncements of concern with the Brazilian market, the Department of State turned a deaf ear to the incessant pleas for funds coming from consuls in Brazil. As with the merchant marine, the U.S. government's refusal to subsidize a more effective consular information gathering service reflected a preoccupation with the exigencies of domestic politics: U.S. voters in the congressional election of 1890 and the presidential election of 1892 voted out the Republicans in good part because the "Billion Dollar Congress" was perceived as spendthrift. This was for expenditures on domestic public works, not something so arcane as the foreign service.

The Limits of Success

Although there were obviously some very serious barriers to the growth of U.S. exports to Brazil, some goods did burgeon during the treaty years. They were not, in general, the agricultural products Blaine had promised to sell to win the support of Midwestern farmers. Between 1890 and 1895 absolute agricultural exports declined by some 2 percent, and their share of U.S. exports to Brazil fell from 68 to 52 percent.[107] The only agricultural goods whose export in dollar terms increased were bacon and cottonseed oil, though one could argue that both were industrial products.

American wheat farmers and flour exporters had held out great hopes of expansion toward Brazil, which already before the treaty was the second largest foreign market for flour for the United States. The heralded market for flour proved to be something of a mirage, however. On the one hand, between 1890 and 1894 there was an increase of 3,399,300 barrels over the previous four-year total. The British-owned Rio Flour Mills, Brazil's main flour manufacturer, was badly hurt by American imports, a fact that must have pleased Blaine.[108] However, the success of U.S. flour was as much due to a drought in Argentina, Brazil's main supplier of wheat, as to the Blaine-Mendonça Accord. Moreover, the price of flour dropped so much that the dollar earnings for flour exports grew little. Increasingly the Brazilian flour market became segmented: the populous and prosperous Southeast was captured by the Argentines, while the United States held the poorer area from Pernambuco north; domestically milled flour soon came to predominate.[109]

Most of the U.S. exports that did increase during the treaty years were manufactured products. Table 5 lists those exports whose average total during the treaty was significantly higher than their average for the three prior years. A note of caution should be interjected however: The totals for the three pretreaty years are biased because the treaty was in effect during the three months of fiscal 1891. Thus they are a little inflated. At the same time, Table 5 does not accurately record the dynamic of the growth of North American exports because much of it occurred in 1891, after the treaty's promulgation but before it went into effect. For a breakdown of United States exports by year consult Appendix 1.

Although many U.S. exports displayed large percentage gains, in general their gross sales remained minimal. Considering that total U.S. exports in 1892 were some $1.032 billion, a $50,000 increase would not be felt in the U.S. economy, though it might have some political weight.[110] The only exports whose totals were sufficiently large to contribute to the amelioration of the glutted American market were steel and iron products and cotton manufactures. The former recorded an average of almost $1,000,000 a year over pretreaty totals, and cotton textiles rose about $100,000.[111]

U.S. manufacturers did dump surplus stock in Brazil during the Depression, but they did not, for the most part, perceive the Brazilian market as an extension of the American market, one that could help solve the structural

TABLE 5
Growth of U.S. Exports to Brazil, 1889–94

Goods	Yearly Average 1889–91	Yearly Average 1892–94
Duty-free goods		
Books, maps, and engravings	$164,200	$296,700
Wheat flour	3,598,600	4,052,900
Cars for railroad	405,300	810,400
Canned fish	6,200	26,900
Saws and tools	160,600	233,200
Locomotives	489,500	674,800
Rosin	105,300	158,900
Cottonseed oil	8,700	146,600
Bacon	430,800	705,300
Reduced-duty goods		
Colored cloth	363,900	508,900
Uncolored cloth	277,200	637,004
Wearing apparel	36,800	85,200
Butter	15,200	18,900
Goods with no duty reductions		
Brass and its manufactures	7,400	28,500
Patent medicine	155,100	199,000
Twine and cord	24,900	33,400
Cutlery	20,700	31,500
Firearms	34,600	61,300
Locks	33,800	70,500
Sewing machines	72,600	88,200
Wire	7,800	44,400
Lard oil	43,200	73,900
Lubricating oil	55,700	89,900

SOURCE: U.S. Treasury Dept., *The Foreign Commerce and Navigation of the United States, 1893,* vol. 2, and *1897,* vol. 2 (Washington, D.C.: Government Printing Office, 1893, 1897), passim.

problems of oversupply. Those American industrialists who did establish a commercial infrastructure in Brazil were such companies as Singer, Baldwin, Diamond Match, and Standard Oil. They either enjoyed a technical advantage abroad and at home or had crafted combinations to dominate their domestic market; they were not the firms that suffered from overproduction and a declining profit rate in the U.S. market.[112] Reciprocity was advertised as a solution for farmers, smaller merchants, and manufacturers beset by competition within the United States, but the export trade was becoming increasingly competitive and complicated with growing barriers to entry. A man who should have known, Charles Flint, eloquently explained the transformation of international commerce:

> During the first three quarters of this century margins of profit in foreign commerce were so large that merchants with only moderate capital entered the field successfully. . . . During the past twenty-five years, however, the margins of profit in foreign trade and transportation have been reduced at least seventy-five percent. . . . While in foreign trade the middleman is more useful than in domestic commerce, the tendency of the times is, by bringing together producer and consumer, to eliminate him. . . . All this

makes necessary large aggregations of capital; and the tendency to consolidation, which is the striking feature of industrial enterprise, is finding its way into international commerce.[113]

The consignment trade was dying. U.S. Minister E. H. Conger (a man Flint later recommended for a consular position) pointed out that in any new line of trade "no good can be sold here by sample. The competition is now too sharp." Warehouses and credit were necessary.[114] It is not surprising then that William Becker found that "the industries with the largest exports of manufactured goods had some of the highest levels of concentration."[115]

Other U.S. manufacturers corrected the problem of oversupply by forming trusts and pooling agreements rather than looking abroad. Large companies in areas such as petroleum, sugar, rubber, tin, and wire were more inclined to absorb and limit competition than enter foreign markets.[116] These manufacturers saw Brazil as a market of last resort. They were "only interested in dumping goods when a surplus in the U.S. occurs to drive prices down."[117] This strategy alienated Brazilian and Portuguese merchants who sold the American products because "when the domestic market improves, they [U.S. manufacturers] ignore Latin America so delivery is uncertain."[118] Conger criticized the American textile industry in particular for such a lack of concern for the Brazilian merchant and market. Since, "as a general rule it is only surplus that is offered here," the goods that were exported were manufactured "especially for the home market with no reference to the needs, customs, or desires of this Brazilian people."[119] Former consul general C. C. Andrews observed that although "American manufacturers generally have a good name in Brazil," their practices in the Brazilian market drove Brazilian importers to conclude that "the Americans have such a great home market that they don't wish to trouble themselves about exporting."[120]

An examination of the *Rio News*, the English-language commercial newspaper in Rio de Janeiro, reveals that the American producers who advertised were primarily companies with technological advantages and success in the United States, not companies facing gluts at home seeking to relieve them abroad.[121] A check of the *O Estado de São Paulo*, a Brazilian Portuguese-language daily from São Paulo, produced the advertisement of only one additional American product: lard. American producers of goods that tried to stay afloat in a flooded home market apparently made no special effort to reach the English or Portuguese reading publics.

The failure of American producers to find a safe harbor in Brazil demonstrated that worries of Brazilian industrialists were unfounded. The years of the treaty coincided with some of the greatest Brazilian industrial expansion of the nineteenth century. The textile industry, the most important and best studied, experienced rapid growth because of easy money, a booming stock market, and protection from the devalued milreis. Sugar did not much benefit from the agreement, but this meant that the effort to create usinas (central sugar mills) to modernize the sector was not undermined by

U.S. demand for raw sugar. In some states, particularly Pernambuco, numerous usinas were mounted in the 1890's, but they abandoned their long hopes of finding an export market and concentrated instead on the swelling domestic market, a tactic long advised by foreign investors. Total Brazilian sugar production and productivity rose even while its share of exports fell. Thus despite the dire predictions of the treaty's opponents and the hopes of its supporters, the Blaine-Mendonça treaty did not increase Brazilian dependence on international commerce. Rubber and coffee exports continued to expand, but because of world demand, not state policy. In fact, the first Republic would witness the steady decline of exports' share of GNP.

Conclusion

The Blaine-Mendonça treaty did not ignite an explosion of commercial activity during its short lifetime. The pact's limited concessions were insufficient and the times too unsettled to alter comparative advantage. Still, the experiment was not a failure. As the Tariff Commission's eminent economist Frank Taussig reflected, "Exports from the United States to the reciprocity States, favored by special reductions of duty, showed a substantial increase in spite of the handicap of severe industrial depression and revolutionary disturbances existing in many of these States, while at the same time there were decreases in the aggregate exports to all other countries."[122]

Blaine, with Flint's help, had correctly identified the barriers to the entry of U.S. goods and had crafted a comprehensive package of reforms that would have gone a long way toward selling American goods in Brazil. Unfortunately, congressional intransigence, built as much on suspicion of special interests as antistatism, doomed ample steamship subsidies, the creation of the Inter-American Bank, and consular reform. The lack of sufficient public assistance was critical because market conditions soured just as the trade agreement came into force. Brazilian economic and political turmoil as well as an unprecedented expansion of industry reduced Brazil's imports and dampened American enthusiasm for the market. Nonetheless, it would be wrong to conclude that U.S. producers and traders were not very interested in the Brazil market. On the contrary, tremendous curiosity was whetted, but, unfortunately, without a commercial infrastructure, too little of that curiosity was translated into new commerce. Then the crippling depression in the United States between 1893 and 1896 turned merchants' eyes away from Brazil. Nonetheless, the termination of the reciprocity treaty created a storm of resentment from those who believed that it was the correct formula for U.S. economic expansion abroad.

CHAPTER 10

Aftermath

Neither Pan-Americanism, the Blaine-Mendonça Accord, nor Flint's Fleet brought the political acclaim their authors had hoped. Instead of providing James G. Blaine with the laurels to capture the presidential nomination, as some rival Republicans feared, Pan-Americanism died as a political issue. Ill health forced Blaine to resign his post at the State Department in June 1892, and he died in January 1893. His Brazilian policy was left as a legacy rather than a political rallying point.

Benjamin Harrison secured renomination, but failed in his bid for re-election and retired from politics. A rather drab, stoic man, he had relied on the party for his first presidential election. Lacking charisma, he could not resist the tide of resentment against the Republican "Billion Dollar Congress," their links to special interests such as the trusts, and the high tariff. Reciprocity or the appeal to a closer alliance with South America won him few extra votes in 1892.

Cleveland and the Democrats who rode to victory in 1892 on the engine of a lower tariff and honest government did not fare better. In fact, the national uproar caused by the repeal of the Sherman Silver Purchase Act and the interest-dominated Wilson Tariff compounded by the 1893 depression and unrest such as the Pullman strike cost Cleveland his party's nomination in 1896. William Jennings Bryan, a silverite and strong antiexpansionist, captured the Democratic mantle in 1896, while Cleveland retired from politics. The Democrats would not return to the White House until 1912 when Woodrow Wilson reasserted Cleveland's aggressive Latin American policy.

The one man to profit politically from the Harrison years, ironically, was William McKinley. A strong opponent of reciprocity and expansion in 1890, by 1896 he had become converted to both causes. His call for both protection and expansion helped win him two presidential elections and demonstrated that Harrison's intuition was correct even if his timing was bad. It took the disastrous depression of the 1890's to convince the mass of businessmen and others of the necessity of looking abroad. McKinley pushed through a weak reciprocity plank with the 1897 Dingley Tariff, but congressional logrolling, jealousy of legislative prerogatives, and fear of executive power prevented him from using reciprocity to gain meaningful trade concessions abroad. Still, he remained committed to it. In the last speech he ever made—delivered at the Pan American Exposition in Buffalo—McKinley averred that his belief in reciprocity was stronger than ever. The next day he was shot. McKinley's stress on economic expansion transformed the Republicans from the party of reform to the party of prosperity. His legacy was to end the age of equilibrium by making the Republicans the majority party until the next great depression demanded new policies.[1]

The day after McKinley's tragic death, the National Association of Manufacturers called for a national reciprocity conference. Despite the strong advocacy of the NAM (which had originally been created by Midwestern manufacturers to protest the termination of the McKinley Tariff) and Theodore Roosevelt's support, interest in reciprocity began to wane. Protectionism returned triumphant until the Payne-Aldrich Tariff of 1909 weakly reasserted the principle of using tariff concessions to open foreign markets. The Democrats took up the same principle in 1913.[2] Protectionism's resurgence is unsurprising. Even its defenders had never regarded reciprocity as an alternative to protection, but rather an extension of it. Charles Flint, one of its intellectual parents, testified to a congressional committee in 1901, "I regard the reciprocity theory as being the highest evolution of the protective policy."[3] After World War I, nationalism and concerns with self-sufficiency and preparedness further strengthened the protectionist tendency.[4]

Brazil was one of the few countries to agree to a special reciprocal trade agreement with the United States during the prewar years, though this did not evidence the special Brazilian "deference" to the United States that France's minister had worried about in 1894.[5] After all, the Brazilian representative refused the U.S. offer of a reciprocity treaty in 1898, for fear of having to offer similar concessions to other trading partners. When Brazil's president did offer lower duties on a host of U.s. goods in 1904, the Brazilian Congress in Rio initially repealed the legislation, though it was later reinstated. Moreover, the French received privileges similar to those extended to the United States.[6] Despite ritual obeisance to free trade, Brazilian politicians aggressively defended their own exports with the world's first successful state-run export price-support program, the valorization of coffee.[7] More serious for American exporters, they also maintained, according to an agent of the U.S. Department of Commerce, the highest tariff rate in the western hemisphere and one of the highest in the world.[8]

Trade with Brazil grew nonetheless, but it is not clear that trade agreements were much responsible for the growth. Even though, in absolute amounts, U.S. exports to Brazil in 1906–10 were almost triple the 1888–90 totals and even 75 percent above the reciprocity years, the U.S. share of the Brazilian market remained a constant 12 percent. Only the crippling of trade with Europe provoked by World War I helped American producers widen their niche; by 1915 the United States was providing 40 percent of Brazil's imports. That experience allowed U.S. traders to maintain a central place in the Brazilian market even once European competitors rebuilt and resumed trade.[9] In a sense, the commercial transformation during World War I proved Blaine's original point: if American exporters were provided with a privileged position for sufficiently long to establish a commercial, financial, and transport infrastructure, they could compete with the Europeans even once those privileges expired. But the Blaine-Mendonça treaty had prevailed for too short a time and over a time too troubled in both Brazil and the United States to arouse American exporters to launch a full-scale commercial invasion. The next time the opportunity arose they were ready.

Just as trade slowly swelled before the war, so too did American direct investment. As already noted, the United States was a net debtor in the early 1890's. Yankees did not begin to invest abroad in substantial amounts until the end of the depression of the 1890's. Even then, the bulk of investments went to adjoining countries—Mexico, Canada, and Cuba—and generally represented spillovers from domestic undertakings. Certainly the Blaine-Mendonça pact did not seduce American capital to immigrate. The Encilhamento fizzled by the end of 1891 and with it disappeared the fevered stock market dealings and visionary schemes. Only one U.S. corporation was established in Brazil between 1889 and 1896, and no U.S. loans were offered.[10] Beginning in 1906 some large American companies were begun in Brazil, particularly those organized by the entrepreneur Percival Farquhar, but the massive wave of American capital swept over the country only after World War II.[11]

Charles Flint failed to mastermind the Brazilian empire he had envisioned, but he played an important part in one of the most important early American companies in Brazil: U.S. Rubber. The trust that Flint had organized in the early 1890's was a prototype of the vertical and horizontal integration he advocated for American business in general. The company placed its own buying agents in Brazil and its own shipping fleet on the seas. It made purchases with its own letters of credit, saving importer commissions and discount charges.[12] Rubber goods were manufactured in the United States by U.S. Rubber's factories. In the late 1890's Flint also won or bought concessions to pave the streets and run the streetcars in the capital of the Amazonian rubber country, Manaus, but his connections to the Brazilian government did not always help his rubber empire. The biggest coup achieved by his U.S. Rubber Company, a concession to 30 million acres of the province of Acre, which then belonged to Bolivia, was canceled when Brazilian nationalists and Yankeephobes conquered the province and worked it themselves.[13] (It is striking that the two largest U.S. companies in Brazil before World War I and the only two companies in the country that attempted widescale integration, U.S. Rubber and Farquhar's Brazil Railroad, both became involved in wars. The war with Bolivia and the Contestado revolt that attacked the Brazil Railroad demonstrated that many Brazilians were willing to put their lives on the line to fight the effects of monopoly capitalism.) Brazil was not yet a country for a trust organizer.

With the death of the Encilhamento's dreams of incorporating Brazil, Flint's ties to the country became tenuous. His trading company did much more business with other Latin American countries. In 1900 the Brazilian accounts receivable of the Flint, Eddy and American Trading Company represented just 2 percent of the total.[14] Although Salvador de Mendonça attempted in 1906 to win the extremely lucrative concession to direct Brazil's first state valorization of coffee program for himself and Flint, there is no evidence that he succeeded.[15] Flint's trust building, which continued unwavering, was concentrated in the United States where he put together dozens of large and small combinations, including the precursor of IBM.

Flint's military links to Brazil also ended once his fleet was disbanded. The Brazilian government eventually reimbursed him for his expenses, but, he calculated, the payment was $150,000 short of his outlay. Since, as he pointedly remarked, he had not entered the venture for philanthropic purposes, he maneuvered to recoup his loss. He sold the ship he had purchased from Huntington, the *Nichteroy*, to the U.S. Navy, which employed it in the Spanish-American War as the USS *Buffalo*.[16] (The renaming came before McKinley was assassinated in Buffalo, so no irony was intended, though one emerged.) This ended his ties to Flint's Fleet but not to the arms industry. Already before the war with Spain, Flint supposedly arranged with Cleveland to create another private navy and "infest the seas with American privateers when the Venezuelan tangle threatened war with England."[17] During the war with Spain he cooperated with his friend Cornelius Bliss, then secretary of the interior, to supply munitions to the U.S. forces and to prevent the Spanish from acquiring ships. Later he sold twenty submarines and torpedo boats to Russia when it was on the verge of war with Turkey and sold the Japanese a Chilean man-of-war for the Sino-Japanese War.[18] He supplied uniforms and weapons for Colombia, served as the agent for the Wright brothers, trying to sell aeroplanes to the French and Germans, and there is evidence he might have armed rebels in the Mexican Revolution. By 1910 he had supplied vessels and war munitions to ten governments. During World War I he provided weapons and ammunition to the U.S. Army. He came to own some of the weapons companies he represented, making him one of the early representatives of the military-industrial complex.[19]

Despite Flint's success as a broker and manufacturer of weapons of war, he was not able to convince Brazil to turn from its traditional suppliers in Europe to the United States. His mercenary fleet's American-made experimental weapons did not impress the Brazilian navy. (Indeed, even the U.S. Navy gave up on the dynamite gun for arming ships, converting its one ship armed with pneumatic guns, the *Vesuvius*, into a torpedo ship capable of only small eruptions.)[20] Despite the destruction of the Brazilian navy which, according to the minister of the navy, had reduced its "naval power to almost nothing," they did not want the ships Flint had purchased. The minister disdainfully dismissed them as "not having the qualities of warships."[21] Of course, he may have reflected the general naval ire that their state-of-the-art ships such as the *Aquibadan* were defeated by converted merchantmen. Most of Flint's Fleet did remain and served in the Brazilian navy. However, when the Brazilian navy contracted for eight new ships it turned to its traditional suppliers: England, France, and Germany.[22] It may well be that sailors partly turned away from the United States because they resented the U.S. role in defeating the naval revolt. After all, Admiral Wandenkolk, who had initiated the rebellion against Floriano, became the navy's chief of staff in 1898. (Admiral de Mello, unable to quit his inclination for insurrection, was jailed for conspiracy and insubordination on his old base on the Isla das Cobras a couple of years later.)[23] The Brazilian navy's most notable gesture of friendship came during the Spanish-American War when it sold the United States not only the *Nictheroy* but also two of its new ships just being finished in England, which the Spanish also coveted.[24]

Toward the end of his life, Flint prided himself on his Brazilian adventure, reflecting that "I think that I did as much as any other man to preserve Brazil as a republic."[25] While there is no doubt about the importance of his contribution, it is much less clear what he preserved. A monarchist restoration was simply not possible in 1894 because of lack of support from the royal family and lack of organization. Rather, the struggle was between different republican elements based on class and regional and factional lines. Although Floriano Peixoto and the radical republican wing emerged victorious from the war, they could not retain control of the state. To secure Paulista support, and possibly because of American urging, Floriano had recognized Prudente de Morais as his successor while the naval revolt was still active. With the war over, Floriano had second thoughts about relinquishing control to this conservative representative of the planter bourgeoisie. But he stuck to his pledge, no doubt largely because he was very ill (he died the next year) and there was no apparent successor with a national following.

Jacobin influence grew under Prudente because of the war in the backlands of Canudos that fed fears of a monarchist restoration, but after 1897

Jacobinism went into sharp decline. The Historical Republicans and landed oligarchs assumed power. When a self-styled Jacobin group surfaced in the 1920's under the title of the Acção Social Nacionalista (ASN) it resembled the earlier group only in name and in its presumed reverence for the Iron Marshal. In fact, it was composed of men who had opposed Floriano when he was alive. The new Jacobins saw the enemy as the politicized working class, not the semifeudal elite as in the 1890's. ASN leaders attempted to manipulate nationalism for the conservative goal of steering the working class away from anarchism, rather than creating a more developed, just society.[26]

Floriano's victory was thus a pyrrhic one; in order to "save" the Republic he had to strike deals that doomed the Republic of his dreams. The next to share his vision and who were able to gain political power were the *tenentes* who decided that the only solution to the Republic's oligarchic rule was its overthrow. They were joined by a few aging Florianistas such as Lauro Sodré and Alexandre Barbosa Lima. Together they played a major role in the 1930 Revolution that ended the First Republic.

For Salvador de Mendonça, the treaty was not the crowning act of his diplomatic career. Instead, as one student of Brazilian diplomacy in the period put it, "In the history of international relations it would be difficult to find a commercial agreement that provoked such a clamor and generated such unsavouriness."[27] Mendonça continued as Brazilian minister to the United States until 1898, so he clearly gained the confidence of successive regimes. Nonetheless, Brazilian diplomatic history has accorded him virtually no credit in establishing closer relations with the United States. Araujo Jorge, for example, does not even mention Mendonça in his discussion of diplomacy of the first years of the Republic, and Amado Luiz Cervo gives him scant attention.[28] Ironically, men such as Jorge, who applauded Floriano as the consolidator of the Republic, praised the Barão de Rio Branco and Joaquim Nabuco for forging closer ties to the United States. These two diplomats, both strong monarchists at the time of Floriano, were staunch enemies of the Iron Marshal. Nabuco, who succeeded Mendonça as minister to the United States and became the first Brazilian ambassador there, wrote a book denouncing the U.S. participation in the naval revolt.

Later in life, Mendonça published his own self-defense that was also an indictment of Nabuco and Rio Branco; but now the worm had turned. He accused them of being too pro-American! According to Mendonça, the two diplomats had become lackeys of the United States and slavish devotees of the Monroe Doctrine (the precise criticism Nabuco had earlier leveled at Mendonça). By this time (1911) Mendonça had become a vocal nationalist. Joining the chorus of other nationalists such as Alberto Torres and Nicanor Nascimiento and socialist Mauricio Lacerda, the former minister to the United States decried Yankee imperialists such as the capitalist Percival Farquhar, who created the largest company Brazil had ever known. Mendonça also became suspicious of the Dollar Diplomacy of Roosevelt and

Taft. He had not, however, become anti-American. On the contrary, Mendonça argued in the same volume attacking Farquhar and Roosevelt that the Democratic Party was a peace-loving one respecting the sovereignty of Latin America. He continued to be a disciple of Pan-Americanism, holding that an inter-American diet should replace the arrogant application of the Monroe Doctrine.[29] Ironically, the actions of McKinley, Roosevelt, and Taft that so outraged Mendonça were prepared by Blaine's Pan-Americanism. Blaine, whom Mendonça befriended and trusted (and continued to revere to the end of his life), no doubt would have approved of their expansionist policies.

Conclusion

The lessons were neither simple nor clear-cut. On the U.S. side there was clearly no consensus over the importance of foreign markets or the proper role of the state in promoting trade. Indeed, the state was sharply divided between the executive and Congress, and even the parties were internally riven along regional and sectoral lines. James G. Blaine, sensing the evolving needs of the U.S. economy and, even more pressing, the growing impatience with protectionism felt by consumers and opponents of trusts, saw reciprocity and Pan-Americanism as rallying points. He was also concerned that the great colonial powers were dividing the world among themselves, leaving out the United States. He hoped to lead the Republicans away from their reformist Civil War heritage stressing ethnic loyalties and waving the bloody shirt to become the party of national economic development under the aegis of corporate liberalism. Blaine was not responding to a great tide of American pressure for expansion, however. Most Americans, businessmen and workers alike, were preoccupied with the home economy and its social problems. Thus the state was not acting as an agent of the ruling class in seeking foreign markets. To the extent that one can conflate Blaine and the state—which is problematic because of the diffuse and contradictory nature of the state—he seems to have been acting rather autonomously. The "Plumed Knight" anticipated future needs more than responded to current business demands, but he was not acting alone.

Although business in general was not yet enamored of overseas markets or encouraging of state assistance, a clique of businessmen was deeply involved in formulating policy. Charles R. Flint, Thomas Jefferson Coolidge, and Cornelius Bliss not only helped pressure Congress, they participated in crafting the reciprocity provision of the McKinley Tariff, resolutions at the Pan American Congress, and the Blaine-Mendonça Accord. These men were not captains of industry concerned by growing evidence of glut nor representatives of ailing Midwestern farmers. Rather, they were men with interests in many sectors but centered in trade and transportation who sought to retain the commercial leadership of New York and Boston and, of course, to profit themselves. To do so, they mobilized commercial and trade associations throughout the country. An inchoate interest in foreign markets jelled; new organizations were formed such as the National Association of Manufacturers, while old ones began to clamor for commercial expansion.

Flint and friends sought state action because they themselves hoped to benefit from the steamship subsidies, isthmian canal company, Inter-American Bank, and Pan American railroad concessions they were promoting. They extended the old politics of pork barrel to the international sphere. To succeed, however, they had to convert a sizable share of Congress, and for that they needed voices from civil society. While many of their projects ultimately failed, it is striking how close they came to success. I am not posing here a secret cabal that actually ran the state. Flint and his colleagues were able to exert so much influence precisely because they staked out an area that, while promising and consonant with Republican ideology, was not of great importance to most politicians or of great expense to the Treasury. In this context, a small shove by a knowledgeable, single-minded, and well-connected group could bring impressive results. Although they were operating on the margins of the central political concerns of their day, by attaching their star to the most influential and eloquent politician of their times, Blaine, they were able to help bring commercial expansion closer to the center of national discourse.

Even Grover Cleveland, who won reelection in 1892 on a platform of small government and opposition to jingoism, found that he could not entirely abandon the expansionist legacy Harrison left him. Initially he did restrain or end many initiatives, but when tested in Brazil, he decided to commit the U.S. Navy to protecting American commerce and permit Flint to mount his own flotilla, even in the face of British opposition. He attempted in part to divert public attention from the woes of the great depression that hit in 1893 by playing on Anglophobia and holding out the promise of foreign markets. Little appreciated in most diplomatic histories of the period, the U.S. action in Brazil pushed Cleveland to a wider and more aggressive enforcement of the Monroe Doctrine.

It was not just coincidence that the later controversy with the British over Venezuela began when the British occupied the small Brazilian island of Trinidad and French soldiers attempted to occupy the Brazilian Amazon.[1] The broader interpretation of U.S. Latin American policy that began in

Brazil was given voice in the 1895 Olney Doctrine, which boasted to the British that "today the United States is practically sovereign on this continent, and its fiat is law upon the subjects to which it confines its interposition."[2] Secretary of State Olney based U.S. authority on the Monroe Doctrine, Washington's Farewell Address, and the twenty-inch gun that had proved so convincing in Guanabara Bay. Although no blood was shed and only one salvo was fired by the *Detroit*, the actions of the New Navy in Guanabara Bay—as well as the Blaine-Mendonça agreement—had great symbolic significance. They forcefully rearticulated Gunboat Diplomacy and foreshadowed Dollar Diplomacy.

The actions of Admiral Benham and Flint's Fleet in Guanabara Bay also demonstrated the overlap of commercial, strategic, diplomatic, and industrial motives. The navy's corporate interest was to prove the value of its new fleet and win support for further buildup. The navy appealed to the American public and Congress by promising to protect U.S. trade, force back John Bull, and show the stars and stripes around the world. Nascent arms manufacturers also wanted to see their combat wares proven and publicized, perhaps opening new international markets for U.S. weapons and vessels. The navy was driven by a technological imperative as much as by the Monroe Doctrine, and to a considerable degree it was the navy, not the State Department, that dictated American actions during the naval revolt. Private diplomacy was conducted by Flint through his fleet. He extended to the field of foreign affairs the private appropriation of state attributes characteristic of corporate liberalism, making himself grander—and more dangerous—than the tinsel filibusterers of the mid–nineteenth century.

In Brazil too, the Blaine-Mendonça treaty issued from domestic concerns and became caught up in internal struggles. The Republic's birth did not signal the hegemony of the exporter class and laissez-faire economic liberalism as is too often assumed. There were sharp differences over economic policy. Industrialism and corporate liberalism appealed to many of the bourgeoisie who had emerged with the Encilhamento. Patrimonial tendencies of the Empire were also slow to decline.

Signed in part to win a market for Northeastern sugar and partly in return for U.S. recognition of the new Republic, this pact for freer trade was supported initially by interests tied to the monarchy, the military, and the more traditional Northeast. Historic Republicans and Paulista coffee planters in general, despite their Pan-Americanism and dedication to free trade, opposed the agreement. Conventional wisdom notwithstanding, Southeastern republicans did not initially seek closer relations with the United States. They were wary because they saw Marshal Deodoro da Fonseca manipulating United States friendship for autocratic ends. Decentralization was the battle cry when they ultimately overthrew the republic's first president.

His successor, Marshal Floriano Peixoto, allied with the Paulistas, but did not relax his grip on the central government. His regime, backed by young military officers and the urban middle class, attacked many of the financiers and speculators who had profited from the Encilhamento. Floriano's supporters, particularly the radical Jacobins, were nationalist, xenophobic, and favorable to industrialism. Nonetheless, they believed in Pan-Americanism and the Monroe Doctrine. They viewed the United States as the anti-imperialist alternative. Yet the very aspects of the U.S. political and economic models that attracted them—federalism, industrialism, protectionism, and opposition to European imperialism—were jeopardized by the trade pact. Consequently, Floriano undermined many of the advantages promised by the Blaine-Mendonça Accord, but he retained, and even strengthened, the arrangement with the United States because he feared that the European powers were aiding the insurgents in the naval revolt and the civil war in the south. It was a good decision. The New Navy and Flint's Fleet played a key, and perhaps decisive, role in defeating the rebellion by preventing the European recognition of rebel belligerency.

Neither Marshal Deodoro nor Marshal Floriano acted as compradors, beholden to foreigners. They used U.S. interests in creating an American sphere of influence to counterbalance European influence in Brazil. The result was that British hegemony in Brazil ended. British traders and investors continued to be leaders, but they were no longer in a commanding position even though the United States was not able to fully supplant them until the 1930's.[3]

Brazilian regimes continued to be friendly to the United States. They usually supported the United States in the Pan American Union and sided with the United States in both world wars, but they did not cede Americans any special economic privileges in Brazil. Blaine and others sought advantages, even free trade imperialism, but the Brazilian regime enjoyed sufficient internal cohesion and international support once the Republic was consolidated to be able to fend off Yankee pressures.

What does all of this have to do with our modern enlightened world? The parallels are striking. The United States again finds itself a debtor nation unable to compete with Europeans—and now Japanese—who are forming trade blocks at the same time that they speak of free markets. The United States turns to Latin America to create its own trading block. The Latin American nations, feeling somewhat left out by·the European common market and by Southeast Asia, are forming their own trading unions.

Within the United States, of course, conditions have changed considerably. Protectionism is in retreat, and foreign markets and international competition are the new mantras. The Republicans now call for limited government, decentralization, and free trade, while the Democrats have adopted much of the former Republican position, calling for state coordination of economic policy. But the central concerns of capital accumulation, job creation, and foreign competition persist. Foreign trade is now viewed as a savior.

This study of the U.S. experience with Brazil under reciprocity cautions against optimistic expectations from trade agreements such as the North American Free Trade Agreement. The Blaine-Mendonça Accord itself was not sufficient to change the calculations of comparative advantage. Without a transportation, sales, and financial infrastructure in place, American exporters could not take advantage of treaty privileges. As Blaine had noted, access to foreign markets alone was not enough. Without a state industrial policy to promote and coordinate exports, the venture was doomed to failure.

U.S. exports also failed to expand as expected because Brazil's internal conditions were unpredictable. The treaty itself was a pawn in Brazilian political struggles and subject to the vicissitudes of its champions, and the Brazilian leaders were nationalists whose foremost concern was with their own country's welfare. They were not especially compliant. The economy also suffered severe reverses reducing its attractiveness and hindering long-range planning. Tied closely into the same world economy, Brazil suffered the same cycles as the United States, so its markets could not provide a countercyclical boost in times of downturn in the United States. The most serious structural problem of all was Brazilian poverty. A poor country with a maldistributed income, Brazil lacked the purchasing power to make much difference in the huge American economy. All of these problems persist today.

Expanding the bilateral agreement to a Pan American trading union was an impossible dream. Brazil had entered the pact precisely because it wanted special privileges over other Latin American sugar producers, not out of a sense of inter-American brotherhood. In fact, the interests of the Latin American countries competed with each other—and with the United States—more than they complemented each other. For example, special interests in the United States such as wool producers and iron smelters refused to see their protection reduced so the other two big Latin American countries, Argentina and Mexico, refused to sign reciprocity treaties.

Mexico's experience underscores the limited value of trade treaties. While Mexico was signing numerous commercial agreements with its Central American and Caribbean neighbors in the 1890's, it turned down the United States. That did not matter much, though. Trade and foreign investment between the two countries grew rapidly even without a treaty. The reason for the boom was that Mexico benefited from a spillover effect of U.S. companies moving south and creating some of the first transnational companies there. The unique geographic relationship of Mexico and the United States militated against extending this model to other Latin American countries, however. Even in Mexico, the gains for the U.S. economy were quite limited. Very few new jobs were created.

The lack of growth within the United States deriving from Latin American trade in general and the Blaine-Mendonça Accord in particular would not have surprised Blaine or Flint. They probably realized that many of their arguments in favor of agricultural exports were hollow. Blaine cared more about farmers' votes than finding them markets. In fact, there was really little effort in any corner to find markets for companies suffering from agricultural or industrial glut. The only companies that were able to expand their business in Brazil—and in Mexico—were large, successful ones that did not need government aid. The large innovative companies such as Singer Sewing Machines or Standard Oil that prospered in the United States also did well abroad because they could establish their own infrastructure.

Consequently, the reciprocity treaties should be seen as intended more for political consumption within the United States than as agents of economic expansion. They were sops to the farmers and small industrialists who were being left behind by monopoly capitalism and an appeal to the nationalism of workers who owned an ever smaller slice of the American pie. As home markets shrank or were dominated by large corporations, the promise of foreign markets was held out. "Competition" and "free markets" became the watch words at precisely the time that they were under attack at home. The discourse of economic expansion and international competition was the antidote to Populism, trust-busting, and union organizing. So are they still.

That gray, drizzly January day in 1891 Blaine and Mendonça had spoken of a brighter tomorrow with closer ties between their countries cemented by thriving trade. They did not foresee the central role gunboats would play in the arrangement or the extent to which their optimism, in the short run at least, was exaggerated. They did realize, however, that these two giants' futures were becoming increasingly entangled as the age of empire began the intense internationalization of the world whose effects we feel so keenly today and whose consequences are difficult to predict. But it is a world in which trade and some analogue of gunboats will continue to be extremely important—and intimately related.

Appendixes

U. S. Exports to Brazil, 1889–97
(in thousands of dollars)

	Treaty Years								
	1889	1890	1891	1892	1893	1894	1895	1896	1897
Agricultural implements	31.9	49.5	70.5	31.4	35.2	20.1	40.8	35.6	23.6
Books, maps, engravings	130.6	136.6	225.5	330.1	212.2	347.9	170.7	48.9	128.2
Brass and its manufactures	5.4	6.9	9.9	26.2	31.3	28.1	21.6	6.2	5.1
Wheat	384.3	1,616.2	501.2	183.6	58.6	—	—	—	12.1
Wheat flour	3,651.9	3,304.9	3,829.0	4,972.6	3,647.2	3,538.9	2,683.9	3,450.1	3,541.6
Other breadstuffs	38.3	32.8	37.1	41.7	52.4	44.2	53.5	49.0	39.1
Candles	12.8	17.1	17.4	21.5	16.8	16.2	11.2	8.1	5.2
Cars for steam railroad number	221	515	660	797	408	681	316	147	—
$	275.8	347.2	593.2	878.5	296.1	1,256.6	270.3	217.6	104.0
Carriages, horse cars, and parts	32.4	23.3	89.5	62.5	32.8	23.1	21.0	44.3	15.3
Medicine, patent or propietary	154.1	124.7	186.6	170.7	210.2	206.1	229.5	243.4	192.1
All other chemicals and dyes	37.0	39.8	59.1	41.4	44.5	38.3	51.0	52.7	42.7
Clocks and watches	60.5	67.1	79.5	59.4	71.2	64.6	94.0	72.3	59.5
Bituminous coal	0.8	46.7	79.8	105.7	96.6	31.5	71.9	70.6	87.1
Manufactures of colored cloth	412.2	383.6	299.0	323.3	549.0	654.4	703.1	325.1	233.8

Appendix 1, continued

				Treaty Years					
	1889	1890	1891	1892	1893	1894	1895	1896	1897
Manufactures of uncolored cloth	190.6	398.5	232.5	350.4	780.8	781.1	891.6	594.1	373.2
Wearing apparel and other	28.3	31.6	50.5	75.6	76.8	103.1	107.8	73.8	68.0
Perfume and cosmetics	56.5	44.0	52.6	30.5	50.8	38.1	43.1	40.0	19.0
Canned fish	3.4	4.0	11.1	17.1	23.7	40.1	28.1	38.0	47.4
Cord, twine, and other	28.3	23.4	23.2	20.8	38.7	40.6	51.0	78.6	82.8
Manufactures of rubber	7.7	9.3	22.3	25.0	20.8	16.8	19.5	23.2	17.8
Glass and glassware	23.8	24.6	38.4	38.3	35.6	26.6	34.7	44.2	44.8
Scientific instruments, telegraph, and telephone	55.5	85.4	268.8	163.0	140.9	100.8	165.5	282.8	100.5
Car wheels and castings	18.6	17.9	31.4	203.3	13.2	11.9	37.5	15.3	15.5
Cutlery	16.5	17.3	28.4	28.7	28.4	37.3	29.7	25.9	24.2
Firearms	29.2	30.2	44.3	60.6	77.2	46.0	65.8	75.7	89.1
Locks	21.3	29.4	50.6	64.9	75.1	71.6	96.2	116.6	64.3
Machinery (unspecified)	233.2	120.2	489.8	299.5	239.8	235.6	354.3	343.1	321.3
Saws and tools	136.0	161.7	184.1	195.3	205.1	199.1	197.7	189.6	179.6
Scales and balances	8.3	9.1	17.3	16.6	23.2	18.9	21.6	24.0	18.0
Sewing machines	78.7	60.6	78.4	73.0	89.8	101.7	140.0	137.5	114.5
Locomotives	272.1	377.7	818.6	927.0	857.1	190.2	1,648.8	721.4	348.9

Boilers and stoves	14.8	22.7	186.0	20.5	177.0	39.6	125.4	51.6
Wire	8.1	4.5	10.8	46.1	55.6	116.9	130.1	239.3
All other steel manufactures	52.3	60.9	225.8	133.2	63.1	139.5	140.2	133.9
Jewelry	61.0	54.6	70.5	73.0	96.5	101.0	69.5	33.7
Lamps	27.0	28.5	39.4	31.2	45.3	38.6	37.2	29.2
Manufactures of boots and shoes	2.3	1.1	1.2	0.4	1.7	3.0	2.1	2.4
Rosin	66.2	91.7	158.0	166.8	154.3	205.4	233.4	234.5
Turpentine and pitch	38.9	58.3	60.0	64.3	43.3	56.3	65.0	46.7
Lard oil	35.1	39.6	54.8	51.6	74.1	30.3	42.8	23.1
Illuminating oil	890.0	876.6	1,047.6	1,195.2	839.7	1,155.8	1,557.2	1,510.0
Lubricating oil	45.4	49.0	72.7	81.9	98.5	101.7	153.3	129.0
Cottonseed oil	7.2	8.8	20.1	90.7	221.8	233.1	173.9	172.9
Plated ware	32.4	22.7	63.4	45.8	23.1	27.6	25.5	17.1
Bacon	103.5	387.0	801.8	576.2	1,220.9	1,998.4	1,482.7	1,013.2
Lard	484.8	1,509.2	1,304.9	549.9	1,149.3	1,140.1	938.6	714.8
Butter	5.3	19.6	20.8	14.9	16.1	67.6	36.5	40.3
Silk	25.6	22.1	37.6	33.4	27.8	31.6	39.0	21.1
Soap	37.1	54.7	31.6	13.4	12.7	14.4	15.3	10.0
Wood boards	340.8	380.2	683.7	548.0	425.3	536.2	823.7	700.7
House furniture	50.8	50.9	125.8	118.7	70.3	79.9	72.9	51.5
TOTAL	9,276.5	11,902.5	14,049.3	12,388.1	13,866.0	15,165.1	14,258.2	12,441.1

SOURCE: U.S. Treasury Department, *The Foreign Commerce and Navigation of the United States, 1893*, vol. 2, and *1897*, vol. 2 (Washington, D.C.: Government Printing Office, 1893, 1897), passim.

U. S. Imports from Brazil, 1889–97
(in thousands of dollars)

	Treaty Years								
	1889	1890	1891	1892	1893	1894	1895	1896	1897
Chemicals and dyes	21.5	32.7	62.0	117.9	56.0	61.4	90.2	154.9	80.6
Cocoa	321.0	192.9	502.5	608.0	939.1	122.9	374.2	291.3	332.6
Coffee									
lbs.	373,920.8	310,005.0	327,403.9	453,011.0	429,423.6	377,825.9	435,871.7	395,106.6	542,857.3
$	44,891.7	45,664.1	62,022.0	95,751.7	57,136.7	60,377.8	60,316.7	54,019.9	52,792.9
Diamonds	31.6	3.8	62.4	157.4	162.4	57.2	25.6	—	2.3
Fruit	182.7	62.4	282.8	450.6	405.8	296.1	181.8	173.9	197.3
Hair	112.3	139.8	178.5	208.8	268.7	92.7	101.0	92.7	73.3
Goat skins	1,306.3	1,783.0	2,033.5	2,111.6	1,501.5	1,154.6	1,146.8	1,180.7	1,304.6
Other skins	925.8	394.8	476.9	663.3	697.6	286.5	470.4	986.4	439.7
Rubber									
lbs.	19,502.9	20,819.9	21,340.8	25,506.5	26,749.7	23,386.1	26,489.2	22,035.6	21,858.0
$	7,569.0	9,157.2	12,304.2	13,723.7	11,692.0	11,058.8	13,195.3	10,205.3	11,401.0
Unmanufactured wood	63.8	35.3	47.4	90.9	101.9	17.8	46.5	17.8	13.1
Free sugar									
lbs.	—	—	100,120.3	177,520.6	114,599.0	258,447.1	51,842.2	—	—
$	—	—	2,860.4	4,468.1	2,921.9	5,688.7	980.4	—	—
Dutiable sugar									
lbs.	223,925.9	73,801.0	102,701.0	883.5	—	—	128,419.8	191,457.9	140,773.7
$	4,838.1	1,659.2	2,280.9	41.0	—	—	1,720.9	3,776.5	2,137.0
Total sugar									
lbs.	223,925.9	73,801.0	203,821.3	178,404.1	114,599.0	258,447.1	180,262.0	191,457.9	140,773.7
$	4,838.1	1,659.2	5,141.1	4,509.1	2,921.9	5,688.7	2,701.3	3,776.5	2,137.0
TOTAL	60,323.5	59,318.8	83,161.8	118,633.6	76,222.1	79,360.2	78,831.5	71,060.0	69,039.4

SOURCE: U.S. Treasury Department, Foreign Commerce and Navigation of the United States, 1893, vol. 2, and 1897, vol. 2 (Washington, D.C.: Government Printing Office, 1893, 1897), passim.

Reference Matter

Notes

ABBREVIATIONS

AEMEUA: Archivo de la Embajada de México en los Estados Unidos de América, Archivo Histórico Diplomático Méxicano, Mexico City
BAR: Bureau of American Republics
Brasil MF: Ministério da Fazenda
Brasil MIVOP: Ministério da Indústria, Viação, e Obras Publicas
Brasil MJ: Ministério da Justiça
Brasil MM: Ministério da Marinha
Brasil MRE: Ministério das Relaçiones Exteriores
Brasil MV: Ministério da Viação e Obras Públicas
BzLUS: Brazilian Legation in the United States to the Department of State
CFBH: Council of Foreign Bond Holders, Guild Hall Collection, Newspaper Clipping File, microfilm
CGBEU: Consulado Geral do Brasil nos Estados Unidos, Arquivo Histórico de Itamaraty, Rio de Janeiro
CGBL: Consul Geral do Brasil em Londres, Arquivo Histórico de Itamaraty, Rio de Janeiro
DGE: Diretoria Geral de Estatística
FCRB: Fundação Casa Rui Barbosa, Rio de Janerio
FIBGE: Fundação Instituto Brasileiro de Geografia e Estatística
F.O.: Foreign Office, Kew Gardens, London
JGBA: James G. Blaine Family Archive, Library of Congress, Washington
MAE CC: Ministère d'Affaires Etrangères, Correspondance Commerciale, Quai d'Orsay, Paris
MAE CP: Ministère d'Affaires Etrangères, Correspondance Politique, Quai d'Orsay, Paris

MDBEU: Missão Diplomática Brasileira nos Estados Unidos, Arquivo Histórico de Itamaraty, Rio de Janeiro

MDLIS: Missão Diplomática Lisboa

MDPort: Missão Diplomática do Conde de Paço d'Arcos no Brasil, 1891–1893

NRA: Nathaniel Rothschild and Sons Archive, London

NYT: New York Times

PO: Public Opinion

QBA: Quintino Bocayuva Archive, Centro de Pesquisa e Documentação (CPDOC), Fundação Getúlio Vargas, Rio de Janeiro

RS: Raul Soares Archive, CPDOC, Fundação Getúlio Vargas, Rio de Janeiro

USBC: United States Bureau of the Census

USDS: United States Department of State

USNav: United States Navy area file 4, RG 45, National Archives, Washington

USNav.Int: United States Navy, "Naval Intelligence Reports Concerning Affairs in Brazil," Navy Subject File, 1790–1910, VI Box 663, Record Group 45, National Archives

USNav.Letters: United States Navy, South Atlantic Squadron, 1892–1905, "Letters and Telegrams Sent to the Navy Department and Others," Record Group 313, Records of Naval Operating Forces, entry 79. National Archives

USTC: United States Tariff Commission

WQG: Walter Q. Gresham Papers, Library of Congress, Washington

INTRODUCTION

1. USBC, pp. 550, 552. Even Field, who discounts the economic basis of U.S. imperialism, acknowledges that the "importance of Brazilian trade—which greatly exceeded that of China, may be conceded" (p. 660).

2. Burns, *Unwritten Alliance*. See also McCann; Wesson.

3. Fagg, p. 30.

4. I use the word "American" to refer to citizens of the United States even though it also applies to the residents of two continents. I apologize, but there is no better word.

5. See the debate between Field, LaFeber, "Comment," and Beisner, "Comment." Benjamin, pp. 91, 95, turns the accidental argument on its head when he notes that in fact the United States in the nineteenth century was "the most consistently expansionist nation in modern times" because rather than negotiating with citizens of adjacent countries, the United States simply conquered them. Only at the end of the nineteenth century was physical occupation no longer deemed necessary or justifiable. Commerce, foreign investment, and missionaries were employed instead.

6. See Bemis, *Diplomatic History*, chap. 30; Holbo; Fields; Graebner, chap. 1. Noted also in Gardner et al.

7. W. A. Williams, *Tragedy* and *Roots*; LaFeber, *New Empire* and *The American Search*; McCormick.

8. Rosenberg. A number of other historians of foreign relations have noted the steady rise of expansionism in the 1890's, for example, Beisner, *Old Diplomacy*, Campbell, *Transformation*, Tompkins.

9. Luxemburg; Hobson; Bukharin; Lenin.

10. Gallegher and Robinson. For a good discussion of this position see W. R. Lewis.

11. Rosenberg, p. 64.   12. LaFeber, *New Empire*, p. 60.

13. Beisner, *Old Diplomacy*, p. 138.   14. LaFeber, *New Empire*, p. 102.

15. Bemis, *Latin American Policy*, p. 112; Grenville and Young, p. 87.

16. Pletcher, "Reciprocity."

17. Pletcher, in a review article "United States Relations with Latin America," p. 59, notes how few studies of inter-American relations deal with economic questions.

18. Thanks to Ken Hagan for the felicitous phrase.

19. Some of the works that adopt this perspective include Bandeira, Frank, *Capitalism*, and T. Santos.

20. Gill, p. 22.

21. An excellent study of international regimes is Krasner, *Structural Conflict*.

22. Putnam, p. 436.

23. Lake, p. 87 and passim.

24. Frank, *Lumpenbourgeoisie*, p. 70.

25. A strong statement to this effect is Burns's *The Poverty of Progress*.

26. Good examples of this trend can be seen in Love and Jacobsen, Gootenberg, *Between Silver and Guano* and *Imagining Development*, and Jacobsen.

27. This is somewhat ironic since, as Ken Hagan has pointed out, the United States itself had undergone considerable centralization since the Civil War.

28. Sklar.

29. The old navy, of course, had a long and rich history of gunboat interventions as shown in Hagan, *Gunboat Diplomacy*, and there had been a less successful effort in Chile in 1891 and a small-scale adventure in Honolulu in January 1893.

30. W. A. Williams, *American Empire*, pp. 35.

31. Campbell, *Transformation*, p. 141; Holbo, pp. 219, 220; Becker, *Dynamics*, pp. xiv, 182; May, p. 58.

32. See Nelson, who notes that the outcry against the marriage of imperialism and militarism began in the 1890's.

33. Kiernan, p. 105.

34. Krasner, p. 11. See also Becker, *Dynamics*, who argues, p. ix, "The government bureaucracy that grew up to promote the expansion of American commerce was not created simply in response to business pressures. American economic expansion was part of a larger bureaucratic struggle."

I. THE UNITED STATES IN THE GILDED AGE

1. USBC, p. 278.

2. Ibid., pp. 297, 301, 302.

3. Ibid., pp. 141, 402, 409. See also Hession and Sardy, pp. 411, 422.

4. USBC, p. 423.

5. Calculated from USBC, pp. 12, 13.

6. Jones, pp. 351–89; Berkhofer, pp. 153–66.

7. Markusen, p. 33.

8. Gallman, pp. 26, 30; Hession and Sardy, pp. 433–34.

9. USBC, pp. 115, 297, 302.

10. Friedman and Schwartz, pp. 91–93.

11. Beaud, p. 120.

12. Reported in the *Springfield Republican* in *PO* 13, no. 10 (June 11, 1892): 241.

13. Between 1875 and 1892, according to Phillips, p. 239, the number of millionaires quadrupled from 1,000 to 4,047, and the number of decamillionaires did the same, from 50 to 200.

14. Becker, pp. 20, 25, points out that oil was one of the few products that was sold more abroad than in the United States. The major manufactured exports were ma-

chinery, processed foods, oil, and metal products. For many producers of these goods, exports were vital.

15. *NYT*, Oct. 22, 1888: 4-4.

16. Rostow, *World Economy*, pp. 72–73; Wilkins, *Foreign Investment*, p. 145.

17. *Economist*, Nov. 28, 1891: 1520.

18. Davis and Huttenback, p. 11.

19. Hobsbawm, *Age of Empire*, p. 51; Hayem, *Congress international de 1889*, pp. 39–47.

20. Great Britain had purchased half of the exports of Asia, Africa, and America in 1850, but Platt, p. 116, shows its total by 1900 had fallen to 25 percent. The British turned increasingly to their own colonies for trade.

21. Report of Louis Strauss in Hayem, *Congress international*, p. 79.

22. Schumpeter, pp. 430–31.

23. W. A. Lewis, p. 178; Wilkins, *Foreign Investment*, p. 151.

24. USBC, p. 565. See Healy for expansionist arguments.

25. In 1889 the Englishman Robert Griffen estimated Great Britain's per capita wealth at $1,450, France at $950, and the United States at $500. The *San Francisco Chronicle* argued that this was an undervaluation of the United States, which was in fact ahead of France; *PO* 8, no. 12 (Dec. 28, 1889): 319. In a recent estimate, Paul Bairoch in "How not Why," p. 33, finds the U.S. per capita GNP second only to Australia's in 1880 and first in the world in 1900, 10 percent greater than Great Britain's.

26. Quoted in Schivelbusch, p. 10.

27. Hobsbawm, *Age of Empire*, chap. 3; Palmer, pp. 103–13.

28. Hobsbawm, p. 62.

29. *Congressional Record*, vol. 33 (Jan. 9, 1900), p. 711.

30. See Crapole.

31. Missouri's Champ Clark illustrated the fear of assimilating colonies when he protested, "How can we endure our shame when a Chinese senator from Hawaii with his pigtail hanging down his back, shall rise from his chair and in pidgin English proceed to chop logic with Senator Henry Cabot Lodge, oh woe." Quoted in H. W. Morgan, *America's Road*, p. 107. See also Pratt; Healy; Hunt; and Pike, *United States and Latin America*.

32. Coolidge, p. 117.

33. See Rostow's discussion of the *Economist's* recognition of business cycles in *British Economy*, pp. 161–78.

34. Hayem, *Congress international*, p. 90.

35. Thimm, pp. 68–71, 116–27.

36. See Lamoreaux, pp. 187–90, and Chandler, pp. 287–376.

37. Becker, p. x, argues that the dependence on the state was inversely correlated to businesses' capacity for creating independent solutions.

38. *Export and Finance*, Jan. 18, 1890: 58; see also Holbo; Cochran and Miller, pp. 164–96.

39. "Why Harrison Was Elected," *North American Review*, vol. 147 (Dec. 1889): 690; *NYT*, Apr. 7, 1887: 4-3.

40. Dubofsky, pp. 55–69; Haywood.

41. *Economist*, Oct. 13, 1888, Monthly Trade Supplement, p. 6.

42. Faulkner, p. 91; see also King, pp. 72–87.

43. Jensen, pp. 2, 7, notes that politics in this era were heated and popular. All male citizens could vote, and in parts of the country a greater percentage of the electorate, many of whom were farmers, voted than in any prior or subsequent period.

44. *Washington Post,* July 21, 1890, in *PO* 9, no. 16 (July 26, 1890): 361.

45. W. A. Williams, *American Empire;* see also Pollack; Woodward; Morgan, "Populism."

46. Keller, p. viii, notes that "these [1880's and 1890's] were not so much years of government lethargy and subservience to vested interests—the customary view—as a time of intense conflict between old values and the pressures generated by massive change [because of industrialization]." See also Sklar.

47. Terrill, p. 32; see also Gould, "Republican Search," pp. 176–82.

48. *NYT,* Feb. 1, 1888: 4-3, Apr. 8, 1890: 4-2.

49. Cited in Gould, "Republican Search," p. 177.

50. *NYT,* Dec. 20, 1887: 4-4.

51. Davis and Huttenback, p. 38; W. A. Williams, *Roots,* p. 26. Chernow observes that the Morgan Bank was "something of a cross between a central bank and a private bank" (p. xii) and was closely tied to the British banking house.

52. R. Alger to James G. Blaine, Dec. 26, 1888, JGBA, reel 4.

53. *NYT,* Apr. 7, 1887: 4-3.

54. The *New York Times* reported on Nov. 29, 1887: 4-2, that both parties were vague and divided on the issue. In twelve Democratic state conventions in 1886, four had been silent on the tariff, three cautious, one in favor of protection, and four outspoken for "tariff for revenue only." The twenty Republican state conventions in the same year revealed four states with no reference to the tariff, ten for protection, five more cautious, and one for revision and reduction.

55. *NYT,* June 23, 1888: 4-3. For a fine discussion of the Democrats see R. H. Williams, "Dry Bones," pp. 136–37.

56. *NYT,* Mar. 4, 1888: 5-3. The *Times* commended on Dec. 7, 1887, p. 4-1-3, Cleveland's "great statesmanship" because he "forced upon his party an issue as to which the party is divided." If successful, the Democrats "may find a sound and valid reason for existence . . . substantial principles wholly disconnected with the old and worn out questions that are absolutely and forever settled."

57. No one knows how public opinion stands on tariff reform. It has never been squarely tested." On Nov. 29, 1887: 4-2, the paper observed that the views of the House of Representatives were not known on particular positions. "If it takes any action, it will be in deference to opinion since formed or that may form next year."

58. Stanwood, pp. 227–29; Muzzey, p. 362.

59. *NYT,* Dec. 20, 1887: 4-4, and Sep. 16, 1888: 4-7.

60. R. H. Williams, *Years of Decision,* p. 25.

61. W. L. Scott to Grover Cleveland, Sep. 16, 1887, in Cleveland, *Letters,* pp. 157–58. Scott noted that this was Senator Samuel Randal's position.

62. The Prohibitionist Party's vote grew in New York from 25,000 in 1885 to 42,000 in 1887; "Why Harrison Was Elected," *North American Review* (vol. 147), p. 689.

63. Muzzey, p. 362.

64. Sec Morgan, *William McKinley* and *From Hayes to McKinley.*

65. Grover Cleveland to William A. Fussy, Feb. 2, 1888, in Cleveland, *Letters,* p. 173. In listing his principles, the tariff is not mentioned. See also Welch, pp. 84–87.

66. A leading Democratic proponent of industrial exports, A. B. Farquhar, noted the great change in public concern for export expansion in *NYT,* Feb. 13, 1890: 4-4.

67. The expansionist wing of the Democrats was best represented by Alabama's Senator John Tyler Morgan, strong advocate of steamship subsidies, the Nicaraguan canal, and low tariffs, because, as he wrote John W. Foster (July 21, 1883, in the J. W.

Foster papers), "Our crops are bountiful and our people are full of zeal and confidence and are leaving sentimental politics for something of more importance." See also Fry, "Southern Expansionism" and *Search for Southern Autonomy*, pp. 101–9.

68. R. H. Williams, *Democratic Party*, pp. 127–29.

69. R. H. Williams, *Years of Decision*, p. 13.

70. Socolofsky and Spetter, p. 15. On the fraud see *NYT*, Nov. 4, 1888: 1-2, and A. B. Farquhar to Cleveland, Nov. 15, 1888, in Cleveland, *Letters*, p. 192. Jensen, pp. 27–30, rejects the fraud allegations; he argues that 1888 was the cleanest election in years.

71. See, for example, the article by James Blaine's son, Walker Blaine, "Why Harrison Was Elected," *North American Review* (vol. 147), p. 691. Blaine admitted "The country at large cares little for foreign affairs, so long as we are not at war, and little for a navy or a Navy Department as long as we are at peace." They were not interested in financial matters until Cleveland issued his tariff speech. "Silence on the tariff, an ordinary report on 'the state of the Union' a recommendation that Congress should consider the question of the surplus revenue, would probably have secured him a second term."

72. Jensen, p. 33.

73. Kleppner, pp. 30, 31, 70, 75.

74. C. L. Miller, p. 181.

75. R. H. Williams, *The Democratic Party*, pp. 127–29.

76. H. W. Morgan, *From Hayes to McKinley*, p. 296. See also Campbell, *Transformation*, p. 144.

77. Sherman, pp. 96, 97.

78. When Blaine died, the *New York Tribune* (Jan. 28, 1893) called him "the greatest American of recent times. . . . No other American since Lincoln has commanded in equal measure love, confidence, and loyal devotion of a great political party." The *Chicago Times* (Jan. 29, 1893) said, "Within the memory of this generation no American was more deeply beloved, more enthusiastically followed, more profoundly hated, more cordially condemned, than this one-time candidate for the Chief Magistracy." Both in *PO* 14, no. 13 (Feb. 4, 1893): 419, 420.

79. R. H. Williams, *Years of Decision*, p. 12.

80. Jensen, p. 13.

81. J. G. Blaine, p. 429; Tyler, p. 17. As secretary of state he had said that the foreign policy of the Garfield Administration had two objects: "First to bring about peace and prevent future wars in North and South America; second, to cultivate such friendly, commercial relations with all American countries as would lead to a large increase in the export trade of the United States." Quoted in Lockey, p. 275.

82. Quoted in Terrill, p. 48.

83. Romero, *Reciprocidad*, pp. 71, 27, 28–35. See also LaFeber, *New Empire*, p. 48; Stanwood, pp. 192–93. *Export and Finance* (Jan. 18, 1890: 57–59) gives Abram Hewitt's version of the negotiations.

84. Faulkner, p. 49. For the backwardness of some of the principal competitors of the United States, Argentina and Chile, see Scobbie and Bauer.

85. Eysenbach, pp. 36, 41, 221.

86. May, p. 21.

87. Muzzey, p. 448.

88. *Mexican Herald*, Mar. 14, 1897: 11; U.S. Industrial Commission, vol. 1, *Trusts*.

89. Hobsbawm, *Age of Empire*, p. 39.

90. Rosenberg, p. 51; Pletcher, "Reciprocity," p. 54.

91. Taussig, pp. 185–86.

92. *NYT*, Feb. 8, 1890: 8-3.

93. Lavergne, pp. 184, 186. Hayford and Pasurka also find that the best indicator for duty levels was the level of the previous tariff.

94. Lake, p. 225.

95. *Chicago Inter-Ocean*, Sep. 11, 1890, in *PO* 9, no. 24 (Sep. 20, 1890): 545. Terrill, p. 163.

96. Quoted in Terrill, p. 164.

97. Quoted in Morgan, *William McKinley*, p. 62.

98. Frieden, p. 68; Sklar, p. 67.

99. LaFeber, *New Empire*, p. 188.

100. *NYT*, June 25, 1890: 1-1.

101. *NYT*, Apr. 13, 1890: 5-6, and Sep. 8, 1892: 4-3.

102. Romero to Min. Relaciones Exteriores, July 12, 1890 (AEMEUA), legajo 396, no. 835.

103. Ibid. This view was widely held: *NYT*, Mar. 30, 1890: 4-2, July 17, 1890: 1-1.

104. *NYT*, Aug. 9, 1890: 4-2.

105. Ibid., July 15, 1890: 3-2.

106. *Boston Journal*, Sep. 17, 1890, in *PO* 9, no. 24 (Sep. 20, 1890): 545.

107. The *Philadelphia Press*, Sep. 16, 1890, in *PO* 9, no. 24 (Sep. 20, 1890): 546, believed that the success of reciprocity came because "the lessons of the Pan American Congress have been learned by 64,000,000 of Americans."

108. John W. Foster to Walter Q. Gresham, Dec. 1892, in WQG Papers, vol. 39.

109. *NYT*, Aug. 29, 1889: 5-1 and 8-4.

110. *NYT*, Mar. 28, 1890: 4-1, and Feb. 14, 1934. Albert Mai of the Uruguayan Legation wrote to Flint, June 23, 1890 (in the JGBA, reel 11): "Therefore reciprocity is a desideratum,—and in suggesting this to Senator Hale, I cannot but think that your distinguished Secretary of State was in no small measure prompted by your intervention and activity."

111. Bryce, p. 324.

112. *NYT*, Oct. 23, 1889: 2-3.

113. *NYT*, Feb. 19, 1891: 2-6, and Mar. 28, 1890: 4-1.

114. *Spanish American Commercial Union*, p. 1.

115. Memo from the New York Commercial Company, George Alden, president, Charles R. Flint, treasurer, July 28, 1890, JGBA papers, reel 11.

116. C. Flint to J. G. Blaine, July 29, 1890, in JGBA, reel 11: "I sent out letters . . . to 500 manufacturers last night . . . and will have 500 in form 'B' go out in the name of another merchant who represents manufacturers in the export trade." Flint to W. Curtis, Aug. 8, 1890 (USDS, CorAmRep, box 16): "Put out 2,000 letters to all parts of the country in similar form to the enclosed . . . sending them in the names of four or five important commission houses in this city." Flint also advised Senator Aldrich on the reciprocity provision of the McKinley Tariff. Flint wrote to W. Curtis, Sep. 2, 1890 (USDS, CorAmRep, box 16), that he had "arranged for the sending of telegrams to be signed by the President of the Produce Exchange and others."

117. Flint to J. G. Blaine, July 29, 1890, in JGBA, reel 11.

118. C. Flint to J. G. Blaine, Feb. 6, 1891, JGBA, reel 11. *NYT*, July 28, 1890: 5-2. Flint to W. Curtis, Aug. 27, 1889 (USDS, CorAmRep, box 20).

119. *Baltimore American*, in *PO* 9, no. 25 (Sep. 27, 1890): 569; *Minneapolis Times*, Sep. 11, 1890, and *Philadelphia Press*, Sep. 16, 1890, in *PO* 9, no. 24 (Sep. 20, 1890): 544.

120. See letters in USDS, CorAmRep, box 16.

121. *Baltimore News*, Sep. 1, 1890, in *PO* 9, no. 22 (Sep. 6, 1890): 498.

122. Laughlin and Willis, p. 532.

123. Quoted in Terrill, p. 160.

124. Laughlin and Willis, p. 29.

125. Harrison specifically praised this aspect of reciprocity in his message to Congress, Dec. 1, 1890, in Harrison, *Public Papers*, p. 83.

126. Quoted in Faulkner, p. 107.   127. Stephenson, p. 83.

128. Pomeroy, p. 19.   129. *NYT*, Mar. 1, 1892: 9-1.

130. Although representatives of some of the ten nations that eventually signed reciprocity agreements challenged this interpretation, arguing that they had indeed entered into treaties, Secretary of State Walter Gresham replied in October 1894 when the agreements were terminated that "the so-called treaties or agreements that were entered into, based upon the third section of the McKinley bill, were not treaties binding upon the two Governments." U.S. Trade Commission, p. 160.

131. Quoted in Faulkner, p. 108.

2. TARGET: LATIN AMERICA

1. Hobsbawm, p. 347.   2. Lake, pp. 216, 217.

3. Lipson, p. 17.   4. McGann, p. 93.

5. Davis and Huttenback, pp. 38; Brown, p. 100; Zeitlin, pp. 94, 95.

6. See Bouvier.

7. Blaine noted in "The Foreign Policy of Garfield," *Political Discussions*, p. 419, the "most dangerous movements" of French guardianship of the Panama canal.

8. Laughlin and Willis, p. 186.   9. Pletcher, "Reciprocity," 59.

10. W. A. Lewis, p. 169.   11. J. G. Blaine, p. 429.

12. Harrison to Blaine, Jan. 17, 1889, in Volwiler, p. 46.

13. Sherman, p. 164. Gresham's wife Matilda, in Gresham, vol. 2, pp. 495, 570, believed that Blaine preferred to be secretary of state rather than president because of his concern for foreign affairs.

14. Bastert, pp. 389, 403, 412.

15. Quoted in Grenville and Young, p. 92.

16. Quoted in Pletcher, *Awkward Years*, p. 92. Also see Pike, *Chile*, pp. 48–58, and Kiernan, "Foreign Interests."

17. Hill, pp. 30–31; Whitaker, p. 580.

18. The signatories were Bolivia, Chile, Costa Rica, Ecuador, Honduras, Mexico, Nicaragua, Paraguay, and Peru. See McGann, pp. 68–69.

19. Quoted in ibid., p. 87.

20. J. G. Blaine, "Foreign Policy of Garfield," in *Political Discussions*, p. 411.

21. J. G. Blaine, p. 413; H. Blaine, vol. 2, p. 296. See also Matias Romero, "Pan American Conference," *North American Review*, vol. 151 (July 1890): 354; Campbell, *Transformation*, p. 98.

22. Peskin, p. 79.

23. U.S. Trade Commission, *Report 1886*.

24. Quoted in Parlee, pp. 149, 93. The Monterrey region was eventually tied into central Mexico, but the prosperous northwestern part of Mexico was linked to the center only after 1910.

25. McGann, p. 77.

26. U.K. *Alphabetical Index 1852–1899* and *1900–1949*, passim; *The Economist*, April 21, 1888, p. 502; Uzoigwe, pp. 29–35; Russell, passim.

27. Langer, pp. 238–82.

28. The participants were Argentina, Bolivia, Brazil, Chile, Colombia, Costa Rica, Ecuador, El Salvador, Guatemala, Haiti, Honduras, Mexico, Nicaragua, Paraguay, Peru, the United States, Uruguay, and Venezuela.

29. *NYT*, Feb. 14, 1890: 4-5; Matias Romero to Min. Relaciones Exteriores, Feb. 15, 1890, AEMEUA, legajo 393, no. 206.

30. Romero, 356, reported that the reason that Santo Domingo refused to participate was because her 1884 commercial treaty with the United States had not been ratified by the American Congress, so it was a waste of time to formulate other Latin American policies that Congress would likely reject again.

31. Romero, "Pan-American Conference," p. 357; Fagg, p. 23.

32. Muzzey, p. 145; Swann, pp. 114, 195.

33. Muzzey, pp. 27, 146, 147, 233–35, 304. Muzzey notes that there is very little information available on Blaine's economic activities, but he clearly enjoyed a lifestyle far in excess of what his official salaries could afford him. Swann, pp. 194, 195.

34. Lustig, pp. 100, 102.

35. Thimm, p. 51.

36. Blaine and the officials were absolved. See Lockey, p. 286.

37. Thimm, p. 3.

38. Curtis, *United States and Foreign Powers*, pp. 70, 74.

39. Thimm, p. 10. Becker, *Dynamics*, pp. viii, ix, argues that big businessmen were not interested in government help in foreign trade; only smaller businessmen saw the need for government aid.

40. May, p. 58.

41. Ibid., pp. 57, 61.

42. Coolidge, p. 124.

43. *New York Herald*, Feb. 8, 1891: 9-6; *NYT*, Mar. 1, 1889: 1-7.

44. *Dictionary of American Biography*, vol. 1, pt. 1, p. 369.

45. Coolidge, p. 135.

46. May, p. 45.

47. H. Blaine to M., Nov. 25, 1881, in H. Blaine, *Letters*, p. 257; *NYT*, Mar. 1, 1889: 1-7. See also Coolidge, pp. 9, 76, 82, 276; Chandler, pp. 426, 427; Terrill, p. 263; *Dictionary of American Biography*, vol. 2, pt. 2, pp. 394–95; Wilson, p. 82; May and Plaza, p. 7; Wolfe, p. 223; Overton, pp. 32, 53, 65.

48. Coolidge, p. 8.

49. BAR, *Handbook 1891*, vol. 1, p. 9. Pepper, passim.

50. *NYT*, Aug. 29, 1889: 5-1; Terrill, pp. 138, 189.

51. Wall, p. 452.

52. Springfield (Mass.) *The Union*, Oct. 11, 1889 clipping in *Benjamin Harrison Papers*; Martí, *Obras completas*, vol. 6, p. 98; Coolidge, p. 102; *NYT*, Aug. 29, 1889: 5-1, and June 20, 1888: 4-3; Terrill, p. 263. R. H. Williams, in *Democratic Party*, p. 68, argues that Estée was in fact an "anti-railroad man" who worked with Huntington against Stanford and the Union Pacific.

53. *Dictionary of American Biography*, vol. 4, pt. 2, pp. 528–29.

54. Salvador de Mendonça to Barão de Cotegipe, Apr. 15, 1887, in (CGBEU, NY), 258-3-10. See also Fry, "Southern Expansionism," 332, 334.

55. Chandler, p. 333.

56. Kiernan, *Marxisim*, p. 93.

57. Thimm, p. 136.

58. Flint, *Memories*, pp. 287, 9.

59. Ibid., pp. 286, 66, 85.

60. License, New York Commercial Company, July 21, 1886, memo, Aug. 23, 1890; New York Commercial Company, memo, Apr. 27, 1891; June 19, 1891, in

scrapbook, box 6, Flint Papers; R. Hyermans to W. R. Grace, Feb. 15, 1889, and A. M. Macomber to M. Grace, Feb. 26, 1889, in box 61, Grace papers. The last letter implies that Coolidge and Flint may have been working together in the rubber consolidation.

61. Flint, *Memories*, pp. 289, 309.

62. See Flint's testimony to the U.S. Industrial Commission 1901, p. 89.

63. Claim of Minor C. Keith against the government of Costa Rica includes letter from Flint to Keith June 22, 1898, in Flint papers, box 7; *Brooklyn Daily Eagle*, Oct. 6, 1901, in Flint papers, box 7.

64. Spanish American Commercial Union, p. 20; *NYT*, Mar. 1, 1889: 1-7; R. H. Williams, *Democratic Party*, p. 132. See also *Dictionary of American Biography*, vol. 1, pt. 1, p. 369.

65. Bliss was president of the American Protective League, *NYT*, Jan. 22, 1892: 8-6; Andrew Carnegie, "Summing Up the Tariff Discussion," *North American Review* 151 (July 1890): 55, 67; A. Carnegie to J. G. Blaine, July 22, 1889, in Carnegie papers, vol. 10, supports the idea of a customs union. See also *Boston Journal*, Dec. 14, 1889, in *P.O.* 8, no. 11 (Dec. 21, 1889); Coolidge, p. 102; John Henderson, in Spanish American Commercial Union, p. 42.

66. *NYT*, Apr. 22, 1890: 1-1, and Apr. 23, 1890: 3-5. Martí, *Obras completas*, vol. 6, p. 42.

67. *Charleston News and Courier*, Oct. 8, 1889, in *PO* 8, no. 1 (Oct. 12, 1889): 3.

68. *Chicago Inter-Ocean*, Oct. 4, 1889; *Omaha World-Herald*, Oct. 4, 1889; *San Francisco Examiner*, Oct. 2, 1889; and the *New York Tribune*, Oct. 8, 1889, in *PO* 8, no. 1 (Oct. 12, 1898): 1-3.

69. *St. Paul Press*, Oct. 4, 1889; *San Francisco Chronicle*, Oct. 3, 1889, in *PO* 8, no. 1 (Oct. 12, 1889): 2.

70. *New York Herald*, Oct. 8, 1889; *Bradstreet's*, Oct. 5, 1889; and *Harper's*, Oct. 12, 1889, in *PO* 8, no. 1 (Oct. 12, 1889): 1, 2.

71. Curtis, "Friends in South America."

72. Martí, *Inside the Monster*, p. 340.

73. Romero, "Pan American Conference," p. 356. *El Comercio* of Lima, quoted in *NYT*, Dec. 1, 1889: 4-5, concurred. The *London Spectator*, Oct. 8, 1889, and the *New York Herald*, Oct. 8, 1889, thought Blaine dreamed of a Pan American protectorate, but neither thought it possible in *PO* 8, no. 1 (Oct. 12, 1889): 3.

74. International American Conference, *Reports of Committees*, vol. 1, pp. 9–10; Azevedo, p. 187. Coolidge, p. 120, notes that while an international arbitration plan was important to Blaine, "Questions relating to the improvement of business intercourse . . . [were] the favorite idea of James G. Blaine."

75. Sklar points out (p. 438) that corporate liberalism in the late nineteenth century strengthened the executive and the judiciary in part by creating "extra-electoral bodies of experts and administrators insulated from the fluctuations of electoral politics." See also Mattox.

76. Blaine to Carnegie, June 13, 1889, in Carnegie papers, vol. 10.

77. McGann, pp. 131–33.

78. Romero to Ministério Relaciones Exteriores, Jan. 30, 1890, AEMEUA, legajo 392, no. 132.

79. Quoted in Martí, *Obras completas*, vol. 6, p. 90.

80. International American Conference, *Report of Committees*, vol. 1, p. 83; Brasil MRE, *Relatorio 1891*, pp. 153, 170; Terrill, p. 264.

81. Romero, "Pan-American Conference," p. 419; *NYT*, Aug. 29, 1889: 8-4.

82. Brasil MRE, *Tratado de Arbitramento*, passim; Martí, *Obras completas*, vol. 6, pp. 74, 88, 89, 102; Coolidge, p. 125.

83. International American Conference, *Report of Committees*, vol. 1, pp. 113, 114, 138–52; Brasil MRE, *Relatório, 1891*; USDS, *Foreign Affairs 1890*, p. 4.

84. That Argentina was the strongest defender of the customs union at the conference was unusual, Flint pointed out in International American Conference, *Report of the Committees*, vol. 1, pp. 153, 154; it accounted for only 4 percent of U.S. imports from Latin America. It was true that in 1870 over 90 percent of Latin American imports into the United States were charged duties, but by 1889 fully 87.5 percent of those imports were entering duty free. In other words, the United States was already moving unilaterally into a free trade arrangement with its neighbors.

85. Quoted in Laughlin and Willis, p. 135.

86. J. G. Blaine, pp. 187, 193, 301, 314, 309; Muzzey, p. 151; J. M. Lachlan, president of the U.S. and Brazil Mail Steamship Company, to Blaine, July 31, 1889, in Records of the U.S. Delegation to the First International Conference of American States, box 20, N.A., thanked Blaine for his "zealous advocacy" and ended "personally, I am *glad* that you are connected with this *important* matter" (emphasis in the original).

87. *Frank Leslie's* in *PO* 8, no. 12 (Dec. 28, 1889): 306; Marvin, p. 381.

88. Blaine in *North American Review* in *PO* 8, no. 12 (Dec. 28, 1889): 306.

89. Quoted in Martí, *Obras completas* vol. 6, p. 58, also p. 75. *NYT*, Feb. 7, 1891: 4-2; Swann, p. 194.

90. Brasil MRE, *Relatório, 1891*.

91. Pepper, p. 124.

92. M. Romero to Ministério de Relaciones Exteriores, Feb. 9, 1890, AEMEUA, legajo 393, no. 144.

93. To be fair, the House Committee on Banking and Currency did report favorably on the bank, but the bill died in committee because it was believed that the bank would have enjoyed a monopoly of U.S. commerce in Latin America. Also, Congress allocated $65,000 for plans for an inter-American railroad, but capital was not forthcoming to build it; *NYT*, Apr. 11, 1890: 4-3.

94. Interview with Grace in the *NYT*, Mar. 11, 1890: 9-1.

95. Romero, "Pan-American Conference," p. 421.

96. *Philadelphia Press*, May 31, 1890, and *Boston Post*, May 29, 1890, in *PO* 9, no. 9 (June 7, 1890): 195.

97. The *New York Post*, May 29, 1890, and the *Boston Globe*, May 30, 1890, noted the link between the Pan American recommendations and the legislation going to Congress [*PO* 9, no. 9 (July 7, 1890): 195].

98. The *New York Times* reported July 28, 1890: 1-1, that Blaine was "stealing a march on the silver question" by pushing through Congress a bill to appropriate funds for the international American monetary union meeting recommended by the Pan American Conference.

99. See address of Harrison to Congress, Dec. 1, 1890, Dec. 9, 1891, and Dec. 6, 1892, in *Public Papers*, pp. 83, 86, 99, 101, 146; Hutchins, p. 534; Socolofsky and Spetter, pp. 58, 59.

100. Although interest in the China market peaked in the late 1890's, it began in the late 1880's and early 1890's. See Campbell, *Special Business Interests*, pp. 14, 15, and McCormick, pp. 26–28, 31.

101. So convinced were they of its imminent construction that the Bureau of American Republics (the organization that issued from the Pan American Conference) published in its 1891 handbook a picture of a "Bird's Eye View of the Maritime Canal of Nicaragua" as if it were already fully in operation. BAR, *Handbook 1891*, p. 178. See also *NYT*, Feb. 7, 1889: 1-3, Feb. 25, 1889: 1-3, Apr. 2, 1892: 8-2, and

June 11, 1892: 4-1. The *Boston Journal,* Jan. 25, 1890, in *PO* 8, no. 17 (Feb. 1, 1890): 402, discusses the "unprecedentedly busy" preparations that were being made for the canal in Greytown, Nicaragua. See also Clayton, "The Nicaraguan Canal."

102. Sherman, p. 119.

103. Bliss to Curtis, Dec. 4, 1889; Flint to Curtis, Sep. 4, 1889, Sep. 19, 1889, Nov. 27, 1889; Spencer Borden to Flint, Sep. 18, 1889, all in "Records of U.S. Delegation to First International Conference of American States," box 20.

104. Clipping, no name, Washington, Nov. 25, 1889, in "Records of U.S. Delegation to First International Conference of American States, 1889–1890," box 20.

105. Quoted in Caruso, p. 613. See also Pepper, pp. 121–35.

106. Pepper, pp. 131, 133, 134, 169.

107. George W. E. Dorsey to Flint, July 7, 1890, in JGBA, reel 11; Coolidge, p. 128; *NYT,* Aug. 29, 1889: 5-1; Industrial Commission on Trusts, *Report, 1901,* p. 50; Babcock, pp. 28–30, 34; The *New York Times* reported Mar. 31, 1892: 9-1, that "Flint and Co. of this city is said to have a strong grip on the crude rubber output." Records of U.S. Delegation to First International Conference of American Republics, box 21, is devoted to the Inter-American Bank. It contains almost exclusively letters from Flint discussing his lobbying efforts.

108. Flint finally was able to push the legislation through the House but failed in securing the enabling legislation.

109. *NYT,* Aug. 29, 1889: 5-1; Swann, pp. 123, 237; Hutchins, p. 531.

110. Robert W. Perks, apparently a representative of the British Manchester Ship Canal Works, wrote from London, Mar. 2, 1891, inquiring of Flint if a neutral canal built by Americans and Englishmen together "meets with the approval of the parties advising with Senator Miller." That the letter found its way to the Blaine archive, reel 11, demonstrates that Flint was in contact with the secretary of state on the canal. Claim of Minor C. Keith against the government of Costa Rica in Flint papers, box 7.

3. BRAZIL: FROM MONARCHY TO REPUBLIC

1. Deputy Espirito Santo in Brasil, Congreso Nacional, *Anais,* vol. 2, p. 92, after asking rhetorically, "What is our duty here?" answered, "Is it not simply to turn our eyes to the most advanced nations and transplant their governmental systems to our country without removing the ff and rr expression in the political system of the United States?"

2. Bandeira, p. 117; Burns, "Relações internacionais," p. 378; Silva, *Poder civil,* p. 3; Singer, p. 374.

3. Of course, there were substantial differences in culture and self-perception as well. The best study of these contrasts is Vianna Moog's *Bandeirantes e pioneiros.*

4. FIBGE, *Sérias estatísticas retrospectivas,* vol. 1, pp. 76–84.

5. Rippy, *Rivalry.*

6. Hill, pp. 6, 122, 140; Manchester, pp. 68; Wilgus; Bethell, *Abolição,* pp. 272, 273.

7. Manchester, p. 266, suggests that after 1853 relations became even closer between the United States and Brazil as an "entente cordial" formed. In fact, there was little understanding or cordiality this early.

8. Hill, pp. 219–58; N. Luz, *Amazonia,* passim; Bandeira, pp. 90, 91, 94, 95, 117.

9. USBC, p. 553.

10. A. Gérard to Rebot, Aug. 9, 1891, MAE CC, vol. 23; Hill, p. 170.

11. Rydell, p. 15.

12. Flint, *Memories,* p. 78; Bandeira, p. 120.

13. Freyre, pp. 76–78, 90, 91.

14. LaFeber, *New Empire*, p. 48. LaFeber asserts that the reason Brazil, along with Chile and Argentina, was excluded was because Frelinghusen could not offer duty reductions on the politically sensitive wool. Since Brazil, unlike the other two, was not a wool producer, this seems beside the point. Rather, the problem was that Brazil's main exports to the United States were already duty free, so there was nothing to offer.

15. J. Smith, "Latin American Trade Commission," pp. 12, 18, 22. The commission was originally supposed to inspect Brazil, but when Cleveland replaced Arthur, the Democratic administration ordered the commission to make a hasty return to Washington. Rio newspapers lashed out at the slight.

16. The commercial treaty with Great Britain had allowed British imports a lower duty rate than even Portugal enjoyed, and, more seriously, had guaranteed Englishmen in Brazil special rights of extraterritoriality and inheritance: it restricted Brazilian sovereignty by granting British subjects special rights in Brazil.

17. Mendonça, *Ajuste de contas*, pp. 36, 37, 40; Manchester, p. 306; Azevedo, p. 148.

18. Lafayette Rodrigues Pereira, J. G. do Amaral Valente, and Salvador de Mendonça to B. Harrison, April 1889, BzLUS, vol. 6; Mendonça, *Ajuste de contas*, p. 40.

19. Tavares Bastos, p. 22; Mauá, p. 235.

20. See, e.g., Leclerc, p. 142; Ramalho Ortigao, "Quadro social da revolução brasileira," *Revista de Portugal*, vol. 2 (1890): 84; Prado, "Destinos políticos do Brasil," *Revista de Portugal*, vol. 1 (1889): 469.

21. Mendonça, *Ajuste de contas*, p. 17.

22. M. L. Mulhall, "Brazil: Past and Future," *Living Age*, vol. 184 (Feb. 1, 1890): 301. The *South American Journal*, Aug. 25, 1888, in CFBH, vol. 5, estimated British capital in 1887 at U.S. $300 million in direct and portfolio investments and another U.S. $200 million in commercial credit.

23. Manchester, p. 316; R. Miller, pp. 159–69.

24. *Washington Post*, in PO 8, no. 12 (Dec. 28, 1889): 297, and *Age of Steel PO* 12, no. 1 (Oct. 10, 1891): 18.

25. FIBGE, *Sérias estatísticas retrospectivas*, vol. 1, pp. 46, 86, 87; Suzigan, pp. 123–46.

26. FIBGE, *Sérias estatísticas retrospectivas*, vol. 1, p. 68.

27. Centro Industrial do Brasil, vol. 1, pp. 260, 261.

28. W. A. Lewis, p. 178.

29. *Revue des Deux Mondes*, Jan. 1, 1889, p. 239; Marichal, p. 127.

30. Blondel to Ministère d'Affaires Etrangères, Oct. 18, 1889, MAE CC, vol. 22. The *New York Times* reported, Jan. 5, 1889, 1-5, that a group of American capitalists from New York, Pittsburgh, and Washington had received a concession for 50,000 to 60,000 acres bordering the Amazon River near the Andes Mountains where they sought to invest $2 million in gold and diamond mines.

31. Quoted in Marichal, p. 145.

32. *South American Journal* and *Financial Times*, Mar. 9, 1889, in CFBH, vol. 6.

33. Pernambuco and Minas Gerais also sought European loans, *South American Journal*, Mar. 2, 1889, and Aug. 17, 1889; *London Times* Aug. 30, 1889, in CFBH, vol. 6.

34. Cited in CGBL 254/3/10, 1889–1891. For concurring opinions see Amelos de Chaillou to René Goblet, Ministère des Affaires Etrangères, Mar. 9, 1889, MAE CC, vol. 22, and *South American Journal*, Oct. 1891, in CFBH, vol. 7.

35. *South American Journal*, Dec. 1, 1888, in CFBH, vol. 6.

36. CFBH, vol. 6, passim. The Visconde de Ouro Preto calculated in *A decada republicana*, vol. 1, p. 52, that private companies borrowed 59, 288 contos.

37. James W. Wells wrote in the *New York Sun, PO* 10, no. 5 (Nov. 8, 1890): 12, "It is much in her favor that she (Brazil) has dispensed with the costly aid of London financiers and is carrying out these great enterprises with the aid of native capitalists, engineers, and contractors."

38. *South American Journal*, Mar. 2, 1889, and *Money Market Review*, Nov. 28, 1888, in CFBH, vol. 6.

39. *Financial News*, Oct. 5, 1889, in CFBH, vol. 6.

40. *South American Journal*, Mar. 2, 1889, Apr. 22, Aug. 31, 1889; *London Times*, Aug. 30, 1889, in CFBH, vol. 6; *The Economist*, Sep. 22, 1888, p. 1194.

41. Graham, *Britain*, p. 152; *Financial News*, Sep. 6, 1888, and *Statist*, May 19, 1888, in CFBH, vol. 6; Companie Générale de Chemin de Fer Brésilien prospectus, Mar. 24, 1894, in MAE CP, vol. 26.

42. Balmori et al., pp. 19, 203, 220. Sweigart, p. 227; Vaz, p. 45; Levi, p. 83; Cardoso de Mello, p. 150.

43. *Jornal do Commércio*, Dec. 1889, in "Recortes," FCRB; Juca Faro to Quintino Bocayuva, Jan. 4, 1892, in Quintino archive, QB 891.03.31 cp; Banco Hypotecário to Floriano Peixoto, Oct. 18, 1893, in Floriano archive, Caixa 8L, Pacote 5; *Almanak Laemmert, 1890*, passim.

44. *Revue des Deux Mondes*, Sep. 15, 1889, p. 480; Schantz, p. 349; *South American Journal*, July 3, 1889, in CFBH, vol. 6.

45. Oliveira Lima, *Memórias*, p. 144. As late as 1887, U.S. Consul to Brazil C. C. Andrews in *Brazil*, p. 116, had lamented that Brazilians "concern themselves very little with what takes place in the United States."

46. *London Times*, Nov. 18, 1889, quoted in CGBL 254/3/10. This view was shared, for example, by João Gomes, "Notas do mez," *Revista de Portugal* 1 (1889): 781. See also N. W. Sodré, *Burguesia brasileira*.

47. N. M. Rothschild to Minister of Finance, Nov. 14, 1890, Letter Agency Book 4, NRA; Wileman, pp. 247, 253; J. L. Ardin to Min. d'Affaires Etrangèrs, Dec. 26, 1889, in MAE CC, vol. 22; *Revue des Deux Mondes*, Dec. 1, 1889, pp. 717, 718.

48. George Makepeace Towle, "Spread of the Democratic Idea," *North American Review*, Feb. 1890, abstracted in *PO* 8, no. 18 (Feb. 8, 1890): 424. Luiz de Magalhães, "Revista de política interna," *Revista de Portugal* 3 (1890): 484.

49. *New York Herald*, Feb. 1, 1891: 19-5.

50. *NYT*, Jan. 19, 1890: 17-6.

51. Mendonça de Azevedo, p. 178; "Diplomatic Dispatches U.S. Ministers," Nov. 19, 1889, and Dec. 17, 1889; Hill, p. 265.

52. Frederico de S. (pseudonym of Eduardo Prado), "Prácticas e theorias da dictadura republicana no Brasil," *Revista de Portugal* 3 (1890): 75, 76, 83, and "A república brazileria," *Revista de Portugal* 2 (1890): 830; Leclerc, pp. 99, 116–18; *NYT*, Apr. 28, 1890: 2-1.

53. Frederico de S. (E. Prado), "A república brazileira," *Revista de Portugal* 2 (1890): 858.

54. Abstracted in *PO* 8, no. 12 (Dec. 28, 1889): 280. See also Rippy, "The United States and the Republic."

55. Abstracted in ibid. See also the disapproving clippings sent by Brazil's minister Amaral Valente back to Quintino Bocayuva, Brazil's foreign minister, Jan. 7, 1890, in MDBEU, "Ofícios 1890–92."

56. Abstracted in *PO* 8, no. 12 (Dec. 28, 1889): 280.

57. *The Economist*, London, Nov. 23, 1889: 495.

58. Quoted in Silva, *1889*, p. 88.

59. *South American Journal,* Dec. 14, 1889, p. 757.

60. Porto, *Apontamentos,* passim.

61. Quoted in Freyre, p. 7.

62. Amaral Valente sent to Blaine, Jan. 4, 1890 (BzLUS, reel 7), letters from ten notable imperial statesmen proclaiming for the Republic.

63. In Minas Gerais republicans under the Empire constituted barely 30 percent of the electorate, and in São Paulo 25 percent; in Rio Grande do Sul they were still only the second most powerful party. There was a national republican organization founded in 1887, but article nine of its charter stipulated that "the federal directory can not block the actions of provincial parties on matters of provincial business, interests or aspirations." Under the Republic there was little national coordination. Boehrer, pp. 117, 144, 189, 195.

64. D. Burke to U.S. Dept. of State, June 19, 1890, in "Diplomatic Dispatches Bahia."

65. The first, described by Medeiros e Albuquerque, pp. 173–75, involved only 30–40 men, but seemed to reveal the freedmen's hostility to the Republic. The second, described by the *New York Times,* Jan. 15, 1890: 5-1, included one cavalry and two infantry regiments as well as an artillery battalion.

66. On the military see Hahner, *Civilian-Military Relations;* Schulz; Sodré, *História militar;* Simmons.

67. Medeiros e Albuquerque, p. 171. Constant Magalhães would die one year later and Deodoro the following year.

68. Oliveira Martins, *A circulação fiduciaria,* pp. 179–80; P. M. Campos, "Brasil-Portugal," pp. 211–12.

69. Dec. 7, 1889, MDBL, "Ofícios 1889–1890," 214-3/3.

70. This issue appeared to become moot, however, when Brazil's minister of foreign affairs, anxious for recognition of the Republic by a foreign country and concerned with lessening border tensions since a revolt in the southern Brazilian state of Rio Grande do Sul was feared (which indeed broke out within a year), signed a pact with his Argentine counterpart in Montevideo on Jan. 25, 1890. In exchange for the treaty, Argentina became the first country to recognize Brazil's new republican government. The Missiones controversy was not dead, however; it would reappear later when Brazil renounced the agreement. Mendonça to Harrison, May 9, 1892, in BzLUS, reel 7, has the history of the dispute and considerable correspondence. Also, Belen to Ministère d'Affaires Etrangères, July 21, 1891, in MAE CC, vol. 34, Finances. M. W. Williams; Scenna, pp. 262–66.

71. *NYT,* Sep. 8, 1887: 4-2. See also Burns, *Unwritten Alliance,* pp. 32–33.

72. Brasil, MRE, *Relatório 1891,* pp. 34–43, 67–74; *NYT,* June 15, 1890: 5-2; Frederico de S., "Dictadura no Brasil: Tratados Diplomáticos," *Revista de Portugal* 2 (1890): 415, 418. Max Leclerc reported in *Cartas do Brasil,* pp. 95–97, how unpopular Bocayuva's mission to Argentina was domestically.

73. Harrison to Amaral Valente, Jan. 30, 1890, BzLUS, vol. 7.

74. Harrison, *Public Papers,* p. 67.

75. *NYT,* Jan. 30, 1890: 1-6.

76. Abstracted in *PO* 8, no. 18 (Feb. 8, 1890): 425.

77. *Kansas City Journal,* Jan. 31, 1890, in ibid. With Brazil's republican revolution the *New York Times* began to devote far more space to the southern republic's economic, diplomatic, and political affairs.

78. Amaral Valente had sent to Blaine, Jan. 4, 1890 (BzLUS, reel 7), letters from the leading monarchist politicians who all recognized the Republic as a fait accompli and advised against any restorationist attempts.

79. *NYT,* Jan. 15, 1890: 5-1.

80. Harrison explicitly thanked Mendonça (Mendonça to Araripe, Jan. 30, 1891, MDBEU, "Ofícios 1890–92") for "identifying the Brazilian nation with the measures needed to promote the welfare of the States which make up our great continent [which] has been conspicuous from the time you and your honored colleagues entered the recent International American Conference."

81. The *New York Times* described Mendonça (Jan. 17, 1891: 8-2) this way: "A slight man of middle age. His hair is streaked with grey. His features are resolute and his manner quiet and suave." He was "stylishly attired" and spoke "excellent English."

82. Fontoura Xavier to Prudente de Morais, Feb. 20, 1899, in Coleção Prudente, lata 600, pasta 42.

83. J. G. Amaral Valente to Blaine, Jan. 13, 1890, and Mendonça to Blaine, Aug. 5, 1890, in BzLUS, vol. 7.

84. Flint wrote to Harrison, Dec. 21, 1890, JGBA, "I am delighted that he [Mendonça] has been named minister and I feel that he will be able to carry our negotiations for reciprocity to a satisfactory conclusion."

85. Mendonça, *Ajuste de contas*, pp. 224–25.

86. Flint was particularly hospitable to the Brazilian delegation, inviting them to private dinners and putting them and their country's flag at a special place of honor at a large banquet: *NYT*, Sep. 26, 1889: 9-4, and Spanish American Commercial Union, p. 11.

87. J. Amaral Valente to Q. Bocayuva, Jan. 10, 1890, in MDBEU, "Ofícios 1890–92," *Financial News*, Dec. 28, 1889, in CFBH, vol. 6; *NYT*, Nov. 16, 1889: 1-5.

88. Aceely (?—illegible) to Flint, Jan. 20, 1890, in JGBA, reel 11.

89. *NYT*, Oct. 27, 1890: 5-6.; Amaral Valente to Q. Bocayuva, May 6, 1890, MDBEU, "Ofícios 1890–92."

90. Later, Blaine supposedly supplied four million dollars more. Quoted in Cosío Villegas, *História moderna de México*, vol. 6, p. 700.

91. Mendonça to Constantino Palleta, Dec. 8, 1891, in MDBEU, "Ofícios 1890–92"; Mendonça, *Ajuste de contas*, p. 50; Flint, *Memories*, p. 176; Foster, *Diplomatic Memoirs*, vol. 2, p. 7; Bliss to William R. Day, Feb. 19, 1898, State Department Miscellaneous Letters, reel 992, N.A., RG 59; Azevedo, pp. 164, 165; Hill, p. 266.

92. Ferns, pp. 446–58; Ziegler, pp. 244–67.

93. *Rio News*, Aug. 22, 1892.

94. Quintino Bocayuva, July 31, 1902 in Quintino QB 01.02.05 cp.

95. Tedui to Ministère d'Affaires Etrangères, Nov. 18, 1889, MAE CC, vol. 22; Paço d'Arco to Ayres Gouveia, Nov. 2, 1892, in MDPort.

96. Congress Nacional, *Anais*, vol. 2, p. 6.

97. Quoted in Hahner, *Civilian-Military Relations*, p. 74.

98. Mello, *Governo provisório*, p. 124.

99. Quoted in Abranches, *O Golpe do Estado*.

100. Abranches, *O Golpe do Estado*, pp. 140–41, 150; Carone, *A República Velha*, vol. 2, pp. 19–25.

101. Witter, vol. 1, pp. 88–91; Pan American Union, *Bulletin*, Mar. 1894, p. 665.

102. Cesar Zama in Camara dos Deputados, *Anais, 1896*, vol. 6, p. 86, and A. Lima, *Discursos*, p. 118. Undated manifesto of Rui to Deodoro, NRA, XI-65-78, M. B. Levy, "O Encilhamento," pp. 209. For more on the Encilhamento see Topik, "Brazil's Bourgeois Revolution?"

103. Blondel to Ministère d'Affaires Etrangères, Jan. 3, 1890, MAE CP, vol. 34.

104. Abranches, *Governos e congressos*, passim.

105. Calculated from Abranches, *Governos e congressos*, passim.

106. J. Nabuco to Barão de Rio Branco, July 31, 1890, in Nabuco, *Cartas*, p. 188, said "The republican party disappeared. . . . They lost importance they had under the monarchy; they are suspect to the representatives of the 15th of November [Deodoro's followers] who are jealous of them [the republicans] and completely control the situation."

107. FIBGE, *Sérias estatísticas retrospectivas*, vol. 1, pp. 85, 88, 89; Denslow, pp. 22, 25; Buescu, p. 52.

108. Lewin, pp. 54, 55.

109. J. M. de Carvalho, "Elite and State-Building," pp. 193, 194, 198, and calculated from Carvalho, *A construção da ordem*, p. 170.

110. Merrick and Graham, pp. 94, 96; Denslow, p. 22; Eisenberg, "Abolishing Slavery"; Conrad and Costa, *Da senzala à colônia*.

111. FIBGE, *Sérias estatísticas retrospectivas*, vol. 1, pp. 85, 88, 89. For discussion of sugar in the colonial period see Schwartz.

112. Mintz, p. 73.

113. Beet sugar grew from 4 percent of British imports in 1851 to 65 percent by 1889, consequently the British colonies' share of the market fell from 70 percent to 13 percent during those years. Diaz Miranda, pp. 42–50, 60, 64, 67–69.

114. R. Graham, *Britain*, p. 75; Eisenberg, *Modernization Without Change*, p. 23.

115. The 1887 treaty to restrict state sugar bounty payments was still under consideration when Brazil entered into negotiations with the United States. The British signed it and waited for continental powers to participate; *The Economist*, Apr. 21, 1888, p. 502.

116. Deerr, *History of Sugar*, pp. 506–7. When the sugar agreement was finally reached in 1902, it was indeed a purely European settlement.

117. USBC, p. 548; Mintz, pp. 73, 197.

4. BRAZIL DEBATES THE TREATY

1. Brazil MRE, *Relatório, 1891*, p. 9.

2. Mendonça to Justo Chermont, June 19, 1891, and Mendonça to Constantino Palleta, Dec. 8, 1891, MDBEU, "Ofícios 1890–92." Bocayuva feared that the alliance would endanger his pending Missiones treaty, but other cabinet members thought the U.S. alliance more important than the Argentine treaty. Mendonça to Araripe, Mar. 20, 1891, MDBEU, "Ofícios 1890–92." Brazil's Minister of Foreign Relations, Justo Chermont, agreed that a "young" nation like Brazil needed American friendship and could not afford a tariff war with the United States; Brazil MRE, *Relatório, 1891*, p. 25; Azevedo, p. 159; Abranches, *Golpe de Estado*, p. 200.

3. Paço d'Arco to Min. Conde de Valbom, Aug. 21, 1891, in MDPort, p. 66.

4. Wyndham to Salisbury, Apr. 2, 1890, in F.O. 13/666, warns that the Brazilian army in Rio Grande do Sul might revolt out of anger at the treaty with Argentina.

5. Nabuco directly compared Floriano with Balmaceda in *Balmaceda*, p. 253.

6. Quoted in Burr, p. 199.

7. T. Belen to Ministère d'Affaires Etrangères, July 21, 1891, in MAE CP, vol. 34; Abranches, *Golpe de Estado*, p. 85; Pike, *Chile*, pp. 66–71.

8. Fonseca quote from D. Burke to Dept. of State, Oct. 27, 1890, "Dispatches Bahia." C. Frederick Adams to Salisbury, Dec. 8, 1890, F.O. 13/667; Leal, p. 185; Simmons, p. 153; Cosío Villegas, vol. 6, p. 700. Grenville and Young, pp. 216–17, lend credence to the assertion of Mexico's ambassador Matías Romero that he received intelligence about Blaine's funding of Deodoro's election campaign from a confidant of Blaine.

9. Medeiros e Albuquerque, p. 203.

10. Abranches, *Golpe de Estado*, p. 85; Hahner, "Paulistas' Rise to Power," pp. 154, 157.

11. See R. Graham, "Rio Flour Mills"; Love, p. 47; Bandeira, p. 117.

12. Brazil's coffee valorization programs begun in 1906 proved that the country's market share was indeed so large that it could affect world prices without fearing the competition of other producers.

13. Mendonça, *Situação internacional*, p. 190. Taussig, p. 127, concurred that a rise in the tariff on Brazilian coffee would cause the price of all coffee to rise.

14. Quoted by J. Fenner in letter to Dept. of State, Sep. 2, 1892, "Diplomatic Dispatches U.S. Ministers."

15. E. H. Conger to Dept. of State, Aug. 15, 1891, "Diplomatic Dispatches U.S. Ministers."

16. Quoted in C. de Mendonça, p. 159.

17. Quoted in E. H. Conger to Dept. of State, July 2, 1892, "Diplomatic Dispatches U.S. Ministers."

18. Mendonça to Saraiva, June 8, 1890, Coleção Saraiva; Mendonça to Barbosa, Apr. 2, 1890, FCRB; *Jornal do Commércio*, Rio de Janeiro, May 17, 1892; *Rio News*, Mar. 10, 1891; Barbosa, *Finanças*, pp. 406–13.

19. The United States adopted a limited "most favored nation" clause, arguing that it was not applicable to reciprocal arrangements. This interpretation irritated U.S. trading partners; Laughlin and Willis, p. 15.

20. Barbosa, *Finanças*, pp. 413, 414.

21. Blaine to Harrison, Aug. 10, 1891, in Volwiler, pp. 173–74.

22. Mendonça, *Situação internacional*, p. 143, reports that Blaine finally agreed to signing the compulsory arbitration treaty with the right to conquest renounced because it was interpreted as meaning only that none of the signatory countries could conquer from each other. Cuba would therefore still be fair game.

23. Volwiler, p. 110. Foster, *Diplomatic Memoirs*, vol. 2, p. 3; Terrill, p. 177.

24. *Washington Post*, Feb. 5, 1891.

25. Barbosa, *Finanças*, p. 409.

26. Lima, *Memórias*, p. 148; *The Nation* 53: 1377 (Nov. 19, 1891): 384, and 54: 1397 (Apr. 7, 1892): 262–63.

27. Foster, *Diplomatic Memoirs*, vol. 2, p. 8.

28. Harrison, according to the *New York Times*, Oct. 20, 1891: 4-3, claimed that the pork treaty had nothing to do with reciprocity, but the evidence belies that assertion. See, for example, Harrison to Foster, Sep. 10, 1891, Foster papers. See also Gignilliat, p. 12. A similar agreement would be made in 1898 to open France to pork; see Gould, "Diplomats in the Lobby."

29. Amaral Valente to Q. Bocayuva, Nov. 2, 1890, MDBEU, "Ofícios 1890–1892."

30. *NYT*, July 29, 1890: 4-2.

31. Gerard to Rebot, May 21, 1892, MAE CC, vol. 24. *NYT*, July 17, 1890: 1-1.

32. *New York Sun* in *PO* 13, no. 3 (Apr. 16, 1892): 43.

33. Terrill, p. 163.

34. Harrison, *Public Papers*, p. 71. Blaine to Harrison, July 22, 1890, in Volwiler, p. 110.

35. *Washington Post*, Feb. 5, 1891; see also *New York Herald*, Feb. 6, 1891: 3.

36. Prado, *A illusão americana*, p. 194.

37. Gerard to Rebot, Feb. 26, 1892, MAE CC, vol. 23.

38. Mendonça to Barão de Lucena, May 8, 1891, in Lucena, p. 120.

39. Quoted in Abranches, *Golpe de Estado*, p. 200.

40. Ibid., p. 404. Barbosa himself may have been party to the deception. Mendonça wrote him from New York on July 7, 1890 (CRB), that the basis of the McKinley Tariff had been changed to include sugar from other countries.

41. Gerard to Rebot, May 21, 1892, MAE CC, vol. 24, *NYT*, Feb. 10, 1892: 8-5.

42. Mendonça to Justo Chermont, June 19, 1891, and Mendonça to Constantino Palleta, Dec. 8, 1891, in MDBEU, "Ofícios 1890–92."

43. Flint to Blaine, April 9, 1891, in JGBA, reel 11. Flint ended his letter with a newspaper clipping and the message "By the enclosed from last night's paper you will note that when a head turns up opposed to Reciprocity we hit it as hard as we can."

44. Mendonça, pp. 17, 63, 82–83.

45. *NYT*, Jan. 17, 1891: 8-2.

46. Mendonça to Commissão Brasileira na Exposição de New Orleans, Dec. 21, 1884, in CGBEU, NY, 1881–1894.

47. Memorandum of S. de Mendonça, July 4, 1891, MDBEU, "Ofícios 1890–92."

48. Mendonça, *Situação internacional*, p. 105.

49. Quoted in C. de Mendonça, p. 154.

50. Martí, *Obras completas*, vol. 6, p. 104.

51. Mendonça to Justo Chermont, May 8, 1891, MDBEU, "Ofícios 1890–92."

52. Fontoura Xavier to Prudente de Morais, Feb. 20, 1899, in Coleção Prudente, lata 600, pasta 42; Adams to Salisbury, Jan. 17, 1891, in F.O. Record Group 13: Brazil; Bliss to William R. Day, Feb. 19, 1898, State Dept. Misc. Letters, reel 992. Joaquim Nabuco, later Brazilian ambassador to the United States, believed in 1893 that Mendonça was receiving a large commission from Flint for the purchase of armaments; Graham, *Britain*, p. 312.

53. *Rio News*, June 3, 1891.

54. E. H. Conger to Dept. of State, Mar. 6, 1891, "Diplomatic Dispatches U.S. Ministers"; *Jornal do Commércio*, Feb. 12, 1891, in F.O., Record Group 13: *Brazil*, Mar. 7, 1891. Paço d'Arco to Min. Conde de Valbom, July 21, 1891, in MDPort, p. 83.

55. M. Gresham, vol. 2, p. 651.

56. Sociedade Auxiliadora da Agricultura de Pernambuco, passim; Diaz Miranda, passim. For modernization in Cuba see Morena Fraginals, and for Louisiana see Heitman.

57. Where the imperial central government set aside only 500 contos (about U.S. $250,000) for interest guarantees in 1889, the state government of Pernambuco alone lent mill owners some 16,000 contos by 1896. Brasil, Contadoria Geral do Império, *Balanço geral, 1889*. Eisenberg; *Modernization without Change*, pp. 92–114; Carone, *República velha*, vol. 1, pp. 54, 55.

58. Bianconi, *Cartes*, pp. 10, 16. Diegues Júnior, *População e açucar*, pp. 143, 186; Guerra, p. 264; Diaz Miranda, pp. 185–239; Carone, *A República velha*, vol. 1, pp. 55, 57.

59. Brasil, Congresso Nacional, *Anais*, vol. 3, p. 65.

60. All of these authors stress the developmental policies of the first republican governments: Villela and Suzigan, p. 127; H. Bastos, *O pensamento industrial*, p. 9; N. W. Sodré, *Burguesia Brasileira*, p. 76; N. Luz, *A luta*, p. 66; Fishlow, pp. 8, 12; Cano, p. 145; Lobo, *História do Rio de Janeiro*, vol. 2, p. 456; Stein, *Brazilian Cotton Manufacture*, p. 91; F. Versiani, 9; Suzigan, pp. 138–41.

61. *NYT*, Oct. 14, 1888: 4-5.

62. Blondel to Ministère d'Affaires Etrangères, Dec. 7, 1889, and Amelos to Mon. Spuller, Ministère d'Affaires Etrangères, Mar. 14, 1889, MAE CC, vol. 22; Luz, *Luta*, p. 161.

63. H. Bastos, *Rui Barbosa*; H. Silva, *1889*, p. 73. See also Pelaez and Suzigan, p. 179.

64. N. Luz, *A luta*, pp. 168–69.

65. Pan American *Bulletin*, July 1895, pp. 13, 14, and June 1892, p. 1437. The *South American Journal* of May 4, 1889, reported that "emancipation [of slaves] has improved trade" and singled out boots, shoes, corsets, and cotton prints as areas of expansion.

66. Reuter, p. 94.

67. H. Bastos, *O pensamento industrial*, p. 135.

68. Ibid., p. 28; Brasil, MRE, *Relatório, 1891*, pp. 28, 29.

69. Ibid., and Mendonça to R. Barbosa, Apr. 2, 1890, in CRB.

70. Brazil, MRE, *Relatório, 1891*, p. 28.

71. Mendonça to Araripe, Mar. 20, 1891, MDBEU, "Ofícios 1890–92." Mendonça, in *Situação internacional*, pp. 187–88, written years later, was even clearer about his position: "The era was one of many hopes for the creation of new manufacturing industries in Brazil; the national good sense was subordinated to the erroneous doctrine of protectionism which was fed by two illusions: one, that a voluminous issue of paper money could ultimately produce . . . the capitalization that we lacked; and second, that customs tariffs could aid national industries against foreign imports, even though they [national industries] lacked the essential conditions for vitality such as native raw materials, good workers, transportation facilities, etc."

72. Custódio de Mello in Congresso Nacional, *Anais*, vol. 1, p. 52.

73. *Rio News*, June 30, 1891. See also Congresso Nacional, *Anais*, vol. 3, pp. 82, 92, 198, 200, 222, 741; L. de Albuquerque, *Amazonia em 1893*, p. 86.

74. Camara dos Deputados, *Anais*, 1893, vol. 2, p. 464.

75. This legislation sparked heated objections by the European consuls in Brazil. Brasil, *Leis do Brasil*, decree 277, Mar. 22, 1890.

76. Only Brazilian-owned ships with two-thirds Brazilian crews could engage in the coastal trade. The law was suspended for five years but put into practice in 1895, though never closely enforced. See Congresso Nacional, *Anais*, vol. 3, p. 704.

77. This was aimed mostly at Portuguese dry-goods dealers. Camara dos Deputados, *Anais*, 1891, vol. 2, p. 77.

78. *NYT*, Jan. 21, 1890: 2-3.

79. Feb. 11, 1891, in Diplomatic Instructions of Department of State to Brazil, vol. 17, p. 502; W. H. Lawrence to Secretary of State, June 17, 1892, "Diplomatic Dispatches U.S. Ministers," vol. 24. S. Mendonça to Wharton, June 11, 1892, BzLUS.

80. Camara dos Deputados, *Anais*, vol. 2, 1892, p. 64.

81. *New York Sun*, Nov. 15, 1891, in *PO* 12, no. 7 (Nov. 21, 1891): 149.

82. Report of Russian agent de Routkowsky in Gerard to Rebot, Mar. 7, 1892, MAE CC, vol. 23; *The Economist*, 1891, p. 307; Paço d'Arco to Min. Hintze Ribeiro, Apr. 13, 1893, *MDPort*, p. 60; Gabriel de Piza to Barão de Lucena, Mar. 22, 1891, *Arquivo Lucena*, p. 106.

83. Conger to Dept. of State, Nov. 13, 1891, "Diplomatic Dispatches U.S. Ministers," vol. 13; Kerby to Dept. of State, May 4 and 5, 1891, in "Dispatches Pará"; Consul in Recife to Dept. of State, Nov. 23, 1891, in "Dispatches Pernambuco"; U.S. Consul in Bahia to Dept. of State, Mar. 26, 1891, in "Dispatches Bahia."

84. Hill, p. 269.

85. Carone, *Primeira República*, p. 162. Graham in "Robinson and Gallegher in Latin America," p. 211, notes that British merchants often preferred to work through Brazilian politicians, men such as Rui Barbosa, than through their own consuls. Diegues Júnior, *Imigração*, p. 201; Boehrer, p. 48; Ridings.

86. Paço d'Arcos reported to Min. Costa Lobo, May 24, 1892, in MDPort, pp. 45, 46, that he had granted the Barão de Alto-Mearim the title of Conde "so we could

take advantage of his influence with his banker colleagues who greatly influenced ["preponderavam"] if indeed they did not dominate the Lucena-Deodoro government."

87. Quoted in Hahner, *Civilian-Military Relations*, p. 49.

88. Brasil, *Leis do Brasil*, decree 1338, Feb. 5, 1891.

89. Congresso Nacional, *Anais*, vol. 2, p. 11.

90. Ibid., vol. 3, p. 741.

91. Memorandum of conversation with Blaine by J. B. Moore, May 29, 1891, in Volwiler, p. 157.

92. Ibid., p. 102.

93. Conger to Dept. of State, Sep. 2, 1892, "Diplomatic Dispatches U.S. Ministers."

94. Mendonça to Araripe, Feb. 27, 1891, MDBEU, "Ofícios, 1890–92"; A. Gerard to Rebot, Aug. 9, 1891, MAE CC, vol. 23.

95. A. Gerard to Rebot, July 24, 1891, and Feb. 20, 1892, MAE CC, vol. 23; Paço d'Arco to Min. Hintze Ribeiro, Apr. 13, 1893, MDPort, p. 60. The British also sought a commercial treaty but with no success, Salisbury to Adams, Feb. 20, 1891, F.O., Record Group 13: Brazil.

96. Deodoro died one year later.

97. Carone, *A República velha*, vol. 1, pp. 38–40.

98. Moore memorandum of Blaine, May 29, 1891, Blaine to Harrison, July 30, 1891, in Volwiler, pp. 157, 166.

99. Quoted in Azevedo, pp. 155–56. *The Economist*, Jan. 14, 1893, p. 9.

100. Paço d'Arco to Min. Conde de Valbom, Aug. 21, 1891, MDPort, p. 88.

101. Calculated from Brasil, Congresso Nacional, *Anais*, vols. 2 and 3, passim.

102. Conger to Dept. of State, Nov. 13, 1891, "Diplomatic Dispatches U.S. Ministers."

5. THE IRON MARSHAL AND THE NORTHERN GIANT

1. Nabuco, *Intervenção estrangeira*, p. 273.

2. Rothschilds to Brazil's Minister of Finance, Jan. 8, 1892, and Mar. 11, 1892 Agency Letter Book no. 4, NRA.

3. *L'Etoile du Sud*, Feb. 17, 1894: 458, claimed the damage was greater than the Panama Canal Company's bust in Paris.

4. *O Operário*, Ceará, Mar. 6, 1892.

5. Brasil MJ, *Relatório*, 1892, p. 3; Leclerc.

6. Wanting to remain both legal and in power, Floriano refused to call new elections for a president but, at the same time, continued to retain the title of "vice president." Technically, Brazil had no president between November 1891 and November 1894. In fact, Floriano assumed all of the prerogatives of the office.

7. Miranda, p. 156.

8. This was Floriano's characterization of the transition of office in Peixoto to Harrison, Nov. 30, 1891, in BzLUS.

9. E. Stevens to W. Wharton, Dec. 19, 1891, and Jan. 5, 1892, "Dispatches Pernambuco"; *NYT*, Dec. 10, 1891: 1-6.

10. *NYT*, Feb. 12, 1892: 4-5, Jan. 21, 1892: 1-5, and Feb. 20, 1892: 1-7; W. Henardock to E. Stevens, Feb. 17, 1892, and Stevens to Wharton, Feb. 27, 1892, "Dispatches Pernambuco." Junta Governista de Sul Mineira to Custódio de Mello, Feb. 20, 1892, in RS, 1892-02-20; and Afonso Pena to F. Rodrigues Alves, Apr. 20, 1892, 2-1.1.513, A. Pena archive; *NYT*, Dec. 10, 1891: 1-6.

11. *La Capital*, Buenos Aires, in *PO* 12, no. 24 (Mar. 19, 1892); *NYT*, Apr. 23, 1892: 4-2; *Financial Times*, London, June 28, 1892, in CFBH, vol. 7.

12. *NYT*, Apr. 12, 1892: 1-3; Hahner, *Civilian-Military Relations*, p. 55.

13. Based on Abranches, *Governos e congressos*, passim.

14. L. Sodré, *Crenças e opinões*, p. 238; Floriano Peixoto, *Mensagem dirigida ao Congresso* (Rio: 1894), pp. 4, 15. Magalhães Júnior, *A espada contra o Império*, vol. 2, p. 338.

15. Abranches, *Governos e congressos*, passim; Carone, *República velha*, vol. 2, pp. 19–25; Hahner, *Civilian-Military Relations*, p. 93.

16. Nabuco, in *Intervenção estrangeira*, p. 260, maintained that Floriano became a Jacobin for political expediency.

17. Quoted in Vianna, *O ocaso do Império*, pp. 130–31.

18. The constitution called for new elections in the event that the president left office before two years of his term had elapsed. Floriano maintained that since Deodoro had not been elected in direct elections anyway, this article did not apply to him, only to his successors. The Supreme Court, probably under military pressure, agreed with Peixoto. Memorandum in Coleção Solon, pasta 30, lata 559.

19. Freire, p. 19.

20. Quoted in Hahner, *Civilian-Military Relations*, p. 74.

21. Nabuco, *Intervenção estrangeira*, p. 259.

22. Lt. Col. Inocêncio Serzedello Corrêa, who served as Floriano's minister of finance as well as other ministries, Lt. Lauro Sodré, governor of Pará, Major Alexandre José Barbosa Lima, governor of Pernambuco, and Lt. Lauro Müller, governor of Santa Catarina, all had middle-class origins.

23. Boiteux, p. 231; Palha, p. 250; J. F. Velho Sobrinho, *Dicionário bio-bibliográfico brasileiro*, vol. 2, p. 338; N. Santos, *Floriano*, vol. 2, p. 86; Abranches, *Governos e congressos*, passim. After originally supporting Floriano's overthrow of Deodoro, Vinhaes turned against him.

24. Data collected from Abranches, *Governos e congressos*, passim; Lins, p. 284; Barreto, pp. 291–93; Luz, *A Luta*, p. 73; Velho Sobrinho, *Dicionário*, vol. 2, pp. 90, 338; Boiteux, pp. 229, 283.

25. Lins, pp. 283, 323; Boiteux, p. 283. Prominent Florianistas Lauro Müller, Lauro Sodré, Barbosa Lima, and Tasso Fragoso all studied under the staunch positivist Benjamin Constant at the Praia Vermelha military academy, and Serzedello Corrêa was a fellow teacher there. Palha, p. 250; A. Lima, p. 8; E. Sodré, p. 17; Brasil, MVOP *Dados biográficos dos ministros*, p. 77. For positivism in the military academies see Costa, pp. 83–87, and *O Positivismo*, p. 158; Oliveira Torres, pp. 71–72.

26. L. Sodré, p. xxviii. Of the 41 military men in Congress between 1890 and 1894, only six had not gone to some military academy. Twenty had degrees in engineering. At least nine of the congressmen were teachers in military academies. This is at a time when 85 percent of all Brazilians were illiterate, and the country's institutions of superior education enrolled only about 2,000 students a year. Abranches, *Governos e congressos*, passim; Lins, p. 284; N. Luz, *A luta*, p. 73; E. Sodré, p. 19.

27. For examples see Camara dos Deputados, *Anais*, 1891, vol. 1, pp. 82, 242; 1891, vol. 4, pp. 379, 551; 1891/1892, p. 171; 1892, vol. 2, p. 464; 1892, vol. 4, p. 220; vol. 5, pp. 13, 16, 42, 160.

28. Quoted in J. M. Carvalho, *Os bestializados*, p. 74.

29. See Topik, "Metropoles macrocéfalas."

30. Calculated from Brasil DGE, *Recenseamento de 1890*, pp. 408–21. I have taken one-fourth of the commercial sector as middle class and removed domestics and the unemployed to determine the influential active work force.

31. DGE, *Recenseamento 1890*, pp. 408–21.
32. Ibid.
33. Drescher, pp. 451–52, maintains that the Brazilian underground railroad was the largest such abolitionist movement anywhere. See also S. Graham; Hahner, *Poverty and Politics*; J. M. Carvalho, *Os bestializados*; Conrad.
34. *Echo Popular*, Rio, July 3, 1890, July 9, 1890, July 16, 1890. J. A. Rodrigues, p. 9; Padua, p. 178.
35. Most notable were Rio Grande do Sul, São Paulo, the Federal District, Rio de Janeiro state, Minas Gerais, Sergipe, Alagoas, Pernambuco, Rio Grande de Norte, Pará, and Amazonas.
36. Nabuco, *A Intervenção estrangeira*, p. 167. Paço d'Arco to Ayres de Gouveia, June 8, 1892, in MDPort, p. 158.
37. Nabuco to Hilario de Gouveia, Sep. 12, 1894, in *Cartas amigos*, p. 245, and Nabuco, *Intervenção estrangeira*, pp. 253, 259.
38. *Echo Popular*, Mar. 15, 1890: 2.
39. *Voz do Operário*, Bahia, May 6, 1894.
40. *O Republicano*, Forteleza Ceará, Nov. 15, 1895, p. 1.
41. A. Lima, p. 120.
42. For an excellent study of the symbols of the Republic see Carvalho, *A Formação das almas*.
43. All Jacobins were followers of Floriano, but many supporters of Floriano did not subscribe to the Jacobins' xenophobia and authoritarianism.
44. Serzedello Corrêa, *O Problema econômico do Brasil*, pp. 5, 8, 9, 95; Brazil, MF, *Relatório, 1893*, p. 124. For other expressions of the same opinion see A. Lima, pp. 115, 218; Camara dos Deputados, *Anais*, 1892, vol. 2, p. 464; Vieira, p. 24; d'Atri, p. 297.
45. Gootenberg, *Imagining Development*.
46. For examples of the pro-industry position of Floriano and his ministers see Brasil, Presidente, *Mensagem ao Congresso Nacional . . . 12 maio, 1892*, p. 17; Brazil, MF, *Relatório, 1893*, p. 126; Camara dos Deputados, *Anais*, 1892, vol. 1, pp. 73, 75.
47. For a study of this transition in France see C. Tilly, *Contentious French*.
48. *O Republicano*, Forteleza, Nov. 15, 1895, p. 1.
49. *O Nacional*, Mar. 17, 1895: 2. See also *O Nativista*, São Paulo, June 14, 1895: 1, 2, and *O Jacobino*, Oct. 13 and 17, 1894.
50. *O Nativista*, Sep. 22, 1895: 3. For more on British speculation see *O Jacobino*, Sep. 22, 1894; *Cahete*, Maceió Alagoas, Oct. 19, 1896: 2, and Nov. 29, 1896: 1; *A Metralha*, Rio, Dec. 5, 1893; *O Republicano*, Forteleza, Feb. 1, 1896; *Gazeta de Commérico e Finanças*, Rio, Oct. 21, 1895: 1.
51. Magalhães Júnior, *A espada contra o Império*, vol. 2, p. 346, and *A Metralha*, Rio, Nov. 23, 1893: 1.
52. *O Nativista*, São Paulo, Sep. 14, 1895: 1; see also *Cahete*, Nov. 9, 1896: 1; *O Jacobino*, Sep. 22, 1895.
53. E. Prado, *A Illusão americana*, pp. 11, 243.
54. Wilkins, *Emergence of Multinational Enterprise*, vol. 1, pp. 39, 44, explains that the Singer Sewing Machine Company was one of the few U.S. companies with representatives in Brazil in the nineteenth century. USDS, *Commercial Relations 1895*, p. 649, and *1895 and 1896*, vol. 2, p. 686.
55. Pan American *Bulletin*, May 1891: 1877; *Rio News*, July 5, 1892, and July 2, 1891; Wileman, pp. 85, 86.
56. Paço d'Arco to Hintze Ribeiro, Apr. 13, 1893, in MDPort, p. 60.

57. Ibid., Rio, June 24, 1893, pp. 219, 226.

58. Paço d'Arco to Min. Hintze Ribeiro, Apr. 13, 1893, May 19, 1893, and June 24, 1893, in MDPort, pp. 60, 63, 201.

59. *Jornal do Commércio*, Feb. 8, 1891, clipping in C. Fredrick Adam to Salisbury, Mar. 7, 1891, F.O. Record Group 13. E. Conger to Blaine, Jan. 11, 1892, in "Diplomatic Dispatches U.S. Ministers." For industrial pressure see C. Sousa Santos.

60. A. Gerard to Rebot, Jan. 5, 1892, MAE CC, vol. 23. Gerard quotes the *Jornal do Brasil* as saying "We are Americans but we want to be most of all Brazilians and we have no need of Mr. Blaine's tutelage."

61. *A Metralha*, Rio, Dec. 5, 1893: 2.

62. Mello, *Governo provisório*, p. 279; Carone, *República velha*, vol. 2, p. 103. See also Topik, "Brazil's Bourgeois Revolution?". Medeiros e Albuquerque, p. 223, reports that the banker offered 300 or 400 contos for Floriano's land worth only ten or twenty contos. Floriano replied that he was pleased that the land was now worth so much and would consummate the deal once he was no longer president. *L'Etoile du Sud*, Feb. 17, 1894: 458; Paço d'Arco to Ayres de Gouveia, June 8, 1892 in MDPort, p. 152; Leoni, p. 26.

63. Salvador de Mendonça, "Memorandum," Jan. 11, 1892, in BzLUS.

64. Ibid.

65. Camara dos Deputados, *Anais*, 1891/1892, p. 96; Stein, *Brazilian Cotton Manufacture*, p. 85.

66. Native industry did not really require the tariff revision because the devaluation of Brazil's currency meant that the milreis price of imports doubled even though the duty component of the price declined. The domestic production cost did not rise as fast because wages were kept down. Hence they could remain competitive.

67. Wileman, p. 215.

68. E. Conger to Blaine, Rio, Jan. 18, 1892, in "Diplomatic Dispatches U.S. Ministers"; A. Gerard to Rebot, Jan. 6, 1892, MAE CC, vol. 23; Brazil MF, *Relatório, 1895*, p. 19. The Pan American Union's *Bulletin* reported in November 1895, p. 262, that the total amount of port tax refunded was U.S. $340,000.

69. Azevedo, p. 155.

6. THE DEMOCRATS TAKE OVER

1. R. H. Williams, *Years of Decision*, p. 46; Jensen, pp. 141, 150–52; Kleppner, pp. 372–73.

2. Socolofsky and Spetter, p. 70.

3. Jensen, p. 141; Kloppner, pp. 12, 13, 18.

4. "The Recent Election," *North American Review*, vol. 151 (Dec. 1890): 642–43.

5. See, for example, the opinion of the *New York Mail and Telegraph*, *St. Louis Globe-Democrat*, *New York Tribune*, *New York Star*, *Baltimore Sun*, *Savannah News*, *Nashville American*, *Kansas City Times*, *St. Paul Press*, *Cleveland Plain-Dealer*, *Harper's Weekly*, *Pittsburgh Dispatch*, and *San Francisco Examiner* in PO 12, no. 6 (Nov. 1890): 122–24.

6. "Message to Congress," Dec. 6, 1892, in Harrison, *Public Papers*. As the *Baltimore American* (Dec. 2, 1890) put it, "Every measure of importance endorsed by the majority of the Fifty-first Congress is endorsed by the President"; in PO 10, no. 9 (Dec. 6, 1890): 195.

7. *NYT*, Feb. 1, 1890: 15, and Apr. 13, 1891: 5-6.

8. Harrison to H. B. Kelly, Apr. 7, 1891, in Harrison, *Public Papers*, p. 285.

9. *NYT*, Feb. 6, 1891: 4-1, and Feb. 7, 1891: 4-2.

10. *New York Tribune*, Feb. 24, 1891, in *PO* 10, no. 21, Feb. 28, 1891: 488.

11. *Engineering and Mining Journal*, Feb. 7, 1891: 161.

12. In *PO* 10, no. 19, Feb. 14, 1891: 437–41. This issue of *PO* contains opinion from some 50 newspapers and journals, almost all of it favorable though the Democrats see the treaty as just a step on the way to the ultimate goal of free trade.

13. *The Economist*, Mar. 7, 1891: 307, and July 16, 1892: 912.

14. *Financial Times*, Feb. 12, 1891, in CFBH, vol. 7.

15. Quoted in Adler, p. 21.

16. Tate, pp. 240–45.

17. Dunning, pp. 285–91.

18. Campbell, *Transformation*, pp. 76–83.

19. Some American sailors in Santiago from the U.S.S. *Baltimore* were beaten in a drunken brawl; two of them died. The Chilean government at first refused to apologize and made remarks that offended Harrison. Harrison gave an ultimatum, recommending war if the slight were not redressed. Fortunately, the Chileans relented before fighting broke out. See Goldberg; Zeitlin.

20. Logan, pp. 397, 401, 405–7, 411, 424, 456; LaFeber, *New Empire*, pp. 127–30.

21. *Boston Journal*, Jan. 25, 1890 (in *PO* 8: 17, Feb. 1, 1890): 402, describes how Greytown, Nicaragua, was "unprecedentedly busy" because of preparations for the canal. See also Clayton, "Canal Morgan."

22. Quoted in W. A. Williams, *American Empire*, p. 345. Socolofsky and Spetter, pp. 96–101; Swann, pp. 194, 200–234. LaFeber, *New Empire*, pp. 121–27.

23. See, for example, Henry Cabot Lodge, quoted in Grenville and Young, pp. 211, 212.

24. Quoted in the *Mobile Register* in *PO* 10, no. 6 (Nov. 15, 1890): 122. See also the opinions expressed by *Memphis Appeal-Avalanche*, *New York Star*, *Savannah News*, *St. Paul Press* in the same *PO*.

25. See *PO* 13, no. 8 (May 28, 1892): 175–76, for Blaine's continuing popularity. *NYT*, Apr. 18, 1892: 4-4. Sherman, pp. 119, 128; Knoles, pp. 38, 52, 53, 62, 68; R. H. Williams, *Years of Decision*, p. 62.

26. Harrison, *Public Papers*, pp. 8–25.

27. Knoles, p. 127.

28. Harrison to McKinley, Sep. 3, 1892; Harrison, *Public Papers*, p. 11. *American Economist*, Apr. 29, 1892: 222, 223, claimed an increase of trade with Brazil and Cuba of $4 million since the advent of reciprocity.

29. *PO* 13, no. 13 (July 2, 1892): 300.   30. Quoted in Terrill, p. 190.

31. Ibid.   32. *NYT*, June 21, 1892: 4-1.

33. It was discovered later that the Treasury had made a statistical error that greatly exaggerated the volume of imports from Brazil.

34. Congressman William L. Wilson in *Forum* in *PO* 14, no. 2 (Oct. 15, 1892): 30. *NYT*, Aug. 4, 1893: 4-5.

35. See Campbell, *Transformation*, pp. 186–200, and LaFeber, *New Empire*, p. 150. Other historians such as Holbo, p. 207, and Tompkins, pp. 63–68, see Cleveland as a "hiatus" from the concern with foreign markets and territorial annexation. Neither group fully appreciates the evolution of Cleveland's policy.

36. Campbell, *Transformation*, p. 186.

37. *NYT*, Aug. 4, 1893: 4-5.   38. *NYT*, July 5, 1892: 5-4.

39. Ibid.   40. Ibid.

41. Quoted in Knoles, p. 187, who also (121) points out that the Socialist Labor Party also wanted greater state ownership of utilities and land but took no position at all on the tariff or foreign trade.

42. Quoted in W. A. Williams, *American Empire*, p. 304; see also Welch, pp. 48, 51, 57, 62–63. Perhaps Cleveland's lack of personal charisma did no harm because his austere, reserved opponent exuded even less warmth. Republican Senator Platt found Harrison "as glacial as a Siberian stripped of his furs"; quoted in Knoles, p. 35.

43. See *PO* 14, no. 3 (Oct. 23, 1892): 51–55, for discussions of the key issues of the election.

44. R. H. Williams, *Years of Decision*, p. 65. Williams contends that had Blaine been able to campaign—and had Harrison campaigned more vigorously—their vision could have carried the day. Certainly the results of the 1896 election support his contention.

45. *New York Sun* in *PO* 14, no. 6 (Nov. 12, 1892): 124; *NYT*, Mar. 4, 1893: 4-2; *St. Louis Globe-Democrat* in *PO* 14, no. 7 (Nov. 19, 1892): 149; R. H. Williams, *Democratic Party*, pp. 120, 162; Welch, pp. 65–73.

46. Kleppner, p. 8.

47. Cleveland's Second Inaugural Address, *Letters of Cleveland*, p. 313; M. Gresham, vol. 2, p. 668.

48. In 1890 he had written Representative John G. Carlisle, Apr. 7, 1890, Cleveland, *Letters*, p. 222, that the Democrats should not propose their own tariff in opposition to the McKinley bill because it would be much easier to simply attack the Republicans.

49. Keller, pp. 298, 299; Welch, pp. 48, 53.

50. C. Clark, vol. 1, p. 233.

51. *St. Louis Globe-Democrat* in *PO* 14, no. 7 (Nov. 19, 1892): 148.

52. Cleveland to Carlisle, Apr. 7, 1890, in Cleveland, *Letters*, p. 222.

53. Gresham to MacVeagh, May 7, 1894, WQG, vol. 48.

54. Gresham to C. E. Dyer, May 2, 1894 in WQG, vol. 48.

55. Gresham to MacVeagh, May 7, 1894, in WQG, vol. 48; Holbo, p. 220.

56. Taussig, pp. 288, 290, 309, 312, 314. M. Gresham, vol. 2, p. 651; Terrill, pp. 185, 192, 193; Welch, pp. 132–35.

57. Cleveland to Thomas C. Catchings, Aug. 27, 1894, Cleveland, *Letters*, pp. 364–66.

58. Ibid.

59. Campbell, *Transformation*, p. 99.

60. Quoted in U.S. Tariff Commission, *Reciprocity*, p. 159.

61. J. W. Foster, *Diplomatic Memoirs*, vol. 2, p. 16.

62. Quoted in W. A. Williams, *American Empire*, p. 350. Other Populist leaders such as Jerry Simpson and the future Democratic presidential candidate William Jennings Bryan also turned their attention to foreign markets; Terrill, p. 199; *NYT*, Apr. 20, 1893: 6-3.

63. 53d Congress, 2d session, House Report no. 234, p. 11.

64. *Louisville Courier-Journal* and *New York Tribune* in *PO* 15, no. 5 (May 6, 1894): 121; *New Orleans Times-Democrat* and *Detroit Tribune* in *PO* 15, no. 4 (Apr. 29, 1894): 96.

65. Quoted in Welch, p. 14.

66. Ibid., pp. 151, 152, 158; Coolidge, p. 125.

67. *PO* 13, no. 13 (July 2, 1892): 299.

68. Gresham wrote Carl Schurz, July 11, 1893, in WQG, vol. 40, about Samoa: "Our Government should not undertake to maintain a protectorate either alone or in conjunction with other Powers in the South Sea Islands or elsewhere." Welch, p. 161. See also Gresham to Thomas Bayard, Feb. 22, 1894, in Bayard papers, box 192; Swann, pp. 200–234.

69. Gresham wrote a confidential note to Thomas Bayard, Oct. 29, 1893, WQG, vol. 48, "The Constitutional Government [of Hawaii] was not overthrown by a revolution of the people on the Islands; on the contrary, the Queen was over-awed by the American Minister and the presence of a body of armed troops landed from one of our war ships. Her submission was thus coerced. . . . It would lower our national standard to endorse a selfish and dishonorable scheme of a lot of adventurers."

70. Gresham to Noble C. Butler, Nov. 23, 1893, WQG, vol. 48.

71. *PO* 13: 13 (July 2, 1892): 299. Tate, p. 253.

72. LaFeber, *New Empire*, pp. 159–62, 197–210.

73. Dunning, p. 283.

7. OF REVOLTS AND GUNBOATS

1. LaFeber, *New Empire*, pp. 202–3, 217–18, and "Depression Era Diplomacy," pp. 107–18; W. A. Williams, *American Empire*, p. 35.

2. J. Smith, *Illusions of Conflict*, p. 183.

3. See, for instance, LaFeber, "Depression Era Diplomacy"; J. Smith, *Illusion of Conflict* and *Unequal Giants*, and "Brazilian Naval Revolt"; Vivian; Clowes; Calhoun, "American Policy"; Bandeira; Hill; Cerro and Bueno.

4. Mendonça, *A situação internacional*, p. 196.

5. Paço d'Arco to Min. Ayres Gouveia, Nov. 2, 1892, in MDPort, p. 176. Love in *Rio Grande do Sul*, p. 63, suggests that a more reasonable 5,000 men crossed the Uruguayan border.

6. See Chasteen.

7. The rebels themselves posed themselves as republicans. General Tavares's manifesto, published in the *Jornal do Commércio* of Porto Alegre, Apr. 2, 1893, said, "The objective of the riograndense revolutionaries is not the restoration of the monarchy; it is to liberate Rio Grande from tyranny . . . reestablish the guarantee of all individual rights, and end the regime of persecutions, of unprecedented violence . . . that unfortunately has been supported by the government of Marshal Floriano Peixoto." Hasslocher, p. 75, argued that the conflict between Castelhos and Silveira Martins was in reality personal, not ideological. Each leader would retain the same following even if they switched programs, but he also believed that Silveira Martins did want to restore the monarchy. Love, *Rio Grande do Sul*, p. 71, notes that Silveira Martins was most concerned about holding power; the form of the regime was secondary, though in a marriage of convenience he did agree with Saldanha da Gama that a national plebiscite should be called, tacitly supporting the restorationist position. Finally, Targa maintains that this was actually a class-based struggle in which Castilhos represented bourgeois and petit bourgeois supporters against the more traditional ranchers of Silveira Martins.

8. Bello, p. 115.

9. Love, *Rio Grande do Sul*, pp. 63, 64.

10. The governor of Minas Gerais and future Brazilian president Afonso Pena wrote to Fernando Lobo Leite from Belo Horizonte, Feb. 25, 1893 (A. Pena archive), "I never doubted that our neighbors were more or less involved in the Rio Grande battles desiring to weaken us."

11. Rogers, p. 376.

12. The final vote was 93 to 52 against impeachment. Thompson to Gresham, May 11, 1893, "Diplomatic Dispatches U.S. Ministers."

13. Schantz, p. 294.

14. See Dudley; Schulz; Hahner, *Civilian-Military Relations*.

15. Clowes, p. 194; Schantz, p. 299; Freire, *História da revolta*, p. 14.

16. Interview in the *New York Herald*, Oct. 3, 1893: 8-1.

17. *NYT*, Oct. 6, 1893: 9; *London Times*, Nov. 17, 1893:9.

18. Lt. C. C. Rogers (p. 380), who had access to all classified U.S. diplomatic and naval correspondence in writing up his intelligence report of the revolt, asserted that "less than one-fourth of the legal effective strength of the navy adhered to Admiral Mello." Given Floriano's need to dragoon civilians, hire foreign mercenaries, and station soldiers on his ships when he was able to finally form a fleet, it is safe to assume that the three-quarters of the Brazilian navy who did not actively support de Mello also did not support Floriano.

19. C. de Mello, *História da revolução*, pp. 20, 60; Schneider, pp. 62, 63.

20. *NYT*, Oct. 26, 1893: 16, and July 6, 1890: 9-3; Clowes, p. 191.

21. Amaral Valente to Quintino Bocayuva, Dec. 14, 1890, MDBEU, "Ofícios 1890–92"; *NYT*, Nov. 16, 1890: 4-2.

22. "Naval Progress during 1893," *Proceedings of the United States Naval Institute*, 1894, 624, notes that the United States had thirteen protected cruisers to Brazil's nine. See also *Jane's All the World's Fighting Ships*, 1898, pp. 22–24, and *NYT*, Mar. 24, 1889: 16-1, which included Brazil with Japan, China, Chile, and Uruguay as countries now having "modern navies." Several of the largest ships were not in the bay at the time of the revolt and would remain beyond de Mello's reach for the duration of the revolt.

23. Clowes, pp. 191–95; Rogers, pp. 377–79.

24. Troops sent from Rio to Paraná overland, a one-to-two-day boat ride, took one day to reach São Paulo by train and then two weeks on horse and foot over poor roads; Luz and Carneiro, vol. 6, p. 38. São Paulo's state army was placed along the coast, so volunteer militias had to defend the interior; Dias de Campos, p. 77.

25. See, for example, the *Financial News* of London, Sep. 9, 1893, and Sep. 12, 1893, and the *Standard*, Sep. 13, 1893, all in CFBH, vol. 8. Picking to Herbert, Oct. 14, 1893, and Nov. 4, 1893, in USNav.

26. De Mello explained personally to U.S. Captain Picking (Picking to Herbert, Rio, Oct. 7, 1893, USNav) that he rebelled for less idealistic reasons: "Peixoto had taken a large amount of money from the government, raised loans, and offered and paid the soldiers large amounts of the money to be true to him and that he sent an infernal machine to Mello in the form of a book."

27. Floriano had explained the veto by accusing the bill of redundancy since the constitution already stipulated that he could not run for reelection.

28. Salvador de Mendonça was an exception. He wrote in the *NYT*, Feb. 4, 1894: 19, "It is curious that instead of appealing to the ballot box . . . the rebel chief should propose to introduce into politics new methods of restoring violated Constitutions, and should attempt to bring back peace and credit by cannon shots and to destroy military dominion by military violence."

29. Brazil, Presidente, *Mensagem dirigida ao Congresso Nacional 4 Outubro, 1894*, pp. 4, 5. Floriano was so suspicious that he complained of people so clever that they left no evidence of aiding the rebels and even had evidence of support for Floriano.

30. C. de Mello, *Governo provisório*, p. 392.

31. Many contemporaries believed that the revolt was nothing more than, in the words of U.S. consul Townes, "a fight between the Army and the Navy in which capture of the loaves and fish is alone incentive for action." Townes to Gresham, Sep. 18, 1893, "Dispatches Rio de Janeiro." Floriano's minister of finance, Freire, in *História da revolta*, p. 16, agreed. The monarchist Joaquim Nabuco wrote to the

Barão de Penedo, Botafogo, Oct. 4, 1892, in *Cartas a amigos*, p. 217, that de Mello was a "pseudo-fanatic" in defending the Republic from restorationist conspiracies. He never believed that de Mello was a defender of the monarchy.

32. See *A Opinão Nacional*, one of the few papers still printing articles sympathetic to the rebels, on Jan. 13, 1894: 1, and Jan. 31, 1894: 1.

33. Frederico Guilherme Lorena, president of the rebels' provisional government in Desterro, Santa Catarina, explained in an undated manifesto to the "people of Santa Catarina" that they were fighting against Floriano's military "tyranny." "The people of Santa Catarina know that this is not, at the moment, a class struggle which the cruel marshal [Floriano] would have them believe." Pasta, "Poder Executivo," Floriano Peixoto archive.

34. Macedo, pp. 16, 17, 19, 26, 79; *O Operário*, Forteleza Ceará, Mar. 27, 1892; Brazil MJ, *Relatório, 1893*, pp. 239–47; J. de Albuquerque, p. 208.

35. In his message to Congress, May 7, 1894, Floriano listed the groups "from all social classes" who aided him: "from the workshops and the schools, from agriculture and commerce"; Presidente do Brasil, *Mensagems*, p. 90; Freire, *História da revolta*, pp. 97, 220–27; Miguel Joaquim Ribeiro de Carvalho, Min. Interior to José Thomaz Porciuncula, Governor Rio de Janeiro state, Jan. 16, 1894, and Feb. 10, 1894, lata 485, doc. 42, Porciuncula archive; Brazil MJ, *Relatório, 1895*, pp. 88, 91. Admittedly, it is difficult to determine to what extent the relative lack of defections reflects mass support for Floriano rather than the efficiency of his secret police and unofficial spies who thwarted several planned defections to the rebels by supposed Florianistas.

36. *NYT*, Feb. 4, 1894: 19. See also Hahner, *Civilian-Military Relations*, p. 114; Reuter, pp. 236–40. C. de Mello, *História da revolução*, p. 35, revealed that the Visconde de Figueiredo had financed the 1891 coup on similar terms.

37. Paço d'Arcos to Gouveia, in MDPort, p. 233. *NYT*, Feb. 23, 1894: 2-4.

38. Juca to Quintino Bocayuva, Rio, Oct. 9, 1890, in pasta 5, folio 1, QB 889.11.16, Quintino; Memorandum, Banco do Brasil to Rui Barbosa, no date, pasta Banco do Brasil, FCRB; Freire, pp. 12, 13, 57; Reuter, pp. 236, 239, 240.

39. The Conde de Mattosinhos, whose son had been deported from Brazil by Floriano, arrived in London on financial business "charged with a delicate mission," *NYT*, Sep. 23, 1893: 5-5, and the Conde de Leopoldina was in Lisbon, *NYT*, Jan. 4, 1894: 1-3.

40. Nabuco, *Intervenção estrangeira*, p. 252; *NYT*, Dec. 8, 1893: 3-1 and Dec. 18, 1893: 3-3; *London Times*, Dec. 18, 1893: 10.

41. Presidente, *Mensagens*, p. 90. A German businessman, Moritz Schantz, p. 327, also believed that the revolt was caused by unhappy soldiers and stock market speculators.

42. Quoted in Thompson, p. 314.

43. Padua, p. 171; Hahner, *Civilian-Military Relations*, pp. 125–48; Topik, "Brazil's Bourgeois Revolution?" p. 268; *Financial Times*, Mar. 1, 1893, in CFBH, vol. 8. Serzedello Corrêa was the "relator" in the House of Deputies for Campos Sales's free trade tariffs between 1898 and 1902.

44. Much of their support may have been simply pragmatic. J. M. dos Santos, pp. 302–3, asserted that the leading Paulista, Prudente de Morais, initially supported the naval revolt. He only switched sides when its failure became evident.

45. W. A. Williams, *American Empire*, p. 365; LaFeber, *New Empire*, p. 210.

46. Thompson to Gresham, Feb. 1, 1894, in "Diplomatic Dispatches U.S. Ministers."

47. Demonstrating the limited reach of the U.S. Navy to that point, the only U.S. Navy ship to regularly call on Rio was the wooden 900-ton *Yantic* that was clearly no

more than a symbolic presence. *NYT*, Sep. 11, 1893: 4-4. To be fair, U.S. naval ships were not strangers in Rio either; ships transiting from the Atlantic to the Asiatic squadron or to the Pacific squadron often put in at Rio en route.

48. S. da Costa, p. 34. By early October when the first American ship, the *Charleston*, arrived, two more Italian and two German men-of-war had also arrived. Picking noted in his report from Rio, Oct. 7, 1893, USNav, the French had a flagship, the *Aréthuse*; the Italians, the *Bausan*, the *Dogali*, and the *Veniero*; the English, the *Sirius*, the *Racer*, and the *Beagle*; the Germans, the *Alexandrine* and the *Arcona*; and the Portuguese, the *Mindello*.

49. Villar, p. 57, who participated as a cadet in the revolt, notes that many of de Mello's ships were ill prepared for warfare at the outset of the rebellion.

50. Stanton to Navy, Oct. 20, 1893, Picking to Herbert, Dec. 24, 1893, and Jan. 5, 1894, and Thompson to Gresham, Oct. 22, 1893, in USNav. U.S. Minister Thompson specifically characterized the German action as a refusal to stop the blockade. See also Beisner, *Old Diplomacy*, p. 97.

51. *London Times*, Oct. 5, 1893, p. 9.

52. Ibid., Nov. 17, 1893: 9.

53. Interview in the *NYT*, Jan. 7, 1894: 16-2.

54. Hagan, *Gunboat Diplomacy*, pp. 9, 10.

55. See, for example, Calhoun, *Gilded Age Cato*, p. 194; Vivian, p. 247.

56. Thompson to Gresham, Rio, Oct. 3, 1893, "Diplomatic Dispatches U.S. Ministers." See also the correspondence between the diplomatic corps and the Brazilian government in "Revolta da Esquadra" in Brazil MRE, *Relatório 1894*, passim.

57. Luz and Carneiro, vol. 6, p. 76.

58. *NYT*, Dec. 19, 1893: 1-4; Ferreira, p. 81; Wehrs, pp. 84–91.

59. Thompson to Gresham, Oct. 5, 1893, "Diplomatic Dispatches U.S. Ministers"; Bello, p. 123.

60. *New York Herald*, Oct. 8, 1893: 8.

61. Captain Picking was "very well pleased that I had instructions from our Government releasing me from any protection of Argentine property"; in Picking to Thompson, Dec. 12, 1893, and Picking to Herbert, Dec. 5, 1893, in USNav. Letters. See also Villalba, p. 66.

62. Quoted in Villar, p. 106.

63. *New York Herald*, Nov. 12, 1893: 8-5.

64. *New York Herald*, Nov. 1, 1893: 9-6; USSD, *Foreign Relations of the United States for 1893*, p. 61; Mendonça to A. C. de Nascimento, Jan. 12, 1894, MDBEU, "Ofícios 1893–96."

65. See, for example, *London Times*, Sep. 22, 1893: 3, which also cites a report in the *Neue Wiener Tagblatt*; see also the *Financial News*, Sep. 22, 1893, the *Standard*, Sep. 21, 1893, *Morning Post*, Sep. 13, 1893, in CFBH, vol. 8. Alcindo Guanabara complained in a letter reprinted in the *NYT*, Dec. 12, 1893: 1-6, that "European, notably British press gives moral support to armed adventurers like Mello." See also the *NYT*, Dec. 14, 1893: 1-1.

66. Nabuco, *Intervenção estrangeira*, p. 149; Thompson, p. 166; Villar, p. 72.

67. Thompson declined to meet with Floriano along with the representatives of France, Great Britain, Germany, Italy, and Portugal; Thompson to Gresham, Sep. 7, 1893, "Diplomatic Dispatches U.S. Ministers." This might explain Floriano's later reluctance to meet with Thompson.

68. Consul Townes demonstrated his disdain for Brazilians and their politics when he wrote to Gresham from Rio, Sep. 18, 1893, "Dispatches Rio de Janeiro," that "I am reliably informed that 50 percent of the people of Rio are subjects of Portugal.

No less than 25 percent of the people are English, French, German, Italian, and American. That leaves 25 percent to the Brazilians, of which 20 percent can neither read or write. We therefore infer that only 5 percent of the people in this city are intelligent citizens, capable of influencing legislation and able to discern the true policy for the good of the Republic. Perhaps nine-tenths of the Army forces are densely ignorant, black negroes, without personal pride or patriotic motives. It is also a fact that the police force of Rio is made up of criminals, who have been placed in the service as a punishment for their crimes."

69. Gresham to Thompson, Oct. 1, 1893, "Diplomatic Dispatches U.S. Ministers."

70. According to Vivian, p. 248, Admiral Benham was given materials on U.S. participation in Chile in 1891 as a guide to what to avoid in his actions in Guanabara Bay.

71. Censorship was so strong that Capt. Picking complained to Herbert, Oct. 14, 1893, USNav: "No authentic news comes to me from other parts of the country." For a monarchist version of newspaper censorship under Floriano see Laet, "A Imprensa," pp. 230–34.

72. *New York Herald*, Oct. 7, 1893: 7, and Oct. 31, 1893: 9. Floriano was so upset by the reporting in the *Herald* that he sent them a message arguing his side, published on Oct. 29, 1893: 5-1. See also *PO* 16, no. 15 (Jan. 11, 1894): 360.

73. *NYT*, Dec. 14, 1893: 1-1.

74. S. da Costa, p. xiv.

75. Freire, *História da revolta*, p. 95.

76. Ibid., pp. 98–102; Villar, p. 83; *New York Herald*, Oct. 24, 1893: 7; Luz and Carneiro, vol. 6, pp. 18–25.

77. See, for example, Calhoun, *Gilded Age Cato*, p. 196.

78. H. Smith, p. 349.

79. Ibid., pp. 334–56.

80. Interview with George Boynton in *The World* of New York, Jan. 18, 1894: 7-1. See also Picking to Herbert, Oct. 7, 1893, and Nov. 17, 1893, USNav, in which Picking notes that Boynton's dynamite tugboat under its top coat of paint had green paint; green is the color of the Brazilian navy. *NYT*, Oct. 25, 1893: 8-6.

81. Flint, *Memories*, p. 101.

82. *NYT*, Sep. 16, 1893: 1-3.

83. Thompson to Gresham, Sep. 19, 1893, "Diplomatic Dispatches U.S. Ministers."

84. Thomas Skidmore is incorrect when he writes in "Brazil's American Illusion," p. 74, that the U.S. fleet found itself "by coincidence" in Guanabara Bay when the revolt broke out.

85. Brazil's minister of foreign relations to Mendonça, Oct. 23, 1893, and Stanton to Herbert, Oct. 25, 1893, USNav. See also Mendonça, *A situaçao internacional*, p. 202; *NYT*, Dec. 30, 1893: 17.

86. *Philadelphia North American*, Oct. 30, 1893, and the *Philadelphia Ledger* as well as the *Philadelphia Record* in *PO* 16, no. 5, Nov. 2, 1893: 117; Gresham to Thomas Bayard, Oct. 29, 1893, in WQG, vol. 48. Calhoun, *Gilded Age Cato*, pp. 197–98.

87. Stanton was reassigned as commander of the North Atlantic Station, which Admiral Benham had left to replace Stanton in the South Atlantic Station. Herbert to Stanton, Dec. 21, 1893, in USNav.Letters. Thompson to Gresham, Rio, Nov. 3, 1893, in "Diplomatic Dispatches U.S. Ministers." Mendonça to Gresham, Oct. 26, 1893, BzLUS.

88. Villar, p. 40.
89. Barão de Itajubá to Thomas Bayard, Apr. 16, 1886, BzLUS.
90. J. Amaral Valente to Quintino Bocayuva, Jan. 10, 1890, MDBEU, "Ofícios 1890–1892."
91. Thompson to Picking, Dec. 16, 1893, in USNav.Letters.
92. Picking to Herbert, Oct. 14, 1893, USNav; Villar, pp. 57, 59; Villalba, p. 91.
93. The three men also disagreed ideologically since da Gama was a monarchist, de Mello a liberal republican, and Lorena a positivist republican.
94. S. Mendonça to C. Carvalho, Dec. 23, 1894, MDBEU, "Ofícios 1890–92"; Documento 117a in Poder Executivo, Floriano Peixoto archive.
95. Picking to Herbert, Oct. 14, 1893, and Nov. 4, 1893, in USNav; Moraes Ferreira, p. 80; Mendonça, *A situação internacional.* Cerait reports to the engineer of Chemin du Fer de Parana, Jan. 18, 1894, in MAE CP, vol. 26, that Paraná was cut off from Rio for five months because the railroad and telegraph had been severed by rebels.
96. *NYT,* Dec. 16, 1893: 1-2.
97. *NYT,* Dec. 23, 1893: 1-1. The *Times* reported on Nov. 10, 1893: 2-3, from Rio that "there is, however, a strong undercurrent of feeling here in favor of the insurgents."
98. D'Auleigny to Perier, Jan. 18, 1894, MAE CC, vol. 25.
99. *NYT,* Dec. 30, 1893: 1-5.
100. The foreign commanders requested the right to unload at another site safe from rebel fire but were denied by Floriano, probably because he hoped that their continuation at the customs house would protect it and the naval arsenal close by from rebel fire. Dauleigny to Perier, Dec. 27, 1893, in MAE CC, vol. 25.
101. Picking to Herbert, Dec. 28, 1893, and Jan. 10, 1893, and Thompson to Picking, Dec. 23, 1893, in USNav; the *New York Times,* Dec. 30, 1894: 17, suggested that Picking "had been too long, perhaps in the harbor, under the influence of naval officers whose sympathies had been enlisted rather for the insurgents than for the republic." See also *London Times,* Jan. 31, 1894: 5.
102. *NYT,* Nov. 29, 1893: 1-2.
103. Hammett, pp. 189, 200–202.
104. Long, p. 6.
105. Karsten, p. 246. I should note that while the U.S. Navy acted independently of the State Department in Rio, in Washington there was considerable communication between Navy and State.
106. *NYT,* Jan. 7, 1894: 8-1. Picking only visited the U.S. consulate in Rio twice when Thompson was in town because he did not "consider the Consulate a very proper place for a gentleman to visit, it being, in my opinion, dirty and disgusting" (Picking to Herbert, Dec. 28, 1893, USNav).
107. Dauleigny to Perier, Jan. 18, 1894, MAE CC, vol. 25.
108. Mendonça, *A situação internacional,* p. 205.
109. Reproduced from the original document found after the end of the revolt in Abranches, *A Revolta da Armada,* pp. 11, 12. Gama also declared that he would "offer my life and those of my companions-in-combat to the holocaust on the altar of the Fatherland," a line almost identical to the moving end of Getúlio Vargas's suicide note some 61 years later.
110. Abranches, *A Revolta da Armada,* pp. 18, 19. The second manifesto, which da Gama approved though he did not actually write it himself, demonstrated one of his goals, "Death to Jacobinism." Villar, pp. 60–65.
111. Villalba, p. 90; *NYT,* Nov. 18, 1893: 1-2. Rogers, p. 389.

112. Mendonça, *A situaçao internacional*, p. 208.

113. J. Smith, *Illusion of Conflict*, pp. 156, 173; R. Graham, *Britain*, pp. 308–11.

114. Thompson to Gresham, Dec. 14, 1893, "Diplomatic Dispatches U.S. Ministers"; S. da Costa, p. 166.

115. Thompson to Gresham, Rio, Feb. 3, 1894, "Diplomatic Dispatches U.S. Ministers."

116. Thompson to Gresham, Feb. 3, 1894, "Diplomatic Dispatches U.S. Ministers."

117. Quoted in S. da Costa, p. 146. See also Abranches, *Revolta da Armada*, p. 30.

118. Mendonça to Gresham, May 30, 1894, BzLUS.

119. Gresham to Thomas Bayard, U.S. Ambassador to Great Britain, June 4, 1894, in the Bayard papers, box 192.

120. *London Times*, Nov. 17, 1893: 4.

121. In late December 80 British ship masters with property worth $1.5 million sent a letter to the British foreign minister protesting the lack of protection for British ships in Guanabara Bay; *NYT*, Dec. 28, 1893: 5-1.

122. See, for example, the *Morning Post*, Sep. 13, 1893; *Statist*, Sep. 23, 1893; *Financial News*, Sep. 9 and 12, 1893, and Dec. 31, 1893; *Standard*, Sep. 13, 1893; *London Times*, Nov. 13, 1893; all in CFBH, vol. 8.

123. J. Smith, *Illusion of Conflict*, p. xiv, notes "Anglo-American economic rivalry in Latin America was a reality, but on the diplomatic level British policy toward Latin America stressed conciliation and co-operation with the United States rather than confrontation or conflict."

124. Wyndham to Roseberry, Jan. 31, 1894, and Feb. 1, 1894, F.O. 13/728; J. Smith, *Illusion of Conflict*, p. 179.

125. The Rothschilds had sought to achieve an arbitrated settlement of the revolt with the president of the United States as arbiter in November so they clearly were not bent on Floriano's overthrow. S. da Costa, p. 136. See also *London Times*, Nov. 13, 1893, and the *Daily Telegraph*, Sep. 16, 1893, in CFBH, vol. 8.

126. Gresham wrote from Washington to T. Bayard, the U.S. ambassador in London, on Jan. 21, 1894 (WQG, vol. 42): "I do not believe Great Britain, or any other European Power, would attempt to re-establish the Monarchy in Brazil. The present state of things at Rio cannot last much longer, and I shall not be surprised at the result, whatever it may be. I do not believe the Brazilian people are very patriotic. Perhaps a majority of them are indifferent to what is now going on."

127. *NYT*, Nov. 19, 1893: 1-4. According to S. Santos, *Rebouças*, p. 501, and Besouchet, p. 379, Dom Pedro II occupied himself aboard the ship that was carrying him to European exile with reading aloud French authors and his own sonnets as well as having literary discussions. He refrained from politics, undercutting the possibility of a restorationist movement.

128. Interview in the *New York Herald*, Nov. 14, 1893: 14-4. See also Abranches, *Revolta da Armada*, p. 29, who opens the possibility that funds were given but never reached da Gama. Princess Isabel's chamberlain, the Barão de Muritiba, also denied any involvement by the royal family in the revolt but acknowledged that the revolt was receiving funding from Europe or Brazil; *St. Louis Post-Dispatch*, Nov. 26, 1893: 6. Perhaps Brazilian financiers used this method of securing repayment of their original loans to the insurgents.

129. *New York Herald*, Nov. 9, 1893: 9. Joaquim Nabuco wrote to the Barão de Penedo, May 22, 1894, in *Cartas*, p. 239, that he regretted that the imperial family had not provided the rebels in Rio Grande do Sul funds, for otherwise "the revolution would have had greater force. . . . The best opportunity possible is lost."

130. Janotti, "Monarchist Response" and *Os subversivos*, pp. 63–84.

131. M. Gresham, vol. 2, pp. 777–81. John W. Foster, the former secretary of state, remembered in *A Century of American Diplomacy*, vol. 1, p. 466, that "the commanders of the European squadrons in the harbor [were] in sympathy with the imperialists [monarchist rebels] and unwilling to do anything to discourage them."

132. See Crapole, pp. 14, 201.

133. Perhaps Gresham's will to stand down the British was steeled by his assistant in the negotiations, Kenesaw Mountain Landis, who 26 years later as the first commissioner of baseball would demonstrate his strength of character by making the unpopular moves of banning the spitball and the Chicago Black Sox, including the great Shoeless Joe Jackson. M. Gresham, vol. 2, p. 781.

134. Cecil Spring-Rice quoted in Hitchens, p. 170.

135. S. de Mendonça to C. Carvalho, Dec. 23, 1894, MDBEU, "Oficíos 1890–1892."

136. M. Gresham, vol. 2, pp. 697, 777, reported that Gresham considered Mendonça a man of "exceptional ability."

137. For examples of this campaign see *NYT*, Feb. 11, 1894: 24.

138. Floriano's minister of foreign affairs, João Felipe Pereira, recollected 50 years later that "the attitude of the American squadron anchored in Rio de Janeiro was due solely to his [Mendonça's] intervention"; in S. da Costa, p. xxviii. See also LaFeber, "Depression Diplomacy," 109, 114.

139. It is interesting to note that all three of these men were from New York and knew Flint. Crossman had been a business associate. Flint cooperated with Standard Oil and invited William's brother John D. Rockefeller to dinner, and he knew Straus as a fellow importer. Flint papers, scrapbook, p. 62; Babcock, p. 56. I have no evidence that Flint put them up to writing the letters, however.

140. Rockefeller to Gresham, Jan. 4, 1894, USNav; *Dictionary of American Biography*, vol. 9, pp. 128–29.

141. Gresham to Isidor Straus, Jan. 6, 1894, in WQG, vol. 48.

142. Hammett, p. 71.

143. *NYT*, Jan. 7, 1894: 16-1.

144. Calculated from Cooling, *Gray Steel*, p. 222.

145. Hotchkiss, for example, was convinced to build a factory in Connecticut to build guns and torpedoes for the navy. Contracts were regionally distributed to broaden the political base. Torpedo ships were constructed in Iowa, while companies from New England (Massachusetts, Rhode Island, and Maine) and the mid-Atlantic (Maryland, New York, New Jersey, and Pennsylvania) to the South (Virginia) and West (California, Oregon, and Washington) contracted to build ships and ordnance. *NYT*, June 23, 1888: 4-5; Aug. 5, 1892: 4-3; Cooling, *Gray Steel*, pp. 77, 135; Herrick, pp. 64–84. Campbell, *Transformation*, p. 72, observes that "in the 1870s, the 1880s, and also the 1890s the economic and strategic factors were inextricably interrelated."

146. Quoted in Roosevelt, p. 521.

147. Karsten, pp. 205–10.

148. Cooling, *Gray Steel*, p. 85.

149. Carnegie to Blaine, May 9, 1891, Carnegie papers, vol. 12; Flint to Carnegie, no date, Carnegie papers, vol. 38; Cooling, *Gray Steel*, p. 135; Flint papers, box 4, memo July 7, 1902. See also Flint, *Memories*, p. 190.

150. Clowes, p. 188.

151. The *San Francisco* embodied the interrelationship of foreign policy in different theaters. It had landed troops in Chile in 1891 to protect the U.S. consulate

there and then served in Hawaii the next year maintaining peace between republicans and monarchists; United States Naval History Division, *Dictionary of American Naval Fighting Ships*, p. 290.

152. Hammett, p. 199; see also Hagan, *This People's Navy*, pp. 203–5.

153. Quoted in Herrick, p. 170.

154. *NYT*, Dec. 28, 1893: 4-5; Sprout and Sprout, p. 190.

155. Castilho, p. 245.

156. Herbert, according to Hammett, p. 141, while not in favor of territorial conquest, favored "a vigorous foreign policy and . . . a Navy which would enable us to enforce that policy."

157. *The National Cyclopaedia of American Biography*, vol. 5, p. 425.

158. *NYT*, Feb. 3, 1894: 2-3.

159. Thompson reported to Gresham, Feb. 1, 1894, in "Diplomatic Dispatches U.S. Ministers," that when Benham broke the blockade "I was not consulted before hand with regard to Benham's action." Benham agreed in his telegram to Herbert, Feb. 1, 1894, USNav. He also did not consult the other foreign commanders.

160. Helm, pp. 22, 25.

161. Long, pp. 419–20, reveals that only 9 percent of the 504 naval diplomatic activities found in the years between 1798 and 1883 were for commercial protection or enhancement and these were "especially frequent in the early years." Hagan, *Gunboat Diplomacy*, demonstrates that the old navy had not entirely abandoned this role, however, as could be seen in Panama in 1885, Samoa in 1889, and Hawaii in 1891.

162. See, for instance, LaFeber, "Depression Era Diplomacy"; J. Smith, *Illusion of Conflict, Unequal Giants*, and "Britain and the Brazilian Naval Revolt of 1893"; Vivian; Clowes; Calhoun, "American Policy"; Bandeira; Hill; Rogers.

163. Benham to Herbert, Feb. 1, 1894, USNav.

164. *London Times*, Jan. 31, 1894: 5, and Feb. 6, 1894: 13; *NYT*, Feb. 9, 1894: 2.

165. Interview in *The World*, Jan. 21, 1894: 13. See also Picking to Herbert, Feb. 18, 1894, USNav.

166. *The World*, Mar. 16, 1894: 7, thought he was "the agent of some big English firm which has speculated in the revolution." He clearly sided with da Gama since he tried to prevent the landing of the American merchantmen that precipitated Benham's firing on the *Trajano*. The *New York Times*, Feb. 3, 1894: 2-3, noted that Rollins was also a representative of the trading house of Willoughby and Weston. He was also "a successful promoter of electrical enterprises" according to the *The World*, Mar. 6, 1894: 2-4. It is suspicious that Flint had also earlier promoted electrical enterprises and he had an office in the same block of New York's Broad Street as Rollins's cousin (number 16). Rollins had come to Rio at the outbreak of the revolt supposedly for the "excitement of viewing naval fights." Was he an agent for Flint?

167. *London Times*, Feb. 6, 1894: 13.

168. *The World*, Feb. 10, 1894: 5-3.

169. Brasil, *Leis do Brasil*, decreto 1549, Sep. 25, 1893, decreto 1745, Oct. 20, 1893, decreto 1608, Dec. 15, 1893; see also Villalba, pp. 137, 140.

170. Hahner, *Civilian-Military Relations*, p. 144; Carone, *República velha*, vol. 2, p. 131; Barreto do Amaral, pp. 193, 194; J. Albuquerque, p. 229.

171. *NYT*, Mar. 5, 1894: 1-2. Souza Lima wrote Prudente de Morais on Mar. 8, 1894, that the election results had just been published in São Paulo; Coleção Prudente, lata 595, pasta 9.

172. Abranches, *Revolta da Armada*, p. 32. Prudente received almost 90 percent of the 336,615 votes cast, less than 3 percent of the national population.

173. USNav correspondence, Jan. and Feb. 1894; personal communication with Gordon Chang and Kenneth Hagan.

174. The *New York Times* reported on Feb. 9, 1894: 2, and Feb. 3, 1894: 2-3, that the British were on the verge of recognizing the rebels' belligerency status when Benham broke the blockade. Thompson to Gresham, Feb. 6, 1894, in "Diplomatic Dispatches U.S. Ministers," reported that strong pressure would be brought to bear on Floriano if he did not hold elections in March and allow a civilian to replace him because that would strengthen the rebel argument that he was a dictator.

175. *NYT*, Feb. 8, 1894: 1-6.

176. Mendonça to C. Carvalho, Dec. 23, 1894, MDBEU, "Ofícios 1893–1896." Thompson wrote Gresham from Rio, Feb. 1, 1894, in "Diplomatic Dispatches U.S. Ministers," that the British minister was going to recommend the recognition of belligerency status: "It has been very clear to me that Europeans, especially the English people, sympathize with the revolters and hope for the establishment of a monarchy upon the ruins of the Republic."

177. Thompson to Gresham, Rio, Feb. 11, 1894, "Diplomatic Dispatches U.S. Ministers."

178. U.S. consul general William T. Townes said in an interview with the *New York Herald*, Feb. 23, 1894: 7, that he first learned of the candidates for the presidential election in American newspapers.

179. Vivian, p. 257. *The World*, Feb. 8, 1894: 1-6.

180. *The World*, Feb. 9, 1894: 11-1.

181. Quoted in Vivian, p. 257.

182. Hahner, "The Paulistas' Rise to Power"; Thompson, pp. 166; Villar, p. 84.

183. Brasil MJ, *Relatório, 1894*, p. 59. Pedro Dias de Campos, who wrote *A Revolta de seis de Setembro* in 1913, admitted (p. 14) that his was the first book in the twenty years since the end of the revolt to discuss the importance of São Paulo's contribution to defeating the rebels. Given the large number of books written extolling Floriano's virtues, and those of São Paulo, this omission is significant. One can infer that few people thought São Paulo's contribution important.

184. Bernardino de Campos to Floriano Peixoto, Feb. 3, 1894, reproduced in Luz and Carneiro, vol. 6, p. 253; see also pp. 67–70, 103, 114.

185. Bernardino de Campos to Min. de Guerra, Feb. 7, 1894, in Luz and Carneiro, vol. 6, p. 255.

186. M. F. Campos Sales to Col. Pires Ferreira, Feb. 26, 1894, in Debes, vol. 2, pp. 379–80.

187. Smith to Thompson, Santos, Feb. 27, 1894, in "Diplomatic Dispatches U.S. Ministers." Campos Sales in Debes, vol. 2, p. 379, also worried about "enemy forces within your own camp."

188. Smith to Thompson, Santos, Feb. 27, 1894, in "Diplomatic Dispatches U.S. Ministers." Even Dias de Campos, whose *Revolta* most lauded São Paulo's contribution to the struggle, admitted that the state was underprepared.

189. "Special Report upon Some of the Events that Took Place in the Harbor of Rio de Janeiro, Brazil between January 12th and March 18th, 1894," Mar. 31, 1894, USNav.Int.

190. Abranches, *Revolta da Armada*, p. 136. Rogers, pp. 398–99.

191. Picking to Herbert, Feb. 18, 1894, USNav. Captain Brownson of the *Detroit* reported to Herbert, Jan. 30, 1894, USNav, that da Gama had indeed offered to surrender to Benham. See also H. Smith, p. 353.

192. Benham had told the Captain of the *Detroit* to return fire, because "other vessels of the squadron will be prepared to support you, if necessary"; Benham to

Herbert, Jan. 31, 1894, USNav. See also *NYT*, Jan. 31, 1894: 1, Feb. 2, 1894: 5-5, Feb. 24, 1894: 1-7 and 15; Clowes, pp. 220–23. Calhoun in *Gilded Age Cato* is typical of the way many have treated the incident. He says, p. 202, "Benham's action was limited, defensive, and in reaction to direct fire by the insurgents." It was only limited because the rebels decided not to resist.

193. Nabuco, *Intervenção estrangeira*, p. 247; *NYT*, Feb. 22, 1894: 5-5; J. Smith, *Illusion of Conflict*, pp. 179, 180.

194. *NYT*, Mar. 15, 1894: 3.

195. Quoted in *PO* 16, no. 19 (Feb. 8, 1894): 449.

196. The *Vossische Zeitung* in the *NYT*, Feb. 2, 1894: 5-5; the *Pall Mall Gazette* in the *NYT*, Feb. 3, 1894: 2-3.

197. W. A. Williams, *American Empire*, p. 35; LaFeber, "Depression Diplomacy," pp. 107–18.

198. Foster, *Century of American Diplomacy*, vol. 1, p. 466.

199. Henry C. Smith to Thompson, Feb. 27, 1894, and Thompson to Smith, Mar. 7, 1894, in "Diplomatic Dispatches U.S. Ministers."

200. J. Smith, *Illusions of Conflict*, p. 208.

201. William McAdoo, "The Navy and the Nation," *Proceedings of the United States Naval Institute* 20, no. 2 (1894): 421.

202. Herrick, pp. 153–55, 170–73. The timing of Benham's act was propitious since Congress was just then considering naval appropriations. Karsten, p. 462, quotes Captain Henry Clay Taylor's letter to Admiral Luce in February of 1894 suggesting "the more you can stir up your friends the better it will be. I am beginning to work up Boards of Trade, Chambers of Commerce and other Commercial bodies all along our coast and lake fronts" for support for the naval war college and navy funds.

203. See Hill, p. 280; Thimm, pp. 119–38; Hammett, p. 201; LaFeber, *New Empire*, pp. 217–18; W. A. Williams, *American Empire*, p. 366; McCloskey, p. 321.

204. J. Smith, *Illusion of Conflict*, pp. 180–81.

8. FLINT'S FLEET

1. Mendonça, *Ajuste de contas*, p. 159; Villalba, pp. 179–86; Villar, pp. 81, 84. Francisco Barbosa's introduction in S. da Costa, p. xvii; Flint, *Memories*, p. 100.

2. The main history of U.S.-Brazilian relations by Bandeira, p. 144, calls it the "cardboard squadron." The two principal histories of the First Republic by Brazilians, Carone, *República velha*, vol. 2, p. 126, and Bello, p. 129, barely treat Flint's Fleet in passing. They both deprecate the legal squadron as small, underarmed, with many useless ships. The enterprise is treated as Brazilian originated and conducted with no appreciation of the role played by American ship makers, technicians, crews, and materiel. Two more recent studies by foreigners make the same mistake. Schneider, p. 76, does recognize that the arrival of the legal squadron in Rio made Gama "throw in the towel," but contends that the squadron consisted of "ships hurriedly purchased in Europe." Joseph Smith, in *Illusion of Conflict*, p. 255, reverses the mistake by recognizing that the ships were purchased in the United States, but they "arrived too late to influence the course of the revolt." In a sequel, *Unequal Giants*, pp. 24, 25, he does not even mention Flint's Fleet, again because he thinks it irrelevant to the contest. This is in line with Hill's first major study of U.S.-Brazilian relations and Hahner's *Civilian-Military Relations in Brazil, 1889–1898*, which completely ignore the mercenary squadron.

3. Cervo and Bueno, pp. 158–59, only mention it in passing. This episode also

could be seen as a continuation of the filibuster tradition of the 1850's except that now in the 1890's industrial and diplomatic interests were more involved.

4. Mendonça to Carlos de Carvalho, Dec. 23, 1894, MDBEU, "Ofícios 1893–1896." See also *New York Herald*, Oct. 15, 1893: 6-1.

5. Already on Oct. 21, 1893: 5, the *New York Times* reported that the two ships were ready to return to Brazil. On Oct. 31, 1893, the *New York Herald*, p. 9, reported that the *Benjamin Constant* was completed and ready to depart. They only actually returned after the naval revolt was ended because of distrust for their crews.

6. Mendonça, *Ajuste de contas*, p. 118. In the *St. Louis Post-Dispatch* of Nov. 8, 1893: 3, Mendonça estimated that outfitting the fleet would not exceed $1.5 million. The estimate is probably low.

7. *NYT*, Oct. 29, 1893: 5.

8. Sprout and Sprout, p. 192.

9. Clipping in Flint papers, box 7.

10. Clayton, *Grace*, pp. 177–80, 196; Eaton, vol. 2, pp. 227–29; "The Shipbuilders of Thomaston: Flint and Chapman," pp. 73–77.

11. Grace to Flint, Oct. 2, 1882, Grace papers, Box 58.

12. Flint, *Memories*, p. 87.

13. Flint had attempted to purchase the USS *Bennington* for Chile; see Flint to Blaine, Mar. 17 and 19, 1891, JGBA archive, reel 11; Flint, *Memories*, pp. 69, 81.

14. Clayton, *Grace*, pp. 212, 213.

15. *Los Angeles Times*, Oct. 27, 1893: 1.

16. In a letter from New York dated Nov. 26, 1889, Arthur F. Bauer of the *New York Tribune* thanked Flint for helping a *Tribune* reporter "learn the exact truth about everything"; Flint papers, box 1.

17. Sulzberger, p. 25. New York Times, *Seventy-Fifth Anniversary Edition*, p. 5; Devine, p. 44; J. Green to Flint, Jan. 20, 1893, and C. N. Miller to Flint, Aug. 16, 1893, in Flint papers. Miller remarks that Flint was again trying to use "memorials and committees from Chambers of Commerce and Boards of Trade" to repeal the Sherman Silver Act.

18. William Wharton to Wallace B. Flint, Mar. 9, 1892, in Flint papers, box 1.

19. Jacob H. Schiff to Flint, Jan. 19, 1893, and August Belmont to Flint, Feb. 3, 1893, in Flint papers; Babcock, p. 47.

20. Flint, *Memories*, p. 91. See also Felisbello Freire to N. Rothschild, Oct. 27, 1893, and the Rothschilds' reply, on Nov. 8, 1893, in which they offer to "ask the friendly intervention of a neutral power"; NRA, "Brazilian Government," XI-65-8B.

21. The *New York Herald*, Feb. 8, 1894: 8-6, reported that the Rothschilds were funding the rebels.

22. Mendonça to Carlos de Carvalho, Dec. 23, 1894, MDBEU, "Ofícios, 1893–1896."

23. Interview in *Human Life*, June 1908, in Flint papers, box 7. In an interview in the *New York Times*, Oct. 27, 1893: 1-2, Huntington maintained that he knew nothing of the *El Cid*'s sale to Brazil.

24. Huntington to Flint, Oct. 16, 1893, in Huntington papers, series 7, reel 52; Flint, *Memories*, p. 96. According to S. da Costa, p. 282, the *World* had argued that Flint paid three times the worth of the *El Cid* while Huntington alleged that he charged $12,000 less than the vessel had cost him. Mendonça, *Ajuste de contas*, p. 164; Clowes; Villalba, p. 128; *London Times*, Oct. 28, 1893: 5.

25. In an unfortunately undated letter from Flint to someone named McCall in the Flint papers, box 5, Flint reported, "I talked to Huntington yesterday for half an hour. He will consider putting business in my hands [and] recognize my experience and

success as negotiator and my special knowledge of ship building." Although this could have been written after 1893, it is more likely that the letter preceded this date since Huntington lived only seven more years afterward and had been a great tycoon for three decades before, when he had been quite friendly with Blaine and other friends of Flint.

26. *NYT*, Feb. 22, 1893: 2-4 and Mar. 19, 1893: 20-5.

27. Statement of stockholders of Flint, Eddy, and the American Trading Company, Flint papers, box 6; M. Grace to Sears, Mar. 4, 1889, and Aug. 30, 1889, in Grace papers, box 62; *Dictionary of American Biography*, vol. 5, pt. 1, p. 522.

28. *New York Herald*, Nov. 4, 1893: 3-5; Mendonça, *Ajuste de contas*, p. 141.

29. Villalba, p. 126. *NYT*, Oct. 29, 1893: 5.

30. The captain of the *Destroyer*, Guy Brick, had worked for Huntington's Pacific Mail Steamship Company; *NYT*, Nov. 27, 1893: 5-3. *Britannia*'s surgeon, Dr. Randall, had previously worked for the USBMSCo.; *NYT*, Nov. 12, 1893: 5-5.

31. Flint to C. Huntington, Nov. 2, 1893, Huntington papers, series 7, reel 52 (1856–1901).

32. *St. Louis Post-Dispatch*, Nov. 23, 1893: 1. I also found reports on the fleet's assembly in *The World, New York Herald, San Francisco Chronicle, Los Angeles Times, Fullerton Tribune*, and *Anaheim Weekly Gazette*.

33. *NYT*, Oct. 28, 1893: 8-3.

34. *NYT*, Oct. 27, 1893: 1-2. *The Marine Journal* reported Sep. 23, 1893, "The latest performance is that of the *El Cid* whose feat on her maiden voyage elicited well-deserved notices from the daily papers and caused no small comment at home and abroad"; in Evans, *Collis*, vol. 2, p. 609.

35. *New York Herald*, Oct. 28, 1893: 5. *San Francisco Chronicle*, Oct. 28, 1893: 1.

36. *New York Herald*, Nov. 2, 1893: 8, lists $225,000, but the memo from Flint, Nov. 1, 1893, in Flint papers, box 4, put the price at $164,000. The discrepancy could be explained by bad reporting, propaganda, or profiteering.

37. *Scientific American*, Dec. 2, 1893; Mendonça, *Ajuste de contas*, p. 135. The *New York Herald*, Nov. 1, 1893: 9, put the cost of the armed *Destroyer* at $85,000. The *New York Herald* reported Oct. 31, 1893: 9, that Admiral Maurity had been advised by men in the U.S. Navy that the *Destroyer* was a "back number" that should not be purchased at any price. Given the ship's unfortunate fate, they well may have been right.

38. See Villalba, pp. 128–31; Clowes, p. 195. *NYT*, Oct. 29, 1893: 5; Flint, *Memories*, p. 92.

39. *New York Herald*, Nov. 1, 1893: 9.

40. *New York Herald*, Nov. 8, 1893: 11-5. *NYT*, Oct. 31, 1893: 5. *NYT*, Nov. 2, 1893: 5-3.

41. Memo, Flint papers, box 7; *NYT*, Nov. 9, 1893: 5-3 and Mar. 19, 1894: 8-3. Flint, *Memories*, p. 142.

42. *Scientific American*, Dec. 2, 1893; Flint, *Memories*, pp. 96, 97; *New York Herald*, Oct. 27, 1893: 7-2, and Nov. 10, 1893: 7. *NYT*, Nov. 18, 1893: 4-4; *San Francisco Chronicle*, Nov. 9, 1893: 1.

43. The *New York Herald*, Oct. 28, 1893: 5, noted, "One Aquibadan or Republica annihilated would be an object lesson in modern naval warfare that would be as startling to foreign naval powers as was the advent of the Monitor in 1861." See also the *San Francisco Chronicle*, Oct. 28, 1893: 1, and the *New York Herald*, Nov. 2, 1893: 8.

44. Excerpted in *PO* 16, no. 6 (Nov. 9, 1893): 138.

45. Mendonça, *Ajuste de contas*, p. 159; Flint, *Memories*, pp. 96, 97; for more on

the dynamite gun see *NYT*, Dec. 9, 1887: 4-3; May 24, 1888: 4-5; Jan. 6, 1889: 2-5; Jan. 16, 1889: 2-3; Feb. 7, 1889: 1-4; Feb. 8, 1889: 8-1; Feb. 10, 1889: 3-5; Feb. 11, 1889: 8-1; Feb. 24, 1889: 8-1; May 11, 1889: 8-5; Jan. 31, 1890: 8-2; July 9, 1890: 1-7; June 8, 1893: 9-6.

46. Carone, *República velha*, vol. 2, p. 126.

47. Flint to Mendonça, Dec. 22, 1893, Flint papers, box 1.

48. Contract in "Business Papers, 1894–1899" file, box 4, Flint papers.

49. Fontoura Xavier to Prudente, Feb. 20, 1899, in Coleção Prudente, lata 600, pasta 42.

50. *New York Herald*, Nov. 1, 1893: 9.

51. Burke to Quincy, Recife, Jan. 20, 1894, in "Diplomatic Dispatches Pernambuco" does not make clear who the intermediary was in the sale of the German torpedo ships. The *New York Times*, Mar. 1, 1894: 3-1, reported the cost of the five torpedo boats at £150,000 (about $650,000). The *Times*, Nov. 1, 1893: 1, also estimated the cost of Flint's Fleet at $3 million but included six ships that Flint optioned but never actually purchased. The other expenses were $500,000 for the *El Cid*, $30,000 for the *Destroyer*, $20,000 for the *Feiseen*, and $50,000 for the Yarrow torpedo boat; equipment from the Hotchkiss company was $400,000, and alterations to convert the ships for war were $400,000. This latter cost presumably included the dynamite gun and torpedoes. This may well be a conservative estimate since the *Britannia*, which cost $225,000, and the *Javelin* are not included nor are the five German torpedo boats.

52. Mendonça, *Ajuste de contas*, p. 174.

53. Flint, *Memories*, p. 96.

54. Ibid., p. 91. Some of the reporting of the revolt had mercenary rather than political ends. The Associated Press reporter invented stories, because, he replied to a disgusted fellow journalist, "that is just the kind of stuff the 'Associated' wants." See also *NYT*, April 15, 1894: 1-6.

55. Flint, *Memories*, p. 91.

56. *Human Life*, June 1908, clipping in Flint papers, box 7; *New York Herald*, Nov. 13, 1893: 4-2.

57. Burke to E. F. Uhl, Jan. 11, 1894, "Diplomatic Dispatches Pernambuco."

58. *London Times*, Oct. 27, 1893: 3.

59. *NYT*, Nov. 5, 1893: 1-4. Other orders came to the United States to outfit Floriano's army. For example, a contract for 3,000 boots was executed in Rhode Island. Ironically, the boots were reportedly manufactured by inmates of the Rhode Island state prison; *New York Herald*, Feb. 4, 1894: 9-5.

60. Buhl, p. 148; *Boston Journal* in *PO* 16, no. 16 (Jan. 18, 1894): 377.

61. *Scientific American*, Dec. 2, 1893.

62. *NYT*, Oct. 9, 1893: 1-4.

63. Mendonça, *Ajuste de contas*, p. 118.

64. Ibid., pp. 117, 120.

65. Ibid., pp. 117, 137.

66. Burke to Uhl, Jan. 11, 1894, "Diplomatic Dispatches Pernambuco." Nabuco in *Intervenção estrangeira*, p. 233, claimed that they were supposedly promised $5,000 if they lost one limb and $10,000 for two. The *New York Times* (Nov. 8, 1893: 8-1) reported that gunners were hired for $50 a day plus two months in advance and shipped out for a year.

67. Stevens to Quincy, Aug. 31, 1893, in "Diplomatic Dispatches Pernambuco." N. W. Aldrich, "The McKinley Act and the Cost of Living," in *Forum*, extracted in *PO* 14, no. 2 (Oct. 15, 1892): 29.

68. *NYT*, Nov. 4, 1893: 5-1. According to the navy's Bureau of Navigation, in 1890 only 47 percent of the navy's men were native born and 58 percent U.S. citizens; in Harrod, p. 17. See also Burke to Quincy, Jan. 11, 1894, "Diplomatic Dispatches Pernambuco."

69. *NYT*, Nov. 8, 1893: 8-1, Nov. 9, 1893: 5-3, Nov. 17, 1893: 7-2, Nov. 21, 1893: 9-3; *New York Herald*, Nov. 11, 1893: 6-6; Mendonça, *Ajuste de contas*, p. 144. Vivian, p. 251, is wrong when he claims the crew of Flint's fleet numbered only 170 men. The *America* alone had that many men.

70. *NYT*, Nov. 14, 1893: 1-3, Nov. 19, 1893: 1-5, Nov. 21, 1893: 1-1, Nov. 22, 1893: 1-1; *New York Herald*, Nov. 27, 1893: 5; Mendonça, *Ajuste de contas*, p. 142. Aboard the *El Cid* were, according to the *New York Times* (Nov. 7, 1893: 8-1), the following Annapolis graduates: a Mr. Macdonough Craven, class of 1880, T. H. Sparling, class of 1883, and John F. Conway, class of 1882. Also H. O. Bingling. Flint, *Memories*, p. 101.

71. *NYT*, Nov. 15, 1893: 5-1.

72. Ibid., Oct. 9, 1893: 1-4. Compare this with the views of the monarchist Joaquim Nabuco, who wrote in *A Intervenção estrangeira*, p. 114, that the crew of Flint's Fleet constituted "the worst scum of Yankee filibusterism," and the leftist nationalist Moniz Bandeira who also denounced the fleet's crew, p. 92, as "riffraff" (*choldra*).

73. *St. Louis Post-Dispatch*, Nov. 11, 1893: 4.

74. Section 5282 of the United States Revised Statutes stated "Every person who, within the territory or jurisdiction of the United States, enlists or enters himself or hires or retains another to enlist or enter himself or to go beyond the limits of or jurisdiction of the United States with the intent to be enlisted or entered in the service of any foreign Prince, State, colony district or people as a soldier or as a marine or seaman on board of any vessel of war, letter of marque or privateer, shall be deemed guilty of high misdemeanor and shall be fined not more than $1000 and imprisoned not more than three years." The *New York Herald* (Nov. 3, 1893: 7) commented, "This seems to be explicit enough."

75. Report of Major W. J. C. Gadsby, Jan. 5, 1894, in MDBEU, "Ofícios 1893–1896"; *NYT*, Nov. 25, 1893: 5-4; Mendonça, *Ajuste de contas*, p. 121. *Dictionary of American Biography*, vol. 5, pt. 1, p. 522. According to the *New York Times*, Nov. 17, 1893: 1-2, the contract read: "It is agreed between the master, officers, seamen, and mariners and crew of the Brazilian steamship, whereof _____ is at present master, or whoever shall go for master, and between Salvador Mendonça, Minister Plenipotentiary of the United States of Brazil to the United States of America, representing the said United States of Brazil as owners of the said steamship, which is now bound from the port of New York to Rio de Janeiro, Brazil. . . . It being expressly stipulated and understood by and between the parties hereto, however, that this agreement does not in any way constitute an enlistment or an agreement to enlist in the Brazilian Navy, or obligate or bind any of the parties thereto to enlist in the Brazilian Navy; neither does it obligate or bind any of the parties thereto to swear allegiance to serve under the Brazilian flag, nor to do or commit any act in violation of the laws of nations, or of the municipal laws of the United States, or interfere with any of the parties hereto appealing to his own Government as a citizen as a subject thereof."

76. Mendonça to Brazilian secretary of state, Dec. 4, 1893, MDBEU, "Ofícios 1893–1896." This operation displayed the duplicity of the entire enterprise. Mendonça put George A. Burt, formerly of the United States and Brazil Mail Steamship Company, in charge of towing the *Destroyer* and another torpedo ship off the coast of São Paulo, while Mendonça would report that the ships had been lost at sea to throw

off the rebels. He told the crews that they should expect $60,000 to share among themselves if they destroyed a rebel ship, but, Mendonça added, he had made "no promise in the name of the [Brazilian] government as to this gratuity, which the government can treat as it sees best, honoring it or refusing it and taking over the torpedo ships with its own officers." On the other hand, Mendonça expected the mercenary crews to honor the agreement and not ask for more. He thought they would act "in an honest and dignified manner," something that Mendonça lacked in' this instance.

77. Los Angeles Times, Nov. 9, 1893: 1.

78. Report from Pinkerton National Detective Agency, N.Y., Nov. 28, 1893, and Dec. 1, 1894, in MDBEU, "Ofícios 1893–1896."

79. Report of Major W. J. C. Gadsby, Jan. 5, 1894, and Mendonça to C. do Nascimento, July 28, 1894, in MDBEU, "Ofícios 1893–1896."

80. Mendonça, Ajuste de contas, p. 121; New York Herald, Nov. 3, 1893: 7-2.

81. NYT, Dec. 22, 1893: 3-3, Jan. 5, 1894: 5-3, Jan. 9, 1894: 1-2, Jan. 10, 1894: 2-4, Jan. 12, 1894: 1-4; New York World, Jan. 1, 1894: 5-2. St. Louis Post-Dispatch, Nov. 28, 1893: 6.

82. Flint, Memories, p. 99.

83. Report from The World correspondent on board the Nictheroy, Jan. 21, 1894: 13. The ship had the anomalous position, when it entered the Danish Virgin Islands, of "a Brazilian ship not engaged in trade."

84. Ibid., p. 99. A sailor-poet on board the Nictheroy penned similar lines, The World, Jan. 21, 1894: 13: "A Yankee ship went out to sea/To fight a man named Mello./Albeit astern she flew the flag/Of blue and green and yellow./Sing hey for Old Glory/For every man in her gallant crew/Was a Yankee seaman, tried and true/Who loved his flag and couldn't forget/Though Hessian he be, he was a Yankee yet."

85. I have come across no explanation for the choices of ship names, but the coincidence of the Nictheroy seems too great to have been fortuitous given its sister ship Andrada (also known as the America) and the great stock Floriano put in symbolic titles and the care he used with words.

86. Bethell, "Independence," pp. 35, 36; and J. H. Rodrigues, vol. 3, pp. 109, 125.

87. Floriano did consult a descendant of Lord Cochrane about hiring mercenaries; H. Smith, p. 336.

88. Mendonça to Cassiano do Nascimento, July 28, 1894, in MDBEU, "Ofícios 1893–1896." See also Anaheim Weekly Gazette, Nov. 16, 1893: 1; Los Angeles Times, Nov. 7, 1893: 1; St. Louis Post-Dispatch, Nov. 8, 1893: 3, and Nov. 9, 1893: 8; San Francisco Chronicle, Nov. 13, 1893: 1.

89. The World, Jan. 21, 1894: 13.

90. NYT, Nov. 9, 1893: 5-3.

91. The World, Jan. 10, 1894: 7.

92. Burke to Josiah Quincy, Dec. 23, 1893, "Diplomatic Dispatches Pernambuco." The World, Jan. 4, 1894; Mendonça, Ajuste de contas, p. 140.

93. Mendonça, Ajuste de contas, p. 140.

94. Interview with 40 returning crew members from the Nictheroy, NYT, Jan. 13, 1894: 1-3, interview with eighteen others, Jan. 21, 1894: 5-1. One crew member admitted that when they reached Recife, the captain "threw overboard $1,000 worth of liquor, and nearly everybody on board was drunk."

95. Quoted in NYT, Jan. 20, 1894: 10-3.

96. See, for instance, The World, Jan. 4, 1894; NYT, Jan. 13, 1894: 1-3. Burke to Quincy, Jan. 11, 1894, "Dispatches Pernambuco."

97. F. Williams, p. 390.

98. Burke to E. F. Uhl, Jan. 13, 1894, "Dispatches Pernambuco."

99. Ibid.

100. Ibid.

101. D. Burke to Quincy, Jan. 31, 1894, "Dispatches Pernambuco."

102. Burke to Quincy, Jan. 11, 1894, and Jan. 20, 1894, "Dispatches Pernambuco." *NYT*, Jan. 23, 1894: 9-4, reported that Flint and Co. responded to returning sailors from the *Nictheroy* seeking back pay that the company "had nothing to do with the enlistment" and that they should see Minister Mendonça.

103. *NYT*, Feb. 3, 1894: 1-7.

104. Ibid., Jan. 11, 1894; Mendonça, *Ajuste de contas*, p. 142.

105. The *New York Times* reported, Jan. 8, 1893: 1-3, that longshoremen in Recife deserted barges used to coal the *Nictheroy* in order to join the insurgents.

106. Burke to Quincy, Jan. 20, 1894, "Dispatches Pernambuco."

107. Villar, p. 73; *NYT*, Feb. 11, 1894: 5-1.

108 Burke to E. F. Uhl, Jan. 13, 1894, "Dispatches Pernambuco." A dispatch from *The World*'s reporter on board the *Nictheroy*, Jan. 10, 1894: 7, reported that the ship took on some 200 Brazilians as well, 100 to 150 of them being cadets. The cadets were there as observers to learn about the vessel. The Brazilian commandant placed on board was only to supervise, as "all orders will be given through her present officers."

109. Interview with Admiral da Gama in the *NYT*, Jan. 16, 1894: 3-2.

110. "Professional Notes" in *Proceedings of the United States Naval Institute* 20, no. 2 (1894): 458. According to Nabuco, in *A Intervenção estrangeira*, p. 234, some of the officers on the torpedo ships were Chilean supporters of Balmaceda, linking even more closely the Chilean and Brazilian revolts.

111. O. Barreto, passim, and Brasil, Serviço de Documentação, *Almirante Gonçalves*, pp. 9–14.

112. Flint, *Memories*, p. 91.

113. Burke to Quincy, Nov. 22, 1893, as well as dispatches of Nov. 11, 1893, and Nov. 15, 1893, "Dispatches Pernambuco."

114. Burke to Quincy, Dec. 4, 1893, "Dispatches Pernambuco." Burke also conjectured that there would be little resistance to a restoration movement in Pernambuco except perhaps by the army.

115. *NYT*, Dec. 14, 1893: 1-1.

116. Burke to Quincy, Jan. 20, 1894, "Dispatches Pernambuco."

117. Captain Picking (Picking to Herbert, Nov. 26, 1893, USNav), who was arguably partial to the rebels and definitely at war with the American diplomats, had dismissed Burke's request for naval aid, claiming that there was no revolt in Pernambuco.

118. D. Burke to J. Quincy, Dec. 30, 1893, "Dispatches Pernambuco."

119. E. Uhl to Navy, Feb. 27, 1894, USNav; *The World*, Feb. 20, 1894: 1-5.

120. Memorandum of General Solon in the Coleção Solon, Rio, lata 614, pasta 19. Also see Dias de Campos, p. 261.

121. Coronel Jardim to Floriano Peixoto, Feb. 3, 1894, in Luz and Carneiro, vol. 6, p. 253.

122. Picking to Herbert, Jan. 10, 1894, USNav.

123. *Baltimore Herald* in *PO* 16, no. 21 (Feb. 22, 1894): 494; *NYT*, Feb. 23, 1894: 2-4.

124. Picking to Herbert, Feb. 18, 1894, USNav; *NYT*, Jan. 16, 1894: 6; Clowes, p. 223.

125. *NYT*, Jan. 14, 1894: 8-3; Villar, pp. 74–75.

126. Abranches, *A Revolta da Armada*, pp. 25, 31, 32, 51, 157.

127. Ibid., pp. 141, 142, 147, 156–57.

128. *NYT*, Jan. 16, 1894: 3-2. According to *New York Times*, Mar. 24, 1889: 16-1, the *Aquibadan* was capable of 15.7 knots at its best, while according to Mendonça, *Ajuste de contas*, p. 160, the *Nictheroy* could do 17 knots. Abranches, *A Revolta da Armada*, p. 147, reports that the *Aquibadan* had trouble with its boilers.

129. *NYT*, Mar. 19, 1894: 8-3.

130. Ibid., Mar. 18, 1894: 3-3. Villar, p. 73, complained that this inaction against the "legal squadron in formation in the north of the country gave Marshal Floriano ever more political and military power."

131. Ibid., p. 73.

132. Ibid., p. 85.

133. G. Burt's interview in the *NYT*, Apr. 24, 1894: 8-3.

134. *NYT*, Jan. 28, 1894: 20-7.

135. Report of Nils de Foch in Mendonça, *Ajuste de contas*, pp. 143–49.

136. *New York Herald*, Feb. 10, 1894: 6-6.

137. *NYT*, Feb. 6, 1894: 1-6.

138. See A. Stevens to Wynham, Bahia, Nov. 19, 1889, FO 13/662; and *NYT*, Feb. 4, 1894: 21-5, whose reporter found no one favorable to Peixoto.

139. Thompson to Gresham, Petrópolis, Feb. 28, 1894, in "Diplomatic Dispatches U.S. Ministers."

140. Clowes, p. 223.

141. Ibid. *NYT*, Feb. 3, 1894: 1-7, and Apr. 16, 1894: 1-3.

142. Castilho, p. 250, says the rebels had no clothes and no food, were listless, and suffered from yellow fever and beri-beri.

143. J. Nabuco to Hilario de Gouveia, Mar. 10, 1894, in *Cartas*, p. 229.

144. Villar, p. 109; *The World*, Feb. 16, 1894: 5-3.

145. Villalba, p. 147.

146. *NYT*, Apr. 17, 1894: 1-5.

147. Villalba, p. 148.

148. Ibid., pp. 150–51. *NYT*, Apr. 17, 1894: 9-5.

149. Interview with Dr. J. A. Tonner in the *NYT*, Dec. 27, 1895, 9-5.

150. Selas Terry to secretary of the navy, Apr. 28, 1894, USNav; Forjaz, pp. 1, 22; Paraty, pp. 49, 58; Nabuco, *Intervenção estrangeira*, pp. 234, 235.

151. Dias de Campos, p. 179.

152. Luz and Carneiro, vol. 6, p. 161; Villalba, p. 191; Thompson, p. 199; Nabuco, *Intervenção estrangeira*, p. 239.

153. *NYT*, Apr. 24, 1894: 8-3.

154. "Professional Notes" in *Proceedings of the United States Naval Institute* 20, no. 3 (1894): 622–23. Edward Brinley, "The Pneumatic Gun on the Brazilian Cruiser Nictheroy," *Proceedings of the United States Naval Institute* 20, no. 72 (1894): 830; memorandum of Captain Alexandrino Faria de Alencar in Thompson, pp. 223–27; *NYT*, Dec. 27, 1894: 9-5.

155. Coleção Solon, lata 614, pasta 19.

156. Mello to General Luiz Salgado, Apr. 10, 1894, and Apr. 11, 1894, in Thompson, pp. 206, 207.

157. Thompson, p. 214.

158. Brasil, Presidente, *Mensagens ao Congresso Nacional*, p. 92.

159. See, for example, Brasil, Serviço de Documentação, *Almirante Gonçalves*, and O. Barreto, passim.

160. Villar, p. 84.
161. *Scientific American*, Dec. 2, 1893.
162. Howard P. Elwell, in "Arming of the Brazilian Cruisers *Nictheroy* and *America*," *Proceedings of the United States Naval Institute* 19, no. 68 (1893): 391, observed that "the recent conversion of the merchant vessels *El Cid* and *Britannia* . . . presents an object-lesson, the value of which can scarsely be overestimated. The two ships . . . were so quickly transformed form their peaceful condition into efficient fighting vessels . . . as to astonish naval officers."
163. The *New York Times* reported, Nov. 5, 1893: 1-4, that "The prompt action of the Brazilian government in purchasing ships in the United States has disconcerted these backers of the insurrectionists in Europe and they fear the collapse of their venture is inevitable."
164. Nabuco, *Balmaceda*, p. 141.
165. Hill, p. 281; *NYT*, Dec. 27, 1894: 9-5.
166. *NYT*, June 23, 1894: 4-2.

9. YANKEE TRADERS IN BRAZIL

1. *Washington Post*, Feb. 5, 1891. The *Post* carried responses to the treaty from businessmen from all over the country; they all saw great advantage in the treaty. The 1892 *Report of the Bureau of American Republics*, p. 9, also found the U.S. business community encouraged by the treaty: "There is most gratifying evidence of an awakened interest among the people of the U.S. in the other American republics and colonies and an increased desire among our merchants and manufacturers to participate in the trade." See also *American Economist*, Feb. 13, 1891: 105, Apr. 3, 1891: 216; *The Engineering and Mining Journal*, 51, no. 10 (Feb. 7, 1891): 161, and 51, no. 10 (Mar. 7, 1891): 279; *New York Tribune*, Feb. 7, 1891; *Boston Journal*, Feb. 9, 1891; *Brooklyn Eagle*, Feb. 9, 1891; *Chicago Inter-Ocean*, Feb. 8, 1891; *Pittsburgh Times*, Feb. 8, 1891; *Wisconsin State Journal*, Feb. 7, 1891; *Iowa State-Register*, Feb. 7, 1891; *Birmingham Age-Democrat*, Feb. 7, 1891; and *Philadelphia Telegraph* Feb. 6, 1891, all in *PO* 10, no. 19 (Feb. 14, 1891): 437–39.
2. Wm. O. Thomas to Wharton, July 14, 1892, "Dispatches Bahia."
3. LaFeber, *New Empire*, p. 60, and *American Search*, pp. 30–31, 103–13.
4. S. Mendonça to Rui Barbosa, Apr. 2, 1890, in CRB; Mendonça, *A Situação internacional*, p. 195.
5. Calculated from U.S. Tariff Commission, *Reciprocity*, p. 186.
6. USBC, *Statistical Abstract of the United States, 1897*, p. 94.
7. Gerard to Deville, June 20, 1893, in MAE CC, vol. 25.
8. Quoted in Wileman, p. 114. See also *NYT*, Aug. 4, 1893: 4-5. Ford, in *Reciprocity*, p. 23, refers to the error as "little less than a blunder and one that would shame a novice in statistics." There is no reason to believe that this mistake was intentional; it was common. In 1888, according to the *Handbook of American Republics, 1891*, p. 78, Brazil claimed to have exported 22 million pounds more coffee to the United States than the latter acknowledged receiving, which was a 9 percent difference.
9. U.S. Tariff Commission, *Reciprocity*, pp. 167, 171.
10. Russ, chap. 25, p. 3.
11. E. Johnson, p. 345.
12. Heitman, p. 288.
13. Russ, chap. 25, pp. 4–7.
14. FIBGE, *Sérias estatísticas retrospectivas*, vol. 1, pp. 85, 87.
15. *Handbook for American Republics*, 1891, pp. 311–13; *Washington Post*, Feb. 11, 1891.
16. *Rio News*, Mar. 24, 1891.

17. Ibid.

18. Ibid., Mar. 24, 1891, and Azevedo, p. 155.

19. Camara dos Deputados, *Anais*, 1892, vol. 2, p. 82.

20. Ibid., 1891, sessão extraordinário, p. 96, shows that the tariff declared a 50 percent increase on all imports except basic necessities such as codfish, dried fish, beans, corn, and rice, as well as a 60 percent increase on wine, beer, and cotton, woolen, and linen goods.

21. Russ, chap. 25, p. 3; *Rio News*, Apr. 12, 1891.

22. *The Economist*, Mar. 7, 1891: 307, and July 16, 1892: 912.

23. A. Gerard to Mon. Ribot, July 24, 1891, and Mar. 7, 1892, in MAE CC, vol. 23, and Gerard to Ribot, Sept. 1892, in MAE CC, vol. 24. Salisbury to Adams, Feb. 20, 1891, FO 13/680.

24. Brazil MF, *Relatório, 1892*, p. 20, mentions the "clamor of relatively important industrial enterprises" for government aid which the administration sought to placate.

25. Topik, "Brazil's Bourgeois Revolution?" pp. 258–63.

26. Anonymous trader to minister of finance, undated (probably 1892), in Brazilian Government letter book XI-65-8B, NRA.

27. Lobo, "Evolução dos preços," pp. 261–62. Wileman, p. 27, estimated the inflation at 30 percent for those years.

28. *Rio News*, Feb. 23, 1892.

29. Ibid., Oct. 25, 1892.

30. Alvey Adee, Acting Secretary to U.S. Legation in Brazil, Washington, May 26, 1891, in "Diplomatic Instructions."

31. *Rio News*, Mar. 24, 1891.

32. C. C. Andrews, p. xiv.

33. Interview with William Ivins, president of the USBMSCo. *NYT*, May 14, 1892: 1-3; Hutchins, p. 519. The British could build ships so much cheaper because of economies of scale. In 1888, according to *PO* 8, no. 4 (Nov. 2, 1889): 95, 88.7 percent of the world's steamship tonnage was built in the United Kingdom Mendonça, *Situação internacional*, p. 195, estimated that U.S. freight, commissions, and insurance cost 5 percent more than in Europe.

34. Rutter, p. 62.

35. Gerard to Rebot, Mar. 7, 1892, in MAE CC, vol. 23. Robert Adams reported to James G. Blaine, Oct. 9, 1889, in USDS CorAmRep box 16, that there were eight British lines and three German as well as three French, two Italian, and two Austrian.

36. Andrews, p. 119; McGann, p. 91. *Handbook of American Republics, 1891*, p. 69.

37. *NYT*, Jan. 9, 1890: 6-4.

38. For example, J. Kerby to Blaine, May 25, 1891, "Dispatches Pará."

39. Quoted in U.S. Treasury Dept., *Commercial Relations of the United States with Foreign Countries during 1894 and 1895*, p. 656.

40. Brasil MRE, *Relatório, 1891*; Marvin, p. 388; Curtis, *Trade and Transportation*, p. 209.

41. Blaine in *North American Review*, *PO* 8, no. 12 (Dec. 28, 1889): 306; Swann, pp. 95, 98, 123; Robert Adams to Blaine, Oct. 9, 1889, in USDS CorAmRep, box 16; *NYT*, Jan. 9, 1890: 6-4. Evans, vol. 2, p. 558.

42. Hutchins, p. 534, Holbo, p. 212, and H. W. Morgan, *From Hayes to McKinley*, p. 363.

43. Interview with William Ivins, *NYT*, Feb. 23, 1893: 10, and May 14, 1892: 1-3.

Ivins claimed that he could have bought equivalent British ships for one-fourth to one-fifth the cost of the U.S. ships but did not because of the subsidy provisions that turned out to be so demanding that the company never received any funds from the new legislation.

44. Hutchins, p. 527.

45. U.S. Treasury Dept., *The Foreign Commerce and Navigation of the United States 1893*, vol. 1, p. 709, and *1897*, p. cxxxviii.

46. *NYT*, Feb. 7, 1891: 4-2.

47. J. Kerby to Blaine, May 25, 1891, in "Dispatches Pará."

48. M. Romero to Marischal, Jan. 18, 1890, in AEMEUA, legajo 392, no. 71, Estados Unidos; Curtis, *Trade and Transportation*, p. 204.

49. See, for example, Fry, *Search for Southern Autonomy*, pp. 94–95, and Fry, "Southern Expansionism."

50. Curtis, *Trade and Transportation*, p. 17; Rutter, pp. 56, 60, 67.

51. Gerard to Develle, Mar. 12, 1893, in MAE CC, vol. 25.

52. Stevens to Wharton, Nov. 19, 1892, "Dispatches Pernambuco."

53. Société Franco-Bresilienne de Travaux Publique to Ministère d'Affairs Etrangères, Paris, Dec. 8, 1891, in MAE CP, vol. 26; *Rio News*, Aug. 25, 1891.

54. Thompson to Gresham, Feb. 28, 1894, in "Diplomatic Dispatches U.S. Ministers"; *Rio News*, May 17, 1891.

55. *NYT*, Sep. 28, 1891: 2-6.

56. J. Kerby to Wharton, Apr. 27, 1891, "Dispatches Pará."

57. D. Burke to Wharton, Apr. 27, 1891, "Dispatches Bahia."

58. Conger to Blaine, Feb. 24, 1891, in "Diplomatic Dispatches U.S. Ministers."

59. *Rio News*, Apr. 26, 1892.

60. J. W. Foster to R. Adams, Sep. 23, 1892, "Diplomatic Instructions."

61. See Stein, *Vassouras*, chaps. 5–7. See also H. Bastos, *O pensamento industrial*, p. 106; Andrews, p. 255. Nabuco to André Rebouças, Jan. 1, 1893, in *Cartas a amigos*, p. 219, complains that the freedman population had been abandoned; it was suffering degradation and death. See also Holloway, *Immigrants on the Land*, and Vaz.

62. Stein, *Brazilian Cotton Manufacture*, p. 26.

63. Ibid., pp. 67–68.

64. Wileman, p. 117.

65. Andrews, p. 121.

66. Conger to Blaine, Feb. 24, 1891, "Diplomatic Dispatches U.S. Ministers."

67. Dockery to Foster, Sep. 9, 1892, "Dispatches Rio de Janeiro."

68. Hoffman, p. 30.

69. Eysenbach, pp. 32, 36.

70. *Rio News*, July 5, 1892.

71. Of the 351,312 foreigners in Brazil in 1890, only 1,500 of them were from the United States, and almost none were merchants according to Brasil MIVOP, Directoria de Estatística, *Sexo, raça, e estado civil*, p. 14. This left the *Rio News*, July 5, 1892, to conclude, "That American products are sold here at all is almost wholly due to the Englishman, German, Portuguese, and Brazilian."

72. W. E. Holloway to John Grace, London, July 12, 1888, in Grace papers, box 5.

73. J. Kerby to Blaine, Feb. 21, 1891, in "Dispatches Pará," U.K. Foreign Office, Consul Walter Hearns, Report of the Year 1892 in Rio Grande do Sul in Apr. 30, CFBH, vol. 8, and *South American Journal*, Aug. 26, 1893, in CFBH, vol. 8.

74. J. Kerby to Blaine, Feb. 13, 1890, and Feb. 10, 1891, "Dispatches Pará"; U.S. Treasury Dept., *Commercial Relations 1895 and 1896*, vol. 2, p. 649.

75. Grace to Sears, Mar. 28, 1890, Grace papers, box 62. Ironically, at the same

time, Grace was negotiating the Grace contract in Peru to take over mines and railroads in that country.

76. J. Kerby to Blaine, Feb. 21, 1891, "Dispatches Pará."

77. Grace to Sears, Apr. 16, 1891, in Grace papers.

78. Ibid. USTC, *Reciprocity and Commercial Treaties*, p. 301, shows that in the thirteen years between 1902 and World War I, U.S. manufacturers supplied only 10 percent of Brazil's rubber manufactures imports.

79. J. Kerby to Blaine, Feb. 10, 1891, in "Dispatches Pará."

80. J. Kerby to Blaine, Feb. 21, 1891, "Dispatches Pará."

81. Andrews, *Brazil*, p. 121.

82. Stein, *Brazilian Cotton Manufacture*, p. 71.

83. Hutchinson, *Report on Trade Conditions*, p. 59.

84. Ibid.

85. Ibid., p. 62.

86. Wileman, pp. 85, 86.

87. U.S. Treasury Dept., *Commercial Relations 1895, 1896*, vol. 2, p. 686.

88. *South American Journal*, Aug. 25, 1888, in CFBH, vol. 6.

89. W. O. Thomas to Gresham, Sep. 30, 1893, "Dispatches Bahia."

90. See Wilkins, *Emergence of Multinational Enterprise*, p. 107, and Wilkins, "Banks over Borders," pp. 231–33, for the reasons U.S. banks failed to expand this early.

91. Hutchinson, *Report on Trade Conditions*, p. 61.

92. José Ayrer Watrims to J. Kerby, May 1, 1891, in J. Kerby to Dept. of State, May 4, 1891, "Dispatches Pará."

93. Conger to Blaine, Feb. 24, 1891, "Diplomatic Dispatches U.S. Ministers."

94. J. Kerby to Blaine, May 1, 1891, "Dispatches Pará."

95. Mattox, p. 37.

96. *NYT*, Jan. 4, 1890: 4-1; Kennedy, p. 215.

97. Edwin Stevens to W. Wharton, Apr. 8, 1891, and Apr. 16, 1891, in "Dispatches Pernambuco."

98. Hard Rand and Co. to U.S. Consulate, Aug. 2, 1890, and Dockery to Foster, Sep. 9, 1892, "Dispatches Rio de Janeiro"; Kerby, p. 56.

99. Stevens to Wharton, Apr. 16, 1891, July 16, 1891, and Dec. 16, 1891, and Wharton to Stevens, Jan. 7, 1892, "Dispatches Pernambuco."

100. Mattox, p. 173; Becker, *Dynamics of Business-Government Relations*, p. 23.

101. Kerby, pp. 47, 56.

102. Ibid., p. 162.

103. Ibid., p. 60.

104. Dockery to Foster, Sep. 9, 1892, "Dispatches Rio de Janeiro"; Charles Negley to Gresham, June 30, 1893, "Dispatches Rio Grande do Sul"; Kerby, p. 59; Curtis, *United States and Foreign Powers*, pp. 13, 21, 34.

105. Dockery to Wharton, Sep. 9, 1892, in "Dispatches Rio de Janeiro"; See also E. Stevens to Wharton, Nov. 16, 1892, "Dispatches Pernambuco"; Kerby, *Amazonia*, p. 98; D. Burke to Quincy, Nov. 7, 1893, "Dispatches Bahia."

106. Dockery to Wharton, Sep. 9, 1892, "Dispatches Rio de Janeiro."

107. U.S. Treasury Dept., Bureau of Statistics, *Statistical Abstract of the United States, 1897*, p. 272.

108. *The Weekly Northwestern Miller*, Aug. 16, 1889: 195; *Bradstreet's* 16, no. 545 (Dec. 8, 1888: 1); United States, *Proceedings of the National Reciprocity Convention*, p. 107, and U.S. Treasury Dept., *The Foreign Commerce and Navigation of the United States, 1893*, vol. 2, p. 635, and *1897*, vol. 2, p. 732; R. Graham, "Rio Flour Mills," pp. 13–38.

109. R. Graham, "Rio Flour Mills," p. 19; Kerby, p. 19; Rutter, pp. 55–56. U.S. Tariff Commission, *Reciprocity*, p. 299, shows that by 1902 Brazilians were milling half of their flour.

110. *The Chautauquan*, 34 (Dec. 1901), 238.

111. U.S. Tariff Commission, *Reciprocity and Commercial Treaties*, p. 189.

112. Becker, "American Manufacturers and Foreign Markets." See also Wilkins, *Emergence of Multinational Enterprise*.

113. Flint, "Our Foreign Trade," p. 63.

114. Quoted in *The Weekly Northwestern Miller*, Oct. 30, 1891: 621.

115. Becker, *The Dynamics*, p. 17.

116. Chandler, pp. 315–72; Lamoreaux.

117. Hutchinson, *Report on Trade Conditions*, p. 62.

118. Ibid.

119. Conger in The Bureau of American Republics, *How the Latin American Markets May Be Reached*, p. 110.

120. Andrews, p. 121.

121. These included the American Bank Note Company, Baldwin Locomotives, Equitable Life Insurance Company, Flint and Company Contractors, New York Commercial Company, Professor Horseford's Acid Phosphate (for nervousness, exhaustion, and diminished vitality), Singer Sewing Machines, St. Jacob's oil (for pain), the Thomson-Houston International Electric Company, and the Westinghouse Air Brake Company.

122. U.S. Tariff Commission, *Reciprocity*, p. 28.

10. AFTERMATH

1. U.S. Tariff Commission, *Reciprocity*, pp. 21, 29–30; Becker, *Dynamics of Business-Government Relations*, pp. 72, 77; Kleppner, p. 369; Terrill, pp. 203, 206.

2. U.S. Tariff Commission, *Reciprocity*, p. 32; Becker, *Dynamics of Business-Government Relations*, p. 44; Gould, "Tariffs and Markets in the Gilded Age"; Pletcher, "Reciprocity," p. 88; Terrill, pp. 207–8.

3. United States Congress, Fiftieth Congress, Second Session, House of Representatives, Report No. 3112: "Report of the Committee on Manufacturers on the Investigation of Trusts," p. 89.

4. Taussig, p. 450.

5. Imbert to Hanstaux, Paris, July 25, 1894, in MAE CC, vol. 25.

6. U.S. Tariff Commission, *Reciprocity*, p. 33; Brazil MRE, *Relatório, 1898*, p. 8; Hayem, *Café du Brésil*, pp. 7, 9.

7. For more see Topik, *Political Economy*, pp. 59–92.

8. U.S. Federal Trade Commission, *Report on Trade and Tariffs in Brazil, Uruguay, Argentina, Chile, Bolivia, and Peru*, p. 57. See also Müller, p. 4.

9. U.S. Tariff Commission, *Reciprocity*, pp. 186, 288.

10. Calculated from Brasil, *Leis do Brasil 1889–1896*, passim, which included the incorporation papers of foreign corporations.

11. Ibid.

12. Babcock, pp. 28, 34, 83.

13. Ibid., p. 83; "Business Papers, Undated," in box 5 of Flint papers.

14. Statement of Flint, Eddy, and American Trading Company in Flint papers, box 6.

15. Mendonça to Flint, Dec. 2, 1905, Flint papers, box 1. Mendonça was apparently involved in an earlier attempt to raise funds for valorization as well; Fontoura Xavier to Prudente de Morais, Feb. 20, 1899, Coleção Prudente, lata 600, pasta 42.

16. Flint, *Memories*, pp. 101, 105; Mendonça to Flint, Mar. 2, 1889.

17. Bridge, p. 279.

18. Flint, *Memories*, pp. 101, 105; Bridge, pp. 279, 282.

19. "Schedule of Matters to be Liquidated by Company Partnership," Mar. 10, 1917, in Flint papers, box 4; Hart O. Berg to Flint and Co., August 1908, Flint papers, box 5; news release, Flint papers, box 4; Flint, *Memories*, p. 189.

20. *NYT*, Aug. 16, 1894: 9-3. The navy continued to believe in the gun for shore batteries, however, where its accuracy was much better; see Lt. Commander Seaton Schroeder, "The USS Vesuvius with Special Reference to her Pneumatic Battery," *Proceedings of the United States Naval Institute*, 20, no. 69 (1894): 1–66. As the *Scientific American* noted on Sep. 15, 1894, "The historical sure-pop shot at the broadside of a barn has been reversed by a system by which the barn itself is shot through the air as a projectile, destined to crush everything that its broad mass may fall upon."

21. Brasil MM, *Relatório, 1895*, p. 6.

22. Ibid.

23. Abranches, *Governos e congressos*, vol. 1, pp. 37, 92.

24. Maclay, vol. 2, pp. 586, 587; Flint, *Memories*, pp. 186–87.

25. Flint, *Memories*, p. 78.

26. Topik, "Middle Class Brazilian Nationalism."

27. S. da Costa, p. 196.

28. Araujo Jorge and Cervo.

29. Mendonça, *A Situação internacional*, p. 255.

CONCLUSION

1. LaFeber, *New Empire*, pp. 240–41.

2. LaFeber, *American Search*, p. 124.

3. See McCann and Hilton for the rise of U.S. influence in the 1930's.

References

ARCHIVES

Brazil

Rui Barbosa Archive, Fundação Casa Rui Barbosa, Rio de Janeiro
Quintino Bocayuva Papers, Centro de Pesquisa e Documentação (CPDOC), Fundação Getúlio Vargas, Rio de Janeiro
Consulado Geral do Brasil na Grã Britania, London, "Ofícios," 1888–94, Arquivo Histórico de Itamaraty (AHI), Rio de Janeiro
Consulado Geral do Brasil no Portugal, Lisbon, "Ofícios," 1888–94, AHI, Rio de Janeiro
Consulado Geral do Brasil nos Estados Unidos, New York, 258-3-10, 1881–94, AHI, Rio de Janeiro
Missões Diplomáticas Brasileiras, Estados Unidos, Ofícios, 1890–96, 233-4-9/11, AHI, Rio de Janeiro
Prudente de Morais Archive, Arquivo Nacional, Rio de Janeiro
Floriano Peixoto Archive, Arquivo Nacional, Rio de Janeiro
Afonso Pena Archive, Arquivo Nacional, Rio de Janeiro
José Thomaz Porciuncula Archive, Instituto Histórico e Geográfico Brasileiro (IHGB), Rio de Janeiro
Coleção Saraiva, IHGB, Rio de Janeiro
Raul Soares Archive, CPDOC, Rio de Janeiro
Coleção General Solon, IHGB, Rio de Janeiro

France

Correspondance Commerciale, 1888–94, vols. 22–26, Archives du Ministère des Affaires Etrangères (MAE), Quai D'Orsay, Paris
Correspondance Politique, vols. 26, 34, MAE

Great Britain

Council of Foreign Bond Holders, Clipping Service, Guild Hall Library, vols. 5–8, 1886–94, microfilm

Records of the Foreign Office, Record Group 13: Brazil, 1888–94, Public Records Office, Kew Gardens, London

N. M. Rothschild and Sons Archive, London

Mexico

Archivo de la Embajada de México en los Estados Unidos de América, Archivo Histórico Diplomático Méxicano, 1888–92, Mexico City

United States

Thomas F. Bayard Papers, Library of Congress (LOC), Washington, D.C.

James G. Blaine Family Archive, LOC

Andrew Carnegie Papers, LOC

Grover Cleveland Archive, microfilm

Charles R. Flint Papers, New York Public Library, New York

John W. Foster Papers, LOC

W. R. Grace Archive, Columbia University, New York

Walter Q. Gresham Papers, LOC

Benjamin Harrison Archive, microfilm

Collis P. Huntington Archive, microfilm

Isaac Jefferson Ross ms. held by Prof. Todd Diacon, Univ. of Tennessee, Knoxville

Department of State,

Correspondence for the Organization of the Commercial Bureau of American Republics, Record Group 43, Box 16, NA

Diplomatic Dispatches from U.S. Consuls to Bahia, 1888–94, Records of the Department of State, RG 59, National Archives (NA)

Diplomatic Dispatches from U.S. Consuls to Pará, 1888–94, RG 59, NA

Diplomatic Dispatches from U.S. Consuls to Pernambuco, 1888–94, RG 59, NA

Diplomatic Dispatches from U.S. Consuls to Porto Alegre, 1888–94, RG 59, NA

Diplomatic Dispatches from U.S. Consuls to Rio de Janeiro, 1888–94, RG 59, NA

Diplomatic Dispatches from U.S. Consuls to Santos, 1888–94, RG 59, NA

Diplomatic Dispatches from U.S. Ministers to Brazil, 1888–94, RG 59, NA

Diplomatic Instructions of the Department of State to Brazil, 1891–94, RG 59, NA

Notes from the Brazilian Legation to the United States to the Department of State, 1888–94, RG 59, NA

Records of the U.S. Delegation to the First International Conference of American States, 1889–90, Record Group 43, Box 20, National Archives

Department of the Navy,

Area 4 File, South Atlantic Squadron, 1888–94, Record Group 45, National Archives

"Naval Intelligence Reports Concerning Affairs in Brazil," Navy Subject File, 1790–1910, VI Box 663, Record Group 45, NA

South Atlantic Squadron, 1892–1905, "Letters and Telegrams Sent to the Navy Department and Others," Record Group 313: Records of Naval Operating Forces, entry 79, NA

PERIODICALS

Almanak Laemmert, 1888–94

American Economist, 1891, 1892
Anaheim Weekly Gazette, Anaheim, Calif., 1893–94
Army and Navy Journal and Gazette, 1893–95
Banker's Magazine, 1890–94
Bradstreet's, 1889–94
Caheté, Maceio, Alagoas, 1896
Echo Popular, Rio de Janeiro, 1890
The Economist, London, 1888–94
Engineering and Mining Journal, 1891
Estado de São Paulo, São Paulo, 1893, 1894
L'Etoile du Sud, Rio de Janeiro, 1894
Export and Finance, 1890
Fullerton Tribune, Fullerton, Calif., 1893–94
Gazeta de Commércio e Finanças, Rio de Janeiro, 1895
O Jacobino, Rio de Janeiro, 1894–97
Jornal do Commércio, Porto Alegre, 1893
Jornal do Commércio, Rio de Janeiro, 1889–94
London Times, 1888–94
Los Angeles Times, 1893, 1894
A Metralha, Rio de Janeiro, 1893, 1894
O Nacional, Rio de Janeiro, 1895
The Nation, New York, 1888–94
O Nativista, São Paulo, 1895
New York Herald, 1892–94
New York Times, 1888–95
North American Review, 1888–94
O Operário, Forteleza, Ceará, 1892
A Opinião Nacional, Rio de Janeiro, 1894
Pan American Bulletin, 1891–94
Proceedings of the Naval Institute, 1889–94
Public Opinion, 1888–94
O Republicano, Forteleza, Ceará, 1895, 1896
Revista de Portugal, Lisbon, 1889–91
Revue des Deux Mondes, Paris, 1889–94
Rio News, Rio de Janeiro, 1891–94
St. Louis Post-Dispatch, 1893–94
San Francisco Chronicle, 1893–94
Scientific American, 1893, 1894
South American Journal, London, 1889
Voz do Operário, Bahia, 1894
Wall Street Journal, New York, 1891
Washington Post, Washington, D.C., 1891
The Weekly Northwestern Miller, 1889, 1891
The World, New York, 1893, 1894

PUBLISHED SOURCES

Abranches, [João] Dunshee de. *Brazil and the Monroe Doctrine*. Rio: Imprensa Na-
cional, 1915.
——. *O Golpe de Estado: Atas e atos do Governo Lucena*. Rio: Oficinas Gráficas do
"Jornal do Brasil," 1954.

———. *Governos e congressos da República*. Rio: M. Abranches, 1918.

———. *A Revolta da Armada e a Revoluçao Rio Grandense*. (*Correspondência entre Saldanha da Gama e Silveira Martins*.) Rio: Gráfica do "Jornal do Brasil," 1955.

Adler, Jacob. *Claus Spreckels, the Sugar King of Hawaii*. Honolulu: University of Hawaii Press, 1966.

Aguiar, Pinto de. *Rui e a economia brasileira*. Rio: Fundação Casa Rui Barbosa, 1973.

Aguilar, Alonso. *Pan-Americanism from Monroe to the Present: A View from the Other Side*. New York: Monthly Review Press, 1968.

Albuquerque, José Joaquim de C.C. Medeiros e. *Minha vida de infância a mociedade, memórias, 1867–1893*. Rio: Calvinho Filho, 1933.

Albuquerque, Luís R. Cavalcanti de. *Amazonia em 1893*. Rio: Imprensa Nacional, 1894.

Amaral, Antônio Barreto do. *Prudente de Moraes, uma vida marcada*. São Paulo: Instituto Histórico e Geográfico de São Paulo, 1971.

Andrews, C. C. *Brazil: Its Conditions and Prospects*. New York: D. Appleton, 1891.

d'Arcos, Conde de Paço. *Missão diplomática do Conde de Paço d'Arcos no Brasil, 1891 a 1893*. Lisbon: n.p., 1974.

d'Atri, Allesandro. *Quintino Bocayuva, pages d'histoire contemporaine*. Paris: Alcan-Levy, 1901.

Azevedo, José Afonso Mendonça. *Vida e obra de Salvador de Mendonça*. Rio: Ministério das Relações Exteriores, Imprensa Nacional, 1971.

Babcock, Glenn D. *History of the United States Rubber Company*. Indianapolis: Indiana University Graduate School of Business, Bureau of Business Research, Indiana Business Report no. 39, 1966.

Bairoch, Paul. "How, not Why: Economic Inequalities between 1800 and 1913: Some Background Figures." In Jean Batou, ed., *Between Development and Underdevelopment 1800–1870*, pp. 1–42. Geneva: Droz and Center of International Economic History, 1991.

Balleiro, Aliomar. *Um estadista no ministério da fazenda*. Rio: Casa Rui Barbosa, 1952.

Balmori, Diana, Stuart F. Voss, and Miles Wortman. *Notable Family Networks in Latin America*. Chicago: University of Chicago Press, 1984.

Bandeira, Moniz. *Presença dos Estados Unidos no Brasil (Dois séculos de história)*. Rio: Civilização Brasileira, 1967.

Barbosa, Rui. *Finanças e política da República*. Rio: Companhia Impressora, 1892.

Barreto, João de Deus Menna. *Os Menna Barretos*. Rio: Laemmert, 1950.

Barretto, Orozimbo Muniz. *Biografia do Almirante Jeronymo Francisco Gonçalves*. Rio: Typografia Leuzinger, 1894.

Bastert, Russell H. "A New Approach to the Origins of Blaine's Pan-American Policy." *Hispanic American Historical Review* 34 (1959): 375–413.

Bastos, A. C. Tavares. *Cartas do solitário*. 1863. Reprint, São Paulo: Editora Nacional, 1975.

Bastos, Humberto. *O pensamento industrial no Brasil*. São Paulo: Livraria Martins, 1954.

———. *Rui, ministro da independência econômica do Brasil*. São Paulo: Martins Editora, 1951.

Bauer, Arnold. *Chilean Rural Society from the Spanish Conquest to 1930*. New York: Cambridge University Press, 1975.

Beaud, Michel. *A History of Capitalism, 1500–1980*. New York: Monthly Review Press, 1983.

Becker, W. "American Manufactures and Foreign Markets." Unpublished ms.

———. *The Dynamics of Business-Government Relations: Industry and Exports, 1893–1921*. Chicago: University of Chicago Press, 1982.

Beisner, Robert L. "Comment." *American Historical Review* 83, no. 3 (June 1978): 674–79.

———. *From the Old Diplomacy to the New, 1865–1900*. New York: Thomas Y. Crowell, 1975.

Bello, José Maria. *A History of Modern Brazil*. Trans. James Taylor. Stanford, Calif.: Stanford University Press, 1966.

Bemis, Samuel Flagg. *A Diplomatic History of the United States*. New York: Henry Holt, 1936.

———. *The Latin American Policy of the United States*. New York: Harcourt, Brace World, 1943.

Benjamin, Jules R. "The Framework of U.S. Relations with Latin America in the Twentieth Century: An Interpretive Essay." *Diplomatic History* 11, no. 2 (spring 1987): 91–112.

Besouchet, Lídia. *Exílio e morte do Imperador*. Rio: Nova Fronteira, 1975.

Bethell, Leslie. *A abolição do trafico de escravos no Brasil*. Trans. Vera Neves Pedrosos. São Paulo: Universidade de São Paulo e Editora Expressão e Cultura, 1976.

———. "Independence." In L. Bethell, ed., *The Independence of Latin America*, pp. 155–94. New York: Cambridge University Press, 1987.

Bianconi, Alfred Marc. *Cartes commerciales, physiques, politiques, administratives*. Paris: Imprimerie Chaix, 1889.

Blaine, Harriet Bailey Standwood. *Letters of Mrs. James G. Blaine*, ed. Harriet S. Blaine Beale. New York: Duffield, 1908.

Blaine, James G. *Political Discussions: Legislative, Diplomatic and Popular, 1856–1886*. Norwich, Conn.: Henry Bill, 1887.

Boehrer, George. *Da monarquia a república*. Rio: Ministério da Educação e Cultura, 1954.

Boiteux, Henrique. *Santa Catarina no exército*. Biblioteca Militar, vols. 51–52. Rio: Bedeschi, 1924.

Bouvier, Jean. *Les deux scandales de Panama*. Paris: Editions du l'Ecole de Hautes Etudes en Sciences Sociales, 1964.

Brasil, Camara dos Deputados. *Anais*, 1891–97. Rio: Imprensa Nacional, 1891–97.

———. Congresso Nacional. *Anais*, 1890–91. Rio: Imprensa Nacional, 1891–92.

———. Congresso. Documentos parlamentares. *Mensagens presidenciais, 1891–1910*. Rio: Typografia Progresso, 1912.

———. Contadoria Geral do Império. *Balanço da receita e despesa do Império, 1888*. Rio: Imprensa Nacional, 1891.

———. Contadoria Geral da República. *Balanço da receita e despesa da República dos Estados Unidos do Brasil, 1890–1895*. Rio: Imprensa Nacional, 1893–98.

———. Diretoria Geral de Estatística. *Leis do Brasil, 1891–95*. Rio: Imprensa Nacional, 1891–95.

———. Diretoria Geral de Estatística. *Sexo, raça e estado civil, nacionalidade, filiação, culto e analphabetismo da população recensada em 31 Dezembro de 1890*. Rio: Officina de Estatística, 1891.

———. Fundação Instituto Brasileiro de Geografia e Estatística. *Séries estatísticas retrospectivas*, vol. 1, *Repertório estatístico do Brasil, quadros retrospectivos*. 1941. Reprint, Rio: FIBGE, 1986.

———. Ministério da Fazenda. *Relatório*, 1891–1895. Rio: Imprensa Nacional, 1891–95.

———. Ministério da Justiça. *Relatório*, 1892–94. Rio: Imprensa Nacional, 1892–94.

——. Ministério da Marinha. *Almirante Jerônimo Gonçalves: Perfil do herói, do chefe militar e do cidadão*. Rio: Serviço de Documentação Geral da Marinha, 1962.
——. Ministério da Marinha. *Relatório*, 1895. Rio: Imprensa Nacional, 1895.
——. Ministério das Relações Exteriores. *Relatório*, 1891–98. Rio: Imprensa Nacional, 1891–98.
——. Ministério das Relações Exteriores. *Tratados de arbitramento*. Rio: Imprensa Nacional, 1891.
——. Ministério da Viação e Obras Públicas. *Dados biográficos dos minístros*. Rio: Ministério da Viação, 1968.
——. Presidente. *Mensagem dirigida ao Congresso Nacional*, May 12, 1892, May 7, 1894, June 17, 1894, June 25, 1894, Oct. 4, 1894. Rio: Imprensa Nacional, 1892, 1894.
Bridge, James Howard. *Millionaires and Grub Street Comrades and Contacts in the Last Half Century*. [1931]. Reprint, Freeport, N.Y.: Books for Libraries Press, 1968.
Brown, Michael Barrat. *Economic Imperialism*. London: Penguin, 1974.
Bryce, James. *The American Commonwealth*. 3d ed. Vol. 2. New York: Macmillan, 1895.
Buescu, Mircea. *Brasil: Disparidades de renda no passado*. Rio: APEC, 1979.
Buhl, Lance C. "Maintaining 'An American Navy' 1865–1889." In Kenneth J. Hagan, ed., *In Peace and War*, pp. 145–73. Westport, Conn.: Greenwood Press, 1978.
Bukharin, Nikolai. *Imperialism and the World Economy*. 1929. Reprint, New York: Monthly Review Press, n.d.
Bureau of American Republics. *Handbook of the American Republics*, nos. 1 and 2. Washington, D.C.: 1891.
——. *How the Latin American Markets May Be Reached*. Washington, D.C.: Government Printing Office, 1893.
——. *Report, 1892*. Washington, D.C.: Government Printing Office, 1893.
Burns, E. Bradford. "As relações internacionais do Brasil durante a Primeira República." In Boris Fausto, ed., *História geral da civilização brasileira*, vol. 9, pp. 377–400. São Paulo: DIFEL, 1977.
——. *The Poverty of Progress: Latin America in the Nineteenth Century*. Berkeley: University of California Press, 1985.
——. *Unwritten Alliance: Rio Branco and Brazilian-American Relations*. New York: Columbia University Press, 1966.
Burr, Robert N. *By Reason or Force: Chile and the Balancing of Power in South America, 1830–1905*. Berkeley: University of California Press, 1965.
Calhoun, Charles W. "American Policy Toward the Brazilian Naval Revolt of 1893–1894: A Reexamination." *Diplomatic History* 4, no. 1 (winter 1980): 39–56.
——. *Gilded Age Cato: The Life of Walter Q. Gresham*. Lexington: University of Kentucky Press, 1988.
Campbell, Charles S. *Special Business Interests and the Open Door Policy*. New Haven, Conn.: Yale University Press, 1951.
——. *The Transformation of American Foreign Relations, 1865–1900*. New York: Harper and Row, 1976.
Campos, Pedro Dias de. *A Revolta de seis de Setembro (A acção de São Paulo)*. Paris: Typografia Aillauld, Alves & Cia., 1913.
Campos, Pedro Moacyr. "Brasil-Portugal, 1826/1889." In Sérgio Buarque de Holanda, ed., *História geral da civilização brasileira*, vol. 6, pp. 204–16. São Paulo: DIFEL, 1974.
Cano, Wilson. *Raizes da concentração industrial em São Paulo*. São Paulo: DIFEL, 1977.

Carone, Edgard. *A primeira república*. São Paulo: DIFEL, 1973.

——. *A República velha*, vol. 1, *Instituições e classes sociais*. São Paulo: DIFEL, 1970.

——. *A República velha*, vol. 2, *Evolução política*. São Paulo: DIFEL, 1974.

Caruso, John Anthony. "The Pan American Railway." *Hispanic American Historical Review* 31, no. 4 (1951): 608–39.

Carvalho, José Murilo de. *Os bestializados: o Rio de Janeiro e a República que não foi*. São Paulo: Companhia das Letras, 1987.

——. *A construção da ordem: a elite política imperial*. Rio: Editora Campus, 1980.

——. "Elite and State-Building in Imperial Brazil." Ph.D. diss., Stanford University, 1974.

——. *A formação das almas*. São Paulo: Companhia das Letras, 1990.

Casalecchi, José Enio. *O partido republicano paulista (1889–1926)*. São Paulo: Brasiliense, 1987.

Cashman, Sean Dennis. *America in the Gilded Age*. New York: New York University Press, 1984.

Castilho, Auguste de. *Le Portugal e le Brésil: conflit diplomatique*. Paris: L. Larose, 1894.

Cavalcanti, Hildiberto Ramos, Jr. "Os republicanos fluminense na legislatura fluminense de 1888." In R. Graham, ed., *Ensaios sobre a política e a economia da provincia fluminense no século xix*, pp. 245–87. Rio: Arquivo Nacional, 1974.

Centro Industrial do Brasil. *O Brasil: suas riquezas naturais, suas indústrias*. 2 vols. Rio: Impressa M. Orosco, 1907, 1908.

Cervo, Amado Luiz. *O parlamento brasileiro e as relações exteriores*. Brasilia: Editora Universidade de Brasilia, 1981.

Cervo, Amado Luiz, and Clodoaldo Bueno. *História da política exterior do Brasil*. São Paulo: Atica, 1992.

Chandler, Alfred D., Jr. *The Visible Hand: The Managerial Revolution in American Business*. Cambridge, Mass.: Belknap Press of Harvard University, 1977.

Chasteen, John Charles. "Background to Civil War: The Process of Land Tenure in Brazil's Southern Borderland, 1801–1893." *Hispanic American Historical Review* 71, no. 4 (Nov. 1991): 737–60.

Chernow, Ron. *The House of Morgan: An American Banking Dynasty and the Rise of Modern Finance*. New York: Atlantic Monthly Press, 1990.

Clark, Champ. *My Quarter Century of American Politics*, vol. 1. New York: Harper, 1920.

Clayton, Lawrence A. "Canal Morgan," *Alabama Heritage* 25 (summer 1992): 6–19.

——. *Grace: W. R. Grace and Company, The Formative Years, 1850–1930*. Ottawa, Ill.: Jameson Books, 1985.

——. "The Nicaraguan Canal in the Nineteenth Century." *Journal of Latin American Studies* 19, no. 2 (Nov. 1987): 323–52.

Cleveland, Grover. *Letters of Grover Cleveland, 1850–1908*. Boston: Houghton Mifflin, 1930.

Clowes, William Laird. *Four Modern Naval Campaigns, Historical, Strategical and Tactical*. London: Unit Library, 1902.

Cochran, Thomas C., and William Miller. *The Age of Enterprise: A Social History of Industrial America*. Rev. ed. New York: Harper and Row, 1961.

Conrad, Robert. *The Destruction of Brazilian Slavery, 1850–1888*. Berkeley: University of California Press, 1972.

Coolidge, Thomas Jefferson. *Autobiography*. Boston: Houghton Mifflin, 1923.

Cooling, Benjamin Franklin. *Benjamin Franklin Tracy, Father of the Modern American Fighting Navy*. Hamden, Conn.: Archon Books, 1973.

——. *Gray Steel and Blue Water Navy: The Formative Years of America's Military-Industrial Complex, 1881–1917.* Hamden, Conn.: Archon Books, 1979.

Corrêa, Inocencio Serzedello. *O problema econômico do Brasil.* 1903. Reprint, Rio: Fundação Casa Rui Barbosa, 1980.

Cosío Villegas, Daniel. *Historia moderna de México*, vol. 6. Mexico D.F.: Editorial Hermes, 1955–74.

Costa, Emília Viotti da. *Da senzala à colonia.* São Paulo: DIFEL, 1966.

Costa, João Cruz. *History of Ideas in Brazil.* Trans. Suzette Macedo. Berkeley: University of California Press, 1964.

——. *O positivismo na República: Notas sobre a história do Positivismo no Brasil.* São Paulo: Companhia Editora Nacional, 1956.

Costa, Sérgio Corrêa da. *A diplomacia do Marechal: Intervenção estrangeira na Revolta da Armada.* Brasilia: Universidade de Brasilia, 1979.

Crapole, Edward P. *America for Americans: Economic Nationalism and Anglophobia in the Late Nineteenth Century.* Westport, Conn.: Greenwood Press, 1973.

Curtis, William E. "Friends in South America." *North American Review* 149 (Sep. 1889): 377–78.

——. *Trade and Transportation Between the United States and Latin America.* U.S. 51st Congress, first session, Senate Executive Document 54. Washington, D.C.: Government Printing Office, 1890.

——. *The United States and Foreign Powers.* Meadville, Penn.: Chautauqua Century Press, 1892.

Davis, Lance E., and Robert A. Huttenback. *Mammon and the Pursuit of Empire.* Cambridge: Cambridge University Press, 1986.

Dean, Warren. "A industrialização durante a República Velha." In Boris Fausto, ed., *Historia geral da civilização brasileira*, vol. 8, pp. 249–84. São Paulo: DIFEL, 1975.

Debes, Célio. *Campos Sales, perfil de um estadísta.* 2 vols. Rio: Livraria Francisco Alves and MEC, 1978.

Deerr, Noel. *The History of Sugar.* London: Chapman and Hall, 1949–50.

Denslow, David. "As exportações e a origem do padrão de industrialização regional do Brasil." In Werner Baer et al., eds., *Dimensões do desenvolvimento brasileiro*, pp. 21–64. Rio: Editora Campus, 1978.

Devine, Michael J. *John W. Foster: Politics and Diplomacy in the Imperial Age, 1873–1917.* Athens: Ohio University Press, 1981.

Diaz Miranda, Mariano. "Dilemmas in the Brazilian Sugar Industry: 1850–1900: The Obsession with Exports and the Failure of Foreign Investors in Pernambuco." Ph.D. diss., University of Texas, Austin, 1988.

Diegues Júnior, Manoel. *Imigração, urbanização, industrialização.* Rio: Centro Brasileiro de Pesquisas Educacionais, 1964.

——. *População e açucar no Nordeste do Brasil.* Rio: Comissão Nacional de Alimentação, 1954.

Drescher, Seymour. "Brazilian Abolition in Comparative Perspective." *Hispanic American Historical Review* 68, no. 3 (Aug. 1988): 429–60.

Dubofsky, Melvyn. *Industrialism and the American Worker, 1865–1920.* New York: Thomas Y. Crowell, 1975.

Dudley, William S. "Institutional Sources of Officer Discontent in the Brazilian Army, 1870–1889." *Hispanic American Historical Review* 55, no. 1 (Feb. 1975): 44–65.

Dunning, William Archibald. *The British Empire and the United States.* New York: Charles Scribner's Sons, 1914.

Eaton, Cyrus. *History of Thomaston, Rockland, and South Thomaston, Maine from Their First Exploration AD 1605; with Family Genealogies*. 2 vols. Hallowell, Maine: Masters, Smith, 1865.

———. "The Shipbuilders of Thomaston." *Log Chips* 2, no. 7 (July 1951): 73–76.

Eisenberg, Peter. "Abolishing Slavery: The Process on Pernambuco's Sugar Plantations." *Hispanic American Historical Review* 54, no. 4 (Nov. 1972): 580–97.

———. *The Sugar Industry in Pernambuco: Modernization Without Change, 1840–1910*. Berkeley: University of California Press, 1974.

Evans, Cerinda W. *Collis Potter Huntington*. 2 vols. Newport News, Va.: Mariner's Museum, 1956.

Eysenbach, Mary Locke. *American Manufactured Exports, 1879–1914: A Study of Growth and Comparative Advantage*. New York: Arno Press, 1976.

Fagg, John Edwin. *Pan Americanism*. Malabar, Fla.: Robert Krieger, 1982.

Faulkner, Harold Underwood. *Politics, Reform, Expansion, 1890–1900*. New York: Harper, 1959.

Fernandes, Heloisa Rodrigues. "A força pública do Estado de São Paulo." In B. Fausto, ed., *História geral da civilização brasileira*, vol. 9. São Paulo: DIFEL, 1977.

Ferns, H. S. *Britain and Argentina in the Nineteenth Century*. Oxford: Clarendon Press, 1960.

Ferreira, Marieta de Moraes, ed. *A República na velha província*. Rio: Rio Fundo, 1989.

Ferrez, Marco. *A marinha*. Rio: Editora Index, 1986.

Field, James A., Jr. "American Imperialism: The 'Worst Chapter' in Almost Any Book" and "Response." *American Historical Review* 83, no. 3 (June 1978): 644–69, 679–84.

Fishlow, Albert. "Origens e consequências da substituição de importações no Brasil." *Estudos Econômicos* 2 (1972): 7–75.

Flint, Charles R. "The Gospel of Industrial Steadiness." In James H. Bridge, ed., *The Trust: Its Book*, pp. 81–93. New York: Doubleday Page, 1902.

———. *Memories of an Active Life*. New York: G. P. Putnam's Sons, 1923.

———. "Our Foreign Trade from a Trader's Standpoint." In Chauncey M. Depew, ed., *One Hundred Years of American Commerce, 1795–1895*, pp. 63–66. New York: D. O. Haynes, 1895.

Ford, Worthington C. "Reciprocity under the Tariff Act of 1890." Washington, D.C.: n.p., 1893.

Forjaz, Augusto. *Portugal e Brazil. Apontamentos para a história do nosso conflicto com a república dos Estados Unidos do Brasil*. Lisboa: Typografia Castro Irmao, 1894.

Foster, John W. *A Century of American Diplomacy Being a Brief Review of the Foreign Relations of the United States 1776–1876*. Boston: Houghton & Mifflin, 1900.

———. *Diplomatic Memoirs*. 2 vols. Boston: Houghton & Mifflin, 1909.

Frank, André Gunder. *Capitalism and Underdevelopment in Latin America*. New York: Monthly Review Press, 1969.

———. *Lumpenbourgeoisie, Lumpendevelopment*. New York: Monthly Review Press, 1974.

Freire, Felisbello. *História da revolta de 6 de Setembro de 1893*. Rio: Cunha e Irmão, 1896.

Freyre, Gilberto. *Order and Progress; Brazil from Monarchy to Republic*. Trans. Rod W. Horton. New York: Alfred Knopf, 1970.

Frieden, Jeffrey A. "Sectoral Conflict and U.S. Foreign Economic Policy, 1914–1940," *International Organization* 42, no. 1 (winter 1988): 59–80.

Friedman, Milton, and Anna Jacobson Schwartz. *A Monetary History of the United States, 1867–1960.* Princeton, N.J.: Princeton University Press, 1963.

Fry, Joseph A. *John Tyler Morgan and the Search for Southern Autonomy.* Knoxville: University of Tennessee Press, 1992.

———. "John Tyler Morgan's Southern Expansionism." *Diplomatic History* 9 (fall 1985): 329–46.

Gallegher, John, and Ronald Robinson. "The Imperialism of Free Trade." *Economic History Review* 6, no. 1 (1953): 1–15.

Gallman, Robert. "Gross National Product in the United States, 1834–1909." In National Bureau of Economic Research, *Conference on Research in Income and Wealth, Output, Employment and Productivity in the United States after 1800.* New York: Columbia University Press, 1966.

Gardner, Lloyd C., Walter LaFeber, and Thomas McCormick. *Creation of the American Empire.* Chicago: Rand, McNally, 1973.

Gignilliat, John L. "Pigs, Politics and Protection: European Boycott of American Pork, 1879–1891." *Agricultural History* 34 (1961): 3–12.

Gill, Stephen, ed. *Gramsci, Historical Materialism and International Relations.* London: Cambridge University Press, 1993.

Goldberg, Joyce S. *The Baltimore Affair.* Lincoln: University of Nebraska Press, 1986.

Gootenberg, Paul. *Between Silver and Guano: Commercial Policy and the State in Postindependence Peru.* Princeton, N.J.: Princeton University Press, 1989.

———. *Imagining Development; Economic Ideas in Peru's 'Fictitious Prosperity' of Guano, 1840–1880.* Berkeley: University of California Press, 1993.

Gould, Lewis L. "Diplomats in the Lobby: Franco-American Relations and the Dingley Tariff of 1897." *Historian* 39 (Aug. 1977): 659–80.

———. "New Perspectives on the Republican Party, 1877–1913." *American Historical Review* 77, no. 4 (Oct. 1972): 1074–83.

———. "The Republican Search for a National Majority." In H. Wayne Morgan, ed., *The Gilded Age,* pp. 171–87. Syracuse, N.Y.: Syracuse University Press, 1963.

———. *The Spanish-American War and President McKinley.* Lawrence: University Press of Kansas, 1980.

———. "Tariffs and Markets in the Gilded Age." *Reviews in American History* 2 (1974): 266–71.

Graebner, Norman, ed. *An Uncertain Tradition: American Secretaries of State in the Twentieth Century.* New York: McGraw-Hill, 1961.

Graham, Richard. *Britain and the Onset of Modernization in Brazil, 1850–1914.* Cambridge: Cambridge University Press, 1968.

———. "A British Industry in Brazil: Rio Flour Mills, 1886–1920." *Business History* 8 (1966): 13–38.

———. "Landowners and the Overthrow of the Empire." *Luso-Brazilian Review* 7 (1970): 44–56.

———. "Robinson and Gallegher in Latin America." In W. R. Lewis, ed., *Imperialism,* pp. 217–21.

Graham, Sandra. "The Vintim Riot and Political Culture: Rio de Janeiro, 1880." *Hispanic American Historical Review* 60, no. 3 (Aug. 1980): 431–49.

Grenville, John, and George Young. *Politics, Strategy and American Diplomacy.* New Haven, Conn.: Yale University Press, 1966.

Gresham, Matilda. *Life of Walter Quintin Gresham, 1832–1895.* 2 vols. 1919. Reprint, Freeport, New York: Books for Libraries Press, 1970.

Guerra, Flávio. *Lucena um estadista de Pernambuco.* Recife: Arquivo Público Estadual, 1958.

Hagan, Kenneth. *American Gunboat Diplomacy and the Old Navy, 1877–1889.* Westport, Conn.: Greenwood Press, 1973.

———. *This People's Navy.* New York: Free Press, 1990.

———, ed. *In Peace and War: Interpretations of American Naval History, 1775–1984.* Westport, Conn.: Greenwood Press, 1984.

Hahner, June. *Civilian-Military Relations in Brazil: 1889–1898.* Columbia: University of South Carolina Press, 1969.

———. "The Paulistas Rise to Power: A Civilian Group Ends Military Rule." *Hispanic American Historical Review* 47 (1967): 149–66.

———. *Poverty and Politics: The Urban Poor in Brazil, 1870–1920.* Albuquerque: University of New Mexico Press, 1986.

Hammett, Hugh B. *Hilary Abner Herbert: A Southerner Returns to the Union.* Philadelphia: American Philosophical Society, 1976.

Harrison, Benjamin. *Public Papers and Addresses of Benjamin Harrison, March 4, 1889, to March 4, 1893.* Washington, D.C.: Government Printing Office, 1893.

Harrod, Frederick S. *Manning the New Navy: The Development of a Modern Naval Enlisted Force, 1899–1940.* Westport, Conn.: Greenwood Press, 1978.

Hasslocher, Germano. *A verdade sobre a revolução.* Porto Alegre: Edição de Livraria Mazeron, 1894.

Hayem, Julien. *Le Café du Brésil et le tarif douanier français.* Paris: Librairie Guillaumin, 1903.

———, ed. *Congress international du commerce et l'industrie tenu à Paris du 23 au 28 septembre de 1889.* Paris: Imprimerie Nationale, 1890.

Hayford, Marc, and Carl A. Pasurka. "The Political Economy of the Fordney-McCumber and Smoot-Hawley Tariff Acts." *Explorations in Economic History* 29, no. 1 (Jan. 1992): 30–50.

Haywood, William D. *The Autobiography of Big Bill Haywood.* New York: International Publishers, 1974.

Healy, David. *U.S. Expansionism: The Imperialist Urge in the 1890s.* Madison: University of Wisconsin Press, 1970.

Heitman, John Alfred. "Scientific and Technological Change in the Louisiana Sugar Industry, 1830–1930." Ph.D. diss., Johns Hopkins University, 1983.

Helm, Edith Benham. *The Captains and the Kings.* New York: G. P. Putnam's Sons, 1954.

Herrick, Walter R., Jr. *The American Naval Revolution.* Baton Rouge: Louisiana State University Press, 1966.

Hession, Charles, and Hyman Sardy. *Ascent to Affluence.* Boston: Allyn and Bacon, 1969.

Hill, Lawrence F. *Diplomatic Relations Between the United States and Brazil.* Durham, N.C.: Duke University Press, 1932.

Hilton, Stanley. *Brazil and the Great Powers, 1930–1939: The Politics of Trade Rivalry.* Austin: University of Texas Press, 1975.

Hitchens, Christopher. *Blood, Class and Nostalgia: Anglo-American Ironies.* New York: Farrar, Straus & Giroux, 1990.

Hobsbawm, Eric. *The Age of Capital, 1848–1875.* New York: Scribners, 1975.

———. *The Age of Empire.* New York: Pantheon Books, 1987.

Hobson, J. A. *Imperialism.* 1902. Reprint, Ann Arbor: University of Michigan Press, 1972.

Hoffman, Charles. *The Depression of the Nineties*. Westport, Conn.: Greenwood Press, 1970.

Holbo, Paul S. "Economics, Emotion, and Expansion: An Emerging Foreign Policy." In H. Wayne Morgan, ed., *The Gilded Age*, pp. 199–221. Syracuse: Syracuse University Press, 1971.

Holloway, Thomas. *Immigrants on the Land: Coffee and Society in São Paulo, 1886–1934*. Chapel Hill: University of North Carolina Press, 1980.

Hunt, Michael H. *Ideology and United States Foreign Policy*. New Haven, Conn.: Yale University Press, 1987.

Hutchins, John G. B. *The American Maritime Industries and Public Policy, 1789–1914*. Harvard Economic Studies, vol. 71. Cambridge, Mass.: Harvard University Press, 1941.

Hutchinson, Lincoln. *Report on Trade Conditions*. Washington, D.C.: Government Printing Office, 1906.

———. "The Results of Reciprocity with Brazil." *Political Science Quarterly* 18 (1903): 282–312.

International American Conference. *Reports of Committees and Discussions Thereon*. 51st Congress, first session, Senate Executive Document 232. Washington, D.C.: Government Printing Office, 1890.

Jacobsen, Nils. *Mirages of Transition: The Peruvian Altiplano, 1780–1930*. Berkeley: University of California Press, 1993.

Jane, Fred T., ed. *Jane's All the World's Fighting Ships, 1898*. 1898. Reprint, Newton Abbot, Devon: David & Charles, 1969.

Janotti, Maria de Lourdes Monaco. "The Monarchist Response to the Beginnings of the Brazilian Empire." *The Americas* 48, no. 2 (Oct. 1991): 223–243.

———. *Os subversivos da República*. São Paulo: Brasiliense, 1986.

Jensen, Richard. *The Winning of the Midwest: Social and Political Conflict, 1888–1896*. Chicago: University of Chicago Press, 1971.

Johnson, Emory. *History of Domestic and Foreign Commerce of the United States*. Washington, D.C.: Carnegie Institute of Washington, 1915.

Johnson, John T. *A Hemisphere Apart: The Foundations of United States Policy Toward Latin America*. Baltimore: Johns Hopkins University Press, 1990.

Jones, Stanley L. *The Presidential Election of 1896*. Madison: University of Wisconsin Press, 1964.

Jorge, A. G. de Araujo. *Ensaios de história diplomática do Brasil no regimen republicana, 1889–1902*. Rio: Livraria Editora de Jacintho Silva, 1912.

Karsten, Peter. "The Naval Aristocracy: U.S. Naval Officers from the 1840's to the 1920's, Mahan's Messmates." Ph.D. diss., University of Wisconsin, Madison, 1968.

Keller, Morton. *Affairs of State: Public Life in Late Nineteenth Century America*. Cambridge, Mass.: Belknap Press of Harvard University, 1977.

Kennedy, Charles Stuart. *The American Consul: A History of the United States Consular Service, 1776–1914*. Westport, Conn.: Greenwood Press, 1990.

Kerby, J. Orton. *An American Consul in Amazonia*. New York: W. Edwin Rudge, 1911.

Kiernan, V. G. "Foreign Interests in the War of the Pacific." *Hispanic American Historical Review* 35, no. 15 (Feb. 1955), pp. 14–36.

———. *Marxism and Imperialism*. London: Edward Arnold, 1974.

King, Wilford I. *The Wealth and Income of the People of the United States*. New York: Macmillan, 1915.

Kleppner, Paul. *The Cross of Culture. A Social Analysis of Midwestern Politics, 1850–1900*. New York: Free Press, 1970.

Knoles, George Harmon. *The Presidential Campaign and Election of 1892*. Stanford University Publications in History, Economics and Political Science, vol. 5, no. 1. New York: AMS Press, 1971.

Krasner, Stephen D. *Defending the National Interest: Raw Materials Investment and U.S. Foreign Policy*. Princeton, N.J.: Princeton University Press, 1978.

———. *The Third World Against Global Liberalism: A Structural Conflict*. Berkeley: University of California Press, 1985.

Laet, Carlos de. "A Imprensa." In Visconde de Ouro Preto, Angelo do Amaral, Barão de Loreto, Carlos de Laet, Afonso Celso, and Silva Costa, *Decada republicana*, vol. 1, pp. 197–261. 2d ed. 1899? Reprint, Brasilia: Editora Universidade de Brasilia, 1986.

LaFeber, Walter. *The American Age: United States Foreign Policy at Home and Abroad since 1750*. New York: Norton, 1989.

———. *The American Search for Opportunity, 1865–1913*. The Cambridge History of American Foreign Relations, vol. 2. New York: Cambridge University Press, 1993.

———. "Comment." *American Historical Review* 83, no. 3 (June 1978): 669–74.

———. *The New Empire. An Interpretation of American Expansion, 1860–1898*. Ithaca, N.Y.: Cornell University Press, 1963.

———. "United States Depression Diplomacy and the Brazilian Revolution, 1893–1894." *Hispanic American Historical Review* (Feb. 1960): 107–18.

Lake, David A. *Power, Protection and Free Trade: International Sources of U.S. Commercial Strategy, 1887–1939*. Ithaca, N.Y.: Cornell University Press, 1988.

Lamoreaux, Naomi. *The Great Merger Movement in American Business, 1895–1904*. Cambridge: Cambridge University Press, 1985.

Langer, William L. *Political and Social Upheaval, 1832–1852*. New York: Harper and Row, 1969.

Laughlin, J. Laurence, and H. Parker Willis. *Reciprocity*. New York: Baker and Taylor, 1903.

Lavergne, Réal P. *The Political Economy of United States Tariffs: An Empirical Analysis*. New York: Academic Press, 1983.

Leal, Victor Nunes. *Coronelism, enxada e voto*. São Paulo: Editora Alfa-Omega, 1975.

Leclerc, Max. *Cartas do Brasil*. Trans. Sérgio Milliet. 1890. Reprint, São Paulo: Companhia Editora Nacional, 1942.

Lenin, V. I. *Imperialism, the Highest Stage of Capitalism*. In Henry M. Christman, ed., *Essential Works of Lenin*. 1932. Reprint, New York: Bantam Books, 1966.

Leoni, Arlindo A. *Embargos n. 2,286: Henry Lowndes, Conde de Leopoldina, Embargados Banco do Brasil e a União Federal*. Rio: Typografia do Jornal do Commércio, 1918.

Levi, Darrell. *The Prados of São Paulo*. Athens: University of Georgia Press, 1987.

Levy, Maria Bárbara. "O Encilhamento." In Paulo Neuhaus, ed., *Economia brasileira, uma visão histórica*, pp. 191–256. Rio: Editora Campus, 1980.

Lewin, Linda. *Politics and Parentela in Paraíba*. Princeton, N.J.: Princeton University Press, 1987.

Lewis, W. Arthur. *Growth and Fluctuations, 1870–1913*. London: George Allen & Unwin, 1978.

Lewis, William Roger, ed. *Imperialism: The Robinson and Gallegher Controversy*. New York: New Viewpoints, 1976.

Lima, Alexandre José Barbosa. *Discursos parlamentares*. Brasilia: Camara dos Deputados, 1963.

Lima, Manuel Oliveira. *Memórias, estas minhas reminiscências*. Rio: Livraria José Olympio, 1937.

——. *Pan-americanismo*. 1907. Reprint, Rio: Fundação Casa Rui Barbosa, 1980.

Lima Sobrinho, Alexandre José Barbosa. *Presença de Alberto Torres (sua visão e pensamento)*. Rio: Civilização Brasileira, 1968.

Lins, Ivan. *História do positivismo no Brasil*. São Paulo: Companhia Editora Nacional, 1964.

Lipson, Charles. *Standing Guard: Protecting Foreign Capital in the Nineteenth and Twentieth Centuries*. Berkeley: University of California Press, 1985.

Lobo, Eulália Maria Lahmeyer. "Evolução dos preços e do padrão de vida no Rio de Janeiro, 1820–1930: resultados preliminares." *Revista Brasileira de Economia* 25, no. 4 (Oct./Dec. 1971): 235–65.

——. *História do Rio de Janeiro: do capital comerical ao capital industrial-financeiro*, vol. 2. Rio de Janeiro: IBMEC, 1978.

Lockey, James B. "James G. Blaine." In Samuel Flagg Bemis, ed., *American Secretaries of State*, vol. 7, pp. 263–300. New York: Cooper Square, 1963.

Logan, Rayford W. *The Diplomatic Relations of the United States with Haiti, 1776–1891*. Chapel Hill: University of North Carolina Press, 1941.

Long, David Foster. *Gold Braid and Foreign Relations: Diplomatic Activities of U.S. Naval Officers, 1798–1883*. Annapolis, Md.: Naval Institute Press, 1988.

Love, Joseph L. *Rio Grande do Sul and Brazilian Regionalism, 1882–1930*. Stanford, Calif.: Stanford University Press, 1971.

Love, Joseph L., and Nils Jacobsen, eds. *Invisible Hand: Economic Liberalism and the State in Latin American History*. New York: Praeger, 1988.

Lucena, Barão de. *Arquivo do Barão de Lucena, Catalogo*. Recife: Secretaria do Interior e Justiça, 1956.

Lustig, R. Jeffrey. *Corporate Liberalism: The Origins of Modern American Political Theory, 1890–1920*. Berkeley: University of California Press, 1982.

Luxemburg, Rosa. *The Accumulation of Capital*. 1913. Trans. Agnes Schwarzschild. Reprint, New York: Monthly Review Press, 1964.

Luz, Fábio, and Davi Carneiro. *Floriano: memórias e documentos*, vol. 6, *A Invasão federalista em Santa Catarina e Paraná*. Rio: Imprensa Nacional, 1941.

Luz, Nícea Vilela. *A Amazonia para os negros americanos (as origins de uma controversia internacional)*. Rio: Editora Saga, 1968.

——. *A luta pela industrialização do Brasil*. 1961. Reprint, São Paulo: Alfa Omega, 1975.

Macedo, Roberto. *Barata Ribeiro, administração do primeiro prefeito do Distrito Federal*. Rio: Departamento Administrativo do Serviço Público, 1955.

Maclay, Edgar Stanton. *A History of the United States Navy from 1875 to 1898*, vol. 2. New York: D. Appleton, 1898.

Magalhães Júnior, Raimundo. *Deodoro, a espada contra o Império*. São Paulo: Companhia Editora Nacional, 1952.

Manchester, Alan K. *British Preeminence in Brazil: Its Rise and Decline*. Chapel Hill: University of North Carolina Press, 1933.

Marichal, Carlos. *A Century of Debt Crises in Latin America: From Independence to the Great Depression, 1820–1930*. Princeton, N.J.: Princeton University Press, 1989.

Markusen, Ann. *Regions: The Economics and Politics of Territory*. Totowa, N.J.: Rowman and Littlefield, 1987.

Martí, José. *Inside the Monster: Writings on the United States and American Imperialism*. Trans. Elinor Randall. New York: Monthly Review Press, 1975.

——. *Obras completas*, vol. 6. La Habana: Editorial Nacional de Cuba, 1963–1973.

Martins, J. P. Oliveira. *O Brazil e as colonias portuguezas*. 5th ed. Lisboa: Parceria Antonio Maria Pereira, 1920.

———. *A circulação fiduciaria: memoria apresentada a Academia Real de Sciencias de Lisboa*. Lisboa: Pereira, 1899.

———. *Estudos de economia e finanças*. Lisboa: Guimaraes, 1956.

Marvin, Winthrop Lippit. *The American Merchant Marine from 1620 to 1902*. New York: C. Scribner's Sons, 1902.

Mattox, Henry E. *The Twilight of Amateur Diplomacy: The American Foreign Service and Its Senior Officers in the 1890s*. Kent, Ohio: Kent State University Press, 1989.

Mauá, Visconde de (Irineo Evangelista de Sousa). *Autobiografia*. Rio: Valverde, 1942.

May, Ernest. *American Imperialism: A Speculative Essay*. New York: Atheneum, 1968.

May, Stacy, and Galo Plaza. *The United Fruit Company in Latin America*. Washington, D.C.: National Planning Assoc., 1958.

McCann, Frank D., Jr. *The Brazilian-American Alliance, 1937–1945*. Princeton, N.J.: Princeton University Press, 1973.

McCloskey, Michael B. "The United States and the Brazilian Naval Revolt, 1893–1894." *Americas* 2 (1946): 296–321.

McCormick, Thomas J. *China Market. America's Quest for Informal Empire, 1893–1901*. Chicago: Quadrangle Books, 1967.

McGann, Thomas. *Argentina, the United States and the Inter-American System, 1880–1914*. Cambridge, Mass.: Harvard University Press, 1957.

Mello, Custódio José de. *Apontamentos para a história da revolução de 23 de Novembro de 1891*. Rio: Cunha & Irmão, 1895.

———. *O governo provisório e a revolução de 1893*. São Paulo: Editora Nacional, 1938.

Mello, Zélia Cardoso de. *Metamofoses da riqueza, São Paulo 1845–1895*. São Paulo: Hucitec, 1985.

Mendonça, Carlos Süssekind de. *Salvador de Mendonça: Democrata do Império e da República*. Rio: Instituto Nacional do Livro, 1960.

Mendonça, Salvador de. *Ajuste de contas*. Rio: Jornal do Commércio, 1899–1904.

———. *A situação international do Brasil*. Rio: Livraria Garnier, 1913.

Merrick, Thomas W., and Douglas H. Graham. *População e desenvolvimento econômico no Brasil*. Trans. Waltensir Dutra. Rio: Zahar, 1981.

Miller, Clarence Lee. *The States of the Old Northwest and the Tariff, 1865–1888*. Emporia, Kans.: Emporia Gazette Press, 1929.

Miller, Rory. *Britain and Latin America in the Nineteenth and Twentieth Centuries*. London: Longman, 1993.

Mintz, Sidney W. *Sweetness and Power: The Place of Sugar in Modern History*. New York: Penguin, 1985.

Miranda, Salem de. *Floriano*. Rio: Biblioteca do Exército, 1963.

Moog, Vianna. *Bandeirantes e pioneiros*. Rio: Editora Globo, 1954.

Morena Fraginals, Manuel. *El ingenio: complejo económico social cubano del azucar*. 3 vols. La Habana: Editorial Ciencias Sociales, 1978.

Morgan, H. Wayne. *America's Road to Empire: The War with Spain and Overseas Expansion*. New York: John Wiley, 1968.

———. *From Hayes to McKinley*. Syracuse: Syracuse University Press, 1969.

———. "Populism and the Decline of Agriculture." In H. Wayne Morgan, ed., *The Gilded Age*, pp. 149–79. Syracuse, N.Y.: Syracuse University Press, 1963.

———. *William McKinley and His America.* Syracuse, N.Y.: Syracuse University Press, 1963.

Müller, Manoel Jansen. *Ainda sobre a tarifa das alfandegas.* London: Kegan, Paul, Trench, Trübner, 1914.

Muzzey, David Saville. *James G. Blaine.* New York: Dodd Mead, 1934.

Nabuco, Joaquim. *Balmaceda.* São Paulo: Companhia Editora Nacional, 1937.

———. *Cartas a amigos.* Ed. Carolina Nabuco. São Paulo: Instituto: Progresso Editorial, n.d.

———. *A intervenção estrangeira durante a Revolta de 1893.* São Paulo: Companhia Editora Nacional, 1939.

Nelson, Keith. "The 'Warfare State': History of a Concept." *Pacific Historical Review* 40, no. 2 (May 1971): 127–43.

New York Times. Seventy-Fifth Anniversary Issue, Sept. 18, 1926.

Osborne, Thomas J. *Empire Can Wait: American Opposition to Hawaiian Annexation, 1893–1898.* Kent, Ohio: Kent State University Press, 1981.

Overton, Grant. *Portrait of a Publisher and the First Hundred Years of the House of Appleton, 1825–1925.* New York: D. Appleton, 1925.

Padua, José Augusto Valladares. "A Capital, a República e o sonho: a experiência dos partidos operários de 1890." *Dados* 28, no. 2 (1985): 163–92.

Palha, Amêrico. *Soldados e marinheiros do Brasil.* Rio: Biblioteca do Exército, 1962.

Palmer, Michael. *De petite journeaux aux grandes agences: naissance du journalisme moderne, 1863–1914.* Paris: Aubier, 1983.

Paraty, Conde de. *Portugal e Brazil. Conflicto diplomático, breves explicações.* Lisboa: M. Gomes, 1895.

Parlee, Lorena M. "Porfirio Diaz, Railroads and Development in Northern Mexico: A Study of Government Policy Toward the Central and National Railroads, 1876–1910." Ph.D. diss., University of California, San Diego, 1981.

Pelaez, Carlos Manuel, and Wilson Suzigan. *História monetária do Brasil.* Rio: IPEA/INPES, 1976.

Pepper, Charles M. *Life and Times of Henry Gassaway Davis.* New York: Century, 1920.

Peskin, Allen. "Blaine, Garfield and Latin America: A New Look." *Americas* 36, no. 1 (July 1979): 78–89.

Phillips, Kevin. *The Politics of Rich and Poor: Wealth and the American Electorate in the Reagan Aftermath.* New York: Random House, 1990.

Pike, Fredrick B. *Chile and the United States 1880–1962: The Emergence of Chile's Social Crisis and the Challenge to United States Diplomacy.* South Bend, Ind.: University of Notre Dame Press, 1963.

———. *The United States and Latin America: Myths and Stereotypes.* Austin: University of Texas Press, 1992.

Platt, D. C. M. *Latin America and British Trade, 1806–1914.* New York: Harper and Row, 1973.

Pletcher, David M. *The Awkward Years: American Foreign Policy under Garfield and Arthur.* Columbia, Mo.: University of Missouri Press, 1962.

———. "Reciprocity and Latin America in the Early 1890s: A Foretaste of Dollar Diplomacy." *Pacific Historical Review* 47 (Feb. 1978): 53–89.

———. "United States Relations with Latin America: Neighborliness and Exploitation." *American Historical Review* 82, no. 1 (Feb. 1977): 39–59.

Pollack, Norman. *The Populist Response to Industrial America.* New York: Norton, 1962.

Pomeroy, William J. *American Neo-Colonialism: Its Emergence in the Philippines and Asia.* New York: International Publishers, 1970.

Porto, Manoel Ernesto de Campos. *Apontamentos para a história da República.* Rio: Imprensa Naiconal, 1890.

Prado, Eduardo. *A illusão americana.* São Paulo: Editora Nacional, 1933.

Pratt, Julian. *Expansionists of 1898.* Chicago: Quadrangle Books, 1964.

Preto, Visconde de Ouro. "Finanças." In Visconde de Ouro Preto et al., eds., *Década republicana,* vol. 1, pp. 7–145. Brasilia: Editora Universidade de Brasilia, 1986.

Putnam, Robert D. "Diplomacy and Domestic Politics: The Logic of Two-Level Games." In Peter B. Evans, Harold K. Jacobsen, and Robert D. Putnam, eds., *Double-edged Diplomacy: International Bargaining and Domestic Politics,* pp. 431–68. Berkeley: University of California Press, 1993.

Queiroz, Suely R. R. *Os radicais da République.* São Paulo: Brasiliense, 1986.

Reuter, Elisabeth Cattapan. "L'encilhamento au Brèsil." These de troisieme cycle, Université de Paris X, 1973.

Ridings, Eugene W. "Business, Nationality and Dependency in Late Nineteenth Century Brazil." *Journal of Latin American Studies* 14, no. 1 (May 1982): 55–96.

Rippy, J. Fred. *Rivalry of the United States and Great Britain over Latin America, 1808–1830.* Baltimore: Johns Hopkins University Press, 1928.

———. "The United States and the Establishment of the Republic of Brazil." *Southwestern Political Science Quarterly* 111, no. 1 (1922): 1–15.

Rodrigues, José Albertino. *Sindicato e desenvolvimento no Brasil.* São Paulo: 1968.

Rodriguez, José Honório. *Independência, revolução e contrarevolução.* Rio: Livraria Francisco Alves Editora, 1975–76.

Rogers, C. C. "The Revolt in Brazil." In Office of Naval Intelligence, General Information Series No. 13, Information from Abroad: *Notes on the Year's Naval Progress,* July 1894, Washington, D.C.: Government Printing Office, 1894.

Romero, Matías. "The Pan American Conference." *North American Review* 151 (July 1890): 354–66.

———. *Reciprocidad comercial entre México y los Estados Unidos.* Mexico: Banco Nacional de Comerico Exterior, 1971.

Roosevelt, Theodore. "The Naval Policy of America as Outlined in the Messages of Presidents of the United States from the Beginning to the Present Day." *Proceedings of the United States Naval Institute* 21, no. 83 (1899): 509–22.

Rosenberg, Emily. *Spreading the American Dream: American Economic and Cultural Expansion, 1890–1945.* New York: Hill and Wang, 1982.

Rostow, Walt Whitman. *British Economy of the Nineteenth Century.* Oxford: Oxford University Press, 1948.

———. *The World Economy: History and Prospects.* Austin: University of Texas Press, 1978.

Russ, William Adam, Jr. *The Hawaiian Revolution (1893–1894).* Selens Grove, Penn.: Susquehanna University Press, 1959.

Russell, Henry Benajah. *International Monetary Conferences.* New York: Harper and Bros., 1898.

Rutter, Frank. *South American Trade of Baltimore.* Johns Hopkins University Studies in Historical and Political Science 15, no. 9 (Sep. 1897).

Rydell, Robert W. *All the World's a Fair: Visions of Empire at American International Expositions, 1876–1916.* Chicago: University of Chicago Press, 1984.

Saes, Décio. *A formação do Estado burguês no Brasil (1888–1891).* Rio: Paz e Terra, 1985.

Santos, Creusa Coelho de Sousa. "Os industrialistas como grupo de pressão, 1880–1898." M.A. thesis, Universidade Federal do Rio de Janeiro, 1985.

Santos, José Maria dos. *A política geral do Brasil*. São Paulo: J. Magalhães, 1930.

Santos, Noronha. *Floriano: memórias e documentos*, vol. 2. Rio: n.p., 1939.

Santos, Sydney M. G. dos. *André Rebouças e seu tempo*. Rio: n.p., 1985.

Santos, Theotonio dos. "Brazil, the Origins of a Crisis." In Ron Chilcote and Joel Edelstein, eds., *Latin America: The Struggle with Dependency and Beyond*, pp. 409–90. New York: John Wiley, 1974.

Scenna, Miguel Angel. *Argentina-Brasil: cuatro siglos de rivalidad*. Buenos Aires: Ediciones La Bastilla, 1975.

Schantz, Moritz. *Das heutige Brasilien*. Hamburg: W. Maukesöhne, 1893.

Schivelbusch, Wolfgang. *Railway Journey: The Industrialization of Time and Space in the 19th Century*. Berkeley: University of California Press, 1977.

Schneider, Ronald M. *"Order and Progress": A Political History of Brazil*. Boulder, Colo.: Westview Press, 1991.

Schulz, John. "The Brazilian Army and Politics: 1850–1895." Ph.D. diss., Princeton University, 1973.

Schumpeter, Joseph. *Business Cycles: A Theoretical and Statistical Analysis of the Capitalist Process*, vol. 1, New York: McGraw-Hill, 1939.

Schwartz, Stuart. *Sugar Plantations in the Formation of Brazilian Society: Bahia 1550–1835*. New York: Cambridge University Press, 1985.

Scobbie, James. *Revolution on the Pampas*. Austin: University of Texas Press, 1964.

Sherman, Thomas H. *Twenty Years with James G. Blaine: Reminiscences by His Private Secretary*. New York: Grafton Press, 1928.

Silva, Hélio. *1889: A República não esperou o amanhecer*. Rio: Civilização Brasileira, 1972.

———. *O Poder civil*. Porto Alegre: L&PM Editores, 1985.

Simmons, Charles Willis. *Marshal Deodoro and the Fall of Dom Pedro II*. Durham, N.C.: Duke University Press, 1966.

Singer, Paul. "O Brasil no contexto do capitalismo internacional." In Boris Fausto, ed., *História geral da civilização brasileira*, vol. 8, pp. 345–90. São Paulo: DIFEL, 1975.

Skidmore, Thomas. "Brazil's American Illusion: From Dom Pedro II to the Coup of 1964." *Luso-Brazilian Review* 23, no. 2 (winter 1986): 71–84.

Sklar, Martin. *The Corporate Reconstruction of American Capitalism, 1890–1916: The Market, the Law and Politics*. New York: Cambridge University Press, 1988.

Smith, Horace. *The War Maker, Being the True Story of Captain George B. Boynton*. Chicago: A. C. McClung, 1911.

Smith, Joseph. "Britain and the Brazilian Naval Revolt of 1893–94." *Journal of Latin American Studies* 2, no. 2 (Nov. 1970): 175–98.

———. *Illusions of Conflict: Anglo-American Diplomacy Toward Latin America, 1865–1896*. Pittsburgh, Penn.: University of Pittsburgh Press, 1979.

———. "The Latin American Trade Commission of 1884–85." *Interamerican Economic Affairs* 24, no. 4 (spring 1971): 3–24.

———. *Unequal Giants: Diplomatic Relations Between the United States and Brazil, 1889–1930*. Pittsburgh, Penn.: University of Pittsburgh Press, 1991.

Sociedade Auxiliadora da Agricultura de Pernambuco. *Trabalhos do Congresso Agrícola do Recife, Outubro de 1878*. 1879. Reprint, Recife: Fundação Estadual de Planejamento Agrícola de Pernambuco, 1978.

Socolofsky, Homer E., and Allan B. Spetter. *The Presidency of Benjamin Harrison*. Lawrence: University Press of Kansas, 1987.

Sodré, Emmanuel. *Lauro Sodré na história da República*. Rio: Edição do Autor, 1970.
Sodré, Lauro. *Crenças e opinoes*. Belem: Typografia do Dicionário Oficial, 1896.
Sodré, Nelson Werneck. *História da burguesia brasileira*. Rio: Civilização Brasileira, 1976.
———. *História militar do Brasil*. Rio: Civilização Brasileira, 1965.
Spanish American Commercial Union. *Banquet Given in Honor of the Delegates of the International American Conference at Delmonicos, Friday Evening December 20, 1889*. New York: Press of El Avisador Hispano-Americano, 1890.
Sprout, Harold, and Margaret Sprout. *The Rise of American Naval Power, 1776–1918*. Princeton, N.J.: Princeton University Press, 1939.
Stanwood, Edward. *American Tariff Controversies in the Nineteenth Century*. Boston: Houghton, Mifflin, 1903.
Stein, Stanley. *The Brazilian Cotton Manufacture: Textile Enterprise in an Underdeveloped Area*. Cambridge, Mass.: Harvard University Press, 1957.
Stephenson, Nathaniel Wright. *Nelson W. Aldrich—A Leader in American Politics*. New York: Charles Scribner's Sons, 1930.
Sulzberger, Iphigene Ochs. (As told to Susan W. Dryfoss.) *Iphigene*. New York: Dodd, Mead, 1979.
Suzigan, Wilson. *Indústria brasileira*. São Paulo: Hucitec, 1986.
Swann, Leonard Alexander, Jr. *John Roach, Maritime Entrepreneur: The Years as Naval Contractor, 1862–1886*. Annapolis, Md.: U.S. Naval Institute, 1965.
Sweigart, Joseph. "Financing and Marketing Brazilian Export Agriculture: The Coffee Factors of Rio de Janeiro, 1850–1888." Ph.D. diss., University of Texas, Austin, 1980.
Targa, Luís Pecoits. "1893. Rio Grande do Sul: Violência revolucionaria e a fundação do Estado burguês." Presented at the 14th Jornadas de História Económica, Córdoba, Argentina, May 5, 1994.
Tate, Merze. *Hawaii: Reciprocity or Annexation*. East Lansing: Michigan State University Press, 1968.
Taussig, Frank. *The Tariff History of the United States*. 8th ed. New York: G. P. Putnam's Sons, 1931.
Terrill, Tom E. *The Tariff, Politics and American Foreign Policy, 1874–1901*. Westport, Conn.: Greenwood Press, 1973.
Thimm, Alfred I. *Business Ideologies in the Reform-Progressive Era, 1880–1914*. Tuscaloosa: University of Alabama Press, 1976.
Thompson, Almirante A. *Guerra civil do Brasil de 1893 a 1895: vida e morte do Almirante Saldanha da Gama*. 3d ed. Rio: Serviço de Documentação Geral da Marinha, 1958.
Tilly, Charles. *The Contentious French: Four Centuries of Popular Struggle*. Cambridge, Mass.: Belknap Press of Harvard University, 1986.
Timm, Charles A. "The Diplomatic Relations Between the United States and Brazil During the Naval Revolt of 1893." *Southwestern Political and Social Science Quarterly* 5 (Sep. 1924): 119–38.
Tompkins, E. Berkeley. *Anti-Imperialism in the United States: The Great Debate, 1890–1920*. Philadelphia: University of Pennsylvania Press, 1970.
Topik, Steven C. "Brazil's Bourgeois Revolution?" *The Americas* 48, no. 2 (Oct. 1991): 245–72.
———. "Metropoles macrocéfalas: Uma comparação entre a primazia do Rio do Janeiro e a da Cidade do México entre 1800 a 1910." *Dados* 34, no. 1 (1991): 53–78.
———. "Middle-Class Brazilian Nationalism, 1889–1930: From Radicalism to Reaction." *Social Science Quarterly* 59 (1978): 93–104.

——. *The Political Economy of the Brazilian State, 1889–1930*. Austin: University of Texas Press, 1987.

Torres, João Camillo de Oliveira. *O Positivismo no Brasil*. Petrópolis: Editora Vozes, 1957.

Tyler, Alice Felt. *The Foreign Policy of James G. Blaine*. Hamden, Conn.: Archon Books, 1965.

United Kingdom. House of Commons. *General Alphabetical Index to the Bills, Reports, Estimates, Accounts and Papers Printed by Order of the House of Commons and to the Papers Presented by Command 1852–1899*. London: His Majesty's Stationary Office, 1909.

United States. Bureau of the Census. *Historical Statistics of the United States: Colonial Times to 1957*. Washington, D.C.: Government Printing Office, 1961.

——. Bureau of Statistics. *Statistical Abstract of the United States, 1897*. Washington, D.C.: Treasury Dept., Bureau of Statistics, 1897.

——. Congress. *Congressional Record*. Washington, D.C.: Government Printing Office, 1888–1900.

——. Forty-Ninth Congress, First Session. House of Representatives. Executive Document no. 50, "Report of the Commission Appointed to Report upon the Commercial Relations Between the United States and Several Countries of Central and South America." Washington, D.C.: Government Printing Office, 1886.

——. Fiftieth Congress, Second Session. House of Representatives. Report no. 3112, "Report of the Committee on Manufactures on the Investigation of Trusts." Washington, D.C.: Government Printing Office, 1888.

——. Fifty-Sixth Congress, First Session. House Document no. 476, "Industrial Commission Reports," vol. 1, "Trusts: Preliminary Report." Washington, D.C.: Government Printing Office, 1900.

——. Department of State. *Commercial Relations of the United States with Foreign Countries 1890–1895*. Washington, D.C.: Government Printing Office, 1891–96.

——. Department of State. *Foreign Affairs of the United States 1890–1895*. Washington, D.C.: Government Printing Office, 1890–95.

——. Federal Trade Commission. *Report on Trade and Tariffs in Brazil, Uruguay, Argentina, Chile, Bolivia and Peru*. Washington, D.C.: Government Printing Office, 1916.

——. Naval History Division. *Dictionary of American Naval Ships*. Washington, D.C.: Naval History Division, Dept. of the Navy, 1976.

——. *Proceedings of the National Reciprocity Convention*. Washington, D.C.: Government Printing Office, 1901.

——. Tariff Commission. *Reciprocity and Commercial Treaties*. Washington, D.C.: Government Printing Office, 1919.

——. Treasury Department. *The Foreign Commerce and Navigation of the United States 1891–1897*. Washington, D.C.: Government Printing Office, 1891–97.

Uzoigwe, G. N. "European Partition and Conquest of Africa: An Overview." In A Adu Boahen, ed., *General History of Africa*, vol. 7, *Africa under Colonial Domination, 1880–1935*, pp. 19–44. Berkeley: University of California Press, 1985.

Vaz, Alisson Mascarenhas. "Cia. de Fiação e Tecidos Cedro e Cachoeira: L'evolution d'une affaire familiale, 1872–1972." Thesis, Université de Paris X, 1973.

Velho Sobrinho, J. F. *Dicionário bio-bibliográfico brasileiro*, vol. 2. Rio: Oficinas Gráficas Irmaos Pongetti, 1937.

Versiani, Flavio R. "Industrialização e economia de exportação: a experiência brasileira antes de 1914." *Revista Brasileira de Economia* 34 (1980): 3–40.

Vianna, Oliveira. *O ocaso do Império*. 3d ed. Rio: Livraria José Olympio, 1959.

Vieira, Dorival Teixeira. *A obra econômica de Amaro Cavalcanti.* São Paulo: Universidade de São Paulo, 1960.
Villalba, Epaminondas. *A Revolta da Armada de 6 de Setembro de 1893.* Rio: Laemmert, 1894.
Villar, Frederico. *As revoluções que eu vi. (O Almirante Luiz Felipe de Saldanha da Gama).* Biblioteca do Exército, vol. 160. Rio: Gráfica Editora Aurora, n.d.
Villela, Anníbal, and Wilson Suzigan. *A política do governo e crescimento da economia brasileira, 1889–1945.* Rio: IPEA/INPES, 1973.
Vivian, James F. "United States Policy During the Brazilian Naval Revolt 1893–94: The Case for American Neutrality." *American Neptune* (Oct. 1981): 245–61.
Volwiler, Albert, ed. *The Correspondence Between Benjamin Harrison and James G. Blaine, 1882–1893.* Philadelphia, Penn.: American Philosophical Society, 1940.
Wall, Joseph Frazier. *Andrew Carnegie.* Pittsburgh: University of Pittsburgh Press, 1970.
Wehrs, Carlos. *Niterói, cidade sorriso: a história de um lugar.* Rio: n.p., 1984.
Welch, Richard E., Jr. *The Presidencies of Grover Cleveland.* Lawrence: University Press of Kansas, 1988.
Wesson, Robert. *The United States and Brazil: Limits of Influence.* New York: Praeger, 1981.
Whitaker, Arthur. *The United States and the Independence of Latin America, 1800–1830.* New York: Russell & Russell, 1962.
Wileman, J. F. *Brazilian Exchange: The Study of an Inconvertible Currency.* 1896. Reprint, New York: Greenwood Press, 1969.
Wilgus, A. Curtis. *A Brief Survey of the Political Relations Between Brazil and the United States.* Boston: Brazilian Section of the Latin American Economic Institute, 1941.
Wilkins, Mira. "Banks over Borders." In Geoff Jones, ed., *Banks as Multinationals,* pp. 217–47. London: Routledge, 1990.
———. *The Emergence of Multinational Enterprise.* Cambridge, Mass.: Harvard University Press, 1970.
———. *The History of Foreign Investment in the United States to 1914.* Cambridge, Mass.: Harvard University Press, 1989.
Williams, Frank B., Jr. "A Tennessean Abroad with His Magic Soldier." *Tennessee Historical Quarterly* 34, no. 4 (winter 1975): 383–91.
Williams, Mary W. "The Treaty of Tordisillas and the Argentine-Brazilian Boundary Dispute." *Hispanic American Historical Review* 5 (1922): 3–23.
Williams, R. Hal. *The Democratic Party and California Politics, 1880–1896.* Stanford, Calif.: Stanford University Press, 1973.
———. "'Dry Bones and Dead Language': The Democratic Party." In H. Wayne Morgan, ed., *The Gilded Age,* pp. 129–48. Syracuse, N.Y.: University of Syracuse Press, 1963.
———. *Years of Decision: American Politics in the 1890s.* New York: John Wiley, 1978.
Williams, William Appleman. *The Roots of the Modern American Empire.* New York: Vintage Books, 1969.
———. *The Tragedy of American Diplomacy.* Cleveland: World Publishing, 1959.
Wilson, Charles Morrow. *Empire in Green and Gold: The Story of the American Banana Trade.* New York: Henry Holt, 1947.
Witter, João Sebastião, ed. *Ideías políticas de Francisco Glycério.* Rio: Fundação Casa Rui Barbosa, 1982.
Wolfe, Gerard R. *The House of Appleton.* Metuchen, N.J.: Scarecrow Press, 1981.

Woodward, C. Van. *Tom Watson, Agrarian Rebel*. New York: Oxford University Press, 1963.

Zeitlin, Maurice. *Civil Wars in Chile (or the Bourgeois Revolutions That Never Were)*. Princeton, N.J.: Princeton University Press, 1984.

Ziegler, Philip. *The Sixth Great Power: A History of One of the Greatest of All Banking Families, the House of Baring, 1762–1929*. New York: Knopf, 1988.

Index

In this index "f" after a number indicates a separate reference on the next page, and "ff" indicates separate references on the next two pages. A continuous discussion over two or more pages is indicated by a span of numbers. *Passim* is used for a cluster of references in close but not consecutive sequence.

Library of Congress Cataloging-in-Publication Data

Topik, Steven.
Trade and gunboats : the United States and Brazil in the age of
empire / Steven C. Topik.
    p.   cm.
Includes bibliographical references.
ISBN 0-8047-2602-7 (cl.) : ISBN 0-8047-4018-6 (pbk.)
    1. United States—Relations—Brazil.   2. Brazil—Relations—United
States.   I. Title.
E183.8.B7T66   1996
327.73081—dc20
96-10467   CIP

Original printing 1996
Last figure below indicates year of this printing
05 04 03 02 01 00